State Names, Seals, Flags, and Symbols

STATE NAMES, SEALS, FLAGS, AND SYMBOLS

A HISTORICAL GUIDE
Revised and Expanded

Benjamin F. Shearer
and
Barbara S. Shearer

Illustrations by
JERRIE YEHLING SMITH

GREENWOOD PRESS
Westport, Connecticut
London

Library of Congress Cataloging-in-Publication Data

Shearer, Benjamin F.
State names, seals, flags, and symbols : a historical guide / Benjamin F. Shearer and Barbara S. Shearer ; illustrations by Jerrie Yehling Smith.—Rev. and expanded.
p. cm.
Includes bibliographical references and index.
ISBN 0–313–28862–3 (alk. paper)
1. Names, Geographical—United States—States. 2. Seals (Numismatics)—United States—States. 3. Flags—United States—States. 4. Capitols. 5. Mottoes—United States. 6. State flowers—United States. 7. State birds—United States. 8. State songs—United States. 9. United States—History, Local—Bibliography. I. Shearer, Barbara Smith. II. Title.
E155.S44 1994
929.9'2'0973—dc20 93–49552

British Library Cataloguing in Publication Data is available.

Library of Congress Catalog Card Number: 93–49552
ISBN: 0–313–28862–3

First published in 1994

Greenwood Press, 88 Post Road West, Westport, CT 06881
An imprint of Greenwood Publishing Group, Inc.

Printed in the United States of America

The paper used in this book complies with the Permanent Paper Standard issued by the National Information Standards Organization (Z39.48–1984).

10 9 8 7 6 5 4 3 2 1

Copyright Acknowledgments

The authors and the publisher gratefully acknowledge permission to use the following copyrighted materials:

Georgia flag and seal designs courtesy of the Office of the Secretary of State of Georgia; Indiana state seal reproduced with permission of the Indiana State Archives, Commission on Public Records; Kentucky state flag and seal reproduced with permission from the Kentucky Secretary of State; Michigan flag and seal designs courtesy of the Michigan Department of State; permission for use of Pennsylvania flag and seal designs provided by the Commonwealth of Pennsylvania, Department of General Services; approval of the use of Mississippi flag and seal illustrations granted by the Mississippi Secretary of State's Office; New Jersey flag and seal designs courtesy of New Jersey Division of Travel and Tourism; North Dakota flag and seal designs courtesy of North Dakota Secretary of State; New Mexico flag and seal designs courtesy of the New Mexico Department of Tourism; West Virginia seal and flag designs courtesy of the Secretary of State of West Virginia; permission for the use of the New York flag and seal granted by Gail S. Shaffer, Secretary of State; use of the Vermont seal was granted by the Vermont Office of the Secretary of State; permission for use of Nebraska state seal was granted by Allen J. Beermann, Secretary of State, Nebraska; permission for use of Montana state flag granted by Travel Montana; permission for use of the Alaska flag granted by Alaska Division of Tourism; permission for use of Delaware state seal and flag granted by Delaware Secretary of State—these may not be reproduced without permission from the Secretary of State of the State of Delaware (see Delaware Code, Title 29, Chapter 23, section 2306). Use of the Hawaii flag and seal authorized by Lieutenant Governor Benjamin Cayetano. Use of the Hawaii seal is governed by section 5–6 of Hawaii Revised Statutes, which states: "Whoever uses any representation of the great seal or the coat of arms of the State in any manner likely to give the impression of official State approval shall be guilty of a misdemeanor. The preceding sentence shall not be construed to apply to the use of the seal or coat of arms in any newspaper, periodical, book or pamphlet wherein the seal or coat of arms is printed for informational purposes only."

Reproduction of stamp designs allowed by the U.S. Postal Service.

Color photography of license plates by Richard Deemer.

Materials from annotated statutory compilations published by West Publishing Company are reprinted with the permission of West Publishing Company.

The statutes reprinted or quoted verbatim from the following pages are taken from the Hawaii Revised Statutes, Idaho Code, Maryland Annotated Code, Nevada Revised Statutes, North Carolina General Statutes, North Dakota Centennial Code, Utah Code Annotated, Virginia Code, West Virginia Code, and the District of Columbia Code, copyright by the Michie Company, and are reprinted with the permission of the Michie Company. All rights reserved.

Sections of Arkansas Code Annotated reprinted with permission of the State of Arkansas, the copyright holder, by the Arkansas Code Revision Commission.

Material from Kansas Statutes Annotated used with the permission of the Revisor of Statutes of the State of Kansas.

Permission for the publication of sections of Tennessee Code Annotated was granted by the State of Tennessee.

Sections 1–4–5, 1–4–6, 1–6–2, and 1–6–4.1 of the South Dakota Codified Laws copyright © by the State of South Dakota, reprint authorized by the Code Counsel, South Dakota Legislative Research Council.

Contents

Introduction

This second edition of *State Names, Seals, Flags, and Symbols* incorporates the numerous changes and additions that have occurred since the publication of the first edition in 1987. Information provided in this edition has been expanded to include the District of Columbia, American Samoa, Guam, the Commonwealth of the Northern Mariana Islands (CNMI), Puerto Rico, and the U.S. Virgin Islands, all homes to citizens of the United States. Four new chapters have also been added. They cover a selection of U.S. postage stamps issued about states and territories, samplings of fairs and festivals, lists of legal holidays and special observances, and short histories as well as descriptions of passenger-car license plates.

State publications and state codes have provided much of the documentation for state symbols and other official designations. State officials—governors, secretaries of state, attorneys general—as well as librarians in state libraries and archives and officers in state motor vehicle departments have provided invaluable assistance as work progressed on this volume. Special thanks is due to Terence G. Villaverde, Special Assistant to the Governor, Washington Office of the Governor of Guam; Ivonne G. Cervoni, Executive Assistant to the Director, Puerto Rico Federal Affairs Administration; Page Stull, Press Secretary to Ron de Lugo, Member of Congress from the U.S. Virgin Islands; Isapela Enesi in the office of Eni Faleomavaega, Member of Congress from American Samoa; and Pete A. Torres in the Office of the Resident Representative to the United States for the Commonwealth of the Northern Mariana Islands.

The United States Postal Service was especially helpful in granting permission for the reproduction of stamp designs, and its publication *United*

States Postage Stamps has been referred to for information about the stamps listed. United States government publications also provided rich sources of descriptive material. John P. Harrington's extensive scholarship on the origin of state names, found in the *Annual Report of the Smithsonian Institution, 1954,* summarizes years of debate on many names and convincingly discards some long-held misinformation. The *Yearbook of Agriculture, 1949* provided descriptive information on state trees. *Bulletins of the United States Museum,* numbers 50, 107, 113, 121, 162, 174, 176, 179, 191, 195, 196, 211, and 237 provided behavioral and descriptive information on state birds.

1 State and Territory Names and Nicknames

The names of the states taken all together honor the important players in the early exploration and history of the nation. Georgia, the Virginias, the Carolinas, New Jersey, New Hampshire, and Maryland, among others, were named by the English. Maine, Vermont, and Louisiana were named by the French. The Spanish left their names to Florida, Colorado, California, Nevada, and Texas. The Dutch were responsible for naming Rhode Island. The United States honored the first president when it created the state of Washington and the Native Americans displaced by the country's westward expansion when it named Indiana. In fact, the majority of state names are derived from Indian names. From the Choctaw in Alabama, to the Aleuts in Alaska, to the Massachusetts on the East Coast, Indian tribes left their mark on the naming of the states.

Nicknames for the states have come out of particular incidents and events or in an effort to promote state industries, businesses, and tourism. The nicknames listed below are those that have stood the test of time and illustrate some historical or economic fact. Not included here are the many slogans devised by the states to promote a particular industry or image.

ALABAMA

The Alabama River was named after the Indian tribe that was settled in central Alabama when early European explorers first arrived there. The state received its name from the river. The name Alabama first occurs in chronicles of DeSoto's 1540 expedition, spelled variously Alibamu, Limamu, and Alibamo. Numerous other variant spellings were set down by English, French, and Spanish explorers.[1]

The origin of the name Alabama is probably in two Choctaw words. "Alba" in Choctaw means vegetation, herbs, plants, or weeds. "Amo" means a gatherer, picker, or shearer. It was not unusual that a tribe would accept a descriptive name from a contiguous tribe. The description "vegetation gatherers" was appropriate for the Alabama Indians, who cleared land for agricultural purposes.[2]

While the state of Alabama has no officially adopted nickname, Alabamians proudly display the nickname "The Heart of Dixie" on their license plates. Alabama is also known as the Yellowhammer State. The state bird is the yellowhammer, chosen because of the color of the uniforms of a company of Alabama confederate soldiers. The NASA-Marshall Space Flight Center in Huntsville has provided Alabama with another nickname—The Pioneer Space Capital of the World.

ALASKA

Alaska is taken directly from the Aleut "aláxsxaq," meaning "the object toward which the action of the sea is directed," or the mainland.[3] Alaska was known as Russian America until its purchase by the United States in 1867. The Russians had used the term Alaska to refer only to the Alaskan peninsula. The name was appropriated by the United States to refer first to the Territory of Alaska and then to the state.[4]

The American purchase of Alaska, negotiated by Secretary of State William Seward, gave Alaska two of its first American nicknames—Seward's Folly and Seward's Ice Box. While obviously meant to be derisive, Seward's purchase of Alaska for $7,200,000 has proved a fine investment. Alaska has also been spoken of more fondly as the Land of Midnight Sun and America's Last Frontier.

ARIZONA

The name Arizona is derived from two words in the Papago Indian dialect of the Pima language—"Aleh-zon," which means "little spring." Spaniards used the term as early as 1736. The springs, now located in Mexican territory, are near a large silver find made in 1735 in the Arizona Creek. Arizona was chosen as the territorial name, in part owing to Charles D. Poston. Poston was a mining speculator who claimed to have first suggested the name Arizona in a petition to Congress to make Arizona a territory.[5]

Arizona is known as the Copper State because of its large copper production and as the Apache State because of the large number of Apache Indians who once lived there. Arizona's most familiar nickname today is the Grand Canyon State.

ARKANSAS

The pronunciation of the word Arkansas is actually prescribed by an 1881 state statute. Although Arkansas is actually another form of Kansas, the Arkansas legislature declared that the correct pronunciation of the three-syllable word should have the final "s" silent, all "a's" with the Italian sound, and the accent on the first and third syllables. This pronunciation follows from the fact that Arkansas was first written in French, as Frenchmen tried to record the sounds they heard from native American Indians.[6] The Kansas Indians are a tribe of the Sioux. Fr. Marquette first used the word Arkansas in a 1673 map.[7]

Arkansas has many nicknames, including the Bowie State and the Toothpick State, which refer to Bowie knives and to the handles for them. The Hot Water State is a nickname that refers to the hot springs in the state.[8] Arkansas also has an officially designated nickname: The Land of Opportunity.[9] The slogan "Arkansas Is a Natural" is also used to promote recreation and tourism.[10]

CALIFORNIA

California was an island filled with gold in an early sixteenth century novel, *Las Sergas de Esplandian*, by Garcia Ordonez de Montalvo. Although the eleventh century *Song of Roland* mentions a capital city called Califerne, it is most probable that Spanish explorers Ortuno Ximenez and Hernando Cortez were familiar with the contemporary Spanish novel and drew their inspiration for naming California, which they thought to be an island, from Montalvo's book. By 1541, California had become an established place name and location on the maps.[11]

Although several slogans have been used by the state of California over the years to promote business and tourism, the only official nickname, designated by the California legislature in 1968, is The Golden State.[12] This nickname was chosen not only in reference to the discovery of gold in 1848, but also to the fields of yellow poppies that bloom in California in the spring.[13]

COLORADO

The Pike's Peak Region, land attained originally from the Louisiana Purchase, Mexican cession, and Texas, became the Colorado Territory soon after gold was discovered near Denver. A number of names were suggested for the territory, including Osage, Idaho, Jefferson, and Colona; however, the name Colorado, Spanish for red, referring to the color of the Colorado River whose headwaters lie within the boundaries of the state, was chosen over the others. Local native Indians from a number of tribes had referred to the river's color in naming it even before the Spanish arrived.[14]

Colorado is known as the Centennial State because it attained statehood in 1876, the one-hundred-year anniversary of the signing of the Declaration of Independence. It is also known as the Highest State and the Switzerland of America for its elevation and mountainous terrain. Many slogans have also been used over the years to promote skiing and tourism in Colorado.

CONNECTICUT

The name Connecticut was clearly established in the early seventeenth century as applied to the Connecticut River.[15] The native Indian word "Quinnehtukqut" was translated into the current English spelling and means "beside the long tidal river."[16]

In 1959, the Connecticut legislature officially adopted the nickname The Constitution State[17] because Connecticut was the first of all the states to have a written constitution. Connecticut is also known unofficially as the Nutmeg State, not because the state produces the spice in large quantities, but because its early citizens were so skilled and industrious that they could make and sell wooden nutmegs.[18]

DELAWARE

The state of Delaware and the Delaware Indians are both named after the Delaware River. The Delaware River was named by the English after Sir Thomas West, Lord de la Warr, who was the Virginia Company's first governor.[19]

Delaware was the first state to ratify the United States Constitution, thus earning it the nickname the First State. Delaware is also known as the Diamond State, a sobriquet originated by Thomas Jefferson, who referred to Delaware as like a diamond—small but of great value.[20]

FLORIDA

Florida was named for the day on which it was discovered by Spanish explorer Ponce de Leon. On Easter Sunday in 1513, de Leon named the new land La Florida in honor of Pascua Florida, the Spanish Feast of the Flowers at Eastertime.[21]

Florida has a number of nicknames owing to its geographical location and the importance of tourism. Florida is commonly known as the Sunshine State. It is also called the Alligator State, the Everglades State, and the

Southernmost State for obvious reasons. The Orange State is still another nickname that acknowledges the importance of the citrus industry to Florida's economy.

GEORGIA

Georgia was founded in 1733 by James Oglethorpe, who had been granted a charter by King George II in 1732 to found a colony named after the king. Oglethorpe carried out the terms of the charter by naming the last of the thirteen British colonies in America Georgia.[22]

The state of Georgia has no officially designated nickname, although it recognizes the use of several unofficial nicknames. Georgia is known as the Peach State and the Goober State for the importance of peaches and peanuts in the state's agricultural economy. Two nicknames refer to the determination and will of Georgia's citizens to lead the South in industrial and economic development—the Empire State of the South and the Yankee-land of the South. Georgia is also known as the Cracker State and the Buzzard State. Crackers, originally a derogatory term meaning braggarts, was the term used to describe immigrants into Georgia who came from the mountains of Virginia and North Carolina. The Buzzard State refers to the fact that buzzards were once protected by law in Georgia.[23]

HAWAII

Captain James Cook named the islands he discovered in 1778 the Sandwich Islands in honor of his patron, the Earl of Sandwich. By 1819, however, King Kamehameha I had united the formerly independent islands under his rule in the Kingdom of Hawaii. In 1893, Hawaii became a republic and a territory in 1898 when the islands were annexed by the United States. Statehood came in 1959.

The name Hawaii itself is said to have come from the traditional discoverer of the islands, Hawaii Loa. Another explanation is that Hawaii means a small or new homeland. "Hawa" means a traditional homeland, and "ii" means both small and raging. The latter meaning may refer to Hawaii's volcanoes.[24]

The state of Hawaii recognized the Aloha State as its official popular name in a 1959 legislative act.[25] Hawaii is also known unofficially as the Pineapple State for its extensive pineapple industry, the Paradise of the Pacific for its natural beauty, and the Youngest State because it is the last state to join the Union.

IDAHO

Contrary to long-held common belief, Idaho is not a Shoshone word meaning "gem of the mountains." In fact, the name Idaho was invented by George M. Willing, who unsuccessfully sought to become a delegate from what would become the territory of Colorado. The more traditional name of Colorado was maintained when Colorado became a territory, partly because the name Idaho was discovered to have been a coined term. Nevertheless, the name Idaho took hold in settlements such as Idaho Springs and gold discoveries on the Salmon and Clearwater rivers known as the Idaho mines. Even a Columbia River steamship was christened *The Idaho*. In 1863, Congress designated the Idaho Territory with the erroneous understanding that Idaho meant "gem of the mountains," while Montana, another name proposed for the territory, was said to mean nothing.[26] In spite of the misunderstanding concerning the origin of the name Idaho, the state of Idaho continues to be known as the Gem State and the Gem of the Mountains.

ILLINOIS

When La Salle traveled up the Illinois River in 1679, he named it after the native Americans he found living along its banks. Illinois is a French spelling for the Illinois and Peoria Indian word "ilini," the plural of which is "iliniwok," meaning a man or a warrior and also possibly a member of the Illinois tribe.[27]

The Illinois legislature officially adopted "Land of Lincoln" as its slogan in 1955, referring to Illinois as the state where Abraham Lincoln began his political career.[28] Illinois is also known unofficially as the Prairie State, a fitting sobriquet for a state that sets aside the third full week of September each year as Illinois Prairie Week "to demonstrate the value of preserving and reestablishing native Illinois prairies."[29] The Corn State is another fitting nickname for Illinois, owing to the importance of that crop to the state's agricultural economy.

INDIANA

The United States Congress created the name Indiana, meaning "Land of the Indians," when it created the Indiana Territory out of the Northwest Territory in 1800.[30]

"Crossroads of America" was designated by the Indiana legislature as the state's official motto or slogan.[31] Indiana is popularly known, however, as the Hoosier State. The origin of the term Hoosier is unclear. It may be a corruption of the terse pioneer question "Who's here?" Another explanation has it that the men who worked for an Indiana contractor, Sam Hoosier, became known as Hoosiers. Still another explanation is that the term Hoosier is a corruption of "husher," a term applied to early riverboat workers who could hush anyone with brute force.[32]

IOWA

The Iowa District was the name of the territory of Wisconsin west of the Mississippi. The district became first a territory and then, in 1846, a state. The Iowa River was named for the Iowa Indians who inhabited the area, and the name of the state was derived from the river. The tribal name " 'Ayuxwa" means "one who puts to sleep." The French spelled Iowa as Ayoua and the English, as Ioway.[33]

Iowa's most enduring but unofficial nickname, the Hawkeye State, was first suggested in an 1838 newspaper article by James G. Edwards as a tribute to Chief Black Hawk. Black Hawk had come back to Iowa to die after his release from prison, where he had served a sentence for fighting the encroachment of white settlers on Indian land.[34]

KANSAS

Kansas is the French spelling of the Kansas, Omaha, Kaw, Osage, and Dakota Sioux Indian word "KaNze." In the language of the Kansas, the word Kansas means the "south wind." The tribal name was applied to the Kansas River and also to the territory occupied by the tribe.[35]

Kansas has several nicknames that describe its history, resources, and weather. Kansas was known at one time as "Bleeding Kansas," an apt appellation for pre–Civil War Kansas and the carnage that occurred there at the time. In a sense, Kansas was a precursor of things to come as the United States was about to embark on civil war. Kansas is also called the Squatter State for the squatters who settled the new territory. The Cyclone State is a nickname that calls to mind the worst of Kansas weather; the Sunflower State calls to mind the wild sunflowers of the plains, the official flower of the state. Finally, Kansas is called the Jayhawk State for the unruly irregulars and pillagers who first occupied the Kansas borders. Kansas soldiers came to be known as a result as Jayhawkers.[36]

KENTUCKY

The name Kentucky, the Wyandot word for "plain," referring to the central plains of the state, was first recorded in 1753. Kentucky, which had been a province of Virginia, became a territory in 1790, a state in 1792.[37]

Kentucky is commonly nicknamed the Bluegrass State, in spite of the fact that it is officially a commonwealth. Bluegrass is actually green, but its bluish-purple buds, when seen from afar, give a field of bluegrass a bluish tint.[38] Kentucky is also nicknamed for two crops that have figured in its economic history—the Hemp State and the Tobacco State. Finally, Kentucky has been called the Dark and Bloody Ground, a nickname passed down by Daniel Boone from an Indian chief to describe the battles Indians and whites fought in Kentucky.[39]

LOUISIANA

In 1682, explorer Sieur de La Salle was the first European to descend the Mississippi River all the way to its delta. He named the area he discovered La Louisianne after Louis XIV of France. The state of Louisiana was carved out of the New Orleans Territory, which was only a portion of the Louisiana Purchase.[40]

Nicknames for Louisiana are plentiful and descriptive. Louisiana is known as the Bayou State for its numerous bayous and the Fisherman's Paradise for the variety of excellent fishing available in the state. The Child of the Mississippi is a nickname that describes the state's geological origin. The Sugar State is a tribute to Louisiana's sugar industry, and the Pelican State is a tribute to the state bird, the brown pelican, which is native to Louisiana.[41]

MAINE

The origin of the name Maine is uncertain. French colonists may have named the area after the French province of Mayne. "Main" was also a common term among early explorers to describe a mainland.[42]

The state of Maine recognizes the nickname the Pine Tree State. The white pine is the state tree and Maine possesses 17 million acres of forest.[43] Maine is also known as the Lumber State for its lumber industry and as the Border State for its geographical position below Canada. The Old Dirigo State refers to the state's motto "Dirigo," which means "I lead" or "I direct."[44]

MARYLAND

When Lord Baltimore received the charter for the colony from Charles I of England, it contained the proviso that the colony be named Maryland in honor of Charles I's wife, Queen Henrietta Maria, who was popularly known as Queen Mary.[45]

Maryland is known as the Free State and the Old Line State. The first of these nicknames originated in 1923. Hamilton Owens, editor of the *Baltimore Star,* coined the term after Maryland refused to pass an enforcement act for Prohibition. He continued to use the nickname in his editorials. The second nickname, by some accounts, was created by George Washington in praise of Maryland's regular line troops who served well in many Revolutionary War skirmishes.[46]

MASSACHUSETTS

Massachusetts was named after the Massachusetts Indian tribe, which populated the Massachusetts Bay region before Columbus first arrived in the New World. Massachusetts means "large hill place." The tribe was named after Great Blue Hill, which lies south of Milton.[47]

Massachusetts Bay lends the state two common nicknames—the Bay State and the Old Bay State. Massachusetts' early settlers were responsible for two more nicknames—the Pilgrim State and the Puritan State. The Old Colony State is a nickname that refers to the original Plymouth Colony. Finally, the Puritan practice of serving baked beans for Sunday meals gives Massachusetts the nickname the Baked Bean State.[48]

MICHIGAN

The name Michigan first appeared in written form in 1672 in connection with a clearing on the west side of the lower peninsula. In Chippewa, the word "majigan" means "clearing." European explorers named Lake Michigan after the clearing. The attribution of Michigan's name to the Chippewa word "micigami," meaning "large water," is not accurate.[49]

Michigan has long been known as the Wolverine State for the large numbers of wolverines that once roamed the peninsula. The Great Lakes that surround Michigan lend it the nicknames the Lake State and the Lady of the Lake. Michigan's extensive auto industry, centered in Detroit, also gives Michigan another nickname, the Auto State.[50]

MINNESOTA

The state of Minnesota received its name from the Minnesota River in southern Minnesota. The Dakota word "mnishota" means "cloudy" or "milky water."[51]

Minnesota is known as the North Star State; its motto is translated from the French as the "Star of the North." Although having many more lakes than the nickname suggests, Minnesota is also called the Land of 10,000 Lakes. Minnesota is nicknamed the Gopher State for the many gophers that roamed its prairies and also the Bread and Butter State for its extensive production of wheat and dairy products.[52]

MISSISSIPPI

The state of Mississippi is named after the Mississippi River, although the river itself has had a number of names throughout history. Indians on the Gulf Coast called the river Malabouchia. Spaniards called it Rio del Espiritu Santo and Rio Grande del Florida during the sixteenth and seventeenth centuries. The French called it the Colbert River after La Salle explored it and then, after the founding of the colony at Fort Maurepas in 1699, the St. Louis River. Mississippi, the name given the river by Northwest Indians visited by La Salle and Marquette, is the name that finally won out. La Salle's map of 1695 actually uses the name Mississippi. Mississippi, contrary to common opinion, means "large river" in Chippewa, not "the father of waters."[53]

Mississippi is nicknamed the Magnolia State for the state flower and tree and the abundance of magnolias in the state. The state coat-of-arms, which depicts an American eagle, lends the nicknames the Eagle State and the Border-Eagle State to Mississippi. The numerous bayous in Mississippi, like Louisiana, lend the nickname the Bayou State to Mississippi. Finally, Mississippi is known as the Mud-cat State for the catfish that are abundant throughout the state's streams and swamps.[54]

MISSOURI

The Missouri Territory was named for the Missouri River, which, in turn, was named for the Missouri Indians. The earliest use of the word in writing occurs on the Marquette map of 1673. The Missouri, a small tribe, lived along the Missouri River with the Illinois to the east and the Little Osage to the west. The name means "canoe haver."[55]

The state of Missouri is commonly known as the Show Me State, a nickname attributed to Representative Willard Vandiver of Missouri. It connotes a certain self-deprecating stubbornness and devotion to simple common sense. Another politician, Thomas Hart Benton, gave Missouri the nickname the Bullion State for his advocacy of hard money, that is, gold and silver. Missouri is also called the Cave State for its numerous caves and caverns open to the public, the Lead State for its lead production, and the Ozark State for the Ozark Mountains in southern Missouri.[56]

MONTANA

Montana's name is derived from the Latin word *montaanus* meaning "mountainous." Montana Territory was created in 1864 out of Idaho Territory.[57]

Montana is popularly known as the Big Sky Country, an allusion to its immense area of mountains and valleys. The Stub Toe State, another nickname, refers to the state's mountainous terrain. The Bonanza State and the Treasure State refer to the importance of mining in Montana. "Naturally Inviting Montana" is a slogan used to promote Montana tourism.[58]

NEBRASKA

The state of Nebraska is actually named after the Platte River, a French name meaning "broad river." The Omaha Indians called the river Nibôápka, or "broad river." When Fremont was in Nebraska in 1842, he first used the word Nebraska in reference to the Platte River, and this name was applied to the territory created in 1854.[59]

Nebraska has had two official nicknames. In 1895, the legislature designated Nebraska as the Tree Planters' State because it is "preeminently a tree planting state."[60] In 1945, the legislature changed Nebraska's official nickname to the Cornhusker State in recognition of Nebraska football.[61] Nebraska is also unofficially nicknamed the Antelope State for the herds of antelope that once roamed its territory and the Bug-eating State for its numerous bull bats, which eat insects.[62]

NEVADA

Seventeenth and eighteenth century Spanish sailors traveling between the Philippines and Mexico saw mountain ranges in California from out at sea. They named these mountains Sierra Nevada or "snowy range." When a new territory was designated out of Utah, it was decided to name it Sierra Nevada, but the territory was named simply Nevada in 1859.[63]

Nevada is nicknamed the Sage State and the Sagebrush State for the wild sage that grows there prolifically. It is also known as the Silver State and the Mining State for its silver mines. Because Nevada was admitted to the Union in 1864 while the Civil War was raging, it has the additional nickname of the Battle Born State.[64]

NEW HAMPSHIRE

Captain John Mason of the Royal Navy received a grant in 1629 for the part of the land that became the state of New Hampshire. He named the area New Hampshire after the central English county of Hampshire, where he had spent a number of years of his youth.[65]

New Hampshire is nicknamed the Granite State for its extensive granite formations and quarries and the White Mountain State for the range of that name in northern New Hampshire. New Hampshire's mountains also lend it the nickname of the Switzerland of America. The mountains, which spawn five of New England's rivers, lend New Hampshire still another name, The Mother of Rivers.[66]

NEW JERSEY

New Jersey was named after the island of Jersey in the English Channel by Sir John Berkeley and Sir George Carteret. Berkeley and Carteret obtained a royal charter for this colony. Carteret was born on the island of Jersey and had been its lieutenant governor.[67]

New Jersey is known as the Garden State for its truck farms which provide produce to nearby cities and as the Clam State for the clams taken in off its coast. The Camden and Amboy State is an old nickname that recalls the influence of the Camden and Amboy Railroad in New Jersey. Two other nicknames are derived from an even earlier period: the Jersey Blue State recalls the blue uniforms of the New Jersey soldiers in the Revolutionary War,[68] and the Pathway of the Revolution recalls the many battles fought on New Jersey soil in the American Revolution.[69]

NEW MEXICO

The upper region of the Rio Grande was called "Nuevo Mexico" as early as 1561 by Fray Jacinto de San Francisco in the hope that this area would hold the riches of Mexico. Mexico, which is the Aztec spelling, means "place of Mexìtli," one of the Aztec gods. When New Mexico came under American control, the Spanish name was anglicized.[70]

New Mexico is nicknamed the Cactus State for the numerous cacti that grow there and the Spanish State in honor of its history as a Spanish-speaking state.[71] While New Mexico has an official slogan for business, commerce, and industry—"Everybody Is Somebody in New Mexico"—the sobriquet the Land of Enchantment adorns automobile license plates and is used frequently in the state publications that promote tourism.[72]

NEW YORK

When the British took over New Amsterdam from the Dutch in 1664, the city's new name was proclaimed to be New York in honor of the brother of England's Charles II, the Duke of York and Albany. The Dutch Colony was called New Netherlands, but New York became the name of both the city and the state.[73]

New York is commonly nicknamed the Empire State for its wealth and variety of resources. It is also known as the Excelsior State because the state motto is *Excelsior*. New York is also called the Knickerbocker State in reference to the breeches worn by early Dutch settlers.[74]

NORTH CAROLINA

North Carolina and South Carolina were one colony until they were divided in 1729. Carolina was originally named in honor of France's Charles IX and then in honor of England's Charles I and Charles II, both of whom made grants of Carolina. Carolina is the feminine form of the Latin word *Caroliinus,* an adjective derived from the name *Carolus,* or Charles.[75]

North Carolina is known as the Old North State in reference to its separation from South Carolina in 1729. It has also been called the Turpentine

State for its large production of turpentine. Possibly the most familiar nickname of North Carolina, however, is the Tarheel State. Originally a derisive term, "tarheels" is said to have been a name given to North Carolina Civil War soldiers by soldiers from Mississippi when the Carolina soldiers were routed from a position on a hill. They had forgotten to "tar their heels" and could not maintain their position.[76] Today the term has lost its derogatory inference.

NORTH DAKOTA

The Dakotas were divided into North and South Dakota by an omnibus bill passed in 1889.[77] Dakota is a Sioux word meaning "friends" or "allies." When Dakota Territory was created in 1861, it was named for the Dakota tribe which inhabited the region.[78]

North Dakota recognizes two nicknames. The Sioux State is a nickname that recognizes the Dakota tribe, also called the Sioux. The Flickertail State is a nickname referring to the flickertail squirrel which inhabits North Dakota. North Dakota is also sometimes called the Land of the Dakotas.[79]

OHIO

The state of Ohio is named after the Ohio River. The French explorer La Salle noted as early as 1680 that the Iroquois called the river "Ohio," meaning "large" or "beautiful river."[80]

Ohio is commonly called the Buckeye State for the buckeye trees that grow abundantly in the state and for an incident that occurred in 1788 when a very tall Colonel Sproat led a procession to a fort and the onlooking Indians, impressed by his stature, referred to him as "Big Buckeye." Ohio is also sometimes referred to as the Mother of Modern Presidents, having spawned seven American presidents.[81]

OKLAHOMA

The word Oklahoma first appears in the 1866 Choctaw-Chickasaw Treaty. Allen Wright, a native American missionary who spoke Choctaw, made up the word by combining two Choctaw words: " 'ukla" or person and "humá" or red. Oklahoma therefore means "red person."[82]

Oklahoma is known as the Sooner State and as the Boomer's Paradise. Both of these nicknames derive from the opening of the Oklahoma Territory for settlement in 1889. Boomers were those who came in hordes to settle the new land and sooners were those who illegally entered the territory to stake claims before the designated date and time.[83]

OREGON

The origin of the name Oregon is unclear. There are at least three possibilities, each quite different. Oregon may come from the French Canadian word "ouragan" meaning "storm" or "hurricane." The Columbia River was probably at one time called "the river of storms" by Canadian fur traders. Another possibility is that the name Oregon comes from the Spanish word "orejon" or "big-ear." This term was applied to a number of tribes of the region. Still another possibility is that the name of Oregon comes from the Spanish word "orégano" or wild sage, which was corrupted to Oregon. Sage grows abundantly in eastern Oregon.[84]

Oregon is known as the Beaver State because the beaver has been declared the state animal and is depicted on the state flag and as the Webfoot State in reference to its abundant rainfall. The Hard-case State is a nickname that was given to Oregon because of the difficulties encountered by early settlers.[85]

PENNSYLVANIA

When William Penn was granted a charter in 1680 by England's Charles II, the king gave the name Pennsylvania to the land. *Sylvania* is Latin for woods or woodland and, thus, Pennsylvania means "Penn's woods."[86]

Pennsylvania is sometimes called the Quaker State in reference to William Penn's religious affiliation and the Quakers who settled the state.[87] More commonly, Pennsylvania is nicknamed the Keystone State. Although the origin of this nickname has been lost, it was used and accepted by the turn of the eighteenth century. The term probably refers to Pennsylvania's geographical location in the original thirteen colonies that straddled the Atlantic Ocean.[88]

RHODE ISLAND

When Dutch explorer Adrian Block came upon an island with red clay shores, he named it in his native tongue "Roodt Eylandt," meaning "red island." Under English rule, the name was anglicized in the then current spelling.[89]

Rhode Island's status as the smallest state lends it the nicknames Little Rhody and the Smallest State. Roger Williams, who founded Providence Plantation in 1636, is honored by the sobriquet the Land of Roger Williams. Rhode Island, whose full name is actually The State of Rhode Island and Providence Plantations, is also known as the Plantation State. Finally, Rhode Island uses the nickname the Ocean State to promote tourism.[90]

SOUTH CAROLINA

The Carolinas were originally named in honor of Charles IX of France and then in honor of Charles I and Charles II of England. The Carolinas were divided into north and south in 1729.[91]

South Carolina's rice production lends it the nicknames the Rice State and the Swamp State. Its shape, that of a wedge, gives it the nickname of the Keystone of the South Atlantic Seaboard. The Iodine State is a nickname that refers to the iodine content of South Carolina plants, and the Palmetto State refers to South Carolina's state tree, the palmetto.[92]

SOUTH DAKOTA

The Dakota Territory was named for the Dakota tribe that inhabited the region. The territory was divided into north and south in 1889. Dakota is a Sioux word meaning "friends" or "allies."[93]

South Dakota recognizes two nicknames: the Sunshine State and the Coyote State.[94] The former nickname is frequently used in state publications promoting tourism, and the latter nickname refers to South Dakota's large population of coyotes.[95] South Dakota has also been called the Blizzard State for its severe winter weather and the Artesian State for its artesian wells.[96]

TENNESSEE

The original form of the name Tennessee was the Cherokee name "Tanasi." The Cherokee called two villages on the Little Tennessee River "Tanasi." The river was named after the villages and the region after the river. The meaning of the Cherokee name is unknown.[97]

Tennessee is widely known as the Volunteer State, a nickname resulting from the valor displayed by Tennessee volunteer soldiers fighting under Andrew Jackson in the Battle of New Orleans. Tennessee is also called the Big Bend State in reference to the Tennessee River and the Mother of Southwestern Statesmen for the three United States presidents it has spawned. At one time, Tennessee was called the Hog and the Hominy State for its pork and corn product production, but this nickname is no longer used.[98]

TEXAS

Texas, or "teysha" in the language of the Caddo, means "hello friend." The Spanish used this term to refer to friendly tribes throughout Louisiana, Oklahoma, and Texas. The tribes of the Caddo confederacy, who lived in Louisiana and eastern Texas, came to be called "the kingdom of the

Texas." The name of Texas was firmly established in 1690 when the Spanish named their first mission St. Francis of the Texas.[99]

Texas is popularly called the Lone Star State. The lone star on the state flag connotes the history of Texas as an independent republic fighting alone against great odds for its freedom. Texas is also called the Beef State for its cattle production and the Banner State for its leading position in many pursuits.[100]

UTAH

The White Mountain Apache referred to the Navajo as "Yuttahih" or "one that is higher up." European settlers and explorers understood the Apache term to refer to the Utes, who dwelled farther up the mountains than the Navajo. The land of the Utes came to be called Utah.[101]

Utah's state emblem, the beehive, gives it the nickname of the Beehive State. The beehive is a symbol of industry. Utah's Mormon heritage provides Utah with two nicknames: the Mormon State and the Land of the Saints (the Mormon church is officially called The Church of Jesus Christ of the Latter-Day Saints). Finally, Utah's Great Salt Lake gives it the additional nickname of the Salt Lake State.[102]

VERMONT

The French explorer Champlain, who saw Vermont's Green Mountains only from a distance, designated them as "Verd Mont" or "green mountain" in a 1647 map. The English name Vermont is therefore directly derived from Champlain's naming of the Green Mountains.[103] Vermont's mountains lend it the nickname of the Green Mountain State.[104]

VIRGINIA

Virginia was named in 1584 in honor of Queen Elizabeth of England, who was popularly called the "Virgin Queen." The name Virginia is the feminine form of the Latin word *virginius*.[105]

Virginia has long been nicknamed the Old Dominion or the Ancient Dominion. Charles II of England quartered the arms of Virginia on his shield in 1663 thus adding Virginia to his dominions of France, Ireland, and Scotland. Virginia is often called the Cavalier State for its early settlers who were loyal to England and the Mother of States because it was the first to be colonized. The predominance of the Virginia aristocracy in early United States politics and diplomacy lends Virginia the additional nicknames of the Mother of Presidents and the Mother of Statesmen.[106]

WASHINGTON

Washington Territory was carved out of Oregon Territory in 1853. It was named in honor of George Washington.[107]

The state of Washington is best known as the Evergreen State for its many large fir and pine trees. The Chinook State, a nickname referring to Washington's salmon industry and the Chinook Indians, is no longer in common use.[108]

WEST VIRGINIA

West Virginia was not separated from Virginia until 1861. West Virginia, as part of Virginia, was named after Queen Elizabeth of England, who was called the "Virgin Queen."[109]

West Virginia's scenic Allegheny Mountains lend it the nicknames the Switzerland of America and the Mountain State. Its shape gives it the additional name of the Panhandle State.[110]

WISCONSIN

The state of Wisconsin is named after the Wisconsin River. In Chippewa, Wisconsin means "grassy place." When Hennepin first recorded the name in 1695, it referred either to the river itself or to a place on the river.[111]

Wisconsin is popularly, but unofficially, called the Badger State after the early lead miners who lived underground and were called badgers. The badger is also the state animal of Wisconsin. Wisconsin is also known as the Copper State for its copper mines in the north.[112]

WYOMING

The name Wyoming comes from two Delaware words "mecheweamiing" meaning "at the big flats." A popular interpretation translates the Delaware words as "large plains." Legh Richmond Freeman, publisher of *The Frontier Index* in Kearney, Nebraska, claimed to have been the first to suggest the name Wyoming for the southwest half of the Dakota Territory.[113]

Wyoming has three nicknames currently in use. The Equality State recognizes Wyoming as the first state to extend women the right to vote; "Equality" is also the state motto. Wyoming is also called Big Wyoming and the Cowboy State.[114]

DISTRICT OF COLUMBIA

The District of Columbia was carved out of Maryland and Virginia and created on January 24, 1791. Columbia is feminine, as used for a country, derived from a neo-Latin adjective "columbius," or pertaining to Columbus. The practice of calling the district "Washington" honors the nation's first president.

AMERICAN SAMOA

What is now American Samoa is thought to have been settled around 600 B.C. by Polynesians coming from Fiji, the New Hebrides, and Indonesia. Samoan people were, therefore, quite established when Dutch explorer Jacob Roggeveen ended Samoa's isolation from the Western world in 1722. American Samoa, named for its inhabitants and its association with the United States since 1900, consists of seven islands 2,300 miles south-southwest of Honolulu. It is the only United States territory below the equator.[115]

COMMONWEALTH OF THE NORTHERN MARIANA ISLANDS

Ferdinand Magellan was the first Western explorer to sail through the Mariana Islands in 1521. He named the archipelago the "Island of the Latin Sails" because of the shape of the islanders' canoe sails. But when the islanders robbed his ship, he decided to call the place the "Islands of the Thieves." The islands were not renamed until 1668, when Spain established its first colony on Guam. They were named for the widow of King Philip IV of Spain, Queen Mariana of Austria. Germany bought the Northern Marianas from Spain in 1899 and fifteen years later, Japan seized the islands. After World War II, the U.S. Naval Administration governed until 1962 under a United Nations act making the Northern Marianas a trust territory of the United States. In 1976, a commonwealth was established and in 1986, the trusteeship was ended and the people of the Commonwealth of the Northern Mariana Islands (CNMI) became full U.S. citizens. The Commonwealth calls itself "Micronesia's Sun Belt."[116]

GUAM

Guam, or Guahan, is the southernmost island of the Mariana Archipelago. It was discovered and settled by Chamorros, who were probably of Indo-Malayan and Filipino descent, sometime before 1500 B.C. Magellan arrived there in 1521, but it was Miguel Lopez de Legaspi who claimed the Marianas for Spain. Jesuit missionaries arrived in Agana in 1668. The mission was funded by Queen Mariana of Spain, and the Mariana Islands were christened in her name. Agana became the capital of Guam and the Northern Mariana Islands.

The United States took possession of Guam from Spain in 1898. Except for the Japanese occupation from late 1941 to July 1944, the United States has administered the island. Citizenship rights were granted to Guamanians by the 1950 Organic Act of Guam. The unincorporated territory of Guam is America's westernmost frontier, which is why it is known both as "Where America's Day Begins" and "America's Paradise in the Pacific."[117]

PUERTO RICO

In 1493, during his second voyage, Christopher Columbus discovered an island called Boringuen, which was inhabited by several Indian tribes. He named the island San Juan in honor of St. John the Baptist. The city was called Puerto Rico, meaning "rich port." Later, the names were switched. Puerto Rico has been an American territory since 1898. Puerto Ricans became U.S. citizens in 1917, and in 1952, the island became a semi-autonomous commonwealth voluntarily associated with the United States.[118]

U.S. VIRGIN ISLANDS

The U.S. Virgin Islands lie 1,500 miles south-southeast of New York in the Lesser Antilles. St. Croix, St. Thomas, and St. John are the three principal islands. Columbus found the islands on his second voyage to the New World, naming them "The Virgins," referring to the beauty of the 11,000 seafaring virgins of St. Ursula. According to legend, St. Ursula agreed to marry a pagan prince at her father's request only after 11,000 of the most beautiful virgins of the two kingdoms were gathered to be her companions for three years. Ursula trained her companions into a fighting force and set off up the Rhine to Basel and from there to Rome on foot. But all were martyred near Cologne in 238 A.D.

The Danish took control of all three islands in 1733. They were purchased on March 31, 1917, by the United States for $25,000,000 from Denmark. Today, the Virgin Islands are an unincorporated territory of the United States and everyone born in the Islands is a U.S. citizen. The Virgin Islands call themselves the "American Paradise."[119]

NOTES

1. *Alabama State Emblems* (Montgomery: Alabama State Department of Archives and History, n.d.), p. 2; "The Name Alabama," *Arrow Points* 10 (January 1925): 19–20.

2. *Alabama State Emblems,* pp. 3–4.

3. J. Ellis Ransom, "Derivation of the Word 'Alaska,'" *American Anthropologist* 42 (July–September 1940): 551.

4. John P. Harrington, "Our State Names," *Smithsonian Institution Annual Report* (1954): 376.

5. *Welcome to Arizona* (Phoenix: Arizona Office of Tourism, n.d.); Harrington, "Our State Names," p. 376; Adlai Feather, "Origin of the Name Arizona," *New Mexico Historical Review* 39 (April 1964): 90–100.

6. Ark. Stat. Ann. § 5–102.
7. Harrington, "Our State Names," p. 376.
8. *A Brief History of Arkansas* (n.p., n.d.).
9. Ark. Stat. Ann. § 5–110.
10. *A Brief History of Arkansas.*
11. *California's Legislature, 1984,* pp. 212–13.
12. Cal. Gov't. Code § 420.75 (West).
13. *California's Legislature, 1984,* p. 203.
14. *Colorado State Capitol* (Denver: Colorado Department of Education, n.d.); Harrington, "Our State Names," p. 377.
15. Harrington, "Our State Names," p. 377.
16. *State of Connecticut Register and Manual, 1983,* p. 909.
17. Conn. Gen. Stat. Ann. § 3–110a (West).
18. George Shankle, *State Names, Flags, Seals, Songs, Birds, and Flowers, and Other Symbols,* rev. ed. (Westport: Greenwood Press, 1970, c 1938), pp. 105–6.
19. Harrington, "Our State Names," pp. 377–78.
20. *Delaware; Small Wonder* (Dover: Delaware State Travel Service, n.d.).
21. Harrington, "Our State Names," p. 378; *A Short History of Florida* (Tallahassee: Florida Department of State, n.d.), p. 1.
22. *Georgia's Capitol* (Atlanta: Max Cleland, n.d.).
23. Ibid.; Shankle, *State Names,* pp. 109–10.
24. *Hawaii, The Aloha State* (Honolulu: State of Hawaii, Hawaii Visitors Bureau, Chamber of Commerce of Hawaii, n.d.).
25. Haw. Rev. Stat. § 5–7.
26. *Idaho Blue Book, 1981–1982,* pp. 14–15.
27. Harrington, "Our State Names," p. 379.
28. Ill. Ann. Stat. ch. 1, § 3007 (Smith-Hurd).
29. Ibid., ch. 1, § 3131.
30. *Here Is Your Indiana Government,* 18th ed. (Indianapolis: Indiana State Chamber of Commerce, 1977), p. 135.
31. 1937 Indiana Acts, 1389.
32. *Here Is Your Indiana Government,* p. 135.
33. Benjamin F. Shambaugh, "The Naming of Iowa," *The Palimpsest 38* (March 1957): 97–98; Harrington, "Our State Names," p. 379.
34. Shambaugh, "The Naming of Iowa," p. 98.
35. Harrington, "Our State Names," pp. 379–80.
36. Shankle, *State Names,* pp. 115–16; *Kansas Directory 1982,* pp. 134–35.
37. Harrington, "Our State Names," p. 380.
38. *Oh! Kentucky* (Frankfort: Department of Travel Development, n.d.).
39. Frederick W. Lawrence, "The Origin of American State Names," *National Geographic 38* (July 1920): 129.
40. *Louisiana Facts* (Baton Rouge: Louisiana Department of State, n.d.); Harrington, "Our State Names," p. 380.
41. Shankle, *State Names,* p. 119.
42. *Quick Facts About Maine* (Augusta: John L. Martin, n.d.).
43. Ibid.
44. Shankle, *State Names,* pp. 119–20.
45. Harrington, "Our State Names," p. 380.

46. Gregory A. Stiverson and Edward C. Papenfuse, *Maryland and Its Government in Brief* (Annapolis: Archives Division, Hall of Records Commission, Department of General Services, n.d.), p. 14.
47. Harrington, "Our State Names," p. 381.
48. Shankle, *State Names,* p. 123; information provided by the Citizen Information Service, State of Massachusetts.
49. Harrington, "Our State Names," p. 381.
50. Shankle, *State Names,* p. 124.
51. *Minnesota Facts* (St. Paul: Minnesota Historical Society, Education Division, December 1983); Harrington, "Our State Names," p. 381.
52. Shankle, *State Names,* pp. 125–26.
53. *Souvenir of Mississippi* (Jackson: Dick Molpus, n.d.), p. 19; Harrington, "Our State Names," p. 382.
54. Shankle, *State Names,* p. 127.
55. Harrington, "Our State Names," p. 382.
56. Shankle, *State Names,* pp. 128–29.
57. *Montana Highway Map, 1985–86* (Helena: Montana Promotion Division, 1985).
58. Ibid.; Shankle, *State Names,* p. 130.
59. Harrington, "Our State Names," p. 383.
60. 1895 Neb. Laws, 441.
61. *Nebraska Blue Book, 1982–1983,* p. 12.
62. Shankle, *State Names,* p. 130.
63. Harrington, "Our State Names," p. 383.
64. Shankle, *State Names,* pp. 131–32.
65. Harrington, "Our State Names," p. 383.
66. Shankle, *State Names,* pp. 132–33.
67. Harrington, "Our State Names," p. 383.
68. Shankle, *State Names,* pp. 133–34.
69. *Your Miniguide to New Jersey* (Trenton: New Jersey Department of Commerce and Economic Development, Division of Travel and Tourism, 1985).
70. Harrington, "Our State Names," pp. 383–84.
71. Shankle, *State Names,* p. 135.
72. *New Mexico USA: Where to Go, What to Do* (Santa Fe: Marketing Services Division, New Mexico Economic Development and Tourism Department, 1986); N. M. Stat. Ann. § 12-3-9.
73. Harrington, "Our State Names," p. 384.
74. Shankle, *State Names,* p. 136.
75. Harrington, "Our State Names," p. 384.
76. Shankle, *State Names,* pp. 137–38.
77. *Facts About North Dakota* (Bismark: North Dakota Economic Development Commission, 1983), p. 32.
78. Harrington, "Our State Names," p. 384.
79. *Emblems of North Dakota* (Bismark: Ben Meier, n.d.), n.p.; Shankle, *State Names,* pp. 138–39.
80. Harrington, "Our State Names," pp. 384–85.
81. Shankle, *State Names,* pp. 139–40.

82. Harrington, "Our State Names," p. 385.
83. Shankle, *State Names,* pp. 140–41.
84. Harrington, "Our State Names," p. 385.
85. Shankle, *State Names,* pp. 141–42.
86. Harrington, "Our State Names," p. 385.
87. Shankle, *State Names,* p. 143.
88. *1976–77 Pennsylvania Manual,* p. 846.
89. Harrington, "Our State Names," pp. 385–86.
90. *State of Rhode Island Official Emblems* (Providence: Office of the Secretary of State, n.d.); Shankle, *State Names,* p. 144.
91. Harrington, "Our State Names," p. 384.
92. Shankle, *State Names,* pp. 144–45.
93. Harrington, "Our State Names," p. 384.
94. *Great Seal of South Dakota* (Pierre: Alice Kundert, n.d.).
95. *South Dakota Signs & Symbols,* n.p., n.d.
96. Shankle, *State Names,* pp. 146–47.
97. Harrington, "Our State Names," p. 386.
98. *Tennessee Blue Book, 1985–1986,* p. 341.
99. Harrington, "Our State Names," p. 386.
100. Shankle, *State Names,* pp. 148–49.
101. Harrington, "Our State Names," p. 386.
102. Shankle, *State Names,* p. 150.
103. Harrington, "Our State Names," pp. 386–87.
104. Shankle, *State Names,* pp. 150–51.
105. Harrington, "Our State Names," p. 387.
106. Shankle, *State Names,* pp. 151–52.
107. Harrington, "Our State Names," p. 387.
108. *Our State Seal, Flag, Flower, etc.* (Olympia: Washington State Superintendent of Public Instruction, n.d.).
109. Harrington, "Our State Names," p. 387.
110. Shankle, *State Names,* p. 154.
111. Harrington, "Our State Names," p. 387.
112. Shankle, *State Names,* pp. 154–55.
113. *Wyoming; Some Historical Facts* (Cheyenne: Wyoming State Archives, Museums and Historical Department, n.d.), p. 2.
114. Ibid., p. 1.
115. *American Samoa: Where Polynesia Began . . . and the South Pacific Begins* (n.p., n.d.); pamphlet provided by Office of Congressman Eni Faleomavaega.
116. *The Northern Marianas: Saipan, Tinian, Rota* (Saipan: Marianas Visitors Bureau, n.d.); *History and Geographic Tourist Map of Saipan* (Saipan: Economic Service Counsel, Inc., in cooperation with the Marianas Visitors Bureau, 1992).
117. *Guam and Micronesia* (Agana: Guam Visitors Bureau, 1989), p. 5; *Guam USA Fact Sheet* (Agana: Guam Visitors Bureau, n.d.).
118. *Puerto Rico: The Shining Star of the Caribbean* (San Francisco: Travel and Sports, Inc., 1992), p. 4.
119. *United States Virgin Islands Visitor's Guide* (n.p.: United States Virgin Islands, Division of Tourism, 1993), pp. 5, 8–9.

2 | State and Territory Mottoes

The use of mottoes accompanied the development of heraldry, which began to take hold in the twelfth century. A motto might be considered a terse statement, sometimes humorous, sometimes serious, that describes a certain spirit of the bearer. State mottoes, whether in English, Latin, French, or Spanish, or a native American language, express simply the character and beliefs of the citizenry.

Many state mottoes express a fundamental belief in God. Arizona's motto, *Ditat Deus,* means "God enriches." Florida's motto, taken from United States coinage, states simply "In God We Trust." Colorado's motto states that there is "Nothing without Providence" and Ohio's, that "With God, All Things Are Possible." South Dakota combines two common themes: "Under God the People Rule." Arkansas' motto boldly states that "The People Rule." Some statements of democratic belief are more pugnacious than religious: Alabama, "We Dare Maintain Our Rights," Massachusetts, "By the Sword We Seek Peace, but Peace Only Under Liberty," and New Hampshire, more direct, "Live Free or Die." Still other mottoes are designed as slogans rather than philosophical statements. Alaska promotes itself with the motto "North to the Future." Indiana calls itself "The Crossroads of America." Tennessee touts "Agriculture and Commerce," and Utah's motto is one word—"Industry."

ALABAMA

Motto: Audemus Jura Nostra Defendere[1]

Translation: "We Dare Maintain Our Rights"

Origin: This motto was selected by Marie Bankhead Owen, director of the State Department of Archives and History, when she requested B. J. Tieman to design a cost of arms in 1923. The motto was translated into Latin by University of Alabama Professor W. B. Saffold. The positive statement made by this motto replaced what was considered a negative statement imposed by outsiders during Reconstruction through the motto "Here We Rest."[2]

ALASKA

Motto: "North to the Future"[3]

Origin: In 1963, the Alaska Centennial Commission announced a competition to determine a distinctive centennial motto and emblem for Alaska.[4] During the competition, which carried a $300 prize, 761 entries were received. In December 1963, the commission announced that "North to the Future," the entry submitted by Juneau newsman Richard Peter, had won.[5] The legislature adopted this motto officially in 1967.

ARIZONA

Motto: Ditat Deus[6]

Translation: "God Enriches"

Origin: The motto remains unchanged since its introduction by Richard Cunningham McCormick in 1864. It is an expression, probably biblical in origin, of deep religious sentiment.

ARKANSAS

Motto: Regnat Populus[7]

Translation: "The People Rule"

Origin: A 1907 act changed the motto to its current language from "Regnant Populi," the motto selected in 1864. While the direct origin of this motto is somewhat obscure, it clearly voices the democratic tradition of the state and the nation.

CALIFORNIA

Motto: Eureka[8]

Translation: "I Have Found It"

Origin: The great seal of California, first designed in 1849, included this Greek motto to signify either the admission of the state into the Union or a miner's success.[9] Clearly, this ancient expression refers to the discovery of gold in California.

COLORADO

Motto: Nil Sine Numine[10]

Translation: "Nothing without Providence"

Origin: This motto is credited to William Gilpin, first territorial governor of Colorado. It may actually be an adaptation of a line from Virgil's *Aeneid.*[11]

CONNECTICUT

Motto: Qui Transtulit Sustinet[12]

Translation: "He Who Transplanted Still Sustains"

Origin: This motto, dating back to the early colonial history of Connecticut, was part of the colonial seal that depicted a vineyard. The words are adapted from the Book of Psalms 79:3.

DELAWARE

Motto: "Liberty and Independence"[13]

Origin: This motto was added to the state's great seal in 1847 as an expression of the ideals of American government.[14]

FLORIDA

Motto: "In God We Trust"[15]

Origin: The state seal, adopted in 1868, is declared to be the size of a silver dollar. This motto is evidently taken from the motto used on the silver dollar.

GEORGIA

Mottoes: "Agriculture and Commerce, 1776"; "Wisdom, Justice, Moderation"[16]

Origins: These mottoes appear on the great seal of the state—one on the obverse, the other on the reverse. Agriculture and commerce, of course, describe the mainstay of Georgia's economic well-being. In 1914, the date of 1799 was changed to 1776, the date of national independence rather than the date of Georgia's admission to the Union. Wisdom, justice, and moderation refer to the virtues that should guide legislative, judicial, and executive branches of government.

HAWAII

Motto: Ua Mau ke Ea o ka Aina i ka Pono[17]

Translation: "The Life of the Land Is Perpetuated in Righteousness"

Origin: Before becoming the state of Hawaii's official motto, these words were part of the coat of arms of the Kingdom of Hawaii and the seals of the Republic of Hawaii and the Territory. King Kamehameha III issued this motto upon the restoration of the Hawaiian flag to the kingdom by the British in 1843.[18]

IDAHO

Motto: Esto Perpetua[19]

Translation: "It Is Forever"

Origin: This motto is attributed to Venetian theologian and mathematician Pietro Sarpi (1552–1623) who, in 1623, applied it to the Republic of Venice.[20] This motto was chosen by the Grange in 1867 and by the state of Idaho in 1891.

ILLINOIS

Motto: "State Sovereignty, National Union"

Origin: These words were inscribed on the original state seal adopted in 1818. The seal that came into use in 1868, contrary to an amendment disallowing it, reversed the motto and placed "National Union" above "State Sovereignty." Nevertheless, the official motto places "State Sovereignty" first.[21]

INDIANA

Motto: "The Crossroads of America"[22]

Origin: The 1937 law designates "The Crossroads of America" as Indiana's official state motto or slogan. When this motto was chosen, the theoretical center of the United States was in Indiana; furthermore, a number of north-south and east-west routes intersect in Indiana.

IOWA

Motto: "Our Liberties We Prize, and Our Rights We Will Maintain"[23]

Origin: This motto, expressing the sentiment of Iowans as they entered the Union in 1846, was placed on the state seal by the first General Assembly in 1847.

KANSAS

Motto: Ad Astra per Aspera[24]

Translation: "To the Stars Through Difficulties"

Origin: John J. Ingalls was responsible for including this motto in the design of the great seal in 1861. He was at the time secretary of the Senate. Ingalls claimed the phrase was "as old as Josephus," quite common in heraldry, and the most melodious of various phrases that express similar sentiments. He had first noticed it in the office of the gentleman under whom he had read law.[25]

KENTUCKY

Motto: "United We Stand, Divided We Fall"[26]

Origin: This familiar motto paraphrases a line from John Dickinson's "Liberty Song of 1768," which says "By uniting we stand; by dividing we fall." George Pope Morris, who wrote the poem "The Flag of Our Union," probably got the phrase from the original song.[27]

LOUISIANA

Motto: "Union, Justice and Confidence"

Origin: An exact explanation for the choice of this motto has been lost in time. Clearly, however, it represents the sentiments present at Louisiana's joining the Union. Until 1864, the motto had been "Justice, Union, and Confidence."[28]

MAINE

Motto: Dirigo[29]

Translation: "I Direct" or "I Guide"

Origin: In the design of the seal, the star above the motto is intended to symbolize the state. The motto continues a navigational metaphor to the effect that the state should be a guiding light to its citizens just as the citizens should direct their efforts to the well-being of the state.[30]

MARYLAND

Mottoes: Fatti Maschii Parole Femine; Scuto Bonae Voluntatis Tuae Coronasti Nos[31]

Translation: "Manly Deeds, Womanly Words"; "With Favor Wilt Thou Compass Us as with a Shield"

Origins: The first motto is the motto of the Calvert family, whose history is closely tied to the state. The second motto is derived directly from the twelfth verse of the Fifth Psalm.[32]

MASSACHUSETTS

Motto: Ense Petit Placidam Sub Libertate Quietem[33]

Translation: "By the Sword We Seek Peace, but Peace Only under Liberty"

Origin: This motto was first used on the seal commissioned in 1775, after which time royal authority, and therefore royal seals, lost legitimacy. The motto is attributed to Algernon Sydney, who penned it in 1659.[34]

MICHIGAN

Motto: Si Quaeris Peninsulam Amoenam Circumspice[35]

Translation: "If You Seek a Pleasant Peninsula, Look About You"

Origin: This motto was placed on the 1835 great seal, which was designed by Lewis Cass. Cass, by one story, paraphrased the inscription on the north door of St. Paul's Cathedral in London, so that the lower peninsula took the place of the monument by which Christopher Wren wished to be remembered.[36]

MINNESOTA

Motto: L'Etoile du Nord[37]

Translation: "Star of the North"

Origin: This motto was substituted for the Latin motto on the territorial seal when Governor Sibley designed a new state seal. The seal was approved in 1861. This motto lies behind Minnesota's having become known as the North Star State.[38]

MISSISSIPPI

Motto: Virtute et Armis[39]

Translation: "By Valor and Arms"

Origin: James Rhea Preston, the superintendent of education, suggested this motto when the coat of arms was under consideration in 1894.[40]

MISSOURI

Motto: Salus Populi Suprema Lex Esto[41]

Translation: "The Welfare of the People Shall Be the Supreme Law"

Origin: This motto has always been found on the state seal, which was adopted in 1822. Its source is Cicero's *De Legibus.*[42]

MONTANA

Motto: Oro y Plata[43]

Translation: "Gold and Silver"

Origin: This motto first appeared on the territorial seal adopted in 1865. It had been suggested by a special committee charged with designing the seal. Curiously, it was decided that the motto should be Spanish, but no one knew enough Spanish to formulate the motto correctly in the committee report. The error was corrected before the seal was struck.[44]

NEBRASKA

Motto: "Equality Before the Law"[45]

Origin: This motto was adopted in 1867 along with the state seal. It speaks to the cornerstone of the American system of justice. In 1963, the legislature also adopted a state symbol, a sooner, and a slogan: "Welcome to Nebraskaland, where the West begins."[46]

NEVADA

Motto: "All for Our Country"[47]

Origin: This motto was adopted in 1866 along with the state seal. It is clearly an expression of patriotism.

NEW HAMPSHIRE

Motto: "Live Free or Die"[48]

Origin: These words were written as a toast for a veterans' reunion on July 31, 1809, by General John Stark. The motto was adopted by the legislature in 1945.[49]

NEW JERSEY

Motto: "Liberty and Prosperity"[50]

Origin: The state had used this patriotic, hopeful motto informally for at least a century before it was officially adopted in 1928 along with a new design of the state seal.[51]

NEW MEXICO

Motto: Crescit Eundo[52]

Translation: "It Grows as It Goes"

Origin: This motto, which has its origins in classical Latin literature, has been in use since 1851, when the territorial seal was first designed. It is a statement of belief in growth and progress. True to New Mexico's belief in growth and progress, the legislature adopted a slogan in 1975; the official state slogan for business, commerce, and industry in New Mexico is "Everybody Is Somebody in New Mexico."[53]

NEW YORK

Motto: Exselsior[54]

Translation: "Higher"

Origin: This ancient motto signifying progress has been New York's motto since 1778, when its original coat of arms was adopted.

NORTH CAROLINA

Motto: Esse Quam Videri[55]

Translation: "To Be Rather than to Seem"

Origin: This motto, adopted with the great seal in 1893, can be found in Cicero. It is an expression of the character of the citizens of North Carolina.

NORTH DAKOTA

Motto: "Liberty and Union Now and Forever, One and Inseparable"[56]

Origin: This motto is a quotation from Daniel Webster's *Reply to Hayne.* When the state seal was adopted in 1889, the law changed the wording of the motto used on the territorial seal to its present form.

OHIO

Motto: "With God, All Things Are Possible"[57]

Origin: Ohio's motto, adopted in 1959, is taken from the Bible, Matthew 19:26.

OKLAHOMA

Motto: Labor Omnia Vincit[58]

Translation: "Labor Conquers All Things"

Origin: The classical quotation from Virgil speaks to the virtue of hard work in the settlement and growth of Oklahoma. It was adopted in 1906 as part of the state's seal.

OREGON

Motto: Alis Volat Propriis[59]

Translation: "She Flies with Her Own Wings"

Origin: This motto was first found on the 1849 state seal in spite of the fact that a legislative committee had recommended the motto "The Union" in 1857 and the legislature adopted that motto in 1859. "The Union" remained Oregon's motto until 1987, when the legislature chose to change it back.[60]

PENNSYLVANIA

Motto: "Virtue, Liberty, and Independence"[61]

Origin: This motto was included in the state coat of arms designed in 1778 by Caleb Lownes of Philadelphia. In 1875, it was approved.

RHODE ISLAND

Motto: "Hope"[62]

Origin: The simple motto was added to the seal after the colony received a more liberal charter in 1644. The anchor, the symbol of hope, had been the colonial seal since the beginning.

SOUTH CAROLINA

Mottoes: Animis Opibusque Parati; Dum Spiro Spero

Translations: "Prepared in Mind and Resources"; "While I Breathe I Hope"

Origins: These mottoes and the state seal on which they appear symbolize the June 28, 1776, battle between what is now Fort Moultrie and the British fleet. These mottoes declaring South Carolina's determination, strength, and hope were chosen in 1776 after the colony had declared itself independent.[63]

SOUTH DAKOTA

Motto: "Under God the People Rule"[64]

Origin: This motto was adopted in the 1885 and 1889 South Dakota constitutions at the suggestion of Dr. Joseph Ward, the founder of Yankton College.[65]

TENNESSEE

Motto: "Agriculture and Commerce"

Origin: Tennessee adopted this motto officially in 1987, although it had been used on the state seal since 1801.[66] The legislature also adopted "Tennessee—America at Its Best" as the state slogan in 1965.[67]

TEXAS

Motto: "Friendship"[68]

Origin: This motto was adopted in 1930 in recognition that the name of the state is derived from the Indian word *tejas,* which means friendship.

UTAH

Motto: "Industry"[69]

Origin: This motto, adopted in 1896, is an appropriate motto for a state which uses the beehive as a symbol.

VERMONT

Motto: "Freedom and Unity"[70]

Origin: This motto, on the seal designed by Ira Allen in 1778 and adopted in 1779, expresses the desire that states remain free, but united.

VIRGINIA

Motto: Sic Semper Tyrannis[71]

Translation: "Thus Ever to Tyrants"

Origin: This motto, dating back to the revolutionary times of 1776, evokes the sentiment for independence among the colonists.

WASHINGTON

Motto: Alki

Translation: "Bye and Bye"

Origin: This Indian word appeared on the territorial seal designed by Lt. J. K. Duncan. When settlers landed at Alki Point in Seattle, they named their settlement New York-Alki. They had hoped Seattle would become the New York of the West Coast.[72]

WEST VIRGINIA

Motto: Montani Semper Liberi[73]

Translation: "Mountaineers Are Always Free"

Origin: This motto was adopted with the state seal in 1863. The seal was based on suggestions and designs by Joseph H. Diss Debar.

WISCONSIN

Motto: "Forward"[74]

Origin: This motto, part of the coat of arms, became Wisconsin's motto when the seal and coat of arms were revised in 1851. The seal was designed by Edward Ryan and John H. Lathrop. The motto "Forward" was a compromise between the two men when Ryan objected to Lathrop's Latin motto.[75]

WYOMING

Motto: "Equal Rights"[76]

Origin: This motto, which had been used on the seal, was officially adopted in 1955. It was chosen in recognition of the fact that Wyoming women had attained political rights in 1869, long before they could vote in national elections.

DISTRICT OF COLUMBIA

Motto: Justitia Omnibus

Translation: "Justice for All"

Origin: The first act passed by the District's first legislative assembly on August 3, 1871, created the corporate seal of the District of Columbia, which included this motto.[77]

AMERICAN SAMOA

Motto: Samoa—Muamua le Atua[78]

Translation: "Samoa—Let God Be First"

Origin: This motto, adopted officially in 1975, speaks to the religious fervor of the Chamorros, who populate American Samoa.

COMMONWEALTH OF THE NORTHERN MARIANA ISLANDS

The Commonwealth has not adopted an official motto.

GUAM

Guam has not adopted an official motto.

PUERTO RICO

Motto: Joannes Est Nomen Ejus[79]

Translation: "John Is His Name"

Origin: Christopher Columbus named the island of Puerto Rico San Juan in honor of St. John the Baptist. The coat of arms given by King Ferdinand to Puerto Rico in 1511 prescribed this motto.

U.S. VIRGIN ISLANDS

Motto: "United in Pride and Hope"[80]

Origin: This motto appears on the official seal of the Islands.

NOTES

1. Ala. Code § 1–2–1.
2. *Alabama State Emblems* (Montgomery: Alabama State Department of Archives and History, n.d.), pp. 9–11.
3. Alaska Stat. § 44.09.045.
4. *Centennial Press* 1 (September 1963): 1.
5. *Centennial Press* 1 (December 1963): 1.
6. Ariz. Rev. Stat. Ann. art. 22, § 20.
7. Ark. Stat. Ann. § 5–103.
8. Cal. Gov't. Code § 420.5 (West).
9. *California's Legislature, 1984,* p. 207.
10. Colo. Rev. Stat. § 24–80–901.
11. George E. Shankle, *State Names, Flags, Seals, Birds, Flowers, and Other Symbols,* rev. ed. (Westport: Greenwood Press, 1970, c 1938), pp. 158–59.
12. Conn. Gen. Stat. Ann. § 3–105.
13. Del. Code Ann. tit. 29, § 301.
14. *Official Insignia of Delaware* (Dover: Delaware State Development Department, n.d.).
15. Fla. Stat. Ann. § 15.03 (West).
16. Ga. Code Ann. § 50–3–30.
17. Haw. Rev. Stat. § 5–9.
18. 1959 Haw. Sess. Laws 365.
19. Idaho Code § 59–1005.
20. Shankle, *State Names,* p. 160.
21. *Illinois Blue Book, 1983–1984,* pp. 439–40.
22. 1937 Indiana Acts, 1389.
23. Iowa Code Ann. § 1A.1 (West).
24. Kan. Stat. Ann. § 75–201.
25. *Kansas Historical Collections* 8 (1903–04): 299.
26. Ky. Rev. Stat. Ann. § 2.020 (Baldwin).
27. *Louisville Times,* 19 November 1940 (copy supplied by Kentucky Department for Libraries and Archives).
28. La. Rev. Stat. Ann. § 49–153 (West); information provided by Richard H. Holloway, Archives, State of Louisiana, Division of Archivist, Records Management, and History.
29. Me. Rev. Stat. tit. 1, § 205.
30. *Resolves of the Legislature of the State of Maine . . .* (Portland: Francis Douglas, State Printer, 1820), p. 22.
31. Md. Ann. Code § 13–102.
32. Shankle, *State Names,* p. 162.
33. Mass. Gen. Laws Ann. ch. 2, § 1 (West).

34. "The History of the Seal of the Commonwealth" (copied material supplied by the Massachusetts Secretary of State, Citizen Information Service).
35. Mich. Comp. Laws Ann. § 2.21; § 2.22.
36. *Michigan History Magazine* 13 (1929): 663–64; *The Great Seal of Michigan* (Lansing: Richard H. Austin, n.d.).
37. Minn. Stat. Ann. § 1.135 (West).
38. *Minnesota Legislative Manual, 1985,* p. 11.
39. *Souvenir of Mississippi* (Jackson: Dick Molpus, n.d.), p. 19.
40. *Mississippi Official and Statistical Register, 1980–1984,* p. 27.
41. Mo. Ann. Stat. § 10.060 (Vernon).
42. Shankle, *State Names,* p. 163.
43. Mont. Rev. Codes Ann. § 1–1–501.
44. Rex C. Myers, *Symbols of Montana* (Helena: Montana Historical Society, 1976), p. 4.
45. Neb. Rev. Stat. § 84–501.
46. Ibid., § 90–105.
47. Nev. Rev. Stat. § 235.010.
48. N.H. Rev. Stat. Ann. § 3:8.
49. *Manual for the General Court, 1981.*
50. N.J. Stat. Ann. § 52:2–1 (West).
51. 1928 N.J. Laws 801.
52. N.M. Stat. Ann. § 12–3–1.
53. Ibid., § 12–3–9.
54. N.Y. State Law § 70 (McKinney).
55. N.C. Gen. Stat. § 144–2.
56. N.D. Cent. Code art. XI, § 2.
57. Ohio Rev. Code Ann. § 5.06 (Baldwin).
58. Okla. Stat. Ann. art. 6, § 35 (West).
59. Or. Rev. Stat. § 186.040.
60. "Motto (Oregon's)" (information supplied by the Office of the Secretary of State of Oregon).
61. *Pennsylvania Symbols* (Harrisburg: House of Representatives, n.d.).
62. R.I. Gen. Laws § 42–4–2.
63. *South Carolina State Symbols and Emblems* (Columbia: House of Representatives, n.d.)
64. S.D. Codified Laws Ann. § 1–6–2.
65. *History of the South Dakota State Flag* (Pierre: Bureau of Administration, Division of Central Services, The State Flag Account, n.d.).
66. Tenn. Code Ann. § 4–1–315.
67. Tenn. Code Ann. § 4–1–304.
68. Texas Rev. Civ. Stat. Ann. art. 6143a (Vernon).
69. Utah Code Ann. § 63–13–11.
70. Vt. Stat. Ann. tit. 1, § 491.
71. Va. Code § 7.1–26.
72. *Our State Seal, Flag, Flower, etc.* (Olympia: Washington State Superintendent of Public Instruction, n.d.).
73. W. Va. Code art. 2, § 7.
74. Wis. Stat. Ann. § 1.07 (West).

75. *State of Wisconsin, 1983–1984 Blue Book*, p. 947.
76. Wyo. Stat. Ann. § 8–3–107.
77. *Symbols of the District of Columbia* (Washington, D.C.: Government of the District of Columbia, Office of the Secretariat, Office of Visual Information Management, n.d.).
78. A.S. Code tit. 1, § 1102.
79. P.R. Laws Ann. tit. 1, § 34, § 37.
80. V.I. Code Ann. tit. 1, § 108.

3 | State and Territory Seals

Not merely decorative symbols of statehood, the seals of state have been used to designate official acts of state through the ages, and their use is strictly prescribed by law.

State seals are like snapshots of each state's history. Oklahoma's seal, for example, contains the symbols of the Cherokee, Chickasaw, Creek, Choctaw, and Seminole nations and forty-five small stars around a central star, representing the forty-five existing states before Oklahoma became the forty-sixth in 1907. The seal of Kansas, on which appear thirty-four stars for the thirty-fourth state, depicts a steamboat and a river to symbolize commerce, a settler's cabin and a mare plowing to represent agriculture and prosperity, a train of wagons heading west and a herd of buffalo retreating being chased by two Indians on horseback.

The symbols employed in the seals represent recurring themes—agriculture, commerce, mining, shipping, liberty, and union. These symbols celebrate the economic development of the state, the natural resources on which the state was built, and the freedom of a united people to pursue their lives in peace and harmony.

ALABAMA

In 1939, the Alabama legislature returned to the design of the great seal that had been used before 1868. At the same time, the legislature provided for an official coat of arms. The seal, which celebrates the historical importance of Alabama's river systems, is set out by law to be

> circular, and the diameter thereof two and a quarter inches; near the edge of the circle shall be the word "Alabama," and opposite this word, at the same distance from the edge, shall be the words, "great seal." In the center of the seal there shall be a representation of a map of the state with its principal rivers.[1]

The coat of arms signifies the history of Alabama under five flags, its status as a maritime state, and the courage of its citizens. The law describes the coat of arms as

> a shield upon which is carried the flags of four of the five nations which have at various times held sovereignty over a part or the whole of what is now the state of Alabama: Spain, France, Great Britain and the Confederacy. The union binding these flags shall be the shield of the United States. The shield upon which the flags and shield of the United States are placed shall be supported on either side by an eagle. The crest of the coat of arms shall be a ship representing the "Badine" which brought the French colonists who established the first permanent white settlements in the state. Beneath the shield there shall be a scroll containing the sentence in Latin: "Audemus jura nostra defendere," the English interpretation of which is "We Dare Maintain Our Rights." The word "Alabama" shall appear beneath the state motto.[2]

ALASKA

Alaska's state seal is 2⅛ inches in diameter and consists of "two concentric circles between which appear the words 'The Seal of the State of Alaska.' "[3] The design inside the inner circle represents northern lights, icebergs, railroads, and people native to the state as well as symbols for mining, agriculture, fisheries, and fur seal rookeries. This seal, with the substitution of the word "Territory" for "State," had been used as the territorial seal since 1913.[4] It officially became the state seal in 1960.

ARIZONA

The great seal of Arizona is set in the state's constitution, which was adopted in 1911.

> The seal of the State shall be of the following design: In the background shall be a range of mountains, with the sun rising behind the peaks thereof, and at the right side of the range of mountains there shall be a storage reservoir and a dam, below which in the middle

> distance are irrigated fields and orchards reaching into the foreground, at the right of which are cattle grazing. To the left in the middle distance on a mountain side is a quartz mill in front of which and in the foreground is a miner standing with pick and shovel. Above this device shall be the motto: "Ditat Deus." In a circular band surrounding the whole device shall be inscribed: "Great Seal of the State of Arizona," with the year of admission of the State into the Union.[5]

The seal uses the symbols of Arizona's first primary enterprises: reclamation, farming, cattle raising, and mining.

ARKANSAS

The seal of Arkansas was adopted in 1864. Except for an editorial change affecting the motto made in 1907, the seal has remained the same.

> An eagle at the bottom, holding a scroll in its beak, inscribed "Regnat Populus," a bundle of arrows in one claw and an olive branch in the other; a shield covering the breast of the eagle, engraved with a steamboat at top, a bee-hive and plow in the middle, and sheaf of wheat at the bottom; the Goddess of Liberty at the top, holding a wreath in her right hand, a pole in the left hand, surmounted by a liberty cap, and surrounded by a circle of stars, outside of which is a circle of rays; the figure of an angel on the left, inscribed "Mercy," and a sword on the right hand, inscribed "Justice," surrounded with the words "Seal of the State of Arkansas."[6]

The Arkansas seal celebrates the importance of the steamboat in its development and the industry of its citizens in a peaceful, bountiful land.

CALIFORNIA

The great seal of California was adopted by the 1849 constitutional convention. The code provides a pictorial description.[7] The seal as it now appears is the fourth design, a standardized representation adopted in 1937.

> In the circular design is a seated figure of the goddess Minerva, at her feet a grizzly bear, in the background ships upon a mountain-rimmed bay, in the mid-distance a goldminer at work and, near the top centre, the motto EUREKA (I have found it!) beneath a semi-circle of 31 stars, the number of States in the Union after the admission of California (September 9, 1850).[8]

COLORADO

The Colorado legislature adopted the state seal in 1877. The seal recalls the beauty of the Rocky Mountains and the significance of mining in the state's development.

> The seal of the state shall be two and one-half inches in diameter, with the following device inscribed thereon: An heraldic shield bearing in chief, or upon the upper portion of the same, upon a red ground three snow-capped mountains; above surrounding clouds; upon the lower part thereof upon a golden ground a miner's badge, as prescribed by the rules of heraldry; as a crest above the shield, the eye of God, being golden rays proceeding from the lines of a triangle; below the crest and above the shield, as a scroll, the Roman fasces bearing upon a band of red, white, and blue the words "Union and Constitution"; below the whole the motto, "Nil Sine Numine"; the whole to be surrounded by the words, "State of Colorado," and the figures "1876."[9]

CONNECTICUT

The seal of the state of Connecticut has a history that goes back to colonial times. The seal has undergone several modifications, but essential elements have remained as the 1931 description indicates.

> The great seal of the state shall conform to the following description: It shall be a perfect ellipse with its major axis two and one-half inches in length and its minor axis two inches in length, the major axis being vertical. Within such ellipse shall appear another ellipse with its major axis one and fifteen-sixteenths inches in length and its minor axis one and one-half inches in length. The inner ellipse is separated from the outer ellipse only by a line two points one-thirty-sixth of an inch in width and with the space between the two ellipses, being seven-thirty-seconds of an inch, forming a border. In said space shall appear, letter spaced and in letters one-eighth of an inch in height and of twelve point century Roman, the words "SIGILLUM REIPUBLICAE CONNECTICUTENSIS," beginning and ending one and one-sixteenth inches apart in the lower space along such border. In the center of the inner ellipse shall be three grape vines, two above and one below, each with four leaves and three clusters of grapes intertwined around a support nine-sixteenths of an inch high, and the base of the supports of the two upper vines one inch from the base of the inner ellipse and eleven-sixteenths of an inch apart. The base of the lower support shall be nine-sixteenths of an inch from the base of the inner ellipse and halfway between said bases shall appear the motto "QUI TRANSTU-

LIT SUSTINET," in number three, six point card Roman letters, or engraver's Roman letters, on a ribbon gracefully formed, with the ends of the ribbon turned upward and inward and cleft.[10]

The description of the official arms was revised slightly in 1990 from the original description of 1931.

> The following-described arms shall be the official arms of the state: A shield of rococo design of white field, having in the center three grape vines, supported and bearing fruit. The vine located in the center of the shield and the vine located on the right side of the shield shall ascend in a counterclockwise manner. The vine located on the left side of the shield shall ascend in a clockwise manner. The bordure to the shield shall consist of two bands bordered by fine lines adorned with clusters of white oak leaves (Quercus alba) bearing acorns. Below the shield shall be a white streamer, cleft at each end, bordered with two fine lines, and upon the streamer shall be in block letters the motto, "QUI TRANSTULIT SUSTINET." A drawing of said arms, made in conformity herewith and filed in the office of the secretary, shall be the official drawing of the arms of the state.[11]

DELAWARE

The great seal of Delaware is essentially the same design as the seal of 1777.

> It is emblazoned as follows: Party per fess, or and argent, the first charged with a garb (wheat sheaf) in bend dexter and an ear of maize (Indian Corn) in bend sinister, both proper; the second charged with an ox statant, ruminating, proper; fess, wavy azure, supporters on the dexter a husbandman with a hilling hoe, on the sinister a rifleman armed and accoutred at ease. Crest, on a wreath azure and argent, a ship under full sail, proper, with the words "Great Seal of the State of Delaware" and the words "Liberty and Independence" engraved thereon.[12]

The seal symbolizes the importance of shipping and farming in Delaware's history as well as Delaware's role in carving out American independence.

FLORIDA

The state seal was first designed in 1868 and remains substantially the same except for the substitution of the sabal palmetto for the cocoa tree in 1970.

> The great seal of the state shall be of the size of the American silver dollar, having in the center thereof a view of the sun's rays over a highland in the distance, a sabal palmetto palm tree, a steamboat on water, and an Indian female scattering flowers in the foreground, encircled by the words "Great Seal of the State of Florida: In God We Trust."[13]

The seal signifies Florida's tropical climate and the importance of native Americans in its history and the steamboat in its modern development. In 1985, the seal was officially revised to correct previous errors and to bring it into conformity with the change made in 1970.

GEORGIA

The great seal of Georgia was adopted by the state constitution of 1798. It remains the same today except for changing the date 1799 to 1776.

> The device on one side is a view of the seashore, with a ship bearing the flag of the United States riding at anchor near a wharf, receiving on board hogsheads of tobacco and bales of cotton, emblematic of the exports of this state; at a small distance a boat, landing from the interior of the state, with hogsheads, etc., on board, representing the state's internal traffic; in the back part of the same side a man in the act of plowing; and at a small distance a flock of sheep in different postures, shaded by a flourishing tree. The motto inscribed thereon is "Agriculture and Commerce, 1776."
>
> The device on the other side is three pillars supporting an arch, with the word "Constitution" engraved within the same, emblematic of the Constitution, supported by the three departments of government, namely the legislative, judicial, and executive. The first pillar has engraved upon it "Wisdom," the second, "Justice," the third, "Moderation"; on the right of the last pillar a man stands with a drawn sword, representing the aid of the military in the defense of the Constitution, and the motto is "State of Georgia, 1776."[14]

HAWAII

Except for the legend "Republic of Hawaii" and the size of the seal, Hawaii's state seal is the same as that of the Republic of Hawaii.

> The great seal of the State shall be circular in shape, two and three-quarters inches in diameter, and of the design being described, with the tinctures added as a basis for the coat of arms as follows:
>
> *Arms.* An heraldic shield which is quarterly; first and fourth, stripes of the Hawaiian flag; second and third, on a yellow field, a white ball

pierced on a black staff; overall, a green escutcheon with a five-pointed yellow star in the center.

Supporters. On the right side, Kamehameha I, standing in the attitude as represented by the bronze statue in front of Aliiolani Hale, Honolulu; cloak and helmet yellow; figure in natural colors. To the left, goddess of liberty, wearing a Phrygian cap and laurel wreath, and holding in right hand the Hawaiian flag, partly unfurled.

Crest. A rising sun irradiated in gold, surrounded by a legend "State of Hawaii, 1959," on a scroll, black lettering.

Motto. "Ua mau ke ea o ka aina i ka pono" on the scroll at bottom, gold lettering.

Further accessories. Below the shield, the bird phoenix wings outstretched; arising from flames, body black, wings half yellow, half dark red; also eight taro leaves, having on either side banana foliage and sprays of maidenhair fern, trailed upwards.[15]

IDAHO

The Idaho state seal, designed by Emma Edwards Green, was adopted in 1891.[16] The designer described the seal in these words:

> The question of Woman Suffrage was being agitated somewhat, and as leading men and politicians agreed that Idaho would eventually give women the right to vote, and as mining was the chief industry, and the mining man the largest financial factor of the state at that time, I made the figure of the man the most prominent in the design, while that of the woman, signifying justice, as noted by the scales, liberty, as denoted by the liberty cap on the end of the spear, and equality with man as denoted by her position at his side, also signifies freedom. The pick and shovel held by the miner, and the ledge of rock beside which he stands, as well as the pieces of ore scattered about his feet, all indicate the chief occupation of the State. The stamp mill in the distance, which you can see by using a magnifying glass, is also typical of the mining interest of Idaho. The shield between the man and the woman is emblematic of the protection they unite in giving the state. The large fir or pine tree in the foreground in the shield refers to Idaho's immense timber interests. The husbandman plowing on the left side of the shield, together with the sheaf of grain beneath the shield, are emblematic of Idaho's agricultural resources, while the cornucopias, or horns of plenty, refer to the horticultural. Idaho has a game law, which protects the elk and moose. The elk's head, therefore, rises above the shield. The state flower, the wild Syringa or Mock Orange, grows at the woman's feet, while the ripened

> wheat grows as high as her shoulder. The star signifies a new light in the galaxy of states. . . . The river depicted in the shield is our mighty Snake or Shoshone River, a stream of great majesty.[17]

ILLINOIS

The Illinois state seal, designed by Secretary of State Sharon Tyndale, dates back to 1867 and was first used in 1868. This seal, actually the third since statehood, is considerably altered from the earlier seals.[18]

> The secretary of state is hereby authorized and required to renew the great seal of state, and to procure it as nearly as practicable of the size, form and intent of the seal now in use, and conforming with the original design, as follows: "American eagle on a boulder in prairie—the sun rising in distant horizon," and scroll in eagle's beak, on which shall be inscribed the words: "State Sovereignty," "National Union," to correspond with the original seal of state, in every particular.[19]

INDIANA

Until 1963, Indiana had no officially authorized state seal although pioneer scenes were used on territorial seals as early as 1801.[20] The 1963 law sets out this description:

> The official seal for the state of Indiana shall be described as follows:
>
> A perfect circle, two and five eighths (2⅝) inches in diameter, inclosed by a plain line. Another circle within the first, two and three eighths (2⅜) inches in diameter inclosed by a beaded line, leaving a margin of one quarter (¼) of an inch. In the top half of this margin are the words "Seal of the State of Indiana."
>
> At the bottom center, 1816, flanked on either side by a diamond, with two (2) dots and a leaf of the tulip tree (liriodendron tulupifera), at both ends of the diamond. The inner circle has two (2) trees in the left background, three (3) hills in the center background with nearly a full sun setting behind and between the first and second hill from the left.
>
> There are fourteen (14) rays from the sun, starting with two (2) short ones on the left, the third being longer and then alternating, short and long. There are two (2) sycamore trees on the right, the larger one being nearer the center and having a notch cut nearly half way through, from the left side, a short distance above the ground. The woodsman is wearing a hat and holding his ax nearly perpendicular on his right. The ax blade is turned away from him and is even with his hat.

> The buffalo is in the foreground, facing to the left of front. His tail is up, front feet on the ground with back feet in the air—as he jumps over a log.
>
> The ground has shoots of blue grass, in the area of the buffalo and woodsman.[21]

IOWA

In 1847, the first General Assembly of Iowa adopted the following act designating a state seal:

> The secretary of state be, and he is, hereby authorized to procure a seal which shall be the great seal of the state of Iowa, two inches in diameter, upon which shall be engraved the following device, surrounded by the words, "The Great Seal of the State of Iowa"—a sheaf and field of standing wheat, with a sickle and other farming utensils, on the left side near the bottom; a lead furnace and pile of pig lead on the right side; the citizen soldier, with a plow in his rear, supporting the American flag and liberty cap with his right hand, and his gun with his left, in the center and near the bottom; the Mississippi river in the rear of the whole, with the steamer Iowa under way; an eagle near the upper edge, holding in his beak a scroll, with the following inscription upon it: Our liberties we prize, and our rights we will maintain.[22]

KANSAS

The 1861 resolution creating the great seal of Kansas describes the seal as follows:

> The east is represented by a rising sun, in the right-hand corner of the seal; to the left of it, commerce is represented by a river and a steamboat; in the foreground, agriculture is represented as the basis of the future prosperity of the state, by a settler's cabin and a man plowing with a pair of horses; beyond this is a train of ox-wagons, going west; in the background is seen a herd of buffalo, retreating, pursued by two Indians, on horseback; around the top is the motto, "Ad astra per aspera," and beneath a cluster of thirty-four stars. The circle is surrounded by the words, "Great seal of the state of Kansas. January 29, 1861."[23]

KENTUCKY

Kentucky's seal has remained essentially unchanged since 1792. It combines friendship with a slogan of revolutionary fervor.

> The seal of the Commonwealth shall have upon it the device, two (2) friends embracing each other, with the words "Commonwealth of Kentucky" over their heads and around them the words, "United We Stand, Divided We Fall."[24]

LOUISIANA

The code of Louisiana empowers the governor of the state to devise a public seal to authenticate official governmental acts.[25] In 1902, Governor William Wright Heard prescribed this description of the seal:

> A Pelican, with its head turned to the left, in a nest with three young; the Pelican, following the tradition in act of tearing its breast to feed its young; around the edge of the seal to be inscribed "State of Louisiana." Over the head of the Pelican to be inscribed "Union, Justice," and under the Pelican to be inscribed "Confidence."[26]

The motto and the pelican have been employed in Louisiana seals since at least 1804.

MAINE

In 1820, when Maine became a state, a law was passed describing the state seal. The current law provides a bit more detail and retains all the features of the original seal.

> The seal of the State shall be a shield; argent, charged with a pine tree (Americana, quinis ex uno folliculo setis) with a moose deer (cervus alces), at the foot of it, recumbent; supporters: on dexter side, a husbandman, resting on a scythe; on sinister side, a seaman, resting on an anchor.
>
> In the foreground, representing sea and land, and under the shield, shall be the name of the State in large Roman capitals, to wit: MAINE.
>
> The whole shall be surrounded by a crest, the North Star. The motto, in small Roman capitals, shall be in a label interposed between the shield and crest, viz.:—DIRIGO.[27]

MARYLAND

The Maryland seal, readopted in 1876, is the seal sent from England shortly after the colony was settled. The reverse of the seal is the official state seal. The obverse is used only for decorative purposes.[28]

Description of Great Seal:

(a) Obverse. On the obverse of the Great Seal of Maryland is an equestrian figure of the Lord Proprietary, arrayed in complete armour and bearing a drawn sword in his hand. The caparisons of the horse are adorned with the family coat of arms. On the ground below is represented a sparse growth of grass on sand soil, with a few small blue and yellow flowers. On the circle, surrounding the obverse of the seal, is the Latin inscription "Caecilius Absolutus Dominus Terrae Mariae et Avaloniae Baro de Baltemore" meaning "Cecil Absolute Lord of Maryland and Avalon Baron of Baltimore" (Avalon refers to Lord Baltimore's first settlement in the new world, in Newfoundland).

(b) Reverse. On the reverse of the Great Seal of Maryland is Lord Baltimore's hereditary coat of arms. The 1st and 4th quarters represent the arms of the Calvert family described in heraldic language as a paly of 6 pieces, or (gold) and sable (black) a bend counterchanged. The 1st and 4th quarters are the left-hand top quarter and the right-hand bottom quarter. The 2nd and 3rd quarters show the arms of the Crossland family, which Cecil inherited from his grandmother, Alicia, wife of Leonard Calvert, the father of George, 1st Lord Baltimore. This coat of arms is in quarters also, argent (silver) and gules (red) a cross bottony (boutonne, with a button or a three-leaf clover at the end of each radius of the cross) counterchanged. Above the shield is placed an Earl's coronet (indicating that though only a baron in England, Calvert was an earl or court palatine in Maryland). Above that, a helmet set full faced and over that the Calvert crest, (2 pennons, the dexter or the right one or (gold), the other sable (black) staffs gules (red) issuing from the ducal coronet). The supporters of the shield are a plowman and a fisherman with their hands on the shield, designated respectively by a spade held in the right hand of the plowman and a fish held in the left hand of the fisherman (the fish is heraldic and cannot, therefore, be identified as to any species). The plowman wears a high-crowned, broad-brimmed beaver hat; the fisherman wears a knitted cap (somewhat resembling a stocking cap). The motto in Italian on a ribbon at the feet of the plowman and fisherman is the motto of the Calvert family "Fatti maschii parole femine" loosely translated as "Manly deeds, womanly words." Behind and surrounding both shield and supporters is an ermine-lined mantle and on the circle around this part of the seal are the words "Scuto bonae voluntatis tuae coronasti nos" (5th Psalm, 12th verse: "With favor wilt thou compass us as with a shield") and the date 1632. The date refers to the year the charter was granted.[29]

MASSACHUSETTS

The seal and coat of arms of Massachusetts were adopted in 1885; some revisions were made in 1898 and 1971. The current law holds that the seal

> shall be circular in form, bearing upon its face a representation of the arms of the commonwealth encircled with the inscription within a beaded border, "Sigillum Reipublicae Massachusettensis." The colors of the arms shall not be an essential part of said seal, and an impression from a seal engraved according to said design, on any commission, paper, or document shall be valid without such colors or the representation thereof by heraldic lines or marks.[30]

The coat of arms is described as consisting of

> a blue shield with an Indian thereon, dressed in a shirt, leggings, and moccasins, holding in his right hand a bow, and in his left hand an arrow, point downward, all of gold; and, in the upper right-hand corner of the field a silver star of five points. The crest shall be, on a wreath of gold and blue, a right arm, bent at the elbow, clothed and ruffled, and grasping a broad-sword, all of gold. The motto "Ense petit placidam sub libertate quietem" shall appear in gold on a blue ribbon.[31]

MICHIGAN

The great seal of Michigan, adopted in 1911, is the 1835 seal designed by Lewis Cass. The law now reads that

> the great seal shall be comprised of the coat of arms of the state around which shall appear the words "great seal of the state of Michigan, A.D. MDCCCXXXV."[32]

The coat of arms, simply the seal without the legend, was also adopted in 1911. It is described as follows:

> The coat-of-arms shall be blazoned as follows:
>
> Chief, Azure, motto argent Tuebor;
>
> Charge, Azure, sun-rayed rising sinister proper, lake wavey proper, peninsula dexter grassy proper, man dexter on peninsula, rustic, habited, dexter arm-raised, dexter turned, sinister arm with gun stock resting, all proper;
>
> Crest, On a wreath azure and or, an American eagle rising to the dexter, tips of wings partly lowered to base, all proper, dexter talon holding an olive branch with 13 fruit, sinister talon holding a sheaf

of 3 arrows, all proper. Over his head a sky azure environed with a scroll gules with the motto "E Pluribus Unum" argent;

Supporters:

Dexter, An elk rampant, proper;

Sinister, A moose rampant, proper;

Mottoes, On the scroll unending superior narrow argent, in sable, the motto, "Si quaeris peninsulam, amoenam."

On the scroll unending inferior, broader argent in sable the motto "circumspice."

Observations:

Scroll support and conventional leaf design between shield and scroll superior or;

Escutcheon supporters rest on the scroll supports and leaf design.[33]

MINNESOTA

Even though Minnesota became a state in 1858, the territorial seal remained in use until 1861 when the Minnesota legislature approved Governor Sibley's design for a state seal.[34] The design was revised in 1983 to read as follows:

(a) The seal is composed of two concentric borders. The outside forms the border of the seal and the inside forms the border for the illustrations within the seal. The area between the two borders contains lettering.

(b) The seal is two inches in diameter. The outside border has a radius of one inch and resembles the serrated edge of a coin. The width of the border is 1/16 of an inch.

(c) The inside border has a radius of three-fourths of an inch and is composed of a series of closely spaced dots measuring 1/32 of an inch in diameter.

(d) Within the area between the borders "The Great Seal of the State of Minnesota" is printed in capital letters. Under that is the date "1858" with two dagger symbols separating the date and the letters. The lettering is 14 point century bold.

(e) In the area within the inside border is the portrayal of an 1858 Minnesota scene made up of various illustrations that serve to depict a settler plowing the ground near the falls of St. Anthony while he watches an Indian on horseback riding in the distance.

(f) For the purposes of description, when the area within the inside border is divided into quadrants, the following illustrations should be clearly visible in the area described.

(1) In the upper parts of quadrants one and two, the inscription, "L'Etoile du Nord" is found on the likeness of a scroll whose length is equal to twice the length of the inscription, but whose ends are twice folded underneath and serve to enhance the inscription. The lettering is seven point century bold.

(2) In quadrant two is found a likeness of a rising sun whose ambient rays form a background for a male Indian in loincloth and plume riding on horseback at a gallop. The Indian is sitting erect and is holding a spear in his left hand at an upward 60-degree angle to himself and is looking toward the settler in quadrant four.

(3) In quadrant one, three pine trees form a background for a picturesque resemblance of St. Anthony Falls in 1858.

(4) In quadrants three and four, cultivated ground is found across the lower half of the seal, which provides a background for the scenes in quadrants three and four.

(5) In quadrant three, a tree stump is found with an ax embedded in the stump and a period muzzle loader resting on it. A powder flask is hanging towards the end of the barrel.

(6) In quadrant four, a white barefoot male pioneer wearing clothing and a hat of that period is plowing the earth, using an animal-drawn implement from that period. The animal is not visible. The torso of the man continues into quadrant two, and he has his legs spread apart to simulate movement. He is looking at the Indian.

Additional effects; size. Every effort shall be made to reproduce the seal with justification to the 12 o'clock position and with attention to the authenticity of the illustrations used to create the scene within the seal. The description of the scene in this section does not preclude the graphic inclusion of the effects of movement, sunlight, or falling water when the seal is reproduced. Nor does this section prohibit the enlargement, proportioned reduction, or embossment of the seal for its use in unofficial acts.

Historical symbolism of seal. The sun, visible on the western horizon, signifies summer in the northern hemisphere. The horizon's visibility signifies the flat plains covering much of Minnesota. The Indian on horseback is riding due south and represents the great Indian heritage of Minnesota. The Indian's horse and spear and the Pioneer's ax, rifle, and plow represent tools that were used for hunting and labor. The stump symbolizes the importance of the lumber industry in Minnesota's history. The Mississippi River and St. Anthony Falls are depicted to note the importance of these resources in transportation and industry. The cultivated ground and the plow symbolize the importance of agriculture in Minnesota. Beyond the falls three pine trees represent the state tree and three great pine regions of Minnesota; the St. Croix, Mississippi, and Lake Superior.[35]

MISSISSIPPI

The great seal of the state of Mississippi adopted by the legislature is the same seal that has been in use since statehood was attained in 1817.[36] The 1817 law reads:

> The seal of this state, the inscription of which shall be "the great seal of the state of Mississippi" around the margin, and in the center an eagle, with the olive branch and quiver of arrows in his claws.[37]

MISSOURI

The Missouri state seal, designed by a select committee of legislators, was adopted by the legislature and signed into law in 1822.

> The device for an armorial achievement for the state of Missouri is as follows: Arms, parted per pale, on the dexter side; gules, the white or grizzly bear of Missouri, passant guardant, proper on a chief engrailed; azure, a crescent argent; on the sinister side, argent, the arms of the United States, the whole within a band inscribed with the words "UNITED WE STAND, DIVIDED WE FALL." For the crest, over a helmet full-faced, grated with six bars; or a cloud proper, from which ascends a star argent, and above it a constellation of twenty-three smaller stars, argent, on an azure field, surrounded by a cloud proper. Supporters on each side, a white or grizzly bear of Missouri, rampant, guardant proper, standing on a scroll, inscribed with the motto, "Salus populi suprema lex esto," and under the scroll numerical letters MDCCCXX. And the great seal of the state shall be so engraved as to present by its impression the device of the armorial achievement aforesaid, surrounded by a scroll inscribed with the words, "THE GREAT SEAL OF THE STATE OF MISSOURI," in Roman capitals, which seal shall be in a circular form and not more than two and a half inches in diameter.[38]

MONTANA

The Montana territorial seal, slightly altered since 1865, became the state seal by legislative act in 1893.[39]

> The great seal of the state is as follows: a central group representing a plow and a miner's pick and shovel; upon the right, a representation of the Great Falls of the Missouri River; upon the left, mountain scenery; and underneath, the words "Oro y Plata." The seal must be 2½ inches in diameter and surrounded by these words, "The Great Seal of the State of Montana."[40]

NEBRASKA

The great seal of the state of Nebraska was laid by an 1867 law, which reads in part:

> The eastern part of the circle to be represented by a steamboat ascending the Missouri river; the mechanic arts to be represented by a smith with hammer and anvil; in the foreground, agriculture to be represented by a settler's cabin, sheaves of wheat and stalks of growing corn; in the background a train of cars heading towards the Rocky Mountains, and on the extreme west, the Rocky Mountains to be plainly in view; around the top of this circle to be in capital letters, the motto, "EQUALITY BEFORE THE LAW," and the circle to be surrounded with the words, "Great Seal of the State of Nebraska, March 1st, 1867."[41]

NEVADA

The state seal was officially adopted in 1866. The current law states that

> 1. There shall be a seal of the State of Nevada called The Great Seal of the State of Nevada, the design of which shall be as follows: In the foreground, there shall be two large mountains, at the base of which, on the right, there shall be located a quartz mill, and on the left a tunnel, penetrating the silver leads of the mountain, with a miner running out a carload of ore, and a team loaded with ore for the mill. Immediately in the foreground, there shall be emblems indicative of the agricultural resources of the state, as follows: A plow, a sheaf and sickle. In the middle ground, there shall be a railroad train passing a mountain gorge and a telegraph line extending along the line of the railroad. In the extreme background, there shall be a range of snowclad mountains, with the rising sun in the east. Thirty-six stars and the motto of our state, "All for Our Country," shall encircle the whole group. In an outer circle, the words "The Great Seal of the State of Nevada" shall be engraved with "Nevada" at the

base of the seal and separated from the other words by two groups of three stars each.

2. The size of the seal shall not be more than 2¾ inches in diameter.[42]

NEW HAMPSHIRE

The current seal was adopted in 1931, when a committee was formed to recommend improvements in the seal of 1784. The statute describing the seal is reprinted with permission of Butterworth Legal Publishers.

> The seal of the state shall be two inches in diameter, circular, with the following detail and no other: A field crossed by a straight horizon line of the sea, above the center of the field; concentric with the field the rising sun, exposed above the horizon about one third of its diameter; the field encompassed with laurel; across the field for the full width within the laurel a broadside view of the frigate Raleigh, on the stocks; the ship's bow dexter and higher than the stern; the three lower masts shown in place, together with the fore, main and mizzen tops, shrouds and mainstays; an ensign staff at the stern flies the United States flag authorized by act of Congress June 14, 1777; a jury staff on the mainmast and another on the foremast each flies a pennant; flags and pennants are streaming to the dexter side; the hull is shown without a rudder; below the ship the field is divided into land and water by a double diagonal line whose highest point is sinister; no detail is shown anywhere on the water, nor any on the land between the water and the stocks except a granite boulder on the dexter side; encircling the field is the inscription, SEAL OF THE STATE OF NEW HAMPSHIRE, the words separated by round periods, except between the parts of New Hampshire; at the lowest point of the inscription is the date 1776, flanked on either side by a five-pointed star, which group separates the beginning and end of the inscription.[43]

In 1945, the legislature also adopted a state emblem. The law, slightly amended in 1957, is reprinted with permission of Butterworth Legal Publishers.

> The state emblem shall be of the following design: With an elliptical panel, the longest dimension of which shall be vertical, there shall appear an appropriate replica of the Old Man of the Mountains; surrounding the inner panel, and enclosed within another ellipse, there shall be at the bottom of the design the words of any state motto which may be adopted by the general court; and at the top of the design, between the inner and outer elliptical panels, the words, New Hampshire, appropriately separated from the motto, if adopted, by

> one star on each side. Said emblem may be placed on all printed or related material issued by the state and its subdivisions relative to the development of recreational, industrial, and agricultural resources of the state.[44]

NEW JERSEY

The great seal was authorized in 1776 and its design amended in 1928. The law describes the seal accordingly:

> The great seal of this state shall be engraved on silver, which shall be round, of two and a half inches in diameter and three-eighths of an inch thick; the arms shall be three ploughs in an escutcheon, azure; supporters, Liberty and Ceres. The Goddess Liberty to carry in her dexter hand a pole, proper, surmounted by a cap gules, with band azure at the bottom, displaying on the band six stars, argent; tresses falling on shoulders, proper; head bearing over all a chaplet of laurel leaves, vert; overdress, tenne; underskirt, argent; feet sandaled, standing on a scroll. Ceres: Same as Liberty, save overdress, gules; holding in left hand a cornucopia, or, bearing apples, plums and grapes surrounded by leaves, all proper; head bearing over all a chaplet of wheat spears, vert. Shield surmounted by sovereign's helmet, six bars, or; wreath and mantling, argent and azure. Crest: A horse's head, proper. Underneath the shield and supporting the goddesses, a scroll azure, bordered with tenne, in three waves or folds; on the upper folds the words "Liberty and Prosperity"; on the under fold in Arabic numerals, the figures "1776." These words to be engraved round the arms, viz., "The Great Seal of the State of New Jersey."[45]

NEW MEXICO

The great seal of New Mexico is essentially the one that was designed for the Territory of New Mexico in 1851 and adopted in 1887. After becoming a state in 1912, the state legislature adopted the old territorial seal, appropriately changed for New Mexico's new status, as the state seal.[46]

> The coat of arms of the state shall be the Mexican eagle grasping a serpent in its beak, the cactus in its talons, shielded by the American eagle with outspread wings, and grasping arrows in its talons; the date 1912 under the eagles and, on a scroll, the motto: "Crescit Eundo." The great seal of the state shall be a disc bearing the coat of arms and having around the edge the words "Great Seal of the State of New Mexico."[47]

NEW YORK

The great seal of New York was officially designated in 1882. The 1882 law seeks to describe the seal first adopted in 1778.

> The secretary of state shall cause to be engraved upon metal two and one-half inches in diameter the device of arms of this state, accurately conformed to the description thereof given in this article, surrounded with the legend, "The great seal of the state of New York."[48]

NORTH CAROLINA

North Carolina's seal was adopted first in 1893 and has undergone some modifications since then. The current law is as follows:

> The Governor shall procure for the State a seal, which shall be called the great seal of the State of North Carolina, and shall be two and one-quarter inches in diameter, and its design shall be a representation of the figures of Liberty and Plenty, looking toward each other, but not more than half-fronting each other and otherwise disposed as follows: Liberty, the first figure, standing her pole with cap on it in her left hand and a scroll with the word "Constitution" inscribed thereon in her right hand. Plenty, the second figure, sitting down, her right arm half extended towards Liberty, three heads of grain in her right hand, and in her left, the small end of her horn, the mouth of which is resting at her feet, and the contents of the horn rolling out.
>
> The background on the seal shall contain a depiction of mountains running from left to right to the middle of the seal and an ocean running from right to left to the middle of the seal. A side view of a three-masted ship shall be located on the ocean and to the right of Plenty. The date "May 20, 1775" shall appear within the seal and across the top of the seal and the words "esse quam videri" shall appear at the bottom around the perimeter. The words "THE GREAT SEAL of the STATE of NORTH CAROLINA" shall appear around the perimeter. No other words, figures or other embellishments shall appear on the seal.[49]

NORTH DAKOTA

This North Dakota seal is described in the 1889 state constitution. It is essentially the same as the territorial seal approved in 1863.

> The following described seal is hereby declared to be and hereby constituted the great seal of the state of North Dakota, to wit: a tree in the open field, the trunk of which is surrounded by three bundles of

> wheat; on the right a plow, anvil and sledge; on the left, a bow crossed with three arrows, and an Indian on horseback pursuing a buffalo toward the setting sun; the foliage of the tree arched by a half circle of forty-two stars, surrounded by the motto "Liberty and Union Now and Forever, One and Inseparable"; the words "Great Seal" at the top; the words "State of North Dakota" at the bottom; "October 1st" on the left and "1889" on the right. The seal to be two and one-half inches in diameter.[50]

OHIO

The current seal of Ohio was revised in 1967, but the revision is based on the first seal, adopted in 1803.

> The great seal of the state shall be two and one-half inches in diameter and shall consist of the coat of arms of the state within a circle having a diameter of one and three-fourths inches, surrounded by the words "THE GREAT SEAL OF THE STATE OF OHIO" in news gothic capitals.[51]

The coat of arms used in the seal was also revised in 1967.

> The coat of arms of the state shall consist of the following device: a circular shield; in the right foreground of the shield a full sheaf of wheat bound and standing erect; in the left foreground, a cluster of seventeen arrows bound in the center and resembling in form the sheaf of wheat; in the background, a representation of Mount Logan, Ross county, as viewed from Adena state memorial; over the mount, a rising sun three-quarters exposed and radiating seventeen rays, the exterior extremities of which form a semicircle; and uniting the background and foreground, a representation of the Scioto river and cultivated fields. . . .
>
> When the coat of arms of the state is reproduced in color, the colors used shall be substantially the same as the natural color of the terrain and objects shown.[52]

OKLAHOMA

The design of Oklahoma's seal is laid out thusly in the 1906 state constitution:

> In the center shall be a five pointed star, with one ray directed upward. The center of the star shall contain the central device of the seal of the Territory of Oklahoma, including the words, "Labor Omnia Vincit." The upper left hand ray shall contain the symbol of the ancient seal of the Cherokee Nation, namely: A seven pointed star

partially surrounded by a wreath of oak leaves. The ray directed upward shall contain the symbol of the ancient seal of the Chickasaw Nation, namely: An Indian warrior standing upright with bow and shield. The lower left hand ray shall contain the symbol of the ancient seal of the Creek Nation, namely: A sheaf of wheat and a plow. The upper right hand ray shall contain the symbol of the ancient seal of the Choctaw Nation, namely: A tomahawk, bow, and three crossed arrows. The lower right hand ray shall contain the symbol of the ancient seal of the Seminole Nation, namely: A village with houses and a factory beside a lake upon which an Indian is paddling a canoe. Surrounding the central star and grouped between its rays shall be forty-five small stars, divided into five clusters of nine stars each, representing the forty-five states of the Union, to which the forty-sixth is now added. In a circular band surrounding the whole device shall be inscribed, "GREAT SEAL OF THE STATE OF OKLAHOMA 1907."[53]

OREGON

The seal of the state of Oregon was designed by a legislative committee in 1857 and officially adopted in 1903. The statute describing the seal is reprinted with permission of Butterworth Legal Publishers.

> The description of the seal of the State of Oregon shall be an escutcheon, supported by 33 stars, and divided by an ordinary, with the inscription, "The Union." In chief—mountains, an elk with branching antlers, a wagon, the Pacific Ocean, on which there are a British man-of-war departing and an American steamer arriving. The second—quartering with a sheaf, plow and a pickax. Crest—the American eagle. Legend—State of Oregon, 1859.[54]

PENNSYLVANIA

A seal for the Commonwealth was designed in 1776 and approved in 1791. In 1809, a new die was cut. The seal currently in use was adopted in 1893.[55] The three symbols used in the seal were originally used in county seals. The ship was the crest of Philadelphia County; the plough, the crest of Chester County; and the sheaf of wheat, the crest of Sussex County, which is now in Delaware.[56]

> The shield shall be parted PER FESS, or, charged with a plough, PROPER, in chief; on a sea WAVY; PROPER, a ship under full sail, surmounted with a sky, Azure; and in BASE, on a field VERT, three GARBS, OR. On the SINISTER a stock of maize, and DEXTER an olive branch. And on the wreath of its colours a bald eagle—

PROPER, PERCHED, wings extended, for the CREST. MOTTO: VIRTUE, LIBERTY, and INDEPENDENCE. Round the margin of the seal, COMMONWEALTH OF PENNSYLVANIA. The reverse, Liberty, trampling on a Lyon, Gules, the emblem of Tyranny. MOTTO—"BOTH CAN'T SURVIVE."[57]

RHODE ISLAND

The state seal was adopted in 1875. The anchor was adopted in the 1647 seal by the assembly. The law states that

> There shall continue to be one (1) seal for the public use of the state; the form of an anchor shall be engraven thereon; the motto thereof shall be the word Hope; and in a circle around the same shall be engraven the words, Seal of the State of Rhode Island and Providence Plantations, 1636.[58]

The arms, found on the flag, are officially described as follows:

> The arms of the state are a golden anchor on a blue field, and the motto thereof is the word Hope.[59]

SOUTH CAROLINA

The seal of South Carolina was commissioned in 1776 and first used in 1777. The design for the arms was made by William Henry Drayton and that for the reverse, by Arthur Middleton. The seal is a circle four inches in diameter and is described as follows:

> *Arms:* A Palmetto tree growing on the seashore erect (symbolical of the fort on Sullivan's Island, built on Palmetto logs); at its base, a torn up oak tree, its branches lopped off, prostrate, typifying the British Fleet, constructed of oak timbers and defeated by the fort; both proper. Just below the branches of the Palmetto, two shields, pendant; one of them on the dexter side is inscribed MARCH 26, (the date of ratification of the Constitution of S.C.)—the other on the sinister side JULY 4, (the date of Declaration of Independence): Twelve spears proper, are bound crosswise to the stem of the Palmetto, their points raised, (representing the 12 states first acceding to the Union); the band uniting them together bearing the inscription QUIS SEPARABIT (Who shall separate?) under the prostrate oak, is inscribed MELIOREM LAPSA LOCAVIT (having fallen it has set up a better); below which appears in large figures, 1776 (the year the Constitution of S.C. was passed, the year of the Battle at Sullivan's Island and of the Declaration of Independence, and the year in which the Seal was ordered made). At the summit of Exergue, are the words SOUTH

CAROLINA; and at the bottom of the same ANIMIS OPIBUSQUE PARATI (prepared in mind and resources).

Reverse: A woman walking on the seashore, over swords and daggers (typifying Hope overcoming dangers, which the sun, just rising, was about to disclose); she holds in her dexter hand, a laurel branch, (symbolical of the honors gained at Sullivan's Island), and in her sinister hand, the folds of her robe; she looks toward the sun, just rising above the sea, (indicating that the battle was fought on a fine day, and also bespeaking good fortune); all proper. On the upper part is the sky azure. At the summit of Exergue, are the words DUM SPIRO SPERO (While I breathe I hope) and within the field below the figure, is inscribed the word SPES (Hope).[60]

SOUTH DAKOTA

The design of the state seal was set out in the constitutions of 1885 and 1889. In 1961, the legislature adopted the same design, but specified the colors to be used.

The design of the colored seal of the state of South Dakota shall be as follows: An inner circle, whose diameter shall be five-sevenths of the diameter of the outer circle of any seal produced in conformity herewith; within which inner circle shall appear; in the left foreground on the left bank of a river, a rust-colored smelting furnace from which grey smoke spirals upward and adjacent to which on the left are a rust-colored hoist house and mill, and to the left a grey dump; these three structures being set in a yellow field and above and back of a light green grove on the left bank of the river. In the left background is a series of three ranges of hills, the nearer range being a darker green than the said grove, the intermediate range of a blue-green and the higher range of blue-black coloration.

In the right foreground is a farmer with black hat, red shirt, navy-blue trousers and black boots, holding a black and silver breaking plow, drawn by a matched team of brown horses with a black harness. In the right background and above the horses in a pasture of grey-green, a herd of rust-colored cattle graze in front of a field of yellow-brown corn, part in shock and part in cut rows to the rear and above which are blue and purple hills forming a low background and receding into the distance. Between the right and left foregrounds and backgrounds is a light-blue river merging in the distance into a sky-blue and cloudless sky. Moving upstream on the river is a white steamboat with a single black funnel from which grey smoke spirals upward. Green shrubbery appears on the near bank of the river, in

> the left foreground and on the right bank of the river near the pasture is a yellow field. The farmer is turning black-brown furrows which reach across the circle and in his foreground is a field of brown-green-yellow.
>
> Near the upper edge of the inner circle at the top on a golden quarter circle which is one-fifth in width the distance between the innermost and the outermost circles that compose the seal, shall appear in black, the state motto: "Under God the People Rule." This innermost circle is circumscribed by a golden band one-fourth as wide as the above-described quarter circle, which inner border, shall be circumscribed by a deep blue circle four and one-half times as wide as the above quarter circle, on which in golden letters one-third its width, in height, shall appear at the top the words, "State of South Dakota." In the lower half of the deep blue circle shall appear in words of equal height "Great" and "Seal" between which shall be the numerals "1889." Between the above-stated names and on either side shall appear a golden star one-half in size the width of the deep blue circle. Circumscribing this deep blue circle shall be a band of gold of the same width as of the inner golden band.
>
> Outside of this outer golden band shall be a serrated or saw-toothed edge of small triangles whose base shall be of the same width as the above quarter circle.[61]

TENNESSEE

Tennessee has no officially designated seal. The seal in use now, however, is essentially the same as that recommended in 1801 by a special committee:

> the said seal shall be a circle, two inches and a quarter in diameter, that the circumference of the circle contain the words THE GREAT SEAL OF TENNESSEE, that in the lower part of said circumference be inserted Feb. 6th 1796, the date of the constitution of this State; that in the inside of the upper part of said circle, be set in numerical letters XVI, the number of the state in chronological order; that under the base of the upper semicircle, there be the word AGRICULTURE; that above said base, there be the figure of a plough, sheaf of wheat and cotton plant; that in the lower part of the lower semicircle, there be the word COMMERCE, and said lower semicircle shall also contain the figure of a boat and boatman.

This seal was used until 1829, when a second seal began to come into use. The new seal was used until 1865. The so-called Brownlow Seal was used in 1865, after which time, two new seals came into use. The seal now used is the larger of the two new seals. It differs from the 1801 seal in that the boat is of different design and is pointed in the opposite direction, and the month and day have been dropped from the date.[62]

TEXAS

The seal of Texas is that adopted by the Republic of Texas in 1839. When Texas became a state in 1845, the word "Republic" was changed to "State." The seal is described as follows:

> There shall be a Seal of the State which shall be kept by the Secretary of State, and used by him officially under the direction of the Governor. The Seal of the State shall be a star of five points encircled by olive and live oak branches, and the words "The State of Texas."[63]

UTAH

The state seal of Utah, designed by Harry Edwards, was adopted in 1896. The symbols of the seal include the American eagle (protection in peace and war), the beehive (industry), and sego lilies (peace). The date 1847 represents the year the Mormons came to the Salt Lake Valley, and 1896 is the year in which Utah was granted statehood.[64]

> The Great Seal of the state of Utah shall be 2-½ inches in diameter, and of the following device: the center a shield and perched thereon an American eagle with outstretching wings; the top of the shield pierced by six arrows crosswise; under the arrows the motto "Industry"; beneath the motto a beehive, on either side growing sego lilies; below the beehive the figures "1847"; and on each side of the shield an American flag; encircling all, near the outer edge of the seal, beginning at the lower left-hand portion, the words "The Great Seal of the State of Utah," with the figures "1896" at the base.[65]

VERMONT

In 1821, the original 1779 seal went into disuse. Until 1937, when the design of the first seal was adopted again, Vermont used a number of different seals. The current law reads as follows:

> The state seal shall be the great seal of the state, a faithful reproduction, cut larger and deeper, of the original seal, designed by Ira Allen, cut by Reuben Dean of Windsor and accepted by resolution of the general assembly, dated February 20, 1779. The seal shall be kept by the secretary of civil and military affairs.[66]

The description of the coat of arms was set out in law in 1862:

The coat of arms, crest, motto and badge of the state shall be and are described as follows:

(1) Coat of arms. Green, a landscape occupying half of the shield; on the right and left, in the background, high mountains, blue; the sky, yellow. From near the base and reaching nearly to the top of the shield, arises a pine tree of natural color and between three erect sheaves, yellow, placed diagonally on the right side and a red cow standing on the left side of the field.

(2) Motto and badge. On a scroll beneath the shield, the motto: Vermont; Freedom and Unity. The Vermonter's badge: two pine branches of natural color, crossed between the shield and scroll.

(3) Crest. A buck's head, of natural color, placed on a scroll, blue and yellow.[67]

VIRGINIA

The seal of Virginia is described in a 1930 law:

The great seal of the Commonwealth of Virginia shall consist of two metallic discs, 2¼ inches in diameter, with an ornamental border one fourth of an inch wide, with such words and figures engraved thereon as will, when used, produce impressions to be described as follows: On the obverse, Virtus, the genius of the Commonwealth, dressed as an Amazon, resting on a spear in her right hand, point downward, touching the earth; and holding in her left hand, a sheathed sword, or parazonium, pointing upward; her head erect and face upturned; her left foot on the form of Tyranny represented by the prostrate body of a man, with his head to her left, his fallen crown nearby, a broken chain in his left hand, and a scourge in his right. Above the group and within the border conforming therewith, shall be the word "Virginia," and, in the space below, on a curved line, shall be the motto, "Sic Semper Tyrannis." On the reverse, shall be placed a group consisting of Libertas, holding a wand and pileus in her right hand; on her right, Aeternitas, with a globe and phoenix in her right hand; on the left of Libertas, Ceres, with a cornucopia in her left hand, and an ear of wheat in her right; over this device, in a curved line, the word "Perseverando."[68]

The law also provides for a lesser seal:

The lesser seal. The lesser seal of the Commonwealth shall be 1⁹⁄₁₆ inches in diameter, and have engraved thereon the device and inscriptions contained in the obverse of the great seal.[69]

WASHINGTON

The seal of the state of Washington was prescribed in the 1889 state constitution and added to the body of law in 1967.

> The seal of the state of Washington shall be, a seal encircled with the words: "The Seal of the State of Washington," with the vignette of General George Washington as the central figure, and beneath the vignette the figures "1889."[70]

WEST VIRGINIA

The state constitution of West Virginia designates the seal designed by Joseph H. Diss Debar and chosen by a legislative committee in 1863 as the official state seal.

> The present seal of the State, with its motto, "Montani Semper Liberi," shall be the great seal of the State of West Virginia, and shall be kept by the secretary of state, to be used by him officially, as directed by law.[71]

The report of the committee, which was then adopted by a joint resolution in 1863, described the seal:

> The disc of the Great Seal is to be two and one-half inches in diameter; the obverse to bear the legend "The State of West Virginia," the constitutional designation of our Republic, which with the motto, "Montani Semper Liberi—Mountaineers always free"—is to be inserted in the circumference. In the center a rock with ivy, emblematic of stability and continuance, and on the face of the rock the inscription, "June 20, 1863," the date of our foundation, as if graven with a pen of iron in the rock forever. On the right of the rock a farmer clothed in the traditional hunting garb, peculiar to this region, his right arm resting on the plow handles, and his left supporting a woodman's axe, indicating that while our territory is partly cultivated, it is still in the process of being cleared of the original forest. At his right hand a sheaf of wheat and a cornstalk on the left hand of the rock, a miner, indicated by a pick-axe on his shoulder, with barrels and lumps of mineral at his feet. On his left anvil, partly seen, on which rests a sledge hammer, typical of the mechanic arts, the whole indicating the principal pursuits and resources of the state. In front of the rock and the hunter, as if just laid down by the latter and ready to be resumed at a moment's notice, two hunters' rifles, crossed and surmounted at the place of contact by the Phrygian cap, or cap of liberty, indicating that our freedom and liberty were won and will be maintained by the force of arms.

The reverse of the Great Seal is to be encircled by a wreath composed of laurel and oak leaves, emblematical of valor and strength, with fruits and cereals, productions of the State. For device, a landscape. In the distance, on the left of the disc, a wooded mountain, and on the right a cultivated slope with the log farmhouse peculiar to this region. On the side of the mountain, a representation of the viaduct on the line of the Baltimore & Ohio Railroad in Preston County, one of the great engineering triumphs of the age, with a train of cars about to pass over it. Near the center a factory, in front of which a river with boats, on the bank and to the right of it nearer the foreground, a derrick and a shed, appertaining to the production of salt and petroleum. In the foreground a meadow with cattle and sheep feeding and reposing, the whole indicating the leading characteristics, productions and pursuits of the State at this time. Above the mountain, etc., the sun merging from the clouds, indicating that former obstacles to our prosperity are now disappearing. In the rays of the sun the motto "Libertas et Fidelitate" Freedom and Loyalty—indicating that our liberty and independence are the result of faithfullness to the Declaration and the National Constitution.

The committee further recommend that the above device and motto, for the obverse of the Great Seal be also adopted as the Coat-of-Arms of the State.[72]

WISCONSIN

When Wisconsin became a state in 1848, a new seal was designed to replace the revised territorial seal of 1839. The state seal was itself revised in 1851 and finally prescribed by law in 1881.[73] The law sets out the following description:

The great seal of the state consists of a metallic disc, 2⅜ inches in diameter, containing, within an ornamental border, the following devices and legend: The coat of arms of the state . . . above the arms, in a line parallel with the border, the words, "Great Seal of the State of Wisconsin"; in the exergue, in a curved line, 13 stars.[74]

The coat of arms is prescribed as follows:

The coat of arms of the state of Wisconsin is declared to be as follows:

Arms. Or, quartered, the quarters bearing respectively a plow, a crossed shovel and pick, an arm and held hammer, and an anchor, all proper; the base of shield resting upon a horn of plenty and pyramid of pig lead, all proper; overall, on fesse point, the arms and motto of the United States, namely: Arms, palewise of 13 pieces argent and gules; a chief azure; motto (on garter surrounding inescutcheon), "E pluribus unum."

Crest. A badger, passant, proper.

Supporters. Dexter, a sailor holding a coil of rope, proper; sinister, a yeoman resting on a pick, proper.

Motto. Over crest, "Forward."[75]

WYOMING

Wyoming's seal was adopted in 1893 and revised in 1921. The current law is as follows:

> There shall be a great seal of the state of Wyoming, which shall be of the following design, viz: A circle one and one-half (1-½) inches in diameter, on the outer edge or rim of which shall be engraved the words "Great Seal of the State of Wyoming." The design shall conform substantially to the following description: A pedestal, showing on the front thereof an eagle resting upon a shield, the shield to have engraved thereon a star and the figures, "44," being the number of Wyoming in the order of admission to statehood. Standing upon the pedestal shall be a draped figure of a woman, modeled after the statue of the "Victory of the Louvre," from whose wrists shall hang links of a broken chain, and holding in her right hand a staff from the top of which shall float a banner with the words "Equal Rights" thereon, all suggesting the political position of woman in this state. On either side of the pedestal and standing at the base thereof, shall be male figures typifying the livestock and mining industries of Wyoming. Behind the pedestal, and in the background, shall be two (2) pillars, each supporting a lighted lamp, signifying the light of knowledge. Around each pillar shall be a scroll with the following words thereon: On the right of the central figure the words "Livestock" and "Grain," and on the left the words "Mines" and "Oil." At the base of the pedestal, and in front, shall appear the figures "1869–1890," the former date signifying the organization of the territory of Wyoming and the latter date of its admission to statehood.[76]

DISTRICT OF COLUMBIA

The District's seal was the subject of the first act of the district's first legislative assembly in 1871. The design of the corporate seal became law on August 3, 1871.

> The Corporate Seal of the District of Columbia is a circular design that includes two central figures. One figure depicts George Washington on a pedestal. His right hand rests upon a staff and his left hand rests upon a fasces—an axe within a bundle of rods, which classically symbolizes power. Protruding from behind the fasces are the handles of a plow. Standing on the ground to the right of Washington is the figure of a woman. Blindfolded, she symbolizes justice. Her right hand, extended, holds a wreath, and, in her left hand, is a tablet bearing the word "CONS-TITU-TION" in three lines.
>
> Positioned beneath the presented wreath is an eagle with a shield across its breast. In its left talon are arrows and its right talon holds an olive branch. The eagle's beak clutches a ribbon. To the eagle's immediate left are two hogshead casks of tobacco, a sheaf of wheat and two sacks of agricultural products.
>
> In the background, on the left, the Potomac River is depicted flowing between the Virginia and District of Columbia shores. Crossing the river on a trestle is a smoking, bulbous stack locomotive, emblazed by a radiating sun and trailed by several rail cars. In the background on the right, stands the United States Capitol with rolling hills in the distance.
>
> Centered at the very bottom of the seal is a wreath embracing the year 1871. Flowing on a ribbon from both sides of the wreath are the words "JUSTITIA" (on the left) and "OMNIBUS" (on the right), which together mean "JUSTICE FOR ALL." Arched across the top of the seal are the words "DISTRICT OF COLUMBIA."

The official seal had been used also as the insignia of the District on numerous publications until May 15, 1979, when a mayor's memorandum discussing printing standards declared that it should be replaced "by a logo representing the D.C. flag." This logo, called the "Stars and Bars," employs the three stars over two bars as depicted in the flag.[77]

AMERICAN SAMOA

The territorial seal of American Samoa depicts a fly switch, which represents wisdom, and a staff, which represents authority, crossed above a kava bowl. The kava bowl represents service to the chief and is used in the traditional, formal Kava Ceremony. These symbols lie on a tapa cloth background that represents the artistry of traditional Samoan dress. Around the circumference at the top of the seal are the words "Seal of American Samoa" and the date "17 April 1900," the date on which the United States took possession. The motto *Samoa—Muamua le Atua* appears at the bottom. It means "Samoa—Let God Be First."[78]

COMMONWEALTH OF THE NORTHERN MARIANA ISLANDS

The seal of the Commonwealth employs the latte stone, a symbol of strength and tradition, with the star representing the Commonwealth as the newest star in the Pacific, represented by the field of blue. It was adopted in 1986.

> The official seal of the Commonwealth shall consist of a circular field of blue having in its center a white star superimposed on a gray latte stone, surrounded by the traditional Carolinian mwaar consisting of the following flowers: langilang, flores mayo (seyur) angagha, and teibwo, on the outer border, and the words encircling the imwaar, "Commonwealth of the Northern Mariana Islands" and "Official Seal."[79]

GUAM

The seal of Guam is described in its code of laws:

> The Great Seal of the Territory of Guam shall consist of the Coat of Arms of Guam surrounded by the following words, letters and punctuation, encircling the outer border of the Coat of Arms in such a manner as to be read when the Coat of Arms is in a proper position: "Great Seal of the Territory of Guam, United States of America". The Great Seal shall be approximately two and five-sixteenths (2 5/16) inches long.[80]

The coat of arms is also described in the code of laws:

> The official Coat of Arms of Guam shall consist of an upright, two-pointed oval scene which portrays an ancient flying proa (canoe) approaching the beach near the mouth of the Agana River, with a lone coconut palm tree in the foreground. The colors of the Coat of Arms shall be as follows: yellow, which represents the sand; brown, the tree trunk and canoe; green, the palm fronds; white, the canoe sail; grey, the distant flat-topped mountains; light blue, the sky; dark blue, the water; red, the letters GUAM emblazoned across the Coat of Arms; red, the border around the outer edge and surrounding the oval.[81]

PUERTO RICO

Puerto Rico's official seal is based on the coat of arms adopted in 1952 and amended in 1976, which is illustrated with the seals that King Ferdinand of Spain gave to Puerto Rico by royal order of November 8, 1511. The order described the coat of arms as " 'a green shield bearing in the center a silver lamb resting upon a red book, and bearing a flag with cross and banner, the streamer of the lance showing the device of SANCT JOAN and having for border castles and lions and flags and crosses of Jerusalem, and for a device an F. and a Y. with its crowns and yokes and arrows, and a motto around it reading as follows: Joannes est nomen ejus.' "

Puerto Rico was originally called St. John. Thus the green background, the color used by early Christians for St. John the Baptist, and the red book representing the Apocalypse of John the Apostle. The lamb represents Jesus Christ. Castles and lions symbolize Spain, the Jerusalem flags and crosses St. John the Baptist, and the "F" and "Y," King Ferdinand and Queen Isabella (Ysabella). That the cluster of arrows is made of seven arrows calls up the mystery of the number seven in the Apocalypse. The motto translates as "John is his name."[82]

The official coat of arms is prescribed by law:

> The coat of arms of the Commonwealth of Puerto Rico shall be "a green shield" bearing a silver lamb resting upon a red book and bearing a flag with cross and banner, as shown in the device of Saint John, and having for border castles, lions, flags and crosses of Jerusalem, and having for a device an F and Y with its crown and yoke and arrows, and a motto around it as follows: *Joannes est nomen ejus.*[83]

U.S. VIRGIN ISLANDS

The great seal of the government of the Virgin Islands of the United States as described below came into use on January 1, 1991. The statute is reprinted with permission from Butterworth Legal Publishers.

> In the foreground, a yellow breast (Coereba Flaveola), the official bird of the Virgin Islands, perched on a branch of the yellow cedar (Tecoma Stans), the official flower of the Virgin Islands, on the left end of which are three flowers, three seed pods and, on the right, three leaves of the plant; in the background, surrounding the bird and plant, are three islands representing the three major islands of the United States Virgin Islands, one with a sugarmill located on it, representing St. Croix, another with the Annenberg Ruins, representing St. John, and the third with the Capitol Building, behind which are the flags of the United States of America and the Danneborg, representing St. Thomas; a sailboat is also located in the harbor of the island representing St. Thomas; a scroll bearing the words, "United in Pride and Hope," is located on the lower edge of the design directly below the island representing St. Croix. Encircling the above-described design the words "Government of" are inscribed in the upper portion of the circle, and the words "The United States Virgin Islands" are inscribed in the lower portion of the circle.[84]

NOTES

1. Ala. Code § 1–2–4.
2. Ibid., § 1–2–1.
3. Alaska Stat. § 44.09.010.
4. *Alaska Blue Book, 1977,* p. i.
5. Ariz. Rev. State. Ann. art. 22, § 20.
6. Ark. Stat. Ann. § 5–104.
7. Cal. Govt. Code tit. 1, § 400 (West).
8. *State Emblems* (Sacramento (?): n.d.).
9. Colo. Rev. Stat. § 24–80–901.
10. Conn. Gen. Stat. Ann. § 3–106 (West).
11. Ibid., § 3–105 (West).
12. Del. Code Ann. tit. 29, § 301.
13. Fla. Stat. Ann. § 15.03 (West).
14. Ga. Code Ann. § 50–3–30.
15. Haw. Rev. Stat. § 5–5.
16. Idaho Code § 59–1005.
17. "Description of the Idaho State Seal" (Idaho Historical Society Reference Series No. 61, reissued in 1970).
18. *Illinois Blue Book, 1983–1984,* pp. 439–40.
19. 1867 Ill. Laws 36.
20. *Indiana Emblems* (Indianapolis: Indiana Historical Bureau, 1982), p. 5.
21. Ind. Code Ann. § 1–2–4 (West).
22. Iowa Code Ann. § 1A.1 (West).
23. Kan. Stat. Ann. § 75–201.
24. Ky. Rev. Stat. § 2.020 (Baldwin).
25. La. Rev. Stat. Ann. § 49–151 (West).
26. *Louisiana Facts* (Baton Rouge: Department of State, n.d.).
27. Me. Rev. Stat. tit. 1, § 201.
28. *Maryland Manual, 1981–1982,* p. 9.
29. Md. Ann. Code § 13–302.
30. Mass. Gen. Laws Ann. ch. 2, § 2 (West).
31. Ibid., ch. 2, § 1 (West).
32. Mich. Comp. Laws Ann. § 2.41.
33. Ibid., § 2.22.
34. *Minnesota Legislative Manual, 1985,* p. 11.
35. Minn. Stat. Ann. § 1.135 (West).
36. Miss. Code Ann. § 7–1–9.
37. *Souvenir of Mississippi* (Jackson: Dick Molpus, n.d.), p. 16.
38. Mo. Stat. Ann. § 10.060 (Vernon).
39. Rex C. Myers, *Symbols of Montana* (Helena: Montana Historical Society, 1976), p. 10.
40. Mont. Rev. Codes Ann. § 1–1–501.
41. 1867 Neb. Stats. 863.
42. Nev. Rev. Stat. § 235.010.
43. N.H. Rev. Stat. Ann. § 3:9.
44. Ibid., § 3:1.

45. N.J. Stat. Ann. § 52:2–1 (West).
46. "The Great Seal of the State of New Mexico" (information provided by the New Mexico State Library).
47. N.M. Stat. Ann. § 12–3–1.
48. N.Y. Stat. Law § 73 (McKinney).
49. N.C. Gen. Stat. § 147–26.
50. N.D. Cent. Code art. XI, § 2.
51. Ohio Rev. Code Ann. § 5.10 (Baldwin).
52. Ibid., § 5.04 (Baldwin).
53. Okla. Stat. Ann. art. 6, § 35 (West).
54. Or. Rev. Stat. § 186.020.
55. *Pennsylvania Symbols* (Harrisburg: House of Representatives, n.d.).
56. *Pennsylvania Manual, 1976–1977,* pp. 846–47.
57. *Commonwealth of Pennsylvania Official Documents, 1893,* vol. 4, pp. 215–16.
58. R. I. Gen. Laws § 42–4–2.
59. Ibid., § 42–4–1.
60. *South Carolina State Symbols and Emblems* (Columbia: House of Representatives, n.d.).
61. S.D. Codified Laws Ann. § 1–6–2.
62. *Tennessee Blue Book, 1985–1986,* pp. 337–38.
63. Tex. Gov't. Code art. 4, § 19 (Vernon).
64. *Symbols of the Great State of Utah* (Salt Lake City (?): n.d.).
65. Utah Code Ann. § 67–1a–8.
66. Vt. Stat. Ann. tit. 1, § 493.
67. Ibid., tit. 1, § 491.
68. Va. Code § 7.1–26.
69. Ibid., § 7.1–27.
70. Wash. Rev. Code Ann. § 1.20.080.
71. W. Va. Code art 2, § 7.
72. *The Great Seal of West Virginia* (Charleston: A. James Manchin, n.d.).
73. *State of Wisconsin 1983–1984 Blue Book,* p. 947.
74. Wis. Stat. Ann. § 14.45 (West).
75. Ibid., § 1.07 (West).
76. Wyo. Stat. Ann. § 8–3–101.
77. *Description of the Corporate Seal of the District of Columbia* (n.p., n.d.); *The Corporate Seal of the District of Columbia and the Stars and Bars* (n.p., n.d.); information provided by W. C. Bradley III, Visual Information Specialist, Government of the District of Columbia, Office of the Secretary.
78. *American Samoa* (n.p., n.d.); pamphlet provided by the Office of Congressman Eni Faleomavaega.
79. *Amendments to the Constitution of the Northern Mariana Islands* (Saipan: Marianas Printing Service, Inc., 1986), amendment 43.
80. Guam Code Ann. tit. 1, § 410.
81. Ibid., § 406.
82. *The Coat of Arms of Puerto Rico* (n.p., n.d.); information supplied by Commonwealth of Puerto Rico, Department of State.
83. P.R. Laws Ann. tit 1., § 34, § 37.
84. V.I. Code Ann. tit. 1, § 108.

4 | State and Territory Flags

Flags, like seals, are symbols that legitimize the sovereignty of each state, linked by vote of the people into the union of the United States.

The flags of the states, often displaying the coats of arms, are also tableaux of each state's history. Hawaii's flag proudly symbolizes its founding by displaying Great Britain's Union Jack. New Mexico retains the yellow and red colors of Spain in its flag together with the Zia symbol, an ancient Indian symbol of friendship. The crossed peace pipe and olive branch of Oklahoma's flag and the Indian figure and steamboat of Florida's flag vividly recall the history of these states.

ALABAMA

The state flag of Alabama was officially designated in 1895. The law declares that the flag, reminiscent of the Confederate battle flag, "shall be a crimson cross of St. Andrew on a field of white. The bars forming the cross shall be not less than six inches broad, and must extend diagonally across the flag from side to side."[1]

The governor's flag is the state flag with the addition of the coat of arms or great seal in the upper portion above the cross, and in the lower portion, the military crest of the state.[2]

ALASKA

In 1927, a contest was held among Alaska's school children for the design of a territorial flag. Benny Benson, then thirteen years old, submitted the winning design. In 1959, the territorial flag was declared to be the state flag.[3]

> The design of the official flag is eight gold stars in a field of blue, so selected for its simplicity, its originality and its symbolism. The blue, one of the national colors, typifies the evening sky, the blue of the sea and of mountain lakes, and of wild flowers that grow in Alaskan soil, the gold being significant of the wealth that lies hidden in Alaska's hills and streams.
>
> The stars, seven of which form the constellation Ursa Major, the Great Bear, the most conspicuous constellation in the northern sky, contains the stars which form the "Dipper," including the "Pointers" which point toward the eighth star in the flag, Polaris, the North Star, the ever constant star for the mariner, the explorer, hunter, trapper, prospector, woodsman, and the surveyor. For Alaska the northernmost star in the galaxy of stars and which at some future time will take its place as the forty-ninth star in the national emblem.[4]

The code goes on to describe the color of the stars as that of natural yellow gold and the shade of blue as that used in the United States flag. Standard proportions and size are also delineated.

ARIZONA

Arizona's flag was adopted in 1917. It symbolizes the importance of the state's copper industry.

> The lower half of the flag a blue field and the upper half divided into thirteen equal segments or rays which shall start at the center on the lower line and continue to the edges of the flag, colored alternately light yellow and red, consisting of six yellow and seven red rays. In the center of the flag, superimposed, there shall be a copper-colored five pointed star, so placed that the upper points shall be one foot from the top of the flag and the lower points one foot from the bottom of the flag. The red and blue shall be the same shade as the colors in the flag of the United States. The flag shall have a four-foot hoist and a six-foot fly, with a two-foot star and the same proportions shall be observed for flags of other sizes.[5]

ARKANSAS

In 1913, at the urging of the Pine Bluff Chapter of the Daughters of the American Revolution, the Arkansas legislature adopted a state flag designed by Willie K. Hocker, a member of that chapter. In 1923, an additional star was added to the flag.[6] The current law states that

> (a) The official state flag shall be a rectangle of red on which is placed a large white diamond, bordered by a wide band of blue on which are twenty-five (25) white stars. Across the diamond shall be the word "ARKANSAS" and four (4) blue stars, with one (1) star above and three (3) stars below the word "ARKANSAS." The star above the word "ARKANSAS" shall be below the upper corner of the diamond. The three (3) stars below the word "ARKANSAS" shall be placed so that one (1) star shall be above the lower corner of the diamond and two (2) stars shall be placed symmetrically, parallel above and to the right and left of the star in the lower corner of the diamond.
>
> (b) The three (3) stars so placed are designed to represent the three (3) nations, France, Spain, and the United States, which have successively exercised dominion over Arkansas. These stars also indicated that Arkansas was the third state carved out of the Louisiana Purchase. Of these three (3) stars, the twin stars parallel with each other signify that Arkansas and Michigan are twin states, having been admitted to the Union together on June 15, 1836. The twenty-five (25) white stars on the band of blue show that Arkansas was the twenty-fifth state admitted to the Union. The blue star above the word "ARKANSAS" is to commemorate the Confederate States of America. The diamond signifies that this state is the only diamond-bearing state in the Union.[7]

The code also sets out a salute to the flag: "I salute the Arkansas Flag with its diamond and stars. We pledge our loyalty to thee."[8]

CALIFORNIA

The California Bear Flag was designed by an unknown person sometime between 1875 and 1899. In 1846, however, a bear flag had been chosen as the emblem of the republic. It was adopted by legislative action in 1911. A new color rendering was approved in 1953.

> The Bear Flag is the State Flag of California. As viewed with the hoist end of the flag to the left of the observer there appears in the upper left-hand corner of a white field a five-pointed red star with one point vertically upward and in the middle of the white field a brown grizzly bear walking toward the left with all four paws on a green grass plot,

> with head and eye turned slightly toward the observer; a red stripe forms the length of the flag at the bottom, and between the grass plot and the red stripe appear the words CALIFORNIA REPUBLIC.[9]

The code goes on to specify exact colors and dimensions. The white background symbolizes purity, the red star and bar, courage. The star itself represents sovereignty and the grizzly bear, strength.

COLORADO

The 1911 law, amended slightly in 1929 and 1964, adopting the state flag, describes it as follows:

> The flag shall consist of three alternate stripes to be of equal width and at right angles to the staff, the two outer stripes to be blue of the same color as in the blue field of the national flag and the middle stripe to be white, the proportion of the flag being a width of two-thirds of its length. At a distance from the staff end of the flag of one-fifth of the total length of the flag there shall be a circular red C, of the same color as the red in the national flag of the United States. The diameter of the letter shall be two-thirds of the width of the flag. The inner line of the opening of the letter C shall be three-fourths of the width of its body or bar and the outer line of the opening shall be double the length of the inner line thereof. Completely filling the open space inside the letter C shall be a golden disk; attached to the flag shall be a cord of gold and silver intertwined, with tassels one of gold and one of silver.[10]

CONNECTICUT

The design of the state flag of Connecticut first approved by the General Assembly in 1897 was modified slightly by a 1990 amendment.

> The following-described flag is the official flag of the state. The dimensions of the flag shall be five feet and six inches in length, four feet and four inches in width. The flag shall be azure blue, charged with an argent white shield of rococo design, having in the center three grape vines, supported and bearing fruit in natural colors. The bordure to the shield shall be in two colors, gold on the interior and silver on the exterior, adorned with natural-colored clusters, of white oak leaves (Quercus alba) bearing acorns. Below the shield shall be a white streamer, cleft at each end, bordered by a band of gold within fine brown lines, and upon the streamer in dark blue block letters shall be the motto "QUI TRANSTULIT SUSTINET"; the whole design being the arms of the state.[11]

DELAWARE

The state flag of Delaware was adopted in 1913.

> The design of the official state flag shall be as follows: A background of colonial blue surrounding a diamond of buff in which diamond is placed the correct coat of arms of the State in the colors prescribed by law and in accordance with § 301 of this title, with the words, "December 7, 1787," to be inscribed underneath the diamond.[12]

The code goes on to describe the exact colors of each element of the flag. A governor's flag is also provided by law.[13]

FLORIDA

The Florida state flag makes prominent use of the 1868 seal, which was changed in 1970, when the sabal palmetto replaced the cocoa tree as the state tree.

> The state flag shall conform with standard commercial sizes, and be of the following proportions and description: The seal of the state, in diameter one-half the hoist, shall occupy the center of a white ground. Red bars, in width one-fifth the hoist, shall extend from each corner toward the center, to the outer rim of the seal.[14]

GEORGIA

The Georgia state flag, designed by John Sammons Bell, was adopted in 1956. It replaced the flags adopted in 1799, 1861, 1879, and 1905. The current flag maintains many of the characteristics of the older flags.

> The flag of the State of Georgia shall be a vertical band of blue occupying one-third of the entire flag nearest to the flagstaff. The remainder of the space shall be a square, two-thirds the length of the flag, having a red background with a broad saltire of blue bordered with white on which 13 white mullets or five-pointed stars, corresponding in number to that of the Confederate States of America as recognized by the Confederate States Congress, are emblazoned; so that such remainder shall be the same as the union of the flag of the Confederate States as approved and cited in Statutes at Large of the Confederate States Congress, 1st and 2nd Sessions, 1862–63, 1863–64, and approved May 1, 1863, such remainder being popularly known as the Battle Flag of the Confederacy. On the blue field shall be stamped, painted, or embroidered the coat of arms of the state. Every force of the organized militia shall carry this flag when on parade or review.[15]

The pledge of allegiance to the Georgia flag is set in the state code: "I pledge allegiance to the Georgia flag and to the principles for which it stands: Wisdom, Justice, and Moderation."[16]

HAWAII

The Hawaiian state flag is the same flag that was used for the Kingdom of Hawaii, the Republic of Hawaii, and the Territory of Hawaii. Its alternating white, red, and blue stripes represent the eight islands. The field resembles the Union Jack of Great Britain, from which the flag was originally designed.[17]

IDAHO

The state flag was adopted in 1907. For twenty years, the state flag in actual use did not meet the specifications of the 1907 law. In 1927, this situation was corrected.

> A state flag for the state of Idaho is hereby adopted, the same to be as follows:
>
> A silk flag, blue field, five (5) feet six (6) inches fly, and four (4) feet four (4) inches on pike, bordered with gilt fringe two and one half (2½) inches in width, with state seal of Idaho twenty-one (21) inches in diameter, in colors, in the center of a blue field. The words "State of Idaho" are embroidered in with block letters, two (2) inches in height on a red band three (3) inches in width by twenty-nine (29) inches in length, the band being in gold and placed about eight and one half (8½) inches from the lower border of fringe and parallel with the same.[18]

ILLINOIS

The first Illinois state flag, which incorporated the great seal on the banner, was adopted in 1915. In 1969, the legislature amended the 1915 act to include the name of the state on the flag and to standardize production of the flag. The amended act reads as follows:

> The reproduction of the emblem only on the "great seal of the State of Illinois" is authorized and permitted when reproduced in black or in the national colors upon a white sheet or background and bearing underneath the emblem in blue letters the word "Illinois" and being an actual reproduction of the great seal except for the outer ring thereof for use as a State banner or insignia under the conditions and subject to the restrictions provided by the laws of the United States

and the State of Illinois as to the United States or State flag or ensign.[19]

INDIANA

The Indiana state flag, designed by Paul Hadley of Mooresville, Indiana, was adopted in 1917. In 1979, an amendment standardized the size of the flag, but the 1917 law otherwise remains in force.

> A state flag is hereby adopted, and the same shall be of the following design and dimensions, to-wit: Its dimensions shall be three (3) feet fly by two (2) feet hoist; or five (5) feet fly by three (3) feet hoist; or any size proportionate to either of those dimensions. The field of the flag shall be blue with nineteen (19) stars and a flaming torch in gold or buff. Thirteen (13) stars shall be arranged in an outer circle, representing the original thirteen (13) states; five (5) stars shall be arranged in a half circle below the torch and inside the outer circle of stars, representing the states admitted prior to Indiana; and the nineteenth star, appreciably larger than the others and representing Indiana shall be placed above the flame of the torch. The outer circle of stars shall be so arranged that one (1) star shall appear directly in the middle at the top of the circle, and the word "Indiana" shall be placed in a half circle over and above the star representing Indiana and midway between it and the star in the center above it. Rays shall be shown radiating from the torch to the three (3) stars on each side of the star in the upper center of the circle.[20]

IOWA

The Iowa state banner was designed by Mrs. Dixie Cornell Gebhardt and sponsored by the Iowa Society of the Daughters of the American Revolution. It was approved in 1921.[21]

> The banner designed by the Iowa society of the Daughters of the American Revolution and presented to the state, which banner consists of three vertical stripes of blue, white, and red, the blue stripe being nearest the staff and the white stripe being in the center, and upon the central white stripe being depicted a spreading eagle bearing in its beak blue streamers on which is inscribed, in white letters, the state motto, "Our liberties we prize and our rights we will maintain" and with the word "Iowa" in red letters below such streamers, as such design now appears on the banner in the office of the governor of the state of Iowa, is hereby adopted as a distinctive state banner, for use on all occasions where a distinctive state symbol in the way of a banner may be fittingly displayed.[22]

KANSAS

The Kansas state flag was approved in 1927. In 1961, the name of the state was added to it. The laws describe the flag in this manner:

> The official state flag of the state of Kansas shall be a rectangle of dark-blue silk or bunting, three (3) feet on the staff by five (5) feet fly.
>
> The great seal of the state of Kansas, without its surrounding band of lettering, shall be located equidistant from the staff and the fly side of the flag, with the lower edge of the seal located eleven (11) inches above the base side of the flag. The great seal shall be surmounted by a crest and the word KANSAS shall be located underneath the seal. The seal shall be seventeen (17) inches in diameter. The crest shall be on a wreath or an azure, a sunflower slipped proper, which divested of its heraldic language is a sunflower as torn from its stalk in its natural colors on a bar of twisted gold and blue. The crest shall be six (6) inches in diameter; the wreath shall be nine (9) inches in length. The top of the crest shall be located two (2) inches beneath the top side of the flag. The letters KANSAS shall be imprinted in gold block letters below the seal, the said letters to be properly proportioned, and five (5) inches in height, imprinted with a stroke one (1) inch wide; and the first letter K shall commence with the same distance from the staff side of the flag as the end of the last letter S is from the fly side of the flag. The bottom edge of the letters shall be two (2) inches above the base side of the flag. Larger or smaller flags will be of the same proportional dimensions.
>
> The colors in the seal shall be as follows: Stars, silver; hills, purple; sun, deep yellow; glory, light yellow; sky, yellow and orange from hills half way to motto, upper half azure; grass, green; river, light blue; boat, white; house, dark brown; ground, brown; wagons, white; near horse, white; off horse, bay; buffalo, dark, almost black; motto, white; scroll, light brown.[23]

Kansas also has a state banner, which was approved in 1925. The law holds that the official state banner

> shall be of solid blue and shall be of the same tint as the color of the field of the United States flag, whose width shall be three-fourths of its length, with a sunflower in the center having a diameter of two-thirds of the space.[24]

KENTUCKY

The 1918 act creating Kentucky's state flag was amended in 1962 to read as follows:

> The official state flag of the Commonwealth of Kentucky shall be of navy blue silk, nylon, wool or cotton bunting, or some other suitable material, with the seal of the Commonwealth encircled by a wreath, the lower half of which shall be goldenrod in bloom and the upper half the words "Commonwealth of Kentucky," embroidered, printed, painted or stamped on the center thereof. The dimensions of the flag may vary, but the length shall be one and nine-tenths (1⁹⁄₁₀) times the width and the diameter of the seal and encirclement shall be approximately two-thirds (⅔) the width of the flag.[25]

LOUISIANA

Louisiana's flag was adopted officially in 1912 by the legislature.

> The official flag of Louisiana shall be that flag now in general use, consisting of a solid blue field with the coat-of-arms of the state, the pelican feeding its young, in white in the center, with a ribbon beneath, also in white, containing in blue the motto of the state, "Union, Justice and Confidence."[26]

In 1981, the legislature adopted a state pledge of allegiance.

> I pledge allegiance to the flag of the state of Louisiana and to the motto for which it stands: A state, under God, united in purpose and ideals, confident that justice shall prevail for all of those abiding here.[27]

MAINE

The Maine legislature adopted the state flag in 1909. This flag uses the coat of arms in a field of blue.

> The flag to be known as the official flag of the State shall be of blue, of the same color as the blue field in the flag of the United States, and of the following dimensions and designs; to wit, the length or height of the staff to be 9 feet, including brass spearhead and ferrule; the fly of said flag to be 5 feet 6 inches, and to be 4 feet 4 inches on the staff; in the center of the flag there shall be embroidered in silk on both sides of the flag the coat of arms of the State, in proportionate size; the edges to be trimmed with knotted fringe of yellow silk, 2½ inches wide; a cord, with tassels, to be attached to the staff at the spearhead, to be 8 feet 6 inches long and composed of white and blue silk strands.[28]

Maine law also prescribes a merchant and marine flag.

> The flag to be known as the merchant and marine flag of the State shall be of white, at the top of which in blue letters shall be the motto "Dirigo"; beneath the motto shall be the representation of a pine tree in green color, the trunk of which shall be entwined with the representation of an anchor in blue color; beneath the tree and anchor shall be the name "Maine" in blue color.[29]

MARYLAND

Maryland's flag was officially adopted in 1904, although the flag was first flown in 1888 at Gettysburg Battlefield. The flag described below employs the arms of the Calvert and Crossland families.[30]

> (a) *In general.* The State flag is quartered.
>
> (b) *First and fourth quarters.* The 1st and 4th quarters are paly of 6 pieces, or sable, a bend dexter counterchanged and the 2nd and 3rd, quarterly, are argent and gules, a cross bottony countersigned. Thus, the 1st and 4th quarters consist of 6 vertical bars alternately gold and black with a diagonal band on which the colors are reversed.
>
> (c) *Second and third quarters.* The 2nd and 3rd quarters are a quartered field of red and white, charged with a Greek cross, its arms terminating in trefoils, with the coloring transported, red being on the white ground and white on the red, and all being as represented upon the escutcheon of the State seal.[31]

MASSACHUSETTS

The Massachusetts flag, like many other state flags, includes a representation of the coat of arms. Unlike most other states, the law also prescribes a naval and maritime flag.

> The flag of the commonwealth shall consist of a white rectangular field, bearing on either side a representation of the arms of the commonwealth, except that the star shall be white. The naval and maritime flag of the commonwealth shall consist of a white rectangular field bearing on either side a representation of a green pine tree.[32]

In 1971, the governor's flag was prescribed by law.

> The flag of the governor shall conform to the design of the flag of the commonwealth, except that the field of the flag of the governor shall be triangular in shape.[33]

MICHIGAN

The 1911 law adopting the state flag states simply that "the state flag shall be blue charged with the arms of the state."[34] A pledge of allegiance, written by Harold G. Coburn, was adopted in 1972.

> I pledge allegiance to the flag of Michigan, and to the state for which it stands, 2 beautiful peninsulas united by a bridge of steel, where equal opportunity and justice to all is our ideal.[35]

A governor's flag is also provided in the 1911 law: "The governor's flag shall be white charged with the arms of the state."[36]

MINNESOTA

In 1957, the legislature approved the design for a new flag. The 1893 flag had been a double flag. The new law, revised only for editorial purposes in 1984, simplifies the design of the first flag.[37]

> The design of the flag shall conform substantially to the following description: The staff is surmounted by a bronze eagle with outspread wings; the flag is rectangular in shape and is on a medium blue background with a narrow gold border and a golden fringe. A circular emblem is contained in the center of the blue field. The circular emblem is on a general white background with a yellow border. The word MINNESOTA is inscribed in red lettering on the lower part of the white field. The white emblem background surrounding a center design contains 19 five pointed stars arranged symmetrically in four groups of four stars each and one group of three stars. The latter group is in the upper part of the center circular white emblem. The group of stars at the top in the white emblem consists of three stars of which the uppermost star is the largest and represents the north star. A center design is contained on the white emblem and is made up of the scenes from the great seal of the state of Minnesota, surrounded by a border of intertwining Cypripedium reginae, the state flower, on a blue field of the same color as the general flag background. The flower border design contains the figures 1819, 1858, 1893.
>
> The coloring is the same on both sides of the flag, but the lettering and the figures appear reversed on one side.[38]

MISSISSIPPI

The Mississippi flag was created by a special committee appointed by the legislature in 1894. The original law described a flag

> with width two-thirds length; with a union square, in width two-thirds of the width of the flag; the ground of the union to be red and a broak blue saltier thereon, bordered with white and emblazoned with thirteen (13) mullets or five-pointed stars, corresponding with the number of original states of the Union; the field to be divided into three bars of equal width, the upper one blue, the center one white, and the lower one, extending the whole length of the flag, red—the national colors.[39]

The official pledge of the State of Mississippi reads as follows:

> I salute the flag of Mississippi and the sovereign state for which it stands with pride in her history and achievements and with confidence in her future under the guidance of Almighty God.[40]

MISSOURI

The Missouri flag, designed by Marie Elizabeth Watkins Oliver and Mary Kochtitzky, was approved by the legislature in 1913.[41]

> The official flag of the state of Missouri is rectangular in shape and its vertical width is to the horizontal length as seven is to twelve. It has one red, one white and one blue horizontal stripe of equal width; the red is at the top and the blue at the bottom. In the center of the flag there is a band of blue in the form of a circle enclosing the coat of arms in the colors as established by law on a white ground. The width of the blue band is one-fourteenth of the vertical width of the flag and the diameter of the circle is one-third of the horizontal length of the flag. In the blue band there are set at equal distances from each other twenty-four five pointed stars.[42]

MONTANA

The Montana flag had been the banner of the First Montana Infantry before it was adopted as the state flag in 1905. In 1981, the name of the state was added to the flag.

> The state flag of Montana shall be a flag having a blue field with a representation of the great seal of the state in the center and with golden fringe along the upper and lower borders of the flag; the same being the flag borne by the 1st Montana Infantry, U.S.V., in the Spanish-American War, with the exception of the device, "1st Montana Infantry, U.S.V."; and above the great seal of the state shall be the word "MONTANA" in Roman letters of gold color equal in height to one-tenth of the total vertical measurement of the blue field.[43]

NEBRASKA

A state banner was adopted in 1925 according to a bill introduced by J. Lloyd McMaster. In 1963, the banner was designated the official state flag.[44]

> The banner of the State of Nebraska shall consist of a reproduction of the Great Seal of the State, charged on the center in gold and silver on a field of national blue. The banner shall be the official state flag of the State of Nebraska and may be displayed on such occasions, at such times, and under such conditions as the flag of the United States of America.[45]

NEVADA

The Nevada state flag has been modified several times since 1866, when a flag was first adopted. The current law prescribes the following:

> The official flag of the State of Nevada is hereby created. The body of the flag must be of solid cobalt blue. On the field in the upper left quarter thereof must be two sprays of sagebrush with the stems crossed at the bottom to form a half wreath. Within the sprays must be a five-pointed silver star with one point up. The word "Nevada" must also be inscribed below the star and above the sprays, in a semicircular pattern with the letters spaced apart in equal increments, in the same style of letters as the words "Battle Born." Above the wreath, and touching the tips thereof, must be a scroll bearing the words "Battle Born." The scroll and the word "Nevada" must be golden-yellow. The lettering on the scroll must be black-colored sans serif gothic capital letters.[46]

NEW HAMPSHIRE

New Hampshire's state flag was not adopted until 1909. The original flag was modified in 1931, when changes were made in the state seal. The statute is reprinted with permission of Butterworth Legal Publishers.

> The state flag shall be of the following color and design: The body or field shall be blue and shall bear upon its center in suitable proportion and colors a representation of the state seal. The seal shall be surrounded by a wreath of laurel leaves with nine stars interspersed. When used for military purposes the flag shall conform to the regulations of the United States.[47]

NEW JERSEY

The design of the state flag was adopted in 1896. The law states simply that

> The state flag shall be of buff color, having in the center thereof the arms of the state emblazoned thereon.[48]

In 1965, the official state colors for use in the flag were designated:

> The official colors of the State of New Jersey for use on the State Flag and for other purposes shall be buff and Jersey blue.

For the purposes of this act the specifications, references and designations for the official colors of the state are as follows:

> Jersey Blue (Cable No. 70087, Royal Blue. The Color Association of the United States, Inc.)
>
> Buff (Cable No. 65015, U.S. Army Buff. The Color Association of the United States, Inc.)[49]

NEW MEXICO

The current New Mexico state flag, adopted in 1925, replaced a flag adopted in 1915. The Daughters of the American Revolution had supported the movement for a distinctive new flag, and the design of Dr. Harry Mera was finally chosen.[50] The law reads as follows:

> That a flag be and the same is hereby adopted to be used on all occasions when the state is officially and publicly represented, with the privilege of use by all citizens upon such occasions as they may deem fitting and appropriate. Said flag shall be the ancient Zia sun symbol of red in the center of a field of yellow. The colors shall be the red and yellow of old Spain. The proportion of the flag shall be a width of two-thirds its length. The sun symbol shall be one-third of the length of the flag. Said symbol shall have four groups of rays set at right angles; each group shall consist of four rays, the two inner rays of the group shall be one-fifth longer than the outer rays of the group. The diameter of the circle in the center of the symbol shall be one-third of the width of the symbol. Said flag shall conform in color and design described herein.[51]

In 1953, the legislature adopted both an English and a Spanish salute to the state flag. The official salute to the state flag is:

> I salute the flag of the state of New Mexico, the Zia symbol of perfect friendship among united cultures.[52]

The official Spanish language salute to the state flag is:

> Saludo la bandera del estado de Nuevo Méjico, el símbolo zía de amistad perfecta, entre culturas unidas.[53]

NEW YORK

In 1882, the legislature adopted the arms of the state that had first been designated in 1778. The flag was adopted in 1901 and modified in 1909. The current law reads as follows:

> The device of arms of this state, as adopted March sixteenth, seventeen hundred and seventy-eight, is hereby declared to be correctly described as follows:
>
> *Charge.* Azure, in a landscape, the sun in fess, rising in splendor or, behind a range of three mountains, the middle one the highest; in base a ship and sloop under sail, passing and about to meet on a river, bordered below by a grassy shore fringed with shrubs, all proper.
>
> *Crest.* On a wreath azure and or, an American eagle proper, rising to the dexter from a two-thirds of a globe terrestrial, showing the north Atlantic ocean with outlines of its shores.
>
> *Supporters.* On a quasi compartment formed by the extension of the scroll.
>
> *Dexter.* The figure of Liberty proper, her hair disheveled and decorated with pearls, vested azure, sandaled gules, about the waist a cincture or, fringed gules, a mantle of the last depending from the shoulders behind to the feet, in the dexter hand a staff ensigned with a Phrygian cap or, the sinister arm embowed, the hand supporting the shield at the dexter chief point, a royal crown by her sinister foot dejected.
>
> *Sinister.* The figure of Justice proper, her hair disheveled and decorated with pearls, vested or, about the waist a cincture azure, fringed gules, sandaled and manteled as Liberty, bound about the eyes with a fillet proper, in the dexter hand a straight sword hilted or, erect, resting on the sinister chief point of the shield, the sinister arm embowed, holding before her scales proper.
>
> *Motto.* On a scroll below the shield argent, in sable, Excelsior.
>
> *State Flag.* The state flag is hereby declared to be blue, charged with the arms of the state in the colors as described in the blazon of this section.[54]

NORTH CAROLINA

The flag of North Carolina was adopted in 1885.

> The flag of North Carolina shall consist of a blue union, containing in the center thereof a white star with the letter "N" in gilt on the left and the letter "C" in gilt on the right of said star, the circle containing the same to be one third the width of said union. The fly of the flag shall consist of two equally proportioned bars, the upper bar to be red, the lower bar to be white; the length of the bars horizontally shall be equal to the perpendicular length of the union, and the total length of the flag shall be one third more than its width. Above the star in the center of the union there shall be a gilt scroll in semicircular form, containing in black letters this inscription: "May 20th, 1775," and below the star there shall be a similar scroll containing in black letters the inscription: "April 12th, 1776."[55]

NORTH DAKOTA

The North Dakota state flag was first adopted in 1911. An amendment was made to the original act in 1959. The current law reads as follows:

> The flag of North Dakota shall consist of a field of blue silk or material which will withstand the elements four feet four inches [132.08 centimeters] on the pike and five feet six inches [167.64 centimeters] on the fly, with a border of knotted yellow fringe two and one-half inches [6.35 centimeters] wide. On each side of said flag in the center thereof, shall be embroidered or stamped an eagle with outspread wings and with opened beak. The eagle shall be three feet four inches [101.6 centimeters] from tip to tip of wing, and one foot ten inches [55.88 centimeters] from top of head to bottom of olive branch hereinafter described. The left foot of the eagle shall grasp a sheaf of arrows, the right foot shall grasp an olive branch showing three red berries. On the breast of the eagle shall be displayed a shield, the lower part showing seven red and six white stripes placed alternately. Through the open beak of the eagle shall pass a scroll bearing the words "E Pluribus Unum." Beneath the eagle there shall be a scroll on which shall be borne the words "North Dakota." Over the scroll carried through the eagle's beak shall be shown thirteen five-pointed stars, the whole device being surmounted by a sunburst. The flag shall conform in all respects as to color, form, size, and device with the regimental flag carried by the First North Dakota Infantry in the Spanish American War and Philippine Insurrection, except in the words shown on the scroll below the eagle.[56]

OHIO

The flag of Ohio was first adopted in 1902. An amendment in 1953 was made so that the current law reads as follows:

> The flag of the state shall be pennant shaped. It shall have three red and two white horizontal stripes. The union of the flag shall be seventeen five-pointed stars, white in a blue triangular field, the base of which shall be the staff end or vertical edge of the flag, and the apex of which shall be the center of the middle red stripe. The stars shall be grouped around a red disc superimposed upon a white circular "O." The proportional dimensions of the flag and of its various parts shall be according to the official design on file in the office of the secretary of state. One state flag of uniform dimensions shall be furnished to each company of the organized militia.[57]

In 1963, descriptions of other official flags were passed by the legislature.

> The flag of the governor of this state will be of scarlet wool bunting, six feet eight inches hoist by ten feet six inches fly. In each of the four corners will be a white five-pointed star with one point upward. The centers of these stars will be twelve inches from the long edges and seventeen inches from the short edges of the flag. In the center of the flag will be a reproduction of the great seal of Ohio in proper colors, three feet in diameter, surrounded by thirteen white stars equally spaced with their centers on an imaginary circle four feet three inches in diameter. All stars shall be of such size that their points would lie on the circumference of an imaginary circle ten inches in diameter.
>
> The official colors of the governor of Ohio will be of scarlet silk, four feet four inches on the pike by five feet six inches fly, of the same design as the flag of the governor of Ohio, with the seal and stars proportionately reduced in size and embroidered. The colors will be trimmed on three edges with a knotted fringe of yellow silk two and one half inches wide. Attached below the head of the pike will be a silk cord of scarlet and white eight feet six inches in length with a tassel at each end.
>
> The naval flag of the governor of Ohio will be of scarlet wool bunting, three feet hoist by four feet fly. The design will be the same as the flag of the governor of Ohio with the seal and the stars proportionately reduced in size.
>
> The automobile flag of the governor of Ohio will be of scarlet silk, or wool bunting, one foot six inches on the staff by two feet six inches on the fly. The design will be the same as the flag of the governor of Ohio with the seal and stars proportionately reduced in size. The flag

> will be trimmed on three edges with a knotted fringe of silk or wool one and one half inches wide.[58]

OKLAHOMA

The Oklahoma flag was adopted in 1925 and amended in 1941 to add the name of the state to the flag. The law reads as follows:

> The banner, or flag, of the design prescribed by Senate Concurrent Resolution No. 25, Third Legislature of the State of Oklahoma shall be, and it hereby is superseded and replaced by one of the following design, to-wit:
>
> A sky blue field with a circular rawhide shield of an American Indian Warrior, decorated with six (6) painted crosses on the face thereof, the lower half of the shield to be fringed with seven (7) pendant eagle feathers and superimposed upon the face of the shield a calumet or peace pipe, crossed at right angles by an olive branch, as illustrated by the design accompanying this resolution, and underneath said shield or design in white letters shall be placed the word "Oklahoma," and the same is hereby adopted as the official flag and banner of the State of Oklahoma.[59]

The same section describing the flag also sets out the official salute to the flag: "I salute the flag of the state of Oklahoma: Its symbols of peace unite all people." The salute was adopted in 1982.[60]

In 1957, the legislature approved a governor's flag:

> The flag of the Governor of the State of Oklahoma shall be forest green, bearing on each side the following: the Great Seal of the State of Oklahoma, centered, surrounded by five equidistant white stars with one of the stars placed directly above the Great Seal; and the flag to be edged with golden fringe.[61]

OREGON

The Oregon state flag was adopted in 1925, and the official colors were designated in 1959. The statute is reprinted with permission of Butterworth Legal Publishers.

> (1) A state flag is adopted to be used on all occasions when the state is officially and publicly represented, with the privilege of use by all citizens upon such occasions as may be fitting and appropriate. It shall bear on one side on a navy blue field the state escutcheon in gold, supported by 33 gold stars and bearing above the escutcheon the words "State of Oregon" in gold and below the escutcheon the figures

"1859" in gold, and on the other side on a navy blue field a representation of the beaver in gold.

(2) The official colors of the State of Oregon are navy blue and gold.[62]

PENNSYLVANIA

Pennsylvania's state flag was approved in 1907.

> The flag to be known as the official flag of the commonwealth of Pennsylvania shall be of blue, same color as the blue field in the flag of the United States, and of the following dimensions and design; to wit, The length, or height of the staff to be nine feet, including brass spearhead and ferrule; the fly of the said flag to be six feet two inches, and to be four feet six inches on the staff; in the center of the flag there shall be embroidered in silk the same on both sides of the flag the coat of arms of the commonwealth of Pennsylvania, in proportionate size; the edges to be trimmed with knotted fringe of yellow silk, two and one-half inches wide; a cord, with tassels, to be attached to the staff, at the spearhead, to be eight feet six inches long, and composed of white and blue silk strands.[63]

RHODE ISLAND

The original act designating the state flag was passed in 1897. Although amended, the flag remains essentially unchanged.

> The flag of the state shall be white, five (5) feet and six (6) inches fly and four (4) feet and ten (10) inches deep on the pike, bearing on each side in the centre a gold anchor, twenty-two (22) inches high, and underneath it a blue ribbon twenty-four (24) inches long and five (5) inches wide, or in these proportions, with the motto "Hope" in golden letters thereon, the whole surrounded by thirteen (13) golden stars in a circle. The flag to be edged with yellow fringe. The pike shall be surmounted by a spearhead and the length of the pike shall be nine (9) feet, not including the spearhead, provided, however, that on the 29th day of August, 1978 the flag of the Rhode Island first regiment shall be flown as the official state flag for that day.[64]

The law also allows for a flag and pennant of the governor.

> The flag and pennant of the governor shall be white bearing on each side the following: A gold anchor on a shield with a blue field and gold border; above the shield a gold scroll bearing the words in blue letters "State of Rhode Island"; below the shield a gold scroll bearing in blue letters the word "Hope"; the shield and scrolls to be sur-

> rounded by four (4) blue stars; both the flag and pennant to be edged with yellow fringe.[65]

SOUTH CAROLINA

The first state flag was designed by Colonel William Moultrie at the request of the Revolutionary Council of Safety in 1775. It was in truth a flag for the troops. Moultrie chose the blue of the soldiers' uniforms as the color of the field. A crescent in the upper right of the flag reproduced the silver emblem worn by the soldiers on the front of their caps. A palmetto tree was added in the center of the flag after Moultrie's defense of a palmetto-log fort on Sullivan's Island in 1776. In 1861, with South Carolina's secession, this same flag was chosen as the state's national flag. It became the state flag again when South Carolina rejoined the union.[66]

A 1966 act designated the pledge of allegiance to the state flag.

> The pledge to the flag of South Carolina shall be as follows: "I salute the flag of South Carolina and pledge to the Palmetto State love, loyalty and faith."[67]

SOUTH DAKOTA

South Dakota has two official state flags. The first flag, adopted in 1909, depicted the sun on the obverse and the seal on the reverse. Because of the expense of manufacturing a flag with two emblems, however, a new flag with a single emblem was designed and approved in 1963.[68] The description of the new flag is as follows:

> The state flag or banner shall consist of a field of sky-blue one and two-thirds as long as it is wide. Centered on such field shall be the great seal of South Dakota made in conformity with the terms of the Constitution, which shall be four-ninths the width of the said flag in diameter; such seal shall be on a white background with the seal outlined in dark blue thereon, or, in the alternative shall be on a sky-blue background with the seal outlined in dark blue thereon; surrounding the seal in gold shall be a serrated sun whose extreme width shall be five-ninths the width of the said flag. The words "South Dakota" symmetrically arranged to conform to the circle of the sun and seal shall appear in gold letters one-eighteenth the width of the said field above said sun and seal and the words "The Sunshine State" in like-sized gold letters and in like arrangement shall appear below the said sun and seal. Flags designed of such material as may be provident for outdoor use need have no fringe but flags for indoor and display usage shall have a golden fringe one-eighteenth the width of said flag on the three sides other than the hoist.

> All state flags made in conformity with state law prior to March 11, 1963 shall remain official state flags but the creation of a state flag from and after said date, other than in conformity with § 1-6-4, is prohibited.

In 1987, an official pledge to the state flag was adopted: "I pledge loyalty and support to the flag and state of South Dakota, land of sunshine, land of infinite variety."[69]

TENNESSEE

The Tennessee state flag was designed by LeRoy Reeves and adopted in 1905.[70]

> The flag or banner of the state of Tennessee shall be of the following design, colors, and proportions, to wit, an oblong flag or banner in length one and two thirds (1⅔) times its width, the principal field of same to be of color red, but said flag or banner ending at its free or outer end in a perpendicular bar of blue, of uniform width, running from side to side, that is to say, from top to bottom of said flag or banner, and separated from the red field by a narrow margin or stripe of white of uniform width; the width of the white stripe to be one fifth (⅕) that of the blue bar; and the total width of the bar and stripe together to be equal to one eighth (⅛) of the width of the flag. In the center of the red field shall be a smaller circular field of blue, separated from the surrounding red field by a circular margin or stripe of white of uniform width and of the same width as the straight margin or stripe first mentioned. The breadth or diameter of the circular blue field, exclusive of the white margin, shall be equal to one half (½) of the width of the flag. Inside the circular blue field shall be three (3) five-pointed stars of white distributed at equal intervals around a point, the center of the blue field, and of such size and arrangement that one (1) point of each star shall approach as closely as practicable without actually touching one (1) point of each of the other two (2) around the center point of the field; and the two (2) outer points of each star shall approach as nearly as practicable without actually touching the periphery of the blue field. The arrangement of the three (3) stars shall be such that the centers of no two (2) stars shall be in a line parallel to either the side or end of the flag, but intermediate between same; and the highest star shall be the one nearest the upper confined corner of the flag.[71]

TEXAS

The flag of the Republic of Texas became the official state flag when it was adopted in the 1876 state constitution.

> The Texas flag is an emblem of four sides, and four angles of ninety (90) degrees each. It is a rectangle having its width equal to two-thirds of its length. The flag is divided into three equivalent parts, called bars or stripes, one stripe being bloodred, one white, and the other azure blue. These stripes are rectangles, also, and they are exact duplicates of one another in every respect. The width of each stripe is equal to one-half of its length, or one-third of the length of the Flag, while the length of each stripe is equal to the width of the Flag, or two-thirds of the length of the Emblem.
>
> One end of the Flag is blue, and it is called the Flag's "right." This stripe is a perpendicular bar next to the staff or the halyard, and it is attached by means of a heading made of strong and very durable material. The remaining two-thirds of the Flag is made up of two horizontal bars of equal width, one being white and the other red, and this end of the Emblem is called the Flag's "left." Each one of the stripes is perpendicular to the blue stripe, and when the Flag is displayed on a flagpole or staff, or flat on a plane surface, the white stripe should always be at the top of the Flag, with the red stripe directly underneath it. Thus, each stripe on the Texas Flag touches each of the other stripes, which signifies that the three colors are mutually dependent upon one another in imparting the lessons of the Flag: bravery, loyalty, and purity.
>
> Description of the Star
>
> In the center of the blue stripe is a white star of five points. One point of this star is always at the top, and in a vertical line drawn from one end of the blue stripe to the other, and midway between its sides. This line is the vertical axis of the blue stripe, and it is perpendicular to the horizontal axis at the central point of the stripe. The two lowest points of the star are in a line parallel to the horizontal axis, and the distance from the topmost point of the star to the line through these two points is equal to approximately one third of the length of the blue stripe, or one-third of the width of the Flag. The center of the star is at the point of intersection of the horizontal axis with the vertical axis, or at the central point of the blue stripe. The other two points of the star are above the horizontal axis, and near the sides of the blue stripe.

The salute to the Texas flag is:

> Honor the Texas Flag; I pledge allegiance to thee, Texas, one and indivisible.[72]

UTAH

The Utah state flag was adopted in 1896 and revised in 1933. It was designated the governor's flag in 1911.[73]

> The state flag of Utah shall be a flag of blue field, fringed, with gold borders, with the following device worked in natural colors on the center of the blue field:
>
> The center a shield; above the shield and thereon an American eagle with outstretched wings; the top of the shield pierced with six arrows arranged crosswise; upon the shield under the arrows the word "Industry," and below the word "Industry" on the center of the shield, a beehive; on each side of the beehive, growing sego lilies; below the beehive and near the bottom of the shield, the word "Utah," and below the word "Utah" and on the bottom of the shield, the figures "1847"; with the appearance of being back of the shield there shall be two American flags on flagstaffs placed crosswise with the flags so draped that they will project beyond each side of the shield, the heads of the flagstaffs appearing in front of the eagle's wings and the bottom of each staff appearing over the face of the draped flag below the shield; below the shield and flags and upon the blue field, the figures "1896"; around the entire design, a narrow circle in gold.[74]

VERMONT

The current state flag of Vermont was adopted in 1923. It replaced the state flags adopted in 1803 and 1837. The 1923 law states simply that "the flag of the state shall be blue with the coat of arms of the state thereon."[75]

VIRGINIA

The flag of the Commonwealth of Virginia was adopted by legislative act in 1930.

> The flag of the Commonwealth shall hereafter be made of bunting or merino. It shall be a deep blue field, with a circular white centre of the same material. Upon this circle shall be painted or embroidered, to show on both sides alike, the coat of arms of the State . . . for the obverse of the great seal of the Commonwealth; and there shall be a white silk fringe on the outer edge, furthest from the flagstaff. This shall be known and respected as the flag of Virginia.[76]

WASHINGTON

The state flag of Washington was adopted in 1923 and amended slightly in 1925. The law declares

> That the official flag of the state of Washington shall be of dark green silk or bunting and shall bear in its center a reproduction of the seal of the state of Washington embroidered, printed, painted or stamped thereon. The edges of the flag may, or may not, be fringed. If a fringe is used the same shall be of gold or yellow color of the same shade as the seal. The dimensions of the flag may vary.[77]

WEST VIRGINIA

The current state flag of West Virginia was adopted in 1929, after numerous other flags had come into use and become infeasible. The flag is described as follows:

> The proportions of the flag of the state of West Virginia shall be the same as those of the United States ensign; the field shall be pure white, upon the center of which shall be emblazoned in proper colors, the coat-of-arms of the state of West Virginia, upon which appears the date of the admission of the state into the Union, also with the motto "Montani Semper Liberi" (Mountaineers Always Freemen) above the coat-of-arms of the state of West Virginia there shall be a ribbon lettered, state of West Virginia, and arranged appropriately around the lower part of the coat-of-arms of the state of West Virginia a wreath of rhododendron maximum in proper colors. The field of pure white shall be bordered by a strip of blue on four sides. The flag of the state of West Virginia when used for parade purposes shall be trimmed with gold colored fringe on three sides and when used on ceremonial occasions with the United States ensign, shall be trimmed and mounted in similar fashion to the United States flag as regards fringe cord, tassels and mounting.[78]

WISCONSIN

In 1979, the legislature revised the state flag, which had been adopted in 1913. The 1979 law became effective in 1981 and sets out these requirements:

> (1) The Wisconsin state flag consists of the following features:
>
> (a) Relative dimensions of 2 to 3, hoist to fly.
>
> (b) A background of royal blue cloth.

(c) The state coat of arms, as described under s. 1.07, in material of appropriate colors, applied on each side in the center of the field, of such size that, if placed in a circle whose diameter is equal to 50% of the hoist, those portions farthest from the center of the field would meet, but not cross, the boundary of the circle.

(d) The word "WISCONSIN" in white, capital, condensed Gothic letters, one-eighth of the hoist in height, centered above the coat of arms, midway between the uppermost part of the coat of arms and the top edge of the flag.

(e) The year "1848" in white, condensed Gothic numbers, one-eighth of the hoist in height, centered below the coat of arms, midway between the lowermost part of the coat of arms and the bottom edge of the flag.

(f) Optional trim on the edges consisting of yellow knotted fringe.

(2) The department of administration shall ensure that all official state flags that are manufactured on or after May 1, 1981 conform to the requirements of this section. State flags manufactured before May 1, 1981 may continue to be used as state flags.[79]

WYOMING

The state flag of Wyoming, designed by Mrs. A. C. Keyes of Casper, was adopted in 1917. The colors of the flag carry important symbolism: the red border symbolizes the Indian and the blood of the pioneers; the white signifies purity; the blue symbolizes fidelity and justice.[80] The current law reads as follows:

> A state flag is adopted to be used on all occasions when the state is officially and publicly represented. All citizens have the privilege of use of the flag upon any occasion they deem appropriate. The width of the flag shall be seven-tenths (7⁄10) of its length; the outside border shall be in red, the width of which shall be one-twentieth (1⁄20) of the length of the flag; next to the border shall be a stripe of white on the four (4) sides of the field, which shall be in width one-fortieth (1⁄40) of the length of the flag. The remainder of the flag shall be a blue field, in the center of which shall be a white silhouetted buffalo, the length of which shall be one-half (1⁄2) of the length of the blue field; the other measurements of the buffalo shall be in proportion to its length. On the ribs of the buffalo shall be the great seal of the state of Wyoming in blue. The seal shall be in diameter one-fifth (1⁄5) the length of the flag. Attached to the flag shall be a cord of gold with gold tassels. The same colors shall be used in the flag, red, white and blue, as are used in the flag of the United States of America.[81]

DISTRICT OF COLUMBIA

The flag of the District of Columbia was created by an October 15, 1938, act of the District Commission. Its design was adapted from George Washington's family crest. The insignia, which is illustrated, employs the same design with shorter stripes.

> This flag shall consist of a rectangular white background with two horizontal bars in red, and with three red stars in the upper white space of the flag. The proportions of this design are prescribed in terms of the hoist, or vertical height of the flag as follows: The upper white portion is $\frac{3}{10}$ of the hoist; the two horizontal red bars are each $\frac{2}{10}$ of the hoist; the white space between bars is $\frac{1}{10}$ of the hoist; and the base, or lowest white space, is $\frac{2}{10}$ of the hoist. The three red five-pointed stars have a diameter of $\frac{2}{10}$ of the hoist and are spaced equidistant in the fly or horizontal dimension of the flag. So long as the proportions herein prescribed are observed, the dimensions of the flag both in hoist and fly may vary in accordance with the size of the flag desired.[82]

AMERICAN SAMOA

The flag of American Samoa was adopted in 1960 when internal self-government was introduced. It employs the red, white, and blue of the American flag as well as the United States symbol of the bald eagle and the Samoan symbols of a fly whisk and a ceremonial dancing knife. A white triangle going from the fly to the hoist is defined by a red stripe. Toward the hoist within the white triangle an eagle holds and safeguards the symbols of Samoan culture. The remainder of the flag is blue.[83]

COMMONWEALTH OF THE NORTHERN MARIANA ISLANDS

The design of the flag of the Islands appears in an amendment to the constitution that made them a commonwealth in 1986.

> The official flag of the Commonwealth shall consist, on both sides of a rectangular field of blue, a white star in the center, superimposed on a gray latte stone, surrounded by the traditional Carolinian mwaar. The dimensions of the flag, the mwaar, the star and latte stone shall be provided by law. The field of blue represents the Pacific Ocean; the star represents the Commonwealth as the newest star in the western Pacific; the latte stone represents Chamorro culture; and the mwaar is a headband with flowers used for official ceremonies.[84]

GUAM

> The official territorial flag of Guam consists, on both sides, of a rectangular field of marine blue seventy-eight inches long and forty inches wide, trimmed on all sides with a border of deep red two inches in width and having in its center the Guam Coat of Arms, such Coat of Arms to be twenty-four (24) inches high and sixteen (16) inches wide. The territorial flag may be reproduced for unofficial purposes in smaller or larger sizes, but in such cases, the dimensions shall be in proportion to those stated herein.
>
> The official territorial flag of Guam for holiday uses shall be the same design as stated herein, but shall be fifty percent (50%) larger with identical proportions as the flag described above. The holiday flag shall be displayed on official buildings and flag staffs belonging to the government of Guam on all territorial and national Holidays.[85]

PUERTO RICO

The design of the current Puerto Rican flag became effective on July 25, 1952, although the flag that had been used before commonwealth status remained the flag of the commonwealth.

> The flag of the Commonwealth of Puerto Rico shall be the one traditionally known heretofore as the Puerto Rican Flag, and which is rectangular in form, with five alternate horizontal stripes, three red and two white, and having next to the staff a blue equilateral triangle with a five-point white star. On the vertical side this triangle stretches along the entire width of the flag.[86]

The official salute to the flag of Puerto Rico is as follows: "I swear before the Flag of the Commonwealth of Puerto Rico to honor the fatherland it symbolizes, the people it represents, and the ideals it embodies of liberty, justice and dignity."[87]

U.S. VIRGIN ISLANDS

The design of the U.S. Virgin Islands flag was approved in 1950 and the statute describing it is reprinted with permission of Butterworth Legal Publishers.

> Upon a field argent (white) between the block letters V and I azure (blue) an American Eagle (yellow) displayed and bearing upon his breast the shield of the United States of America and having in his dexter talon a sprig of laurel vert (green) and in his sinister talon a

bundle of three arrows azure (blue). The blue of the letters V.I. and the three arrows shall be azure blue. The blue of the chief of the shield is the blue of the arms and flag of the United States of America.[88]

NOTES

1. Ala. Code § 1–2–5.
2. Ibid., § 31–2–54.
3. *Alaska Blue Book, 1979,* p. 123.
4. Alaska Stat. § 44.09.020.
5. Ariz. Rev. Stat. Ann. § 41–851.
6. *Arkansas Almanac, 1972* (Little Rock: Arkansas Almanac, Inc., 1972), p. 31.
7. Ark. Code Ann. (1987) § 1–4–101.
8. Ibid., § 5–108.
9. Cal. Gov't. Code § 420 (West).
10. Colo. Rev. Stat. § 24–80–904.
11. Conn. Gen. Stat. Ann. § 3–107 (West).
12. Del. Code Ann. tit. 29, § 306.
13. Ibid., tit. 29 § 307.
14. Fla. Stat. Ann. § 15.012 (West).
15. Ga. Code Ann. § 50–3–1.
16. Ibid., § 50–3–2.
17. *Hawaii, The Aloha State* (Honolulu: State of Hawaii, Hawaii Visitors Bureau, Chamber of Commerce of Hawaii, n.d.).
18. Idaho Code § 46–801.
19. Ill. Ann. Stat. ch. 1, § 3001 (Smith-Hurd).
20. Ind. Code Ann. § 1–2–2–1 (West).
21. *1985–86 Iowa Official Register,* vol. 61, p. 236.
22. Iowa Code Ann. § 31.1 (West).
23. Kan. Stat. Ann. § 73–702.
24. Ibid., § 73–704.
25. Ky. Rev. Stat. Ann. § 2.030 (Baldwin).
26. La. Rev. Stat. Ann. § 9–153 (West).
27. Ibid., § 49–167 (West).
28. Me. Rev. Stat. tit. 1, § 206.
29. Ibid., tit. 1, § 207.
30. *Maryland Manual, 1981–82,* p. 10.
31. Md. Ann. Code § 13–202.
32. Mass. Gen. Laws Ann. ch. 2, § 3 (West).
33. Ibid., ch. 2, § 4 (West).
34. Mich. Comp. Laws Ann. § 2–23.
35. Ibid., § 2.29.
36. Ibid., § 2.24.
37. *Official Minnesota Symbols* (St. Paul: Minnesota Historical Society, Education Division, December 1983).
38. Minn. Stat. Ann. § 1.141 (West).

39. 1894 Miss. Laws 154.
40. Miss. Code Ann. § 37–13–7.
41. *State of Missouri Official Manual, 1975–1976,* p. 1438.
42. Mo. Ann. Stat. § 10.020 (Vernon).
43. Mont. Rev. Codes Ann. § 1–1–502.
44. *Nebraska Blue Book, 1982–83,* p. 12.
45. Neb. Rev. Stat. § 90–102.
46. Nev. Rev. Stat. § 235.020.
47. N.H. Rev. Stat. Ann. § 3:2.
48. N.J. Stat. Ann. § 52:3-1 (West).
49. Ibid., § 52:2A-1 (West).
50. Information provided by the New Mexico State Library.
51. N.M. Stat. Ann. § 12–3–2.
52. Ibid., § 12–3–3.
53. Ibid., § 12–3–7.
54. N.Y. State Law § 70 (McKinney).
55. N.C. Gen. Stat. § 144–1.
56. N.D. Cent. Code § 54–02–02.
57. Ohio Rev. Code Ann. § 5.01 (Baldwin).
58. Ibid., § 5.011 (Baldwin).
59. Okla. Stat. Ann. tit. 25, § 91 (West).
60. Ibid., tit. 25, § 92 (West).
61. Ibid., tit. 25, § 93.1 (West).
62. Or. Rev. Stat. § 186.010.
63. Pa. Stat. Ann. tit. 44, § 45 (Purdon).
64. R.I. Gen. Laws § 42–4–3.
65. Ibid., § 42–7–4.
66. *South Carolina State Symbols and Emblems* (Columbia: House of Representatives, n.d.).
67. S.C. Code § 1–1–670.
68. *History of the South Dakota State Flag* (Pierre: Bureau of Administration, Division of Central Services, The State Flag Account, n.d.).
69. S.D. Codified Laws Ann. § 1–6–4, § 1–6–5, § 1–6–4–1.
70. *Tennessee Blue Book, 1985–1986,* pp. 338–39.
71. Tenn. Code Ann. § 4–1–301.
72. Tex. Rev. Civ. Stat. Ann. art. 6142a (Vernon).
73. *Symbols of the Great State of Utah* (n.p., n.d.).
74. Utah Code Ann. § 63–13–5.
75. Vt. Stat. Ann. tit. 1, § 495.
76. Va. Code § 7.1–32.
77. Wash. Rev. Code Ann. § 1.20.010.
78. 1929 W. Va. Acts 495.
79. Wis. Stat. Ann. § 1.08 (West).
80. *Wyoming: Some Historical Facts* (Cheyenne: Wyoming State Archives, Museums and Historical Department, n.d.), p. i.
81. Wyo. Stat. Ann. § 8–3–102.
82. Text provided by W. C. Bradley III, Visual Information Specialist, Government of the District of Columbia, Office of the Secretary.

83. Information provided by the office of Eni Faleomavaega, Member of Congress for American Samoa.

84. *Amendments to the Constitution of the Northern Mariana Islands* (Saipan: Marianas Printing Service, Inc., 1986), amendment 43.

85. Guam Code Ann. tit. 1, § 407.

86. P.R. Laws Ann. tit. 1, § 31.

87. *Regulations to Establish the Official Salute to the Flag of the Commonwealth of Puerto Rico* (San Juan: Commonwealth of Puerto Rico, Department of State, n.d.).

88. V.I. Code Ann. tit. 1, § 101.

5 | State and Territory Capitols

The history of American state and territory capitols is replete with political intrigue, architectural blunderings, frequent destruction by fire, and occasional destruction by war. This history is also, however, a record of the deep and abiding patriotism of the citizens of each state and territory and their respect for and pride in the functions of their governments.

Many of today's capitols were constructed at the end of the nineteenth or beginning of the twentieth century. The architecture of these buildings is clearly informed by the style of the United States Capitol—neoclassical, domed capitols that call to mind ancient democracies. Some states, however, chose contemporary architecture to express their belief in progress. Notable among all the capitols in this regard are the "skyscraper" style capitols of Nebraska and Louisiana, built in the second and third decades of this century. The capitols of Hawaii and New Mexico, completed in the 1960s, are contemporary designs that express the individual history and heritage of those states. But whatever their design, state and territory capitols stand as monuments to the people, to their hard work, and to their belief in the progress of democracy.

ALABAMA

Montgomery was chosen as the capital city of Alabama during the 1845–1846 legislative session. Since becoming a state in 1817, the legislature had met in Huntsville, Cahaba, and Tuscaloosa before choosing Montgomery as a permanent capital. Because the legislative act designating Montgomery stipulated that the state should bear no expense in purchasing land or building a capitol, the city floated a $75,000 bond issue, which paid for the site known as Goat Hill and the erection of a Greek revival capitol designed by Stephen D. Dutton. Completed in 1847, it was destroyed in December 1849. The legislature appropriated $60,000 in 1850 and employed Barachias Holt to design a new building to be erected on the foundation of the destroyed capitol. The new capitol, also in the Greek revival style embellished with Corinthian columns and a towering, white dome, was completed in 1851. In 1885, an east wing was erected at a cost of $25,000. A south wing was added in 1905–1906 for $150,000 and a north wing, in 1911 for $100,000. The wings, constructed of brick with a stucco finish, maintain the box-like, Greek style and are adorned with Ionic columns. Frank Lockwood was the architect for all of the additions.[1]

ALASKA

The six-story Alaska State Capitol in Juneau, begun in 1929, was completed in 1931 as the Federal and Territorial Building. When Alaska became a state in 1958, the state was given possession of the building. In fact, the people of Juneau had donated half of the property to the federal government, as Congress had not appropriated enough money to pay for the building site. Construction and site costs approximated $1 million.

The capitol was designed by James A. Wetmore, who was the federal government's supervising architect. It is made of reinforced concrete with a brick facing. Indiana limestone was used for the lower facade and Tokeen marble, native to Alaska, was used for the four Doric columns of the portico as well as the interior trim.[2]

ARIZONA

The Arizona Capitol, designed by James Riely Gordon, is located in Phoenix. The Victorian four-story structure is made primarily from Arizona materials, as mandated by the legislature. The exterior is made of granite, tuff stone, and malapai. Oak woodwork adorns the interior. The building was completed in 1900 at a cost of $135,744. Today the capitol houses the Arizona State Capitol Museum. Government offices have been moved to nearby or adjacent buildings.[3]

ARKANSAS

The Arkansas State Capitol in Little Rock was begun in 1899 when the existing building became inadequate with the growth of the government.

It was completed after numerous delays in 1916. Final construction costs totalled about $2.5 million, considerably more than the $1 million originally appropriated. The Grecian design of the building, including the dome, which is copied from St. Paul's via the Mississippi Capitol, is essentially that of George R. Mann. Cass Gilbert became the architect toward the end of the project, but he made few changes in the exterior design. The exterior is constructed of Batesville marble and some Indiana Bedford limestone. The interior is finished in Alabama marble.[4]

CALIFORNIA

In 1854, after meeting in San Jose, Vallejo, Sacramento, Vallejo again, and Benicia, the California legislature moved the state capital to Sacramento. Construction of the permanent capitol building, designed by M. F. Butler, began in September 1860, and the cornerstone was laid in May 1861. Although some offices were occupied as early as 1869, the building was not fully completed until 1874. Remodeling work was undertaken from 1906 to 1908 and again in 1928. The capitol was completely restored between 1976 and 1981 at a cost of $68 million.

The "Old Capitol," as it is known today, is a four-story building topped by a copper-clad dome. A cupola extending from the dome is supported by twelve columns. Its roof is covered with gold plate and supports a copper ball, 30 inches in diameter, which is plated with gold coins. The building itself, Roman Corinthian in design, is 219 feet 11½ inches in height, 320 feet in length, and 164 feet wide. The dome rises on a two-story drum. A colonnade of twenty-four Corinthian columns supports the roof, from which a clerestory rises. The first story was constructed from granite out of nearby quarries, and stuccoed brick construction was used for the top three stories.

In 1949 construction of an annex was begun. Completed in January 1952, at a cost of $7.6 million (about three times the cost of the Old Capitol), the annex is 103 feet high, 210 feet long, and 269 feet wide. This six-story building, designed by the State Division of Architecture, is joined to the Old Capitol and, although it is contemporary in style, blends with the lines of the older building.[5]

COLORADO

When Colorado entered the Union in 1876, Denver had been its capital city for nine years. Although a ten-acre site had been donated and accepted for erection of a capitol in 1874, excavation did not begin until 1886. The government continued to operate out of rented quarters until 1894, when offices in the permanent capitol were first used. The building was not completed, however, until twenty-two years after work first began at a cost of almost $3 million.

Colorado's capitol was designed by architect E. E. Myers to resemble the U.S. Capitol. The building measures 383 feet in length and 315 feet in width; its floor plan is in the form of a Greek cross. Gunnison granite was used for the five-foot-thick exterior walls, sandstone from Fort Collins for the foundations, marble from Marble, Colorado for the floors and stairs, and rose onyx unique to Beulah, Colorado for wainscoting. The dome rises 272 feet above the ground. Copper was first used to cover the dome, but, because of the public outcry that copper was not native to Colorado, sheets of gold leaf donated by Colorado miners were applied to the dome. A second coating of gold was applied to the dome in 1950.[6]

CONNECTICUT

The Capitol of Connecticut is located in Hartford, overlooking Bushnell Memorial Park on a site contributed by the city. Funds were appropriated for the building in 1871 and it was completed in 1879 at a cost of $2,532,524. Built by James G. Batterson and designed by Richard M. Upjohn, this Victorian Gothic capitol is constructed of New England marble and granite and is topped by a gold-leaf dome. In 1972, the capitol was declared a national historical landmark.[7]

DELAWARE

In 1787, the Levy Court of Kent County, in which the capital city of Dover is located, decided that the 1722 courthouse had grown too small for county and state offices. Using bricks from the old building as the foundation for the new, the building was finally opened in April 1792 with the proceeds of a state lottery to overcome financial difficulties. The cost was £2107:7:5. In 1795, the General Assembly appropriated £404:4:4 to complete the brick, colonial style state house, including a copper roof.

In 1836, when it was necessary to expand the facility, $3,000 was spent on a two-story plus basement addition that measured 40 by 50 feet. Finally, in April 1873, the legislature purchased the statehouse for its exclusive use at a cost of $15,000. After some remodeling, the capitol was ready for use in 1875. Another addition, built during 1895–1897, added 40 feet to the 1836 addition, and a south wing was added in 1910 at a cost of $62,500. In 1925–1926, a three-story annex was erected to the east side of the original building.[8]

FLORIDA

Tallahassee was chosen to be Florida's capital city in 1824. Two years later, a 40 by 26 foot, two-story masonry building was constructed as the capitol. Although this was to be the wing of a larger building, by 1839, no further addition had been made. Instead, the original structure was razed and a new brick capitol was finally completed in 1845. In 1902, a copper dome was added along with four bay wings. Further enlargements were made in 1923, 1936, and 1947.

By 1972 it was clear that the old capitol did not provide enough space to carry on government operations. A capitol complex was authorized by the legislature that included new legislative chambers and offices as well as a 307-foot, twenty-two-story executive office building. The new concrete and steel capitol, completed in 1977 and dedicated in 1978, cost $43,070,741. It was designed jointly by Edward Durell Stone of New York and Reynolds, Smith and Hills of Jacksonville.[9]

GEORGIA

The people of Georgia voted in 1877 to make the city of Atlanta the state's capital. When Georgia became a state in 1788, Augusta was the capital, and the capital city was subsequently moved to Louisville, Milledgeville, Macon, back to Milledgeville, and, finally, to Atlanta in 1868. In 1883, the legislature appropriated $1 million for the construction of a capitol, to be supervised by a board of five commissioners.

The firm of Edbrooke and Burnham in Chicago was awarded the contract for its Classic Renaissance design. Georgia marble was used for the interior finish and Indiana limestone for the exterior. Construction began in 1884 and was completed within the amount appropriated in 1889. Its largest dimensions are 347 feet, 9 inches in length and 272 feet, 4 inches in width. A rotunda extends from the second floor to a height of 237 feet, 4 inches. The gilded dome is 75 feet in diameter. The cupola is adorned by a 15-foot statue that represents freedom. The main entrance to the capitol is a four-story portico supported by six Corinthian columns.

Renovation work, which included applying native Georgia gold to the dome, was authorized in 1957. In 1981, it was necessary to apply more gold to the dome. The capitol was dedicated as a national historic landmark in 1977.[10]

HAWAII

The Hawaiian State Capitol in Honolulu is certainly one of the most unique of any of the state capitols. The concrete and steel building rises from an 80,000-square-foot reflecting pool to symbolize the creation of the islands out of the water. The legislative chambers are shaped like the volcanoes that gave birth to the islands. The forty columns that surround the capitol are shaped like royal palms.

The architectural firms of Belt, Lemmon and Lo of Honolulu and John

Carl Warnecke and Associates of San Francisco planned and designed the 558,000-square-foot structure. Ground was broken late in 1965 and the capitol was dedicated in 1969. Construction costs came to $21,745,900. Total costs, including construction, equipment, furnishings, design, and fine arts totalled $24,576,900.[11]

IDAHO

The Capitol Building in Boise was designed by the local firm of Tourtellette and Hummell in the same style as the U.S. Capitol. Construction began in 1905. By 1911, the central part of the building was completed, and, by 1920, the east and west wings were ready for use by the legislature. Construction costs totalled nearly $2.3 million.

Idaho sandstone, quarried by convicts, was used for exterior facing. Marble from Vermont, Alaska, Georgia, and Italy was used in the interior. The dome, which rises 208 feet, is topped by a solid copper eagle dipped in bronze, itself standing 5 feet, 7 inches tall. Eight massive columns ring the rotunda and support the dome. The columns are scagliola—a mixture of granite, marble dust, glue, and gypsum that is dyed to look like marble. Artisans from Italy were brought to Boise to do the scagliola veneer.[12]

ILLINOIS

Illinois became a state in 1818. Its capital at that time was Kaskaskia. In 1820, the capital was moved to Vandalia and then, in 1839, with the help of Abraham Lincoln, to its permanent location, Springfield. The building used today is the sixth capitol and the second built in Springfield. Its construction was authorized in 1867, the cornerstone was laid in 1868, and it was completed in 1888 at a cost of $4.5 million. Situated on nine acres of land, the building was designed by John C. Cochrane of Chicago in the form of a Latin cross combining classical Greek and Roman styles. Its height from ground to dome is 361 feet. From north to south the capitol measures, at its extreme, 379 feet and from east to west, 268 feet. The walls supporting the dome are made from granular magnesian limestone. The interior walls are constructed of Niagara limestone. The corridors and walls of the rotunda employ decorative mosaics of marble. Bedford blue limestone and Missouri red granite were used to face the interior stone walls.[13]

INDIANA

In 1824 the Indiana capital was moved to Indianapolis from Corydon, which had been the capital even before Indiana became a state in 1816. The first statehouse, a Greek revival building occupied in 1835, had been outgrown by 1877. Construction of the new Modern Renaissance capitol, designed by local architect Edwin May, began in 1878 and was completed in 1888 at a cost of approximately $2 million. The four-story capitol, constructed of Indiana limestone, contains over twelve acres of floor space. It is distinguished by the dome, 72 feet in diameter, which reaches a height of 234 feet. The inner dome, rising 108 feet above the main floor, is a 48-foot-wide work of stained glass, which was installed in 1887.[14]

IOWA

When the first General Assembly met in Iowa City after Iowa became a state in 1846, it began the search for a new capital. In 1857, the governor finally declared Des Moines to be the capital city. The government occupied temporary quarters in Des Moines until the new capitol was completed in 1884.

A capitol commission was formed in 1870 to construct a capitol for $1.5 million. The commission named John C. Cochrane and A. H. Piquenard architects, and the cornerstone for the traditional, modified Renaissance building was laid in 1871. The cornerstone had to be laid again in 1873 owing to the deterioration of the stone used. The capitol was finally completed eleven years later at a cost of $2,873,294. A fire in 1904, which occurred during repair and modernization work, resulted in additional expenditures for renovation that brought the total cost of the capitol to $3,296,256.

The steel and stone dome, covered with gold leaf that was replaced in 1964–1965, is surmounted by a lookout lantern and terminates in a filial that reaches 275 feet. The capitol was constructed of Iowa stone for the foundation, Iowa granite, Missouri limestone, and Anamosa from Iowa, Ohio, Minnesota, and Illinois. Interior wood came entirely from Iowa hardwood forests, and twenty-nine different foreign and domestic marbles were used for interior facing.[15]

KANSAS

In 1861, the citizens of the new state of Kansas voted to make Topeka their capital city. The next year, the state accepted a donation of twenty acres on which to build a capitol building. In 1866 the cornerstone of the east wing was laid, but it had to be replaced in 1867. By 1870 the building was opened for use by the legislature. In 1879 work started on a west wing with a $60,000 appropriation and a tax increase. The Kansas House of Representatives met in the still unfinished west wing in 1881. Finally, the legislature authorized erection of the central portion, which was completed in 1903. Total costs came to approximately $3.2 million. McDonald Brothers of Louisville were the designing architects.

The classical capitol is 399 feet north to south, 386 feet east to west, and 304 feet to the top of the dome, on which is situated a statue of the goddess Ceres. The central part of the building is five stories high. Each wing is four stories. The interior is decorated with a number of rich marbles, and the rotunda contains eight murals designed by David H. Overmyer. The second floor contains a series of murals by John Stewart Curry.[16]

KENTUCKY

In 1904 the legislature of Kentucky passed a bill providing for the construction of a capitol in Frankfort, thus ending a long debate as to where the permanent capital should be located. Collection of $1 million of debt left from the Civil and Spanish-American wars owed Kentucky by the United States War Department provided the funding. F. M. Andrews and Company had been retained as architects and work commenced in 1905, with the cornerstone having been laid in 1906. The building was dedicated in 1910.

Kentucky's capitol combines French Renaissance and neoclassical designs in a building that measures 402 feet, 10 inches east to west, 180 feet north to south, and 212 feet from the top of the lantern to the terrace floor, on a thirty-four-acre site. The base of the exterior is Vermont granite, and the face-work on the three-story building is Bedford limestone. The exterior walls are adorned with seventy Ionic columns of limestone. The rotunda, 57 feet in diameter, the dome, and the lantern were copied from the Hôtel des Invalides of Napoléon's tomb in Paris. The State Reception Room is a copy of Marie Antoinette's drawing room in the Grand Trianon Palace. Total construction and furnishing costs totaled $1,820,000.[17]

LOUISIANA

When Huey Long became governor of Louisiana in 1928, one of his top priorities was to centralize the state's government under one roof. The 100-year-old neo-Gothic capitol in downtown Baton Rouge had grown inadequate. In 1930, the legislature granted Long's wish and appropriated $5 million for a new capitol building. Work commenced in December 1930 and was completed only fourteen months later.

The New Orleans architectural firm of Weiss, Dreyfous, and Seiferth designed a statehouse that replaced the traditional dome and rotunda with a thirty-four-story, 450-foot tower, and a public hall in accordance with the governor's wishes. The capitol became, at the time, the tallest building in the South, and it remains a fine example of the Art Moderne school of American architecture. The 10 percent savings in building costs were used to embellish the capitol with art deco ornamentation.

The capitol is surrounded by twenty-seven acres of formal gardens, which were once occupied by Louisiana State University. In 1935, Huey Long was assassinated in the very building he had envisioned to be a monument to the people of Louisiana. His grave is located at the center of the formal gardens.[18]

MAINE

Augusta was selected as Maine's capital in 1827, seven years after Maine became a state. Charles Bulfinch was chosen to design the building for a thirty-four-acre plot that had been chosen. The cornerstone of the Greek and Renaissance influenced capitol was laid in 1829 and was completed in time for the legislative session beginning in January 1832. The completed capitol, made of Hallowell granite, cost $139,000, including furnishings and grounds.

The interior was remodeled in 1852 and again in 1860. A three-story wing was added at the rear in 1890–1891. Major remodeling work was accomplished in 1909 and 1910. The length of the structure was doubled to 300 feet, but the original front was maintained. However, a dome that reaches to 185 feet, surmounted by a statue of Wisdom made of copper covered with gold, replaced the original cupola.[19]

MARYLAND

The Maryland State House in Annapolis, begun in 1772 and first occupied in 1779, is the oldest state capitol still used for legislative purposes. The roof was refashioned in 1785 and the dome, designed by Joseph Clark, in 1789. The interior height of the cypress-beamed dome is 113 feet, the largest wooden dome in the country. Annexes were added in 1858 and 1886, but they were replaced between 1902 and 1904. This brick colonial building, trimmed in stone, was built originally for £7500. Most of the rooms of the original building have been restored to their eighteenth-century luster, a task that has occupied most of the years of this century.[20]

MASSACHUSETTS

The site of the statehouse of Massachusetts in Boston was formerly John Hancock's cow pasture. The building was designed by Charles Bulfinch and completed in 1798 after three years of construction. Bulfinch designed the brick capitol after months of studying Greek and Roman temples. The large wooden dome, now covered with 23 karat gold, was originally covered with copper from Paul Revere. Except for two marble wings on each side added in this century and a yellow brick north annex, the original building still looks much as it did in 1798.[21]

MICHIGAN

In 1847, ten years after becoming a state, Michigan moved its capital from Detroit to Ingham township. A new capital city, temporarily named Michigan, was fashioned out of the woods. After only a few months, the city's name was changed to Lansing.

Having quickly outgrown a temporary statehouse, a permanent brick building was erected in 1854 and added to in 1863 and 1865. These buildings were also outgrown within a few years. In 1871, the legislature set a limit of $1.2 million for the construction of a new capitol. Elijah E. Myers, a self-taught architect from Springfield, Illinois, was named the winner of the architectural contest to build the capitol in 1872. The cornerstone was laid in 1873, and the academic-classical structure was completed in 1879.

The capitol building covers more than an acre of land. It is 420 feet long, 274 feet wide, and 267 feet high. It is made of Ohio sandstone, Illinois limestone, Massachusetts granite, and Vermont marble. It has a cruciform floor plan, a high dome in the center, and a two-story portico at the head of the outside stairway above the central entrance. The exterior facade of the top floors is decorated with Corinthian, Tuscan, and Ionic columns.[22]

MINNESOTA

Ground was broken for the Minnesota Capitol in St. Paul in 1896. The legislature had recognized by 1893 that its Romanesque capitol building had become too small to conduct the state's business. Cass Gilbert won the architectural competition with a familiar domed design in the classical Renaissance style. The capitol was ready for occupancy in 1905 at a cost of $4.5 million, including grounds and furnishings.

The basement of the Michigan Capitol is constructed of St. Cloud granite and the rest of the building of Georgia marble. It measures 434 feet from east to west and 229 feet from north to south. The white dome reaches a height of 223 feet.[23]

MISSISSIPPI

In 1822, Mississippi moved its capital to Jackson from Natchez. Eleven years later, a new capitol, Greek revival in style, was planned. What is now referred to as the "Old Capitol" was completed in 1839 and remained in use as the capitol building until the current capitol was completed in 1903.

The "New Capitol," designed by Theodore C. Link of St. Louis, was constructed at a cost of $1,093,641 from 1901–1903. The exterior of this beaux arts classic masterpiece is Bedford limestone and the base course, Georgia granite. Blue Vermont marble, Italian white marble, Belgian black marble, jet black New York marble, and columns of scagliola adorn the interior. The dome rises to a height of 180 feet. An 8-foot eagle of copper coated in gold leaf stands atop the dome.[24]

MISSOURI

Having moved its capital from St. Louis and temporarily to St. Charles, the legislature of Missouri chose Jefferson City to be the capital and appropriated $18,373 in 1825 to construct a permanent capitol there. In 1837, this building was destroyed by fire. A new capital was constructed in 1848 and enlarged in 1888. In 1911 this structure was also destroyed by fire. A $3.5 million bond issue was floated to construct a new capitol. The design contest was won by Tracy and Swartwout and construction began in 1913. Ready for occupancy in 1918, it cost $4,215,000, including furnishings and grounds. The Renaissance-classical capitol, constructed of Burlington limestone, is five stories high, 437 feet east to west, 300 feet wide at the center, and 200 feet wide in the wings. It houses 500,000 square feet of floor space. The dome stretches to a height of 238 feet. Above the dome is a bronze statue of Ceres. Extensive renovation and restoration activities have been completed recently.[25]

MONTANA

Six years after becoming a state in 1889, the Montana legislature authorized $1 million to be spent on a permanent capitol in Helena. Owing to depression and scandal, the original plan was abandoned, and, in 1897, the legislature authorized a less grandiose capitol that would cost, when completed in 1902, only $485,000.

Charles Emlen Bell and John Hackett Kent of Council Bluffs, Iowa were selected as architects. The cornerstone of the Greek Ionic neoclassical capitol was laid in 1899. Sandstone quarried in Columbus, Montana was used for the exterior. The rotunda decoration suggests that of a nineteenth-century opera house. The copper-clad dome above the rotunda was refaced in 1933–1934. East and west wings were added to the original building in 1909–1912. The wings, which maintain the style of the first building, were designed by Frank M. Andrews in association with John G. Link and Charles S. Haire. The facing of the wings is Jefferson County granite, chosen over sandstone for its durability. Some alterations were made in the central and end blocks of the original building during reconstruction in 1963–1965.[26]

NEBRASKA

The Nebraska Capitol, constructed in Lincoln between 1922 and 1932, is unlike any other state capitol building. Rather than imitating the architecture of the U.S. Capitol or harkening back to classical style, this statehouse is thoroughly modern in inspiration, and it received the Building Stone Institute's Award for architectural excellence in 1982. The Indiana limestone building was designed by Bertram Goodhue who, in turn, chose August Vincent Tack to execute the murals, Hildreth Meiere to design the mosaic and tile decoration, and Lee Lawrie to do the sculpture. The base of the capitol is 437 feet square and two stories high. A 400-foot tower, adorned with a bronze statue of "The Sower," rises from the base. The capitol, including grounds and furnishings, was completed at a cost exceeding $10 million.[27]

NEVADA

Early in 1869, the Nevada legislature designated a ten-acre site in Carson City, where it had been using temporary facilities, on which to construct a new capitol for no more than $100,000. The design submitted by Joseph Gosling, which called for a "two-story building in the form of a Grecian Cross, compounded of the Corinthian, Ionic and Doric," was chosen. The plans called for the building to be 148 feet long and 98 feet wide and the cupola to be 30 feet in diameter and 120 feet high.

The cornerstone was laid in 1870, and the capitol was completed on time in 1871. Sandstone from the state prison quarry was used for the facade, and Alaskan marble was used for inlay to the interior arches, floors, and wainscoting. The completed building cost $169,830. An annex was added in 1905, and north and south wings were added in 1913.[28]

NEW HAMPSHIRE

The New Hampshire statehouse in Concord is the oldest state capitol in the country in which the legislature uses its original chambers. The cornerstone for the original building, designed with simple classical lines by Stuart Park, was laid in 1816. The capitol was ready for use in 1819. The two-story New Hampshire granite structure which measures 126 feet wide and 57 feet deep, was completed for $82,000.

In 1864 a project to double the size of the original building was begun using the design of Gridley J. F. Bryant. At this time, a portico was added with Doric and Corinthian columns. A new dome replaced the original, but the gilded eagle that had first been perched on the capitol dome in 1818 was placed on the new dome. In 1909, under the auspices of Peabody and Stearns, the capitol building was again enlarged. The legislature, however, retained its same quarters. The Senate chamber was refurbished in 1974 and the Representatives Hall, in 1976.[29]

NEW JERSEY

The New Jersey statehouse in Trenton is the second oldest in continuous use of all the statehouses in the United States. Traces of the original two-story colonial structure, built in 1792 by Jonathan Doanne, can still be seen. In the mid-1800s, John Notman was employed to do a major restructuring of the capitol, at which time the building attained a Greek revival flavor with the addition of columned porticoes and a rotunda.

When fire destroyed much of the capitol in 1885, repairs and renovation were begun at once under the supervision of architect Lewis Broom. When completed in 1889, the capitol had taken on the French academic classic style popular at the time. Additions were made to the refurbished building in 1891, 1898, 1900, 1903, 1906, 1911–12, and 1917. Major renovations were planned for 1986–1988 to improve the functional aspects of the building and to return it aesthetically to its original design.[30]

NEW MEXICO

Santa Fe, New Mexico's capital city, boasts the oldest capitol building—El Palacio, built in 1610—and one of the newest—the Round House or Bull Pen, completed in 1966. The exterior of the new capitol is modified New Mexico territorial design. The interior is circular and contains four levels. The adobe-colored building with a total area of 232,206 square feet was designed by W. C. Kruger and Associates. Construction costs totaled $4,676,860.

The capitol was designed to include the shape of the Zia, an Indian sun symbol. The Zia, a sign of friendship, is composed of four rays around an inner circle. The entrances to the circular building continue this symbolism. Native marble adorns the interior. The rotunda is 24 feet in diameter and 60 feet high.[31]

NEW YORK

By 1865 the New York legislature had moved to erect a new capitol building in Albany, since Philip Hooker's Greek revival capitol, which had first been occupied in 1809, had clearly become inadequate. Late in 1867, the design of an Italian Renaissance capitol by Arthur D. Gilman and Thomas Fuller was accepted, and ground was broken very shortly thereafter. The 1868 legislature set the spending limit at $4 million, but, by 1874, the commissioners overseeing construction knew that at least $10 million would be needed. The cornerstone was laid in 1871, with architect Fuller still in command. Fuller was dismissed in 1876 and replaced by a board of advisors that included Frederick Law Olmstead and architects Leopold Eidlitz and H. H. Richardson. Plans were redrawn by Eidlitz and Richardson that called for completion of the capitol in 1879 and an additional expenditure of only $4.5 million. Finishing touches were still under way, however, in 1898. As a result of changes in architects and the collaboration of two architects whose styles were quite different, the capitol represents an admixture of Gilman's Italian Renaissance, Richardson's romanesque, Eidlitz's Victorian Gothic, and a bit of Moorish-Saracenic finished with French Renaissance. By 1879, the building was ready for occupancy. The granite building was partially destroyed by fire in 1911. Reconstruction costs amounted to $2 million. From 1978 to 1980, renovation work restored some parts of the building to their original splendor. In 1979, the capitol was designated a national historic landmark.[32]

NORTH CAROLINA

Raleigh was chosen as North Carolina's permanent capital city in 1792, and, by 1796, a two-story brick statehouse had been completed. Between 1820 and 1824, additions were made to this simple building, which was completely destroyed by fire in 1831. The general assembly that met during the 1832–33 session appropriated $50,000 to construct a new capitol, which was to be a larger version of the old statehouse. Architect William Nichols was hired to prepare plans for a building in the shape of a cross with a central, domed rotunda. Nichols was replaced in August 1833 by the New York firm of Ithiel Town and Alexander Jackson Davis. The firm is responsible for giving the capitol its present appearance, although David Paton, who replaced Town and Davis early in 1835, made several changes to the interior.

The cornerstone for the Greek revival capitol was laid in 1833, and soon after construction began another $75,000 had to be appropriated. By the time the building was completed in 1840, its total cost with furnishings came to $532,682. The capitol measures 160 feet by 140 feet. The exterior walls are North Carolina gneiss and the interior walls, stone and brick. The Doric exterior columns are modeled after the Parthenon. The new capitol has been extensively renovated.[33]

NORTH DAKOTA

The "Skyscraper Capitol of the Plains" in Bismarck was completed in 1934 at a cost of $2 million, after the original capitol had been destroyed by fire in 1930. The nineteen-story Indiana limestone building in modern American style was designed by Holabird and Root of Chicago, Joseph Bell De Remer of Grand Forks, and William F. Kurke of Fargo. A four-story judicial wing and state office building was added to the original capitol in the 1970s. The annex, finished in limestone to match the capitol, provides another 100,000 square feet of space. Between 1971 and 1981, over $10 million was spent on various renovation projects.[34]

OHIO

The Ohio legislature voted in 1817, fourteen years after Ohio became a state, to locate the capital in Columbus, which at the time possessed no name. The capital was first located in Chillicothe, moved to Zanesville in 1809, and moved back to Chillicothe in 1812. The desire of the legislature was to fashion a capital city in the center of the state. In December 1916, the legislature moved into the new capital city, Columbus.

The first statehouse, which was destroyed by fire in 1852, had become inadequate by 1838, when the legislature approved a new capitol. The building commission decided on a composite plan, designed from plans received in a competition. The plan decided on was a Greek revival capitol with Doric columns made of native stone. Henry Walter of Cincinnati was named architect, and construction began in 1839. In 1840, construction stopped as the legislature repealed the authorization, and work was not resumed until 1846. In 1848, William R. West was named architect and work was proceeding rapidly. In 1854, when N. B. Kelly became the architect, all the stonework but the cupola had been finished. By 1856, with the appointment of Thomas U. Walter and Richard Upjohn as consulting architects, the legislative chambers had been completed. In 1858, Isaiah Rogers was appointed the architect to complete the interior designs. Finally, the 184 foot by 304 foot capitol was completed in 1861 at a cost of $1,359,121. From 1899 to 1901, an annex was added at a cost of $450,000.[35]

OKLAHOMA

The capitol of Oklahoma, located in Oklahoma City, is unique among state capitol buildings if only for the oil wells that surround the grounds. The structure itself, designed by the firm of Layton-Smith in modern classic style based on Greek and Roman architecture, was begun in 1914 and completed in 1917. The Indiana limestone capitol with a pink and black granite base is six stories high, 480 feet east to west, and 380 feet north to south. There are in fact only five main floors excluding the basement, as the dome and legislative chambers are two stories in height. The exterior facade is ornamented with smooth columns that have Corinthian capitals. The capitol cost approximately $1.5 million. In 1966, a seal was inlaid in the rotunda area at a cost of $4,000.[36]

OREGON

The Oregon statehouse in Salem is the third capitol building in that city; the previous two were destroyed by fire like so many earlier capitols of other states. The first capitol was erected in 1854 at a cost of $40,000. In 1872 another capitol was begun, modeled somewhat after the U.S. Capitol, at a cost of about $325,000. It was destroyed in 1935. Construction began on the present capitol in 1935 and was completed in 1938.

The four-story, modern Greek capitol, designed by Francis Keally of New York, is constructed of white Vermont marble and bronze. It cost approximately $2.5 million. An 8½-ton bronze statue enameled with gold leaf stands atop the capitol tower. The "Golden Pioneer" looks to the west in tribute to Oregon's early settlers. In 1977, wings were added to the capitol, which added 144,000 square feet of usable area to the 131,750 feet in the original building at a cost of $12,025,303.[37]

PENNSYLVANIA

In 1810, the General Assembly passed an act making Harrisburg Pennsylvania's capital city after 1812. Philadelphia was the capital from 1683 to 1799, and Lancaster was the capital from 1799 until the move to Harrisburg. Construction of a capitol was authorized in 1816, and it was occupied in 1821. An addition was authorized in 1864. The main building was destroyed by fire in 1897.

The present capitol was authorized in 1897, supplemented by a 1901 act, and was dedicated by Theodore Roosevelt in 1906. Designed by Joseph M. Houston in the classic style adapted from the Italian Renaissance, the five-story capitol is constructed of Vermont granite. It measures 520 feet in length and 254 feet in width. The dome reaches a height of 272 feet and is surmounted by a figure symbolic of the Commonwealth. The interior is finished in marble, bronze, mahogany, and tiling. Exclusive of furnishings, the building cost $10,073,174.[38]

RHODE ISLAND

In 1895, groundbreaking ceremonies were held in Providence for a new statehouse. Charles Follen McKim designed a capitol in the Greek Renaissance tradition with exterior walls of white Georgia marble. It is 333 feet long and 180 feet wide at the center. The dome, one of four unsupported marble domes in the world, is surmounted by an 11-foot-high, gold-leafed statue of the "Independent Man." Some offices of the capitol were occupied as early as 1900, but the building and grounds were totally completed in 1904 at a cost including furnishings of $3,018,416.[39]

SOUTH CAROLINA

The building of South Carolina's capitol spanned over fifty years owing to war and scandal. In 1851, the legislature began the process of erecting the new capitol. In 1854, the first architect was dismissed and the new architect, Major John R. Niernsee, determined that the workmanship and materials were defective. A new site was chosen and work began, but not according to schedule. Still not completed in 1865, work was suspended when Sherman's army destroyed Columbia. Although the building was not heavily damaged, work did not recommence until 1885. John Niernsee died in the same year. He was succeeded by J. Crawford Neilson and, in 1888, Frank Niernsee replaced Neilson. The younger Niernsee worked primarily on the interior, but work was suspended in 1891. In 1900, Frank P. Milburn was appointed architect. He built the dome and the north and south porticoes. In 1904, Charles C. Wilson became the architect, and the building was finally completed. In the end, the granite capitol was a freely interpreted Roman Corinthian structure that cost $3,540,000.[40]

SOUTH DAKOTA

Pierre had been the temporary capital city since South Dakota became a state in 1889. Not until 1904 did an election determine that Pierre would be the permanent capital. Construction began in 1907 on the capitol building. It was completed in 1910 at a cost of $1 million. C. E. Bell of Minneapolis designed the building, patterning it after Montana's capitol. The exterior is limestone. The rotunda is decorated with marble, scagliola pillars, and mosaic floors. The inner dome rises 96 feet and is made of leaded stained glass. The outer dome rises 159 feet. Its now blackened roof is fashioned from 40,000 pounds of copper. An annex was added to the original building in 1932.[41]

TENNESSEE

Forty-seven years after joining the Union, a bitter debate was ended when Nashville was designated the permanent capital city in 1843. An area known as Campbell's Hill was purchased by the city in the same year for $30,000 and was given to the state for the capitol site. William Strickland, a strong adherent of the Greek revival style, was chosen as architect. The cornerstone for the Tennessee marble structure was laid in 1845. State convicts and slaves performed much of the labor. Although the building was not entirely completed then, it was first occupied by the General Assembly in 1853. By 1857, building costs had amounted to $711,367.

The capitol is designed after an Ionic temple. Eight fluted Ionic columns adorn the north and south porticoes and six adorn the east and west porticoes. The tower rises 206 feet, 7 inches from the parallelogram-shaped structure, which measures 112 feet by 239 feet. Exterior restoration was performed beginning in 1956 and interior restoration and repair, in 1958.

In 1969 and 1970, more restoration work was undertaken in the assembly chambers and in various offices and meeting rooms.[42]

TEXAS

Austin was chosen as the permanent capital of the Republic of Texas in 1839. It remained the capital city after Texas joined the Union in 1845. The present capitol was begun in 1882 to replace an 1852 structure that burned down in 1881. A temporary building, constructed in 1881, was used until the completion of the new capitol in 1888. The temporary structure burned down in 1889. The classical Renaissance capitol, shaped as a Greek cross, was designed by E. E. Myers of Detroit. The exterior walls are Texas pink granite; the interior and dome walls, Texas limestone. The building measures 585 feet, 10 inches in length and 299 feet, 10 inches in width. It is 309 feet, 8 inches from the basement floor to the top of the sixteen-foot statue of the goddess Liberty that stands atop the dome. The capitol provides 273,799 square feet of usable space. The builders of the capitol accepted 3 million acres of land in the Texas Panhandle as payment for constructing the capitol.[43]

UTAH

Utah became a state in 1896, and, although Salt Lake City had long been a capital city, it was not until 1911 that the legislature authorized the construction of a permanent capitol. The Renaissance revival design of Richard K. A. Kletting was chosen for the Utah granite and Georgia marble building. Groundbreaking took place in 1913, and the capitol was completed at a cost of $2,739,528 in 1915.

The capitol is 404 feet in length and 240 feet in width. The ceiling of the copper dome is 165 feet above the floor of the rotunda. The dome itself rises above a pediment and a colonnade of twenty-four Corinthian columns.[44]

VERMONT

Vermont entered the Union in 1791. Its legislature designated Montpelier as the permanent capital city in 1805. The first capitol, in use from 1808 to 1836, was torn down and replaced by a new structure designed by Ammi B. Young after the Greek temple of Theseus. This capitol was destroyed by fire in 1857. The present statehouse, occupied since 1859, was modeled after the building that had burned down except for the dome and larger wings.

The exterior is constructed of Barre granite. The building is accented by a six-columned Doric portico and a 57-foot-high wooden dome. The dome is sheathed in copper and is covered with gold leaf. A statue of Ceres surmounts the dome. The original statue of the goddess of agriculture was replaced in 1938. Construction cost approximately $220,000.[45]

VIRGINIA

The Virginia General Assembly, the oldest law-making body in the western hemisphere, held its first session at Jamestown in 1619. The capitol was moved to Williamsburg in 1699 and then to Richmond in 1779. In 1785, Thomas Jefferson was asked to consult an architect for the design of a capitol. Jefferson chose an architect who shared his interest in classical buildings. Charles Louis Clerisseau, with Jefferson's assistance, modeled a capitol after a Roman temple in France known as "La Maison Carrée." The cornerstone was laid in 1785, and the General Assembly first met in the new capitol in 1788. The two-story brick structure is rectangular with a portico secured by Ionic columns. Between 1904 and 1906, wings were added to each side of the original building. Extensive renovation and remodeling, begun in 1962, was completed in 1963.[46]

WASHINGTON

When Olympia became the territorial capital of Washington in 1855, a wooden capitol was built there. When Washington entered the Union in 1889, a more suitable capitol was desired. In 1893, the design submitted by Ernest Flagg was chosen, and work began in 1894 only to be delayed while the foundation and basement were being constructed. In 1901, what is now known as the "Old Capitol" was purchased by the state and utilized as the statehouse until 1928.

By 1909, the government had decided that the Old Capitol had become inadequate. Ernest Flagg visited Olympia in 1911 and proposed a group concept for the capitol. Architects Walter R. Wilder and Harry K. White of New York were chosen to carry out Flagg's idea. In 1919, work began on an enlarged foundation for Flagg's original building. Construction began in 1922 and continued until completion in 1928.

The Wilkeson sandstone legislative building cost $6,798,596. It is 413 feet long and 179.2 feet wide. The total height is twenty-two stories. The dome, crowned by the "Lantern of Liberty," which rises 287 feet, is the fifth largest in the world. Doric columns adorn the colonnade around the building. Corinthian columns decorate the main north entrance and south portico.[47]

WEST VIRGINIA

Wheeling was the location of West Virginia's first capital. In 1870, the capital was moved to Charleston and, in 1875, back to Wheeling. In 1877, the capital was moved again to Charleston by vote of the people. A capitol was built in 1885 in downtown Charleston, but it was destroyed by fire in 1921 as was the temporary capitol six years later. The capitol now in use was built in stages—the west wing in 1924–1925, the east wing in 1926–1927, the center in 1930–1932—and was dedicated in 1932. Total construction costs came to $10 million.

The capitol was designed by Cass Gilbert, who also designed the U.S. Supreme Court. This Renaissance building provides over fourteen acres of floor space. Porticoes at the north and south entrances are supported by limestone pillars, each of which weighs 86 tons. The exterior of the capitol is buff Indiana limestone, and an assortment of marbles was used to finish the interior. The dome reaches 293 feet, 5 feet higher than the dome of the U.S. Capitol.[48]

WISCONSIN

The state capitol in Madison is Wisconsin's fifth capitol building, the third in Madison. The first Madison capitol was in use from 1838 to 1863. The second building was destroyed by fire in 1904. The current capitol was designed by George B. Post and Sons of New York. Construction began in 1906 and was completed in 1917 at a cost of $7.5 million.

The capitol is situated between Monona and Mendota lakes in a 13.4-acre park. The Roman Renaissance marble and granite structure itself occupies 2.42 acres and rises to a height of 285.9 feet, from the ground to the top of Daniel Chester French's gilded bronze statue "Wisconsin." This capitol boasts the only granite-domed capitol in the nation. The interior is finished in forty-three varieties of stone, glass mosaics, and murals.[49]

WYOMING

Wyoming became a state in 1890. Cheyenne had been the territorial capital, and, in 1886, the first of three separate contracts for a capitol was let, with David W. Gibbs and Company as architect. The cornerstone for the pseudo-Corinthian building, reminiscent of the U.S. Capitol, was laid in 1887, and, by 1888, it was ready for use. The first wings were finished in 1890. New east and west wings were approved in 1915 and completed in 1917. The cost of the original building and its additions totaled $389,569. The sandstone capitol was renovated between 1974 and 1980 at a cost of almost $7 million. The 24-karat gold-leafed dome, 145 feet high, has been leafed four times, most recently in 1980.[50]

DISTRICT OF COLUMBIA

The stately District Building at 1350 Pennsylvania Avenue had been the home to District government for a number of years. However, in November

1992, offices other than those used for Council business were moved and consolidated in a modern concrete, steel, and glass office building at 441 4th Street at Judiciary Square. The building is called One Judiciary Square.[51]

AMERICAN SAMOA

Government House overlooks Pago Pago Bay on the Mountain of Chiefs. Built in 1903 at a cost of $18,651, it has been the home of civilian and naval governors since its construction. The two-story white mansion designed by the U.S. Navy has been enlarged and remodelled over the years, but without losing its original charm as an excellent example of an old South Pacific home.[52]

The Fono or legislature building is a new building that features traditional Samoan architecture. It incorporates both a long oval-shaped residence and a round meeting house.[53]

COMMONWEALTH OF THE NORTHERN MARIANA ISLANDS

Government offices are located on Capitol Hill in Saipan. Capitol Hill is actually a complex of offices and houses that was constructed by the U.S. Naval Technical Training Unit between 1954 and 1956. In fact, these mostly precast concrete buildings were off-limits headquarters for a Central Intelligence Agency program to train Nationalist Chinese for guerrilla warfare against China during the 1950s. Thus the Commonwealth's capitol holds a singular distinction. In 1962, the CIA vacated the complex and the government of the trust territory moved in, to be replaced eventually by the Commonwealth government.[54]

GUAM

The Adelup Complex in Agana is now the site of the governor's office. It had served originally as a school for military children during the naval administration. The school itself had been a rather undistinguished and decaying rectangular structure. The government set out to renovate the school in Spanish style, and in 1985 the governor's office moved to this prime beach location. The renovated complex is replete with Spanish arches, but traditional Chamorro architecture at the front of the complex can be seen in the two porticos supported by latte stones, the pillars on which ancient homes were built, which serve as a symbol of strength.

Government House itself, the official residence of the governor, likewise combines Chamorro and Spanish architecture. It sits on Kasamate Hill in Agana Heights, commanding a beautiful view of Agana and Agana Bay.

Originally constructed in 1952 and completed in 1954, Government House was reconstructed after sustaining damages by Typhoon Pamela in 1976.[55]

PUERTO RICO

The Puerto Rican capitol building in San Juan was authorized in 1907, but not constructed until 1925. It was designed by architect Rafael Carmoega of Puerto Rico. The rotunda was finished at a later date under the architect's supervision. Sixteen columns of rose marble, grouped in fours, form support for the third floor. Four arches reach to the vaulted ceilings. Venetian mosaics, designed from the work of Puerto Rican artists, occupy the vaulting between the arches. The mosaics depict Puerto Rico's conquest, colonization, and discovery as well as the autonomy movement and the abolition of slavery. In the dome's interior are eight figures in mosaic representing freedom, justice, health, the arts, agriculture, education, science, and industry. These figures are surrounded by mythological motifs in a background of rolled gold. The coat of arms, made of leaded glass, is at the center of the dome. Marble friezes occupy the second floor. The north frieze depicts an Indian council, a sixteenth-century Spanish council, and mayors. The west frieze represents the twentieth century. The east frieze depicts Puerto Rican history from 1582 to 1867 and the south frieze, the history for 1671 to 1898, when U.S. forces arrived on the island.[56]

U.S. VIRGIN ISLANDS

There are two government houses in the U.S. Virgin Islands. Government House on St. Croix actually consists of two separate buildings. The older central wing was constructed in 1747 and purchased by the government in 1771 for the governor's residence. The western end of the building was built in the late 1700s and purchased in 1828 for government offices. They were joined together in the 1830s.

Today the capital city of the U.S. Virgin Islands is Charlotte Amalie on St. Thomas. Government House, which is both the home and the office of the governor, was built by the Colonial Council of St. Thomas and St. John, the body that governed under the Danish. It was completed in 1867 at a cost of $33,500 and housed the Vice Governor of the Danish West Indies, who was president of the Colonial Council. Under U.S. administration, Government House became the governor's residence.

Government House is a neoclassical building with Georgian overtones. Danish ballast brick was used in construction. It is stuccoed over in the interior and painted white on the exterior. A two-story cast-iron veranda is its most prominent feature. Native mahogany can be found inside as well as murals painted by Pepino Mangravatti in the 1930s under the Works Progress Administration.

The Legislative Building, home of the Virgin Islands Senate, was planned originally as a marine barracks for the Danish. Although conceived in 1827, construction did not begin until 1829 and was not completed until 1879.[57]

NOTES

1. *Alabama Capitol Complex* (Montgomery: Bureau of Publicity and Information, n.d.); *Alabama Emblems* (Montgomery: Alabama State Department of Archives and History, n.d.), pp. 1–2.
2. *Alaska Blue Book, 1979,* p. 82.
3. Information provided by Anne Wallace, Museum Educator, Arizona State Capitol Museum, Phoenix, Arizona.
4. Clara B. Eno, "Old and New Capitols of Arkansas," *The Arkansas Historical Quarterly* 4 (Autumn 1945): 246–48; John A. Treon, "Politics and Concrete: The Building of the Arkansas State Capitol, 1899–1917," *The Arkansas Historical Quarterly* 31 (Summer 1972): 127, 132.
5. *California's Legislature, 1984,* pp. 135–48.
6. *Colorado State Capitol* (Denver: Colorado Department of Education, n.d.).
7. *State of Connecticut Register and Manual, 1983,* p. 905.
8. *Official Insignia of Delaware* (Dover: Delaware State Development Department, n.d.).
9. *Florida's Capitol* (Tallahassee: Department of State, 1983); *The State of Florida's Heritage and Emblems* (Tallahassee: Department of State, n.d.); information provided by the Florida Legislative Library.
10. *Georgia's Capitol* (Atlanta: Max Cleland, n.d.).
11. *Hawaii State Capitol Fact Sheet* (Honolulu: State Archives, February 1975), pp. 1–2.
12. *Idaho Blue Book, 1981–1982,* p. 214.
13. *Illinois Blue Book, 1983–1984,* pp. 28–32.
14. *The State House, 1888 to Present* (Indianapolis: Indiana Department of Commerce, n.d.); *A Guide to the Indiana State Capitol . . .* (Indianapolis: Indiana Sesquicentennial Commission, 1967).
15. *1985–86 Iowa Official Register,* vol. 61, pp. 228–31.
16. *Kansas Directory, 1982,* pp. 104–113.
17. *Kentucky's Capitol* (Frankfort: Kentucky Department of Public Information, n.d.); *75th Birthday Celebration, State Capitol Building, 1910–1985; Commemorative Program, October 26, 1985,* p. 10.
18. *Louisiana Facts* (Baton Rouge: Louisiana Department of State, n.d.); *The Louisiana State Capitol* (n.p., n.d.).
19. *Maine, the Pine State* (n.p., n.d.).
20. *The Maryland State House, Annapolis* (Annapolis: Maryland Commission on Artistic Property of the State Archives and Hall of Records, Commission for the Maryland Heritage Committee, September 1984).
21. "Additions and Corrections to *Massachusetts*"; material provided by the Massachusetts Citizen Information Service.

22. *Michigan History Salutes . . . The Historic State Capitol Built in 1879* (Lansing: Michigan Department of State, 1980), pp. 3–15.
23. *Minnesota Legislative Manual, 1985,* pp. 2–3.
24. *Souvenir of Mississippi* (Jackson: Dick Molpus, n.d.), pp. 8–16.
25. *Official Manual, State of Missouri, 1975–76,* pp. 1428–30.
26. *The Montana Capitol: A Self-Guiding Tour* (Helena: Montana Historical Society, n.d.), pp. 1–10.
27. *Nebraska Blue Book, 1982–83,* pp. 8–9.
28. *The History of the Capitol Building* (Carson City: Department of Economic Development, n.d.); information supplied by the Nevada State Library.
29. *New Hampshire's State House: A Visitor's Guide* (n.p., n.d.).
30. *New Jersey's Historic State Capitol* (n.p., n.d.); records of the State Capitol Building Commission, 1945–1946 (supplied by John T. Jacobsen, Assistant to the Secretary of State).
31. Information from clippings files provided by Michael Miller, Southwest Librarian, New Mexico State Library, Santa Fe, New Mexico.
32. C. R. Roseberry, *Capitol Story* (Albany: New York State Office of General Services, 1982), pp. 24–25, 45, 126.
33. Information from *North Carolina Manual* provided by Thad Eure, Secretary of State, North Carolina.
34. Lloyd B. Omdahl, *Governing North Dakota, 1981–83* (Grand Forks: Bureau of Governmental Affairs, University of North Dakota, 1981), pp. 72–73; *Facts About North Dakota* (Bismark: North Dakota Economic Development Commission, revised July 1983), p. i; "History of the State Capitol and Grounds Renovations" (n.p., n.d.), one page.
35. *Ohio's Capitals and the Story of Ohio's Emblems* (Columbus: n.p., n.d.), pp. 5–12.
36. *Directory of Oklahoma, 1981,* pp. 36–38.
37. *Oregon Blue Book, 1977–1978,* pp. 141–142.
38. *1976–77 Pennsylvania Manual,* 103 ed., pp. 848–53.
39. *The State of Rhode Island and Providence Plantations 1983–1984 Manual,* pp. 1–5.
40. *South Carolina State Symbols and Emblems* (Columbia: House of Representatives, n.d.).
41. Jan Clark, *South Dakota State Capitol* (Pierre: South Dakota Department of State Development and G. F. Thomsen and Associates, n.d.); *South Dakota History and Heritage* (n.p., n.d.).
42. *Tennessee Blue Book, 1985–86,* pp. 308–12.
43. *Texas Capitol Guide* (Austin: State Department of Highways and Public Transportation, Travel and Information Division, 1983).
44. *Utah: A Guide to Capitol Hill* (n.p., n.d.).
45. *Vermont Legislative Directory and State Manual, 1979–1980,* pp. 4–5.
46. *The Virginia State Capitol, Richmond, Virginia* (Richmond: Division of Engineering and Buildings, 1974).
47. Shanna Stevenson, *A Guide to Washington's Capitol—Walking Tour* (Olympia: Prepared for Office of the Secretary of State, December 1984), pp. 1–4, 11.
48. *State Capitol* (Charleston: Ken Hechler, n.d.).

49. *Wisconsin State Capitol* (Madison: Department of Administration, n.d.); information provided by Kim Varnell, Capitol Tour Guide, Department of Administration, Madison, Wisconsin.

50. *Wyoming Facts* (Cheyenne: Wyoming Travel Commission, n.d.).

51. Information received from the Mayor's Office of Public Information.

52. *Facts about American Samoa* (n.p., n.d.); pamphlet provided by Office of Congressman Eni Faleomavaega.

53. *American Samoa* (n.p., n.d.); pamphlet provided by Office of Congressman Eni Faleomavaega.

54. Information provided by Pete Torres, Federal Relations and Programs, Office of the Resident Representative to the United States, Commonwealth of the Northern Mariana Islands.

55. *Guam and Micronesia* (Agana: Guam Visitors Bureau, 1989), p. 14; personal interview with Terence G. Villaverde, Special Assistant to the Governor, Washington Office of the Governor of Guam.

56. *Capitol of Puerto Rico* (n.p., n.d.); information supplied by Commonwealth of Puerto Rico, Department of State.

57. *Echoes from "Our Journey through History"* (n.p.: United States Virgin Islands Diamond Jubilee Committee, 1992); *Government House, Charlotte Amalie, St. Thomas, U.S. Virgin Islands* (Charlotte Amalie: Government Information Office, n.d.).

6 | State and Territory Flowers

Reasons for selecting a particular state flower are as varied as their colors and varieties. Some flowers have historical significance—the golden poppy caught the attention of early explorers in California who nicknamed the state the Land of Fire upon observing its golden blooms spread across the countryside. The mountain laurel, state flower of Connecticut, was first discovered by the Swedish explorer, Peter Kalm, who sent it to Linnaeus in 1750 for identification. Kansas designated the wild sunflower as a symbolic emblem of early Kansas settlement.

School children and agriculturalists in Delaware lobbied for the peach blossom because the peach was often associated with the state. Florida, of course, named the orange blossom as its state flower in recognition of the orange industry. The apple blossom, named as the state flower of Michigan, pays tribute to their apple industry. Proud of its pine forests, Maine designated the pine cone and tassel as its floral emblem.

A commercial peony grower in Indiana convinced fellow state representatives to name the peony the state flower, in spite of strong opposition. It seems likely, however, that naturalists will try again to see that a flower native to the state will be named the state flower.

Many states seemed to have chosen flowers on the basis of their beauty, such as New York's selection of the rose, Minnesota's pink and white lady slipper, and New Hampshire's purple lilac. Hawaii not only chose a state flower, the hibiscus, but also designated an official flower for each of its eight islands.

Two states selected the apple blossom, Arkansas and Michigan. Nebraska and Kentucky favored the goldenrod, and Louisiana and Mississippi named the magnolia. The mountain laurel was chosen by Connecticut and Pennsylvania. Several states have named varieties of the violet and rose as their state flowers.

ALABAMA

The camellia was named the official state flower of Alabama by the legislature in 1959,[1] repealing the 1927 act designating the goldenrod as the state flower. Unofficially, the red camellia variety with red and white colors similar to those in the state flag is considered the Alabama state flower.[2]

ALASKA

The wild, native forget-me-not, *Myosotis alpestris Schmidt Boraginaceae,* became the state flower and floral emblem of Alaska in 1949 by act of the legislature.[3] Forget-me-nots are sturdy blue perennial flowers, which grow throughout the Arctic region.[4]

ARIZONA

The flower of the saguaro, *Carnagiea gigantea,* was officially designated the state flower of Arizona by legislative act in 1931.[5] The saguaro is a member of the cactus family, which includes around 40 genera and 1,000 species mostly native to North America.[6]

ARKANSAS

The apple blossom, *Pyrus malus,* was declared the state floral emblem of Arkansas by act of the legislature in 1901.[7]

CALIFORNIA

The golden poppy, *Eschscholtzia californica,* was named the official state flower of California by the legislature in 1903. A 1973 amendment designated April 6 of each year as California Poppy Day.[8] Also called the *Copa de Oro,* or "cup of gold," because of the brilliantly colored golden bloom, they grew so widely that early explorers nicknamed California the Land of Fire. Indians used poppy oil on their hair and boiled and consumed the edible portions. As perennials, they bloom several times a year if treated to an occasional trimming.[9]

COLORADO

The white and lavender columbine, *Columbine aquilegia caerulea,* was declared by the legislature to be the state flower of Colorado in 1899.[10] Further provisions of Colorado state law protect the columbine from needless destruction and waste, forbid tearing up the plant by the roots from any public lands, and limit the number of stems, buds, or blossoms that may be picked from public lands to twenty-five.[11] Violation of these provisions is a misdemeanor and is punishable upon conviction by a fine of not less than $5 nor more than $50.[12]

CONNECTICUT

The mountain laurel, *Kalmia latifolia,* was designated by legislative act in 1907 to be the state flower of Connecticut.[13] The Swedish explorer Peter Kalm sent the fragrant white and pink blossomed flower to Linnaeus in 1750 for identification. Linnaeus named it the *Kalmia latifolia,* the first part to honor Kalm and the second to indicate that it had wide leaves. The mountain laurel blooms most brilliantly every two or three years making different sections of the Connecticut countryside host to a beautiful display of blooms depending upon the cycle of a particular growth of plants. Other names for this brightly colored flower are calico bush and spoonwood.[14]

DELAWARE

The peach blossom was adopted as the floral emblem of Delaware by legislative act in 1895. It was also named the official state flower in 1955.[15] Agriculturalists and school children, fearing that the popular goldenrod would be named the state flower, flooded the state legislators with petitions requesting that the peach blossom be adopted as the official state flower. It was felt that the orchards with over 800,000 peach trees were responsible for the Delaware nickname, the Peach State, and had a significant economic impact on the state. As a consequence, the peach blossom was given its due recognition and named the state flower.[16]

FLORIDA

In 1909, the state legislature of Florida adopted the orange blossom as the state flower. A fragrant reminder of Florida's multibillion dollar orange industry, the white blossoms bloom throughout central and southern Florida.[17] Florida has also designated the Coreopsis, which is planted extensively along its highways, as the official state wildflower.[18]

GEORGIA

The Cherokee rose was adopted as the floral emblem of Georgia by legislative act in 1916.[19] Although the Georgia Federation of Women's Clubs supported the adoption of the Cherokee rose, *Rosa sinica,* as the official state flower, they were probably under the mistaken notion that the flower was native to the South. Instead, it is believed that the white, thorny shrub hails from China and was first introduced in England before it arrived in the new world in the latter half of the eighteenth century. The common name of the plant emanates from the Cherokee Indians, who were fond of the plant and were responsible for its widespread propagation. This beautiful plant blooms in the early spring and often in the fall. It is a popular hedge in the South.[20]

In 1979, the Georgia legislature also designated a state wild flower, the azalea.[21]

HAWAII

The *Pua Aloala,* the hibiscus, was designated the flower emblem of Hawaii in 1923.[22] The hibiscus grows abundantly in all color shades throughout the Hawaiian Islands. In addition to a state flower, the Hawaii legislature has designated an official flower for each island:

Hawaii Island	Red *Lehua (Ohia)*
Maui	*Lokelani* (pink cottage rose)
Molokai	White *Kukui* blossom
Kahoolawe	*Hinahina* (beach heliotrope)
Lanai	*Kaumaoa* (yellow and orange air plant)
Oahu	*Ilima*
Kauai	*Mokihana* (green berry)
Niihau	White *Pupu* shell[23]

IDAHO

The syringa, *Philadelphus lewisii,* was designated the official state flower of Idaho by that state's legislature in 1931.[24] The four-petaled syringa blossoms, white and fragrant, cluster at the ends of short branches.[25]

ILLINOIS

The native violet was declared the state flower of Illinois by legislative act in 1908.[26] School children voted in 1907 from among three floral candidates, the violet, wild rose, and goldenrod. The violet won by nearly 4,000 votes.

INDIANA

The flower of the peony, *Paeonia,* was designated by legislative act in 1957 as the official state flower of Indiana.[27] The 1957 act repealed a 1931 act that had named the zinnia the state flower. The 1931 act also repealed a 1923 act that had designated the flower of the tulip tree as the state flower, for in 1931 the tulip tree had been designated the official state tree. From 1919 until 1923, the carnation had been Indiana's state flower.[28]

Since the adoption of the first state flower in 1913, there seems to have been much shuffling of floral emblems and discussions concerning the merits of each candidate. In 1957, a House committee changed a Senate-committee-proposed entry, the dogwood blossom, to the peony.

It has been conjectured that a commercial peony grower, also a state representative, had some influence in this decision. Though the peony is not indigenous to Indiana and, for this reason, has been criticized as inappropriately named as the state flower, it nonetheless continues to be the official state flower. If history repeats itself, however, it will not be long before naturalist agitators try again to change the state floral emblem to one that is native to Indiana.

Blooming in late May or early June, the peony sports its apparel in a variety of shades of pink and red, as well as white.[29]

IOWA

The wild rose was designated the official state flower of Iowa by that state's General Assembly in 1897. Specifically, the *Rośa pratincola,* the wild prairie rose, is considered to be the unofficial selection since there are several species and none was singled out for the designation. The wild rose blooms from June throughout the summer. It has large pinkish flowers with yellow centers.[30]

KANSAS

The *Helianthus,* or wild native sunflower, was designated the state flower and floral emblem of Kansas in 1903. The laws speak to the symbolism of the sunflower as connoting "frontier days, winding trails, pathless prairies" as well as "the majesty of a golden future."[31]

The law's author, Senator George P. Morehouse, very eloquently expressed his love for the flower as well as the people of the state when he addressed the National Guard at Fort Riley after passage of the law. To quote his heartfelt speech:

> This flower has to every Kansan a historic symbolism . . . it is not a blossom lingering a few brief hours, but lasts for a season. It gracefully nods to the caresses of the earliest morning zephyrs. Its bright face greets the rising orb of day and faithfully follows him in his onward course through the blazing noontime, till the pink-tinted afterglow of sunset decorates the western sky and marks the quiet hour of eventide.

It is hard to imagine that the sunflower will ever be dethroned as the state flower.[32]

KENTUCKY

The goldenrod became the official state flower of Kentucky in 1926 by legislative act.[33] Most of the 125 species of goldenrod have yellow flowers, though a few species sport white flowers instead. This perennial herb is also called the yellow-top or flower-of-gold.[34]

LOUISIANA

The magnolia was designated the state flower of Louisiana by act of the legislature in 1900. The magnolia family, which includes about ten genera and seventy-five species, is most commonly found throughout eastern North America. The flower from the magnolia tree or shrub is large and extremely fragrant.[35] Louisiana also designated the Louisiana iris, *Giganticaerulea,* as the official state wildflower in 1990.[36]

MAINE

The pine cone and tassel, *Pinus strobus Linnaeus,* was named the floral emblem of the state of Maine by legislative act in 1895.[37] It is obvious from the state seal, the nickname of the state, and the state tree that Maine is proud of its 17 million acres of forestland. It is no surprise that the pine cone and tassel was designated the official state flower of the Pine Tree State.

MARYLAND

The black-eyed susan, *Rudbeckia hirta,* was proclaimed to be the floral emblem of Maryland by legislative act in 1918.[38] Also called the yellow daisy, this herb is a member of the thistle family, with orange or orange-yellow petals and a purplish brown center.[39]

MASSACHUSETTS

The mayflower, *Epigea repens,* was named the flower or floral emblem of the Commonwealth of Massachusetts by legislative act in 1918. A provision was added in 1925 to protect the mayflower, making it unlawful to dig up or injure a mayflower plant, other than to pick the flower, if growing on public lands. A fine of not more than $50 may be levied upon conviction, unless a person violates this law while in disguise or in the secrecy of night, in which case the punishment is increased to a fine of not more than $100.[40]

Large patches of the mayflower, or ground laurel, may be found growing as far north as Newfoundland and as far south as Florida. The pink or white flowers grow in fragrant clusters at the ends of branches.[41]

MICHIGAN

The apple blossom became the state flower of Michigan by joint resolution of the legislature in 1897. The law cites the apple blossom, in particular the *Pyrus coronaria,* which is native to Michigan, as adding to the beauty of the landscape, while Michigan apples have gained a reputation throughout the world.[42]

MINNESOTA

The pink and white lady slipper, *Cypripedium reginae,* was adopted by the legislature of Minnesota as the official state flower in 1902.[43] The pink and white lady slipper, an orchid, blooms in June and July, thriving in tamarack and spruce marshes. It has been protected by law since 1925.[44]

MISSISSIPPI

The flower of the evergreen magnolia, *Magnolia grandiflora,* was designated the state flower of Mississippi by legislative act in 1952. In 1900 the children of the state had selected the magnolia as the state flower, but their selection was not officially acted on until 52 years later.[45]

MISSOURI

The blossom of the red haw or wild haw, *Crataegus,* was declared the floral emblem of Missouri by the state legislature in 1923. Further, the legislature declared in the same act that the state department of agriculture shall encourage its cultivation because of the beauty of its flower, fruit, and foliage.[46]

The hawthorn's many species are found throughout Missouri and the

Ozarks. The most common species are the margaretta, the turkey apple, and the cockspur thorn. A member of the rose family, the shrubby tree ranges from 3 to 30 feet in height with thorns 3 inches long on some trees. Its white blossoms spring forth in April and May.[47]

MONTANA

The bitterroot, *Lewisia rediviva,* was designated the floral emblem of Montana by legislative act in 1895.[48]

First chosen as the Montana Women's Christian Temperance Union's state flower in 1891, the bitterroot was selected as the official state flower after the Montana Floral Emblem Association held a statewide vote in 1894 and recommended it to the legislature. Of the over 5,800 ballots cast, the bitterroot received 3,621 votes far outdistancing the next runner-up, the evening primrose, which received a mere 787 votes. Early Indians boiled the root of the plant and combined it with meat or berries, making it a nutritious dietary staple.[49]

NEBRASKA

The late goldenrod, *Solidago serotina,* was declared the floral emblem of Nebraska by the legislature in 1895.[50] A member of the thistle family, it is a perennial herb that grows best in moist soil from Canada south to Georgia, Texas and Utah.[51]

NEVADA

The sagebrush, *Artemisia tridentata* or *A. trifida,* was designated the state flower of Nevada by legislative act in 1967. It had been the unofficial state floral emblem since 1917.[52] An odorous silvery-gray member of the thistle family, the sagebrush thrives in the rocky soil or dry plains of the western United States and Canada.[53]

NEW HAMPSHIRE

The purple lilac, *Syringa vulgaris,* was named the state flower of New Hampshire by the legislature in 1919. After months of arguments and committee debates, including an exasperated move by a legislative committee to ask two college botany professors to choose between the Senate preferred purple aster and the House preferred apple blossom, the purple lilac was finally selected. (The two college professors could not agree either, but finally the committee was able to break its deadlock.)[54] In 1991, New Hampshire also designated an official state wildflower, the pink lady's slipper, *Cypripedium acaule.*[55]

NEW JERSEY

The common meadow violet, *Viola sororia,* was designated the state flower of New Jersey by a legislative act in 1971 that became effective during 1972.[56]

NEW MEXICO

The yucca flower was adopted as the official flower of New Mexico by legislative act in 1927.[57] The yucca flower was selected after a vote by school children and subsequent recommendation by the First Federation of Woman's Clubs. Blooming in early summer, the yucca flowers appear at the ends of long stalks. The base of the yucca consists of sharply pointed leaves making the plant both dastardly and delicate as the lower leaves contrast with the gentle ivory colored flowers. Amole, a soap substitute, can be made from its ground roots, a practice still found in some New Mexican Indian villages.[58]

NEW YORK

The rose, in any color or color combination common to it, was designated the official flower of the state of New York by the legislature in 1955.[59]

NORTH CAROLINA

The dogwood was adopted as the official flower of North Carolina by that state's legislature in 1941.[60]

NORTH DAKOTA

The wild prairie rose, *Rosa blanda* or *R. arkansana,* was named the floral emblem of North Dakota by legislative act in 1907.[61] An erect shrub, its stems are usually free of prickles, though sometimes they have a few slender thorns. The pink flowers bloom in June or July.[62]

OHIO

The scarlet carnation was adopted by the Ohio General Assembly in 1904 as that state's official flower in memory of William McKinley. The carnation was considered a good luck piece by McKinley because, during an early campaign for a seat in the U.S. House of Representatives, his opponent gave McKinley a red carnation for his buttonhole. After winning the election, he continued to wear a red carnation during later campaigns.[63]

In 1987, Ohio adopted the large white trillium, *Trillium grandiflorum,* as the official state wildflower.[64]

OKLAHOMA

The mistletoe, *Phoradendron serotinum,* was designated the floral emblem of Oklahoma by legislative act in 1893.[65] A shrub, mistletoe has the dubious distinction of being a tree parasite. There are over 100 American species in the mistletoe family.[66]

OREGON

The Oregon grape, *Berberis aquifolium,* was designated the official flower of Oregon by legislative act in 1899.[67] The Oregon grape, also known as the Rocky Mountain grape or the holly-leaf barberry, is a low trailing shrub. Its spherical berry, about 3 inches in diameter, is blue or purple.[68]

PENNSYLVANIA

The mountain laurel, *Kalmia latifolia,* was adopted as the state flower of Pennsylvania by that state's legislature in 1933.[69] Blooming in June, the laurel's soft pink color is so popular that Tioga County celebrates an annual laurel festival where hundreds attend to soak up its beauty.[70]

RHODE ISLAND

The violet, *Viola palmata,* was designated the state flower of Rhode Island by legislative act in 1968.[71] Also called the early blue violet and Johnny-jump-up, this violet-purple member of the abundant violet family is found from Massachusetts to Minnesota and south to Florida.[72]

SOUTH CAROLINA

In 1924 the General Assembly adopted the yellow jessamine as the official state flower of South Carolina. Reasons given for its selection include its fragrance and resilience. Growing throughout the state, the golden flower's reawakening in the spring has been considered a sign of its constancy and loyalty to the state of South Carolina.[73]

SOUTH DAKOTA

The American pasque flower, *Pulsatilla hirsutissima,* with the motto "I Lead" was made the floral emblem of South Dakota by legislative act in

1903.[74] Also known as the May Day flower, the wild crocus, the April-fools, the rock lily, the badger, and the wind flower, its lavender blooms appear in early spring.[75] It grows best in the arid prairie soil of South Dakota and other midwestern states north to British Columbia.[76]

TENNESSEE

Tennessee has two state flowers, a wild flower and a cultivated flower. The passion flower, *Passiflora incarnata,* officially became the state wild-flower in 1973 by act of the General Assembly.[77] In 1919 a resolution was passed providing that a vote by the state's school children would determine the state flower, and the passion flower was chosen. In 1933, however, the General Assembly passed another resolution adopting the iris as the state flower without rescinding the earlier resolution. This curious situation was finally rectified by the 1973 act that made the passion flower the state wildflower and the iris the state cultivated flower.[78]

The passion flower, also called the maypop, the wild apricot, and the Indian name *ocoee* grows in southern United States and South America. Early South American Christian missionaries gave the flower its name upon seeing such crucifixion symbols as the crown of thorns and three crosses within the flower.[79]

TEXAS

The bluebonnet, *Lupinus subcarnosis,* was adopted as the state flower of Texas by legislative act in 1901.[80] A member of the pea family, the blue-bonnet is one of the over 100 species in this mostly herbaceous family.[81]

UTAH

The sego lily, *Calochortus nuttalli,* was declared to be the state flower of Utah by the legislature in 1911.[82] This slender stemmed member of the lily family has white, lilac, or yellow flowers which bloom in midsummer. It is native from South Dakota to Nebraska and California.[83]

VERMONT

The red clover, *Trifolium pratense,* was designated the state flower of Vermont by legislative act in 1894.[84] The red clover, not native to Vermont, was brought to the United States from Europe.[85] A perennial member of the pea family, it grows wild in fields and meadows. It is also called cow-grass, sugar plum, and honeysuckle clover.[86]

VIRGINIA

The American dogwood, *Cornus florida,* was declared the floral emblem of Virginia by legislative act in 1918.[87] The flowering dogwood is known also as boxwood, white cornel, Indian arrowwood, and nature's mistake. The dogwood is a small tree or large shrub, with greenish yellow flowers and scarlet fruit. Found from Maine to Florida and from Minnesota to Texas, it spruces up the landscape in the fall with its red leaves.[88]

WASHINGTON

The Pink Rhododendron, *Rhododendron macrophyllum* was designated the state flower of Washington by that state's legislature in 1949.[89]

WEST VIRGINIA

The *Rhododendron maximum,* or big laurel, was named the state flower of West Virginia by the legislature in 1903, following a vote by school children.[90] Found from Nova Scotia to Alabama, along streams and in low-lying wooded areas, the big laurel often forms dense thickets. It is also called deer-laurel, cow-plant, rose bay, and spoon-hutch. A tall branching shrub, sometimes a tree, its flowers are rose colored or white, lightly spotted in yellow or orange.[91]

WISCONSIN

The wood violet, *Viola papilionacea,* was officially adopted as the state flower of Wisconsin by legislative act in 1949.[92] The violet won in an election over the wild rose, the trailing arbutus, and the white water lily. After the Arbor Day vote in 1909, the school children's choice was unofficial until voted into law in 1949.[93]

WYOMING

The Indian paintbrush, *Castilleja linariaefolia,* was made the state flower of Wyoming by legislative act in 1917.[94] Other names for this scarlet-leaved member of the figwort family include prairie fire, bloody warrior, and nose-bleed. Parasitic on plant roots, it can be found in meadows and damp thickets from Maine to Wyoming and Texas.[95]

DISTRICT OF COLUMBIA

The District of Columbia commissioners designated the American Beauty rose as the District's official flower on April 17, 1925.[96]

AMERICAN SAMOA

In 1973, the Paogo (Ula-fala) was designated the official flower of American Samoa.[97]

COMMONWEALTH OF THE NORTHERN MARIANA ISLANDS

The Commonwealth designated the Flores Mayo or plumeria (*Plumeria acuminata*) as its official flower in 1986.[98]

GUAM

The official territorial flower of Guam, a local flower called the puti tai nobio, was adopted in 1968. This flower, known also as the bougainvillea, blooms throughout the year on the island.[99]

PUERTO RICO

Puerto Rico has not designated an official flower.

U.S. VIRGIN ISLANDS

In 1950, the *Tecoma stans* was named the official flower of the Virgin Islands. This trumpet-shaped flower is also called the yellow elder or yellow cedar.[100]

NOTES

1. Ala. Code §1–2–11.
2. *Alabama Official and Statistical Register* (Montgomery: Alabama Department of Archives and History, 1979), pp. 24–25.
3. Alaska Stat. §44.09.050.
4. *Alaska Blue Book 1979*, p. 173.
5. Ariz. Rev. Stat. Ann. §41–855.
6. Nathaniel Lord Britton and Addison Brown, *An Illustrated Flora of the Northern United States, Canada and the British Possessions*, 2d ed., rev. and enl. (New York: Scribners, 1913), vol. 2, p. 568.
7. Ark. Stat. Ann. §5–109.
8. Cal. Gov't. Code §421 (West).
9. *California's Legislature 1984*, pp. 202–3.
10. Colo. Rev. Stat. §24–80–905.
11. Ibid., §24–80–906, §24–80–907.
12. Ibid., §24–80–908.
13. Conn. Gen. Stat. Ann. §3–108 (West).
14. *State of Connecticut Register and Manual, 1983*, p. 900.
15. Del. Code Ann. tit. 29, §308.
16. *Delaware State Manual, 1975–1976*, p. 14.

17. 1909 Fla. Laws 688; *The State of Florida's Heritage and Emblems* (Tallahassee: Florida Department of State, 1986).
18. Fla. Stat. Ann. §15.0345 (West).
19. Ga. Code Ann. §50–3–53.
20. *The State of Georgia and Its Capitol* (Atlanta: State Museum of Science and Industry, Department of Archives and History, 1979), p. 16.
21. Ga. Code Ann. §50–3–54.
22. Haw. Rev. Stat. §5–9.
23. *Hawaii, The Aloha State* (Honolulu: State of Hawaii, Hawaii Visitors Bureau, Chamber of Commerce of Hawaii, n.d.).
24. Idaho Code §67–4502.
25. *Idaho Blue Book,* 1981–82, p. 209.
26. Ill. Ann. Stat. ch. 1, §3009 (Smith-Hurd).
27. Ind. Code Ann. §1–2–7–1 (West).
28. George Shankle, *State Names, Flags, Seals, Songs, Birds, Flowers, and Other Symbols,* rev. ed. (Westport, CT: Greenwood Press, 1970, c 1938), pp. 336–37.
29. Information provided by Indiana State Library, Indianapolis, Indiana.
30. *1985–86 Iowa Official Register,* vol. 61, p. 237.
31. Kan. Stat. Ann. §73–1801.
32. *Kansas Directory, 1984,* p. 128.
33. Ky. Rev. Stat. Ann. §2.090 (Baldwin).
34. Britton and Brown, *An Illustrated Flora,* vol. 3, p. 380.
35. La. Rev. Stat. Ann. §49–154 (West); Britton and Brown, *An Illustrated Flora,* vol. 2, pp. 80–83.
36. La. Rev. Stat. Ann. §49–154.1 (West).
37. Me. Rev. Stat. tit. 1, §211.
38. Md. Ann. Code §13–305.
39. Britton and Brown, *An Illustrated Flora,* vol. 3, p. 470.
40. Mass. Gen. Laws Ann. ch. 2, §7 (West).
41. Britton and Brown, *An Illustrated Flora,* vol. 2, p. 692.
42. Mich. Comp. Laws Ann. §2.11.
43. Minn. Stat. Ann. §1.142 (West).
44. Information provided by the Minnesota Historical Society, St. Paul, Minnesota.
45. 1952 Miss. Laws 465.
46. Mo. Ann. Stat. §10.030 (Vernon).
47. *Official Manual, State of Missouri, 1975–1976,* p. 1439.
48. Mont. Rev. Codes Ann. §1–1–503.
49. Rex C. Myers, *Symbols of Montana* (Helena: Montana Historical Society, 1976), p. 12.
50. 1895 Neb. Laws 441.
51. Britton and Brown, *An Illustrated Flora,* vol. 3, p. 394.
52. Nev. Rev. Stat. §235.050.
53. Britton and Brown, *An Illustrated Flora,* vol. 3, p. 530.
54. N.H. Rev. Stat. Ann. §3:5; *Manual for the General Court, 1981.*
55. N.H. Rev. Stat. Ann. §3:17.
56. N.J. Stat. Ann. §52:9 AA-1 (West).

57. N.M. Stat. Ann. §12–3–4.
58. *New Mexico Blue Book 1977–1978,* p. 86.
59. N.Y. State Law §75 (McKinney).
60. N.C. Gen. Stat. §145–1.
61. N.D. Cent. Code §54–02–03.
62. Britton and Brown, *An Illustrated Flora,* vol. 2, p. 283.
63. Ohio Rev. Code Ann. §5.02 (Baldwin); Ohio Almanac (Lorain: Lorain Journal Company, 1977), p. 60.
64. Ohio Rev. Code Ann. §5.021 (Baldwin).
65. Okla. Stat. Ann. tit. 25, §92 (West).
66. Britton and Brown, *An Illustrated Flora,* vol. 1, p. 639.
67. Or. Rev. Stat. §186.
68. Britton and Brown, *An Illustrated Flora,* vol. 2, p. 128.
69. Pa. Stat. Ann. tit. 71, §1006 (Purdon).
70. *Pennsylvania Symbols* (Harrisburg: House of Representatives, n.d.).
71. R.I. Gen. Laws §42–4–9.
72. Britton and Brown, *An Illustrated Flora,* vol. 2, p. 547.
73. *South Carolina State Symbols and Emblems* (Columbia: House of Representatives, n.d.).
74. S.D. Codified Laws Ann. §1–6–10.
75. *South Dakota Legislative Manual, 1981,* p. 145.
76. Britton and Brown, *An Illustrated Flora,* vol. 2, p. 102.
77. Tenn. Code Ann. §4–1–306.
78. Ibid., §4–1–307.
79. *Tennessee Blue Book, 1985–1986,* p. 342.
80. Tex. Rev. Civ. Stat. Ann. art. 6143b (Vernon).
81. Britton and Brown, *An Illustrated Flora,* vol. 2, p. 347.
82. Utah Code Ann. §63–13–6.
83. Britton and Brown, *An Illustrated Flora,* vol. 1, p. 508.
84. Vt. Stat. Ann. tit. 1, §498.
85. *Vermont Legislative Directory and State Manual, 1979–80,* p. 15.
86. Britton and Brown, *An Illustrated Flora,* vol. 2, p. 355.
87. Va. Code §7.1–38.
88. Britton and Brown, *An Illustrated Flora,* vol. 2, p. 664.
89. Wash. Rev. Code Ann. §1.20.030.
90. *West Virginia Blue Book, 1980,* p. 925.
91. Britton and Brown, *An Illustrated Flora,* vol. 2, p. 681.
92. Wis. Stat. Ann. §1.10 (West).
93. *State of Wisconsin, 1983–1984 Blue Book,* p. 948.
94. Wyo. Stat. Ann. §8–3–104.
95. Britton and Brown, *An Illustrated Flora,* vol. 3, p. 214.
96. *Symbols of the District of Columbia* (Washington, D.C.: Government of the District of Columbia, Office of the Secretariat, Office of Visual Information Management, n.d.).
97. A.S. Code tit. 1, §1103.
98. C.M.C. tit. 1, §232.
99. Guam Code Ann. tit. 1, §1022.
100. V.I. Code Ann. tit. 1, §102.

7 | State and Territory Trees

In 1919, Texas became the first state to select a state tree, the pecan. All of the other states have since chosen state trees, and one state, New Jersey, has named a state tree and a state memorial tree.

Out of the thirty-five trees designated by the states, the white oak and the sugar maple tie for first place. Each was named the state tree for four states. Connecticut, Maryland, Illinois, and Iowa named the white oak their state tree. Iowa, in fact, designated all species of the oak. New York, Vermont, West Virginia, and Wisconsin selected the sugar maple. Tying for second place in popularity are the southern pine, designated by Alabama, Arkansas, and North Carolina, and the dogwood, named by Missouri, Virginia, and New Jersey. New Jersey named the dogwood its state memorial tree.

Two states chose the American elm (Massachusetts and North Dakota), the white pine (Maine and Michigan), the cottonwood (Kansas and Nebraska), the palmetto (Florida and South Carolina), the blue spruce (Colorado and Utah), and the tulip poplar (Indiana and Tennessee).

Probably the most frequently cited reason for the selection of a particular state tree is the part that tree played in the early history of a state. The palmetto was used to build colonial forts off the coast of South Carolina. The live oak was used to construct homes by early Georgia settlers. In Tennessee, the tulip poplar was used to construct homesteads and barns. The white oak was chosen by Connecticut in remembrance of a famous tree, the Charter Oak, and its role in the American fight for independence. Kansas recognized the cottonwood planted by pioneers.

New Hampshire's white birch, Maine's white pine, and Oregon's Douglas fir, are but a few examples of trees that are strongly identified with a particular state and, therefore, have been made state emblems. Delaware is proud of the many ornamental uses of its state tree, the American holly.

ALABAMA

The southern pine was designated the official tree of Alabama in 1949.[1]

Scientific name: Pinus palustris Mill.

Synonyms: Longleaf yellow pine, pitch pine, hard pine, heart pine, turpentine pine, rosemary pine, brown pine, fat pine, longstraw pine, long-leaf pitch pine.

Native to: South Atlantic and Gulf coastal plains.

Physical description: The southern pine is a large tree with coarsely scaly, orange-brown bark and slender dark green needles, three in a cluster and from 10 to 15 inches long. The large cones are from 5 to 10 inches long and are dull brown and prickly.

The bill does not specify which species was intended, even though twelve exist in Alabama. However, the person who introduced the bill, Hugh Kaul of Birmingham, has stated that he meant the longleaf pine.[2]

ALASKA

The Sitka spruce, *Picea sitchensis,* became the official tree of Alaska by legislative act in 1962.[3]

Scientific name: Picea sitchensis (Bong.) Carr.

Synonyms: Yellow spruce, tideland spruce, western spruce, silver spruce, coast spruce, Menzies' spruce.

Native to: Pacific coast region north to Canada and Alaska.

Physical description: The bark on this large to very large tree is reddish brown and thin with loosely attached scales. The flat, dark green needles are from ⅝ to 1 inch long, and the light orange-brown cones are from 2 to 3½ inches long with long stiff scales.

ARIZONA

The paloverde, genus *cercidium,* was adopted as the state tree of Arizona in 1954.[4]

Scientific name: Cercidium torreyanum (Wats.) Sargent.

Synonym: Green barked Acacia.

Native to: Southern California and Arizona; south into Mexico.

Physical description: The bark of this short, stout tree is yellow to yellow green. Leaves are oblong in shape and paired with two or three leaflets on each side. Soon after the leaves mature in March or April, they fall, making the tree bare of leaves the rest of the year. The brilliant yellow-gold flowers bloom in early spring, and the pod-shaped fruit ripens in July.

ARKANSAS

The pine tree was designated the state tree of Arkansas in 1939.[5] See the Alabama entry for a description.

CALIFORNIA

Two species of the California redwood, *Sequoia sempervirens* and *Sequoia gigantea,* were named the official state trees of California in 1937.[6]

Scientific names: Sequoia sempervirens (D. Don) Endl. and *Sequoiadendron giganteum (Lindl.) Buchholz.*

Synonyms: Coast redwood and redwood for the first variety; giant sequoia, bigtree, Sierra redwood, and mammoth tree for the second.

Native to: The coast redwood is native to the Pacific coast of California and southwestern Oregon. The giant sequoia is native to the Sierra Nevada in California.

Physical description: The coast redwood is the world's largest species. Its reddish-brown bark is thick, deeply furrowed, and fibrous. The leaves are scalelike and needlelike, flat, slightly curved, and unequal in length ranging from 1/4 to 3/4 of an inch. They are dark green, spreading in two rows. The reddish-brown cones are from 3/4 to 1 inch long and mature in the first year.

The giant sequoia's bark is reddish brown, thick, deeply furrowed, and fibrous. The tree is swollen at the base. The cones range from 1 3/4 to 2 3/4 inches in length, are reddish brown, and mature the second year. The leaves are from 1/8 to 1/4 inch long and may grow from leading shoots 1/2 inch long. The blue-green, sharply pointed leaves grow all around the twig and overlap.

The tallest known *sequoia sempervirens* is 364 feet high. Protected by the state, which matched monies raised by the Save-the-Redwoods League, they are allowed to grow uncut in designated groves.[7]

Located in thirty-two groves on the western slopes of the Sierra Nevada mountains, the *sequoia gigantea* was voted the United States tree by school children across the United States. The largest of these trees, nicknamed "General Sherman" is 36½ feet in diameter, and it is estimated that it could supply enough lumber to build forty houses.[8] It is estimated that this tree is from 3,000 to 4,000 years old.[9]

COLORADO

The unofficial state tree of Colorado is the blue spruce, as designated in 1939.[10]

Scientific name: Picea pungens Engelm.

Synonyms: Colorado blue spruce, balsam, Colorado spruce, prickly spruce, white spruce, silver spruce, Parry's spruce.

Native to: Rocky Mountain region.

Physical description: The four-angled needles of the blue spruce are from ¾ to 1⅛ inches long and are dull blue green. This large tree has gray or brown bark that is furrowed into scaly ridges. Cones are from 2½ to 4 inches long and are light brown with long, thin, irregularly toothed scales.

CONNECTICUT

The white oak, *Quercus alba,* was designated the state tree of Connecticut in 1947.[11]

Scientific name: Quercus alba Linn.

Synonym: Stave oak.

Native to: Eastern half of United States and adjacent Canada.

Physical description: The white oak is a large tree with light gray bark, fissured into scaly ridges. The smooth leaves are oblong, from 4 to 9 inches long, and are deeply or shallowly 5 to 9 lobed. They are bright green above, pale or whitish beneath, and turn a deep red in the fall. The acorns are from ¾ to 1 inch long, with shallow cups.

The Charter Oak, a famous oak of the colonial period, was the inspiration for the oak tree's being named the state tree of Connecticut. In 1687 the Charter Oak was a hiding place for a charter earlier given to the General Court of Connecticut by King Charles II that was rescinded twenty-five years later by King James II. The colonists were not eager to return the charter to James' emissary, and, while they were seated at a table holding the charter, the candles went out. When they were re-lit, the charter was gone.[12]

DELAWARE

The American holly, *Ilex opaca Aiton,* was adopted as the state tree of Delaware in 1939.[13]

Scientific name: Ilex opaca Ait.

Synonyms: Holly, white holly, evergreen holly, boxwood.

Native to: Atlantic and Gulf coasts; Mississippi valley region.

Physical description: A medium-sized to large tree, the American holly's bark is light gray, thin, and smoothish, with wartlike projections. The evergreen elliptical leaves are from 2 to 4 inches long and are coarsely spring toothed, stiff, and leathery. They are green above and yellowish green beneath. The small male and female flowers, which are on different trees, are greenish white. Spherical in shape, the red berrylike fruit is from 1/4 to 3/8 of an inch in diameter.

Holly boughs with their colorful red berries make attractive and lucrative Christmas decorations. It is for this reason that the holly tree is considered one of Delaware's most treasured trees.[14]

FLORIDA

The sabal palmetto palm, known also as the cabbage palm, was designated the state tree of Florida in 1953. This act declares further that such designation should not be construed to limit the use of this tree in any way for commercial purposes.[15]

Scientific name: Sabal palmetto (Walt.) Lodd.

Synonyms: Cabbage palmetto, palmetto, tree palmetto, Bank's palmetto.

Native to: South Atlantic to Gulf coasts from North Carolina to Florida.

Physical description: The trunk of this medium-sized palm tree is stout and unbranched, grayish brown, roughened or ridged, with a cluster of large leaves at the top. The 4- to 7-foot-long evergreen leaves are coarse, fan-shaped, thick, and leathery, much folded and divided into narrow segments with threadlike fibers hanging between. Leafstalks are from 5 to 8 feet long. Fruits are numerous in a much-branched cluster about 7 feet long and are black, 3/8 to 1/2 inch in diameter, and one seeded.

GEORGIA

The live oak was adopted as the official tree emblematic of the state of Georgia in 1937.[16]

Scientific name: Quercus virginiana Mill.

Synonyms: Chêne Vert.

Native to: South Atlantic and Gulf coast regions, lower California, southern Mexico, Central America, and Cuba.

Physical description: The live oak is a medium-sized widespreading tree. Its bark is dark brown, furrowed, and slightly scaly. The leaves are evergreen, shiny dark green above and whitish hairy beneath. They are elliptical or oblong, 2 to 5 inches long, and usually rounded at the apex; their edges are usually smooth and rolled under. There are from one to five acorns on stalks ½ to 3 inches long. The narrow acorns are from ¾ to 1 inch long and have deep cups.

The Edmund Burke Chapter of the Daughters of the American Revolution first introduced the native oak as a candidate for state tree. Many of the earlier settlers lived along the coast or on islands where the oak was plentiful. A few of the better known Georgians who seemed appreciative of the tree's beauty were James Oglethorpe, John Wesley, and Sidney Lanier.[17]

HAWAII

The *kukui* tree, *Aleurites moluccana,* which is also known as the candlenut tree, was designated the official tree of Hawaii in 1959.[18]

Scientific name: Aleurites moluccana (L.) Willd.

Physical description: The sharply pointed or regularly shaped leaves are greyish green due to a grey fur adorning the surface of the leaf, which is especially pronounced beneath. The five-petalled flowers are small, forming delicate white clusters. The nuts are edible if roasted. The fruits were also once used for torch oil.[19]

IDAHO

The white pine, *Pinus monticola,* was declared the state tree of Idaho in 1935.[20]

Scientific name: Pinus monticola Dougl.

Synonyms: Western white pine, Idaho white pine, finger-cone pine, mountain pine, little sugar pine, mountain Weymouth pine.

Native to: Northern Rocky Mountain and Pacific coast regions, including southern British Columbia.

Physical description: The bark on this large tree is gray, thin, and smoothish, becoming fissured into rectangular, scaly plates. The blue-green needles are stout, from 2 to 4 inches long, and are five in a cluster. The cones are long stalked, from 5 to 12 inches long, and yellow brown with thin, rounded scales.

ILLINOIS

Following a vote of school children the Illinois legislature, in 1908, declared the native oak to be the official state tree. Since at least two oaks are native to Illinois, however, another selection was held among school children, this time between the northern red oak and the white oak. The white oak won, and, in 1973, the legislature officially designated the white oak as the official tree of Illinois.[21] See the Connecticut entry for a description.

INDIANA

The tulip tree, *Liriodendron tulipifera,* was designated the official state tree of Indiana in 1931.[22]

Scientific name: Liriodendron tulipifera L.

Synonyms: Yellow poplar, blue poplar, hickory poplar, basswood, cucumber tree, tulipwood, whitewood, white poplar, poplar, old-wife's-shirt-tree.

Native to: Eastern third of the United States and southern Ontario.

Physical description: The tallest eastern hardwood, the tulip tree's bark is brown, becoming thick and deeply furrowed. The unusually shaped leaves are squarish with a broad, slightly notched or nearly straight apex and two or three lobes on each side. They are from 3 to 6 inches long and are shiny dark green above and pale green beneath. The flowers are large and tulip shaped, from 1½ to 2 inches in diameter, and usually green except in the spring when they are orange. The fruit is conelike, from 2½ to 3 inches long and ½ inch thick.

IOWA

The oak, *Quercus spp.,* was officially designated as the state tree of Iowa in 1961.[23] See the Connecticut and New Jersey entries for descriptions.

KANSAS

The cottonwood was designated the official tree of Kansas in 1937.[24]

Scientific name: Populus deltoides Bartr.

Synonyms: Eastern poplar, Carolina poplar, eastern cottonwood, necklace poplar, big cottonwood, Vermont poplar, whitewood, cotton tree, yellow cottonwood.

Native to: Eastern half of the United States and adjacent Canada.

Physical description: A large tree, the cottonwood's bark is at first yellowish green and smooth, becoming gray and deeply furrowed. The leaves are triangular, from 3 to 6 inches long, and wide, long pointed, and coarsely toothed with curved teeth. The smooth leaves are light green and shiny.

The cottonwood has been termed the pioneer tree of Kansas because many homesteaders planted cottonwood. The cottonwood flourished giving the settlers the courage to continue and to lay claim to the land.[25]

KENTUCKY

The coffee tree was named the Kentucky state tree in 1976.[26]

Scientific name: Gymnocladus dioicus (Linn.) Koch.

Synonyms: Kentucky coffee tree, coffeebean tree, coffeenut, mahogany, nickertree, stumptree, virgilia.

Native to: Northeastern United States and southern Ontario; west through Minnesota, Nebraska, and Kansas; southward mainly between the Mississippi River and the Allegheny Mountains to Tennessee.

Physical description: A popular shade tree, the coffee tree grows from 40 to 60 feet in height and lives from 40 to 50 years. Shiny and pale green leaflets turn clear yellow in early autumn. The large seed pods are brown and hang from the tree throughout the winter.

LOUISIANA

The bald cypress, *Taxodium distichum,* commonly called the cypress tree, was designated the official state tree of Louisiana in 1963.[27]

Scientific name: Taxodium distichum (L.) Rich.

Synonyms: Southern cypress, red cypress, yellow cypress, white cypress, black cypress, gulf cypress, swamp cypress, deciduous cypress, tidewater red cypress.

Native to: Swamps and riverbanks of the South Atlantic and Gulf coastal plains and the Mississippi valley.

Physical description: The bald cypress is a large tree with a swollen base and "knees." The bark is reddish brown or gray with long fibrous or scaly ridges. The leaves are light yellow green, whitish beneath, and are crowded featherlike in two rows on slender horizontal twigs. They are flat, from 3/8 to 3/4 of an inch long, and are shed in the fall. The cones are from 3/4 to 1 inch in diameter with hard scales.

MAINE

The white pine was named the official tree of Maine in 1959.[28]

Scientific name: Pinus strobus Linn.

Synonyms: Eastern white pine, northern white pine, soft pine, Weymouth pine, spruce pine.

Native to: Northeastern United States, adjacent Canada, and the Appalachian Mountain region.

Physical description: The largest northeastern conifer, the white pine's bark is gray or purplish and is deeply fissured into broad ridges. Its slender needles are blue green, from 2½ to 5 inches long, and grow five in a cluster. The cones are long stalked, narrow, from 4 to 8 inches long, and yellow brown with thin, rounded scales.

MARYLAND

The white oak, *Quercus alba,* was declared the arboreal emblem of Maryland in 1941.[29] See the Connecticut entry for a description.

MASSACHUSETTS

The American elm, *Ulmus americana,* was named the state tree of Massachusetts in 1941.[30]

Scientific name: Ulmus americana Linn.

Synonyms: White elm, soft elm, water elm, gray elm, swamp elm, rock elm, Orme Maigre.

Native to: Eastern half of the United States and adjacent Canada.

Physical description: The American elm is a large, spreading tree with gray bark that is deeply furrowed with broad, forking, scaly ridges. Twigs are soft and hairy, becoming smooth, not corky winged. Fruits are elliptical and flat, from 3/8 to ½ inch long. Leaves are in two rows, elliptical, from 3 to 6 inches long, and coarsely and doubly toothed with unequal teeth. The two sides of the leaf are unequal. They are dark green and smooth or slightly rough above, and pale and usually soft and hairy beneath.

MICHIGAN

The white pine, *Pinus strobus,* was adopted as the official state tree of Michigan in 1955.[31] See the Maine entry for a description.

MINNESOTA

The red pine or Norway pine, *Pinus resinosa,* was designated the official state tree of Minnesota in 1953.[32]

Scientific name: Pinus resinosa Ait.

Synonyms: Canadian red pine, hard pine.

Native to: Northeastern United States and adjacent Canada.

Physical description: A medium-sized to large tree, the red pine has reddish-brown bark with broad, flat, scaly plates. Needles are two in a cluster, dark green and slender, from 5 to 6 inches long. Cones are 2 inches long and light brown without prickles.

MISSISSIPPI

The magnolia or evergreen magnolia, *Magnolia grandiflora,* was designated the state tree of Mississippi in 1938.[33]

Scientific name: Magnolia grandiflora Linn.

Synonyms: Big laurel, bull bay, great laurel magnolia, bat-tree, laurel-leaved magnolia, large-flowered magnolia, laurel bay.

Native to: South Atlantic and Gulf coastal plains.

Physical description: A medium-sized to large tree, the magnolia has gray to light brown bark, broken into small, thin scales. Leaves are evergreen, oblong or elliptical, from 5 to 8 inches long, short pointed, and leathery with smooth edges. They are shiny bright green and smooth above, rusty and hairy beneath. The flowers are cup shaped, from 6 to 8 inches across, white and fragrant during spring and summer. The fruit is conelike, from 3 to 4 inches long, from 1½ to 2½ inches thick, rusty and hairy.

MISSOURI

The flowering dogwood, *Cornus florida,* was declared the arboreal emblem of Missouri in 1955.[34]

Scientific name: Cornus florida Linn.

Synonyms: Dogwood, boxwood, false box-dogwood, New England boxwood, flowering cornel, cornel.

Native to: Eastern half of the United States and southern Ontario.

Physical description: A small tree, the flowering dogwood's bark is dark reddish brown, broken into small square or rounded blocks. The leaves are paired, elliptical or oval, from 3 to 6 inches long, and short pointed; their edges appear to be smooth but are minutely toothed. They are bright green and nearly smooth above, whitish and slightly hairy beneath; and they turn bright scarlet above in the fall. The greenish-yellow flowers grow in a dense head with four showy, white, petallike bracts from 2¼ to 4 inches in diameter, and bloom in the early spring. The egg-shaped fruits are ⅜ inch long, bright scarlet, shiny, fleshy, and 1 or 2 seeded.

MONTANA

The ponderosa pine was designated the official state tree of Montana in 1949.[35]

Scientific name: Pinus ponderosa Laws.

Synonyms: Western yellow pine, western soft pine, yellow pine, bull pine, foothills yellow pine, red pine, big pine, long-leaved pine, pitch pine, heavy-wooded pine, heavy pine, Sierra brownbark pine, Montana black pine.

Native to: Rocky Mountains and Pacific coast regions, including adjacent Canada; southward to western Texas and Mexico.

Physical description: The ponderosa pine is a large tree with brown or blackish bark, furrowed into ridges. On older trunks, the bark is yellow brown and irregularly fissured into large, flat, scaly plates. The needles are three, or two and three, in a cluster, stout, from 4 to 7 inches long, and dark green. The cones are from 3 to 6 inches long and short stalked with prickly scales, and they are light reddish brown.

NEBRASKA

The cottonwood was declared the state tree of Nebraska in 1972.[36] See the Kansas entry for a description.

NEVADA

The single-leaf piñon, *Pinus monophylla,* was designated the official state tree of Nevada in 1953. In 1987, the bristlecone pine, *Pinus aristata,* was also named the official state tree. The first state tree is described below and illustrated.[37]

Scientific name: Pinus monophylla Torr. and *Frém.*

Synonyms: Nut pine, pinyon, gray pine, Nevada nut pine, singleleaf pinyon pine.

Native to: Great Basin region to California.

Physical description: The single-leaf piñon is a small tree with dark brown bark, furrowed into scaly ridges. The needles are one per sheath, stout, from 1 to 2 inches long, and gray green. The egg-shaped cones are light brown with stout, blunt scales and are from 2 to 2½ inches long. The large, edible seeds, ¾ inch long, are commonly known as pinyon nuts.

NEW HAMPSHIRE

The white birch, *Betula papyrifera,* was named the state tree of New Hampshire in 1947.[38]

Scientific name: Betula papyrifera Marsh.

Synonyms: Canoe birch, silver birch, paper birch, large white birch.

Native to: Northeastern United States; across Canada to Alaska; northern Rocky Mountain region.

Physical description: A medium-sized to large tree, the white birch has smooth, thin, white bark, separating into papery strips. Leaves are oval, from 2 to 4 inches long, long pointed and wedge shaped or rounded at the base. They are coarsely and usually doubly toothed, mostly with five to nine main veins on each side, dull dark green and smooth above, and light yellow green and smooth or slightly hairy beneath. The cones are narrow, from 1½ to 2 inches long and ⅜ inch wide, and hang from slender stalks.

The New Hampshire Federation of Garden Clubs recommended that the white birch be designated the state tree for the obvious reason that it is natively so abundant throughout the state. This graceful and beautiful tree had the practical historical use learned by every school child—its bark was used by Indians to construct their canoes.[39]

NEW JERSEY

The northern red oak was designated the official state tree of New Jersey in 1950.[40]

Scientific name: Quercus rubra Linn.

Synonyms: Red oak, black oak, Spanish oak.

Native to: Eastern half of the United States except the southern border; adjacent Canada.

Physical description: The northern red oak is a large tree with dark brown bark, fissured into broad, flat ridges. The leaves are from 5 to 9 inches long, oblong, and seven to eleven lobed less than halfway to the middle; the lobes have a few irregular bristle-pointed teeth. The smooth leaves are a dull dark green above and pale yellow green beneath, and they turn red in the fall. Acorns have either a shallow or deep cup and are from ⅝ to 1⅛ inch long.

The dogwood was designated the state memorial tree in 1951 by Assembly Concurrent Resolution No. 12.[41] See the Missouri entry for a description of the dogwood.

NEW MEXICO

The nut pine or piñon, *Pinus edulis,* was adopted as the official state tree of New Mexico in 1948.[42]

Scientific name: Pinus edulis Engelm.

Synonyms: Nut pine, pinyon pine, Colorado pinyon pine, New Mexico piñon.

Native to: Southern Rocky Mountain region and adjacent Mexico.

Physical description: A small tree, the nut pine has reddish-brown bark, furrowed into scaly ridges. The needles are two (sometimes three) in a cluster, stout, from ¾ to 1½ inches long, and dark green. The egg-shaped cones are from 1½ to 2 inches long and light brown with stout, blunt scales and large, edible seeds ½ inch long and known as pinyon nuts.

As long ago as the 1500s, when the Spanish first came to New Mexico, they noticed that the piñon nut was a popular food item. People still watch for the periodic overabundant years when there are enough piñons for everyone who is willing to spend some effort to gather them. A close runnerup, the aspen, lost to the piñon after the New Mexico Federation of Women's Clubs selected the piñon for nomination to the state legislature.[43]

NEW YORK

The sugar maple, *Acer saccharum,* was designated the official tree of New York in 1956.[44]

Scientific name: Acer saccharum Marsh.

Synonyms: Hard maple, rock maple, sugar maple, black maple.

Native to: Eastern half of the United States and adjacent Canada.

Physical description: The sugar maple is a large tree with gray bark, furrowed into irregular ridges or scales. The leaves are paired, heart shaped, with three or five lobes, long pointed and sparingly, coarsely toothed. From 3 to 5½ inches in diameter, they are dark green above and light green and usually smooth beneath, turning yellow, orange, or scarlet in the fall. The fruits, 1 to 1¼ inches long, mature in the fall.

NORTH CAROLINA

The pine tree was adopted as the official state tree of North Carolina in 1963.[45] See the Alabama entry for a description.

NORTH DAKOTA

The American elm, *Ulmus americana,* was designated the official tree of North Dakota in 1947.[46] See the Massachusetts entry for a description.

OHIO

The buckeye tree, *Aesculus glabra,* was adopted as the official tree of Ohio in 1953.[47]

Scientific name: Aesculus glabra Willd.

Synonyms: Ohio buckeye, fetid buckeye, stinking buckeye, American horse chestnut.

Native to: Midwestern United States, chiefly Ohio and Mississippi valley regions.

Physical description: The buckeye is a small to medium-sized tree with gray bark, much furrowed and broken into scaly plates. The leaves are paired together with leafstalks from 4 to 6 inches long. Leaflets are five per leafstalk, from 3 to 5 inches long, long pointed, narrowed at the base, and finely toothed. (The shrubby variety of the buckeye tree has from five to seven leaflets.) The showy flowers grow in branched clusters, from 4 to 6 inches long, and are pale greenish yellow with petals nearly as long as the flower, or from ¾ to 1¼ inches long. The one or two poisonous seeds are from 1 to 1½ inches wide and are encased in a prickly fruiting capsule from 1¼ to 2 inches in diameter.

The buckeye got its name because the Indians thought the seed of the tree looked like the "eye of a buck"; in the Indian, the *hetuck.*[48]

OKLAHOMA

The redbud tree, *Cercis canadensis,* was adopted as the official tree of Oklahoma in 1937.[49]

Scientific name: Cercis canadensis Linn.

Synonyms: Judas tree, red Judas tree, salad-tree, Canadian Judas tree.

Native to: North central and eastern United States.

Physical description: A small tree, the redbud branches at 10 to 15 feet from the ground and forms a narrow and erect or a spreading, flattened, or rounded head. An ornamental tree, it flowers in late February to April in a profusion of small, light pink to purple blossoms.

OREGON

The Douglas fir, *Pseudotsuga menziessi,* was declared the official state tree of Oregon in 1939.[50]

Scientific name: Pseudotsuga menziessi (Mirb.) Franco.

Synonyms: Douglas spruce, red fir, yellow fir, Oregon pine, red pine, Puget Sound pine, spruce, fir, Douglas tree, cork-barked Douglas spruce.

Native to: Pacific coast and Rocky Mountain region, including Canada and Mexico.

Physical description: The Douglas fir is a very large tree, next to the giant sequoia and the redwood in size. The bark is reddish brown, thick, and deeply furrowed into broad ridges. The dark yellow-green or blue-green needles are short stalked, flat, and from ¾ to 1¼ inches long. The cones are from 2 to 4 inches long and light brown with thin, rounded scales and long, three-toothed bracts.

The Douglas fir was chosen as the state tree because Oregon is the major supplier of this indispensable lumber tree. Because its wood is relatively lightweight when compared with its strength, it is considered one of the foremost trees in the world for its lumber.[51]

PENNSYLVANIA

The hemlock tree, *Tsuga canadensis,* was adopted as the state tree of Pennsylvania in 1931.[52]

Scientific name: Tsuga canadensis (Linn.) Carr.

Synonyms: Eastern hemlock, Canadian hemlock, hemlock spruce, spruce pine, New England hemlock, spruce.

Native to: Northeastern United States, adjacent Canada, and the Appalachian Mountain region to northern Alabama and Georgia.

Physical description: The hemlock tree is a medium-sized to large tree with brown or purplish bark, deeply furrowed into broad, scaly ridges. The needles are short stalked, flat, soft, blunt pointed, and from ⅜ to ⅝ inch long. They are shiny dark green above and lighter beneath, appearing in two rows. The cones are brownish and from 5/8 to 3/4 inch long.

RHODE ISLAND

The red maple, *Acer rubrum,* was designated the state tree of Rhode Island in 1964.[53]

Scientific name: Acer rubrum Linn.

Synonyms: Soft maple, water maple, scarlet maple, white maple, swamp maple, shoe-peg maple, erable.

Native to: Eastern half of the United States and adjacent Canada; west to the Dakotas, Texas, and Nebraska.

Physical description: A large tree with a large trunk, the red maple's bark is gray, thin, smooth, and broken into long, thin scales. The twigs are reddish, and the leaves are dark green and shiny above, whitish and slightly hairy beneath, turning scarlet or yellow in the fall. The leaves are paired, heart shaped, from 2½ to 4 inches long, and three to five lobed. The lobes are short pointed and are irregularly and sharply toothed. The fruits, 3/4 inch long, mature in the spring.

SOUTH CAROLINA

The palmetto tree, *Inodes palmetto,* was adopted as the official tree of South Carolina in 1939.[54] See the Florida entry for a description.

Palmetto logs, used in the construction of the fort on Sullivan's Island, helped withstand the British attack during the American Revolution. For this reason, the palmetto has been memorialized as the state tree and appears on both the flag and the seal.[55]

SOUTH DAKOTA

The Black Hills spruce, *Picea glauca densata,* was named the state tree of South Dakota in 1947.[56]

Scientific name: Picea glauca (Moench) Voss.

Synonyms: White spruce, single spruce, bog spruce, skunk spruce, cat spruce, spruce, pine, double spruce.

Native to: Northeastern United States, Black Hills, Canada, Alaska.

Physical description: The Black Hills spruce is a medium-sized tree with thin and scaly gray or brown bark. The blue-green needles are four-angled, from ½ to 3/4 inch long, and of disagreeable odor when crushed.

The cones are slender, from 1½ to 2 inches long, pale brown, and shiny with scales that are thin, flexible, and rounded with smooth margins.

TENNESSEE

The tulip poplar, *Liriodendron tulipifera,* was designated the official state tree of Tennessee in 1947.[57] See the Indiana entry for a description.

The tulip poplar is plentiful throughout the state of Tennessee. Early settlers found it particularly useful for dwelling and barn construction.[58]

TEXAS

The pecan tree was designated the state tree of Texas in 1919. An amendment in 1927 made it the duty of the State Board of Control 69 the State Parks Board "to give due consideration to the pecan tree when planning beautification of state parks or other public property belonging to the state."[59]

Scientific name: Carya illinoensis (Wangenh.) K. Koch.

Synonyms: Pecan nut, pecanier, pecan (hickory).

Native to: Mississippi valley region, Texas, and Mexico.

Physical description: A large tree, the pecan tree has deeply and irregularly furrowed and cracked light brown or gray bark. The compound leaves are from 12 to 20 inches long. The leaflets number from eleven to seventeen and are short stalked, lance shaped, and slightly sickle-shaped. They are from 2 to 7 inches long, long pointed, finely toothed, smooth, and slightly hairy. The nuts are slightly four winged, oblong, and pointed, and they have thin husks. From 1 to 2 inches long, they are sweet and edible.

UTAH

The blue spruce was designated the Utah state tree in 1933.[60] See the Colorado entry for a description.

VERMONT

The sugar maple was named the state tree of Vermont in 1949.[61] See the New York entry for a description.

VIRGINIA

The flowering dogwood was designated the state tree of Virginia in 1956.[62] See the Missouri entry for a description.

WASHINGTON

The western hemlock, *Tsuga heterophylla,* was designated the official tree of the state of Washington in 1947.[63]

Scientific name: Tsuga heterophylla (Raf.) Sargent.

Synonyms: West coast hemlock, Pacific hemlock, hemlock spruce, California hemlock spruce, western hemlock fir, Prince Albert's fir, Alaska pine.

Native to: Pacific coast and northern Rocky Mountain regions north to Canada and Alaska.

Physical description: The western hemlock is a large tree with reddish-brown bark, deeply furrowed into broad, flat ridges. The needles are short stalked, flat, from ¼ to ¾ inch long, and shiny dark green above and lighter beneath. The brownish cones are from ¾ to 1 inch long.

WEST VIRGINIA

The sugar maple, *Acer saccharum Marsh.,* was designated the state tree of West Virginia in 1949.[64] See the New York entry for a description.

Because it is used in furniture building and is enjoyed for its maple syrup, the state's school children and civic clubs voted to recommend the sugar maple as West Virginia's state tree.[65]

WISCONSIN

The sugar maple, *Acer saccharum,* was designated the official state tree of Wisconsin in 1949.[66] See the New York entry for a description.

Wisconsin's school children recommended the sugar maple by popular vote in 1948. Though others tried to overrule the 1948 vote by lobbying for the white pine, the legislature followed the recommendation of the Youth Centennial Committee vote.[67]

WYOMING

The cottonwood tree, *Populus sargentii,* was designated the state tree of Wyoming in 1947 and 1961.[68]

Scientific name: Populus deltoides var. *occidentalis Ryb.; P. sargentii Dode* is the name given in the state law.

Synonyms: Plains cottonwood, plains poplar.

Native to: Great plains and eastern border of Rocky Mountains north into Canada.

Physical description: The plains cottonwood is a large tree with gray, deeply furrowed bark. The leaves are smooth, light green, shiny, and broadly oval. They are often wider than long, from 3 to 4 inches long and wide, long pointed, and coarsely toothed with curved teeth. The leafstalks are flat.

DISTRICT OF COLUMBIA

The commissioners declared the scarlet oak to be the official tree of the District on November 8, 1960. This particular oak tree is known for its brilliant color in fall and it can be seen throughout the area around the nation's capital.[69]

AMERICAN SAMOA

American Samoa has designated the Paogo or Pandanus tree as the territorial tree. Samoan chiefs wear necklaces made from the seeds of this tree and its leaves are used to weave mats, baskets, and other items.[70]

COMMONWEALTH OF THE NORTHERN MARIANA ISLANDS

The Commonwealth designated the Trongkon Atbot or flame tree, *Delonix regia,* as its official tree in 1986.[71] Also known as the flamboyant, this tree, as its name suggests, is a beautiful ornamental that may reach almost twenty feet and sports a flat crown adorned by clusters of flowers each with five petals. Four of the petals of each flower are scarlet, one is white, and each flower is about four inches wide.

GUAM

Guam declared the ifit, *Intsia bijuga,* its official tree in 1969. This tree, a member of the ironwood family, was used frequently to build homes on the island and thus symbolizes the strength of the family.[72]

PUERTO RICO

Puerto Rico has not designated an official tree.

U.S. VIRGIN ISLANDS

The U.S. Virgin Islands has not designated an official tree.

NOTES

1. Ala. Code §1–2–12.
2. *Alabama State Emblems* (Montgomery: Alabama State Department of Archives and History, n.d.).
3. Alaska Stat. §44.09.070.
4. Ariz. Rev. Stat. Ann. §41–856.
5. *State Trees and Arbor Days* (Washington, D.C.: Government Printing Office, 1981), p. 4; 1939 Ark. Acts, 1092.
6. Cal. Gov't. Code §422 (West).
7. *State Emblems* (Sacramento: Secretary of State, n.d.).
8. Ibid.
9. *California's Legislature, 1984,* p. 204.
10. *State Trees and Arbor Days,* p. 5.
11. Conn. Gen. Stat. Ann. §3–110 (West).
12. *State of Connecticut Register and Manual, 1983,* p. 907.
13. Del. Code Ann. tit. 29, §305.
14. *Discover Wonderful Delaware!* (Dover: Delaware State Development Department, n.d.).
15. Fla. Stat. Ann. §15.031 (West).
16. Ga. Code Ann. §50–3–55.
17. *The State of Georgia and Its Capitol* (Atlanta: State Museum of Science and Industry, Department of Archives and History, 1979), p. 15.
18. Haw. Rev. Stat. §5–8.
19. Loraine E. Kuck and Richard C. Tongg, *Hawaiian Flowers and Flowering Trees: A Guide to Tropical and Semitropical Flora* (Rutland, VT: Charles E. Tuttle, 1960), p. 12.
20. Idaho Code §67–450.
21. Ill. Ann. Stat. ch. 1, §3009 (Smith-Hurd); *Illinois Blue Book, 1983–1984,* p. 436.
22. Ind. Code Ann. §1–2–7–1 (West).
23. *State Trees and Arbor Days,* p. 8.
24. Kan. Stat. Ann. §73–1001.
25. *Kansas Directory* (Topeka: Secretary of State, 1981), p. 129.
26. Ky. Rev. Stat. Ann. §2.095 (Baldwin).
27. La. Rev. Stat. Ann. §49–160 (West).
28. Me. Rev. Stat. tit. 1, §208.
29. Md. Ann. Code art. 41, §76.
30. Mass. Gen. Laws Ann. ch. 2, §8 (West).
31. Mich. Comp. Laws Ann. §2.31.
32. Minn. Stat. Ann. §1.143 (West).
33. Miss. Code Ann. §3–3–9.
34. Mo. Ann. Stat. §10.040 (Vernon).

35. *State Trees and Arbor Days,* p. 11.
36. Neb. Rev. Stat. §90–113.
37. Nev. Rev. Stat. §235.040.
38. N.H. Rev. Stat. Ann. §3:6.
39. *Manual for the General Court, 1981.*
40. *State Trees and Arbor Days,* p. 12.
41. Edward J. Mullin, ed., *Manual of the Legislature of New Jersey* (Princeton, N.J.: Century Graphics, 1984), p. 11.
42. N.M. Stat. Ann. §12–3–4.
43. *New Mexico Blue Book, 1977–1978,* p. 86.
44. N.Y. State Law §76 (McKinney).
45. N.C. Gen. Stat. §145–3.
46. N.D. Cent. Code §54–02–05.
47. Ohio Rev. Code Ann. §5.05 (Baldwin).
48. *Ohio Almanac* (Lorain, Ohio: Lorain Journal Co., 1977), p. 61.
49. Okla. Stat. Ann. tit. 25, §97 (West).
50. Or. Rev. Stat. §186.
51. *Oregon Blue Book, 1977–1978,* p. 139.
52. Pa. Stat. Ann. tit. 71, §1004 (Purdon).
53. R.I. Gen. Laws §42–4–8.
54. S.C. Code §1–1–660.
55. *1978 South Carolina Legislative Manual,* 59th ed., n.p.
56. S.D. Codified Laws Ann. §1–6–11.
57. Tenn. Code Ann. §4–1–305.
58. *Tennessee Blue Book, 1983–1984,* p. 372.
59. Tex. Rev. Civ. Stat. Ann. art. 6143 (Vernon).
60. Utah Code Ann. §63–13–7.
61. Vt. Stat. Ann. tit. 1, §499.
62. *State Trees and Arbor Days,* p. 16.
63. Wash. Rev. Code Ann. §1.20.020.
64. *State Trees and Arbor Days,* p. 17.
65. *West Virginia Blue Book 1980,* p. 925.
66. Wis. Stat. Ann. §1.10 (West).
67. *Wisconsin Blue Book, 1983–84,* p. 948.
68. Wyo. Stat. Ann. §8–3–106; *State Trees and Arbor Days,* p. 18.
69. *Symbols of the District of Columbia* (Washington, D.C.: Government of the District of Columbia, Office of the Secretariat, Office of Visual Information Management, n.d.).
70. *American Samoa* (n.p., n.d.); pamphlet supplied by the Office of Eni Faleomavaega, Member of Congress from American Samoa.
71. C.M.C. tit. 1, §231.
72. Guam Code Ann. tit. 1, §1024.

8 | State and Territory Birds

Beginning in 1926, when Kentucky officially named the handsome red bird or cardinal as its state bird, campaigns were launched nationwide until each state had selected at least one favorite bird as its avian symbol. Audubon societies and women's clubs from 1926 through the early 1930s were largely responsible for fueling public interest and holding popular votes, many of them among school children. Since then, of course, several states have established or changed state birds.

The cardinal is not only the first to have been proclaimed a state bird, but it also holds the distinction of having been designated by seven states: Illinois, Indiana, Kentucky, North Carolina, Ohio, Virginia, and West Virginia. The western meadow lark holds second place, having been honored by Kansas, Montana, Nebraska, North Dakota, Oregon, and Wyoming. The mockingbird, another favorite, has been named the state bird of Arkansas, Florida, Mississippi, Tennessee, and Texas.

Though the robin is probably the most remembered in idiom and fable, it has surprisingly been selected by only three states: Connecticut, Michigan, and Wisconsin. Maine and Massachusetts concurred that the chickadee was a fine emblem for their states, while Iowa and New Jersey agreed on the Eastern goldfinch.

Both Missouri and New York selected the bluebird in 1927, but New York waited for more than forty years to make it official. Again, over thirty years elapsed between the decisions of Idaho and Nevada to designate the mountain bluebird. Finally, two states, Alabama and South Carolina, chose the wild turkey as the state game bird. Altogether, thirty-two birds have been named as state birds, state game birds, or state waterfowl; four states, Alabama, Georgia, Mississippi, and South Carolina, have designated two birds.

In some cases, it is clear that a state selected a bird for patriotic or economic reasons, but, typically, a bird was selected by sheer popularity based on a number of aesthetic factors. Delaware and Alabama named birds symbolic of Revolutionary and Civil War companies who were nicknamed after the blue hen chicken and the yellowhammer. Utah honored the sea gull for saving farmers' crops in 1848 from pests. On the other hand, the rich blue colors of the mountain bluebird or the bold black and white patterns of Minnesota's loon are reason enough to designate a state symbol.

The names of the birds listed below are a mixture of correct, colloquial, and common names used in the state laws. In some cases, even names once correct have changed. Alabama's yellowhammer is the northern flicker. The California valley quail is properly called the California quail. The robin is the American robin. Georgia's bobwhite quail is actually the northern bobwhite. Hawaii's nene is properly called the Hawaiian goose. The cardinal is the northern cardinal. The eastern goldfinch of New Jersey and Iowa and the willow goldfinch of Washington is the American goldfinch. The chickadee of Maine and Massachusetts is the black-capped chickadee. Minnesota's loon is the common loon. New Mexico's chapparal bird is the greater roadrunner and Utah's sea gull is the California gull.

ALABAMA

The bird commonly called the yellowhammer, *Colaptes auratus,* was designated the state bird in 1927.[1] Other common names for the yellowhammer include the yellow-shafted woodpecker and the flicker.

The Ladies' Memorial Association was responsible for encouraging the legislature to adopt this emblem because the gray and yellow plumage resembled the colors of the Confederate Army uniforms.[2] An incident during the Civil War involving a company from Huntsville, Alabama, resulted in the nickname "yellowhammers" being assigned to all Alabama troops. When the Huntsville company rode into camp at Hopkinsville, Kentucky, newly clad in Confederate uniforms trimmed in bright yellow cloth, they were met with the greeting "Yellerhammer, yellerhammer, flicker, flicker!" When the yellowhammer was adopted as the official state bird in 1927, the old soldiers were pleased, noting that the black breast spots were like bullet holes and the red patch on the neck like a bandana.[3]

Size: Total length: 10 to 11 inches; tail length: 4 inches.

Range: North America except treeless Arctic districts; south to Nicaragua and Cuba; mostly found from Florida and Texas to Kansas, Illinois, Indiana, and North Carolina.

Physical description: The back is grayish brown sharply barred in black; the head and hindneck are plain gray with a red crescent-shaped patch at nape; the shafts of the tail feathers (except the middle pair) are bright pure cadmium yellow as are the underwing feathers and the undersurface of the tail. There is a conspicuous black crescent-shaped patch on the chest; the underparts are pale cinnamon or dull buff-pink fading into pale yellow or white and spotted in black. Males have a broad black stripe across the lower side of the head.

Behavior: While on short flights, flickers glide and dip in rhythmic undulations, but at other times they exhibit a strong and steady flight pattern. As they feed on ants, beetles, grasshoppers, grubs, and other harmful insects, they hop from one choice spot to another within a self-prescribed small perimeter. Flickers consume more ants than any other bird, which in turn keeps enemies of ants, such as the destructive aphid, in check as well. Eggs are white and oval in shape and usually average six to eight per set. If the eggs are destroyed, the persistent flicker will lay another set, sometimes laying as many as forty eggs per season.

Alabama also designated an official state game bird, the wild turkey, in 1980.[4]

The wild turkey, *Meleagris gallopavo,* is the largest of the gallinaceous birds; the males measure from 41 to 49 inches in length, and the females are noticeably smaller.

Size: Body weight: 16 to 40 pounds; tail length: 12½ to 15 inches.

Range: Eastern and south central United States; mountains of Mexico; southern Ontario.

Physical description: The bluish head and red upper neck area is nude, warted, and corrugated in the adult male. The female's head and neck are smoother and are covered with short, dusky, downy feathers. The general color is dusky, glossed with brilliant metallic coppery, golden, and greenish hues. Many of the feathers are margined terminally in velvety black. There is a black pectoral tuft or "beard," greenish at the base and wine-tinted brown gloss distally. The female is duller in color with a smaller beard.

Behavior: Perhaps the most distinctive behavioral trait of the wild turkey is his courtship dance in which he gobbles, struts, spreads his fan-shaped tail, and generally makes a spectacle of himself in order to attract the female. During this season, the male's chest becomes a mass of gooey tissue consisting of oil and fat. From this he may draw nutritional sustenance after his frenzied dances. Wild turkeys feed primarily on fruit, berries, and seeds, and they consume large amounts of insects such as grasshoppers and crickets. Though they travel mostly on foot in flocks, they are able to fly to avoid danger and to cross rivers.

ALASKA

The Alaska willow ptarmigan (*Lagopus lagopus alascensis Swarth*) became the official state bird in 1955.[5]

Size: Wing length: 7½ inches; tail length: 4 inches.

Range: Alaska; Arctic and subarctic regions of North America, Europe, and Asia.

Physical description: Also known as the willow grouse, the male and female have quite different plumages. The male has a hazel to chestnut forehead, crown, and nape; the back feathers are darker with white tips; the upper tail feathers are hazel; the wings are white; the tail feathers are generally brownish gray tipped with white; the sides of the head, throat, and upper breast are hazel becoming darker on the lower breast, barred with gray or black; the scarlet comb over the eyes swells when the bird is sexually aroused; and the underparts are mostly white. In winter, the male plumage is pure white except for the gray or black median pair of tail feathers. The female is mostly tawny olive above; each feather is barred with black and tipped with pale olive buff; the wings are white; the tail feathers are dark brownish gray tipped with white; the sides of the head, chin, and upper throat are cinnamon buff; the lower throat, abdomen, sides, and flanks are yellow buff to yellow tawny and heavily barred with wavy bands of clove brown; the comb is pale vermilion.

Behavior: Typically, a set of willow ptarmigan eggs are laid one day at a time over a period of from seven to ten days. The eggs are oval and shiny, and upon first being laid are a vivid bright red. As they dry, they turn blackish brown flecked with red to brown spots. During the winter, the bird adapts so completely to its environment, that it grows hairlike feathers on its feet allowing it to glide effortlessly across snow as though clad in snowshoes.

ARIZONA

The Arizona legislature adopted the cactus wren, known also as Coues' cactus wren or *Heleodytes brunneicapillus couesi (Sharpe)*, as the state bird in 1931.[6]

Size: Total length: 7 to 7½ inches; tail length: 3 inches.

Range: Desert region of southwestern United States and northern Mexico.

Physical description: The top of the head and hindneck are plain deep brown; the back region is pale, grayish brown conspicuously variegated with white; the tail feathers are brownish gray to black and barred with dusky to white; the sides of the head are mostly white except for a brown postocular stripe occupying the upper portion of the auricular region. The underparts are white deepening into cinnamon buff; the whole surface is heavily spotted with black.

Behavior: The wren's disposition is good; the bird rarely becomes embroiled in battle and is insatiably curious. The interested human bystander is often entertained as the playful little bird energetically inspects cracks, crevices, containers, and trash. The cactus wren builds flask-shaped nests from 3 to 9 feet above the ground on thorny shrubs, trees, or cactus. Cactus wrens feed mostly on beetles, ants, wasps, grasshoppers, and other pests. They also consume a significant amount of fruit.

ARKANSAS

The mockingbird was adopted by the Arkansas legislature as the official state bird in 1929.[7] When it was first introduced to the legislature by the State Federation of Women's Clubs, the legislators thought the issue was a joke. However, they were forthwith presented with rousing speeches enumerating the bird's worth to the farmer. The vote was unanimous, and the issue was settled in favor of the mockingbird.[8]

Size: Total length: 8½ to 9 inches; tail length: 4 to 4½ inches.

Range: Eastern United States and southern Canada; along the Gulf coast to Texas; Bahama Islands.

Physical description: The mockingbird, *Mimus polyglottos,* is mostly plain gray or brownish gray from the top of the head over most of the back region; the lateral tail feathers are white; the wings and tail are dull blackish slate; the middle and greater wing coverts are tipped with dull or grayish white; the primary coverts are white with a subterminal dusky spot or streak; the auricular region is gray; the area beneath the eye and along the side of the head is dull white transversely flecked with gray or dusky; the chin and throat are dull white margined along each side by a distinct dusky streak; the chest is pale smoke gray turning to white on the center of the breast and abdomen; the feathers under the tail are pale buff or buffy white. When the mockingbird is in flight, the broad white spots above can easily be seen against the slate black of the upper wings.

Behavior: Mockingbirds are sturdy creatures which build nests that often last several seasons. From the time when the nest is completed to the time when the fledglings take flight is usually from three to four weeks. Eggs range from bright blue to bluish green or greenish blue spotted with hazel or cinnamon. Both sexes not only build the nests, but also care for the young. Mockingbirds are lively and bellicose, fighting among themselves as well as tormenting cats and dogs. A masterful imitator, the mockingbird is considered one of the most versatile and beautiful songsters, sometimes changing tunes as many as thirty times within a ten-minute period. The diet of the mockingbird consists equally of insects and wild fruit.

CALIFORNIA

The California valley quail, *Lophortyx californica,* was designated the official bird and avifaunal emblem of California by the state's legislature in 1931,[9] winning in a vote involving twenty-four other birds nominated by the California Audubon Society.[10]

Size: Tail length: 3 to 3½ inches; wing length: 4 inches.

Range: Semiarid interior of California as well as the coastal belt south of San Francisco; east to Nevada. (The valley quail has been successfully introduced to other areas.)

Physical description: The adult male is mostly brownish olive on the back and rump; the wings are mostly dark olive brown; the tail feathers are between slate gray and deep mouse gray; the area under the eye, chin, and throat is jet black, the throat bordered by a broad white band extending from each eye to the center throat region in a v-shape; the forehead is pale olive buff with a white line of demarcation across the crown followed by a broader black line. There is a crest on the crown of the head consisting of six forward-drooping, terminally expanded black feathers; a bright design is created by brownish gray feathers of the hindneck speckled with white; the breast is solid deep neutral gray; and the abdomen is warm buff or white with a central bright hazel patch margined in black. The female is the same as the male above but is darker and more brownish; the crest on the crown is smaller and is brownish gray in color; the forehead is a pale buffy brown. There is a light buffy brown speckled pattern on the nape and lower sides of the neck; the chin and throat are grayish white; and the breast is grayish brown.

Behavior: The California valley quail makes little effort to build a safe, sturdy nest for her young. Instead, eggs are found in nests near houses or roads, even in other birds' nests. Traveling in flocks, they feed primarily on seeds, grass, and fruit, consuming minute amounts of flies and insects. Preyed upon by man and animal alike, they make especially easy targets for snakes, raccoons, owls, jays, cats, and dogs. When startled, however, they can make an amazingly quick retreat.

COLORADO

The lark bunting, *Calamospiza melancorys stejneger,* was adopted as the Colorado state bird in 1931.[11] A first statewide vote yielded the name of the meadowlark as the most popular bird in the state. A second vote, spearheaded by the *Denver Post,* the Colorado Mountain Club, and the Colorado Federation of Women's Clubs, determined that the mountain bluebird should receive the title. Finally, the Colorado Audubon Society convinced state legislators that since the bluebird and meadowlark were already state birds of other states, the lark bunting was a more appropriate choice.[12]

Size: Total length: 6 inches; tail length: 2½ inches.

Range: Great plains; migrating south through Texas to the Gulf coast and Mexico.

Physical description: In summer, the adult male is black with a grayish cast on his back; the middle and greater wing coverts are mostly white, forming a conspicuous patch; the tertials are edged with white; and the tail coverts (especially the lower) are margined with white. The adult female is grayish above and brown streaked with dusky; the wing is white patched as in the male but smaller, more interrupted, and tinged with buffy; the underparts are white, streaked with dusky. In winter, the female is less grayish brown with paler markings tinged with buff; the adult male in the winter is similar to the adult female, but the feathers of the underparts and the chin are black beneath the surface.

Behavior: A highly sociable bird, the lark bunting is happiest when safely tucked away in a large flock. During courtship, lark buntings perform a dazzling air show commencing with soaring ascents, then drifting back to earth, all the while whistling a lively tune. From this behavior comes the common expression "happy as a lark." The lark's cheerful life can be tragically cut short by such natural enemies as hawks when his song attracts the attention of those for whom it was not intended. Because larks feed on harmful grasshoppers and waste grain, they are held in high regard by farmers.

CONNECTICUT

The American robin, *Turdus migratorius,* became the state bird of Connecticut by action of the state legislature in 1943.[13]

Size: Total length: 8½ to 9 inches; tail length: 4 inches.

Range: Eastern and northern North America; westward to the Rocky

Mountains; northwestward to Alaska; winters southward to Florida and along the Gulf coast to Texas.

Physical description: The largest thrush in North America, the male is mostly deep mouse gray or brownish slate gray on the back; the head is black with white spots from the eye to the bill and on both the upper and lower eyelids; the chin is white; the feathers of the neck are black in the center, margined with brownish slate gray or mouse gray; the tail is a dull slate black or sooty black with a large and conspicuous white spot; the chest, flanks, breast, and upper abdomen are a plain, deep cinnamon red color; and the lower abdomen is white. The female is much duller in color with gray of upper parts lighter and chest browner than in the male.

Behavior: Named by the English colonists because of the similarity between this and their robin redbreast, the colonists did not notice the close resemblance to their blackbird or the *Turdus,* a thrush. A bird suggestive of the type-A personality, the robin is jittery and easily upset. However, he sails through the air without faltering, chest out and back straight. It is no wonder that we often think of the robin arising early to catch the first worm. A strong singer, he is up at dawn regaling the neighborhood with lengthy, energetic, and cheerful songs. The pale blue eggs (hence the color "Robin's egg blue") are usually laid in sets of three or four. The male cares for the young almost exclusively while the female prepares for a new brood. Sometimes three separate sets of eggs are laid in a year. Robins subsist mostly on beetles and caterpillars supplemented by an intake of spiders, earthworms, and snails. Since the robin also enjoys fruit, both cultivated and wild, he poses a potential threat to orchards. Fortunately, when the preferred insect or wild fruit is available, the robin leaves the fruit crops alone.

DELAWARE

The blue hen chicken was adopted as Delaware's state bird in 1939.[14] During the Revolutionary War, a company of soldiers from Kent County in Delaware entertained themselves between battles by staging cockfights between blue hen chickens. The cockfights became so famous that, when the soldiers fought fiercely in battle, they became known as the Blue Hen's Chickens. This nickname was again adopted during the Civil War by a company from the same county.[15]

Physical description: The throat is nude and wattled; there is a median fleshy "comb" on the forehead; the middle tail feathers are strongly hooked; and the feathers of the rump are elongated and linear, or pointed.

FLORIDA

In 1927, the mockingbird was officially designated the state bird of Florida.[16] The Audubon Society of St. Petersburg was responsible for a statewide vote for a state bird. The mockingbird won by a large margin over such other possibilities as the hummingbird, pelican, and buzzard. One can only imagine the chagrin of the Audubon Society when an entire school voted for the buzzard because the students had been studying the bird as part of an airplane building project.[17] See the Arkansas entry for a description.

GEORGIA

The brown thrasher was designated the state bird of Georgia by the legislature in 1970,[18] even though the governor had officially proclaimed the brown thrasher to be the state bird in 1935.[19]

Size: Total length: 10 inches; tail length: 5 inches.

Range: Eastern United States and southeastern Canada; breeding southward to Florida, Alabama, Mississippi, and Texas and westward to the Rocky Mountains; wintering from North Carolina to Florida and Texas.

Physical description: The plumage above is plain, dull, cinnamon red or tawny red, becoming duller above the eye; the wings are tipped with white or pale buff producing two distinct bands across the wing; the outermost tail feathers are tipped with buff; the auricular region is a light rusty brown, narrowly streaked with dull whitish or pale buffy; the underparts are a pale buff, approaching buffy white on the chin, throat, and abdomen; the chest and sides are streaked with brown or dusky; the throat is margined along each side by a series of blackish streaks forming a distinct stripe along the lower side of the head; the iris is bright lemon or sulphur yellow; and the tail feathers are long.

Behavior: The brown thrasher, *Toxostoma rufum,* is a fickle creature, often changing partners with each new brood during a single mating season. However, both sexes are fiercely protective of their young, launching attacks on any and all creatures, including humans, who dare disturb their nests. Eggs are pale blue, sometimes white, tinged with green, and are evenly spotted in reddish or dull brown. A well-balanced meal consists of the favored beetle, acorns, and wild berries.

Georgia also designated an official state game bird, the bobwhite quail, in 1970.[20] When the thrasher was officially designated the state bird of Georgia, it seemed a proper time to make the bobwhite quail the official state game bird. Known as the "Quail Capital of the World," Georgia was proud to give this designation to a bird so plentiful in Georgia and beloved by sportsmen everywhere.[21]

Size: Wing length: 4½ inches; tail length: 2 to 2½ inches.

Range: Resident of open uplands from Maine through southern New England; westward through Minnesota, North Dakota, and Wyoming; south through northern Florida, the Gulf coast region, northern Texas, and eastern Colorado; southern Ontario.

Physical description: The bobwhite quail, *Colinus virginianus,* is mostly dark amber brown to chestnut above, heavily blotched with fuscous-black and narrowly tipped with pale, warm buff; the lateral feathers of the upper back and the feathers of the lower back and rump are paler, narrowly barred with dusky and crossed by numerous pale warm buffy bands; the tail feathers are gray; the chin, upper throat, and forehead are white with a broad white stripe extending from above the eye to the back of the neck (in the female, the stripe, chin, and throat are pale orange-yellow, and the forehead and crown are between tawny and russet). There is a fairly broad blackish band across the lower throat (auburn in the female), followed by a broader one of cinnamon; the upper abdomen is white washed with pale warm buff; the feathers are crossed by four or five narrow black bars.

Behavior: The bobwhite quail, also commonly referred to as the partridge, feeds on grain left in the field after harvest, as well as locusts, grasshoppers, and potato beetles, making it a popular friend of farmers. The bobwhite quail's plumage makes it possible for the bird to conceal himself quite effectively from hunters and other threats. When it becomes too dangerous to remain stationary, the bobwhite launches himself into sudden flight giving the impression that he is a strong flyer. However, this is not the case, as quail have been known to collapse into the water in failed attempts to cross wide rivers.

HAWAII

The *nene, Nesochen sandwicensis* or *Bernicata sandwicensis,* was designated the state bird in 1957.[22]

Physical description: The *nene,* or Hawaiian goose, is a land goose, only recently saved from extinction by being bred in England and returned to Hawaii by Herbert Shipman and Peter Scott with U.S. financial support. The Hawaiian goose has a long, creme-colored neck, streaked vertically in black, with the light coloring extending upward into the malar region. The back of the neck and head are black. There is a black ring around the neck separating the creme color from the variegated pattern of the grayish brown back.[23]

IDAHO

The mountain bluebird, *Sialia arctica,* was designated and declared to be the state bird of Idaho in 1931.[24] The Idaho State Federation Conservation chairman initially indicated that the western tanager was the best choice for state bird. However, the state's school children felt differently, and the mountain bluebird received the most votes.[25]

Size: Total length: 6½ inches; tail length: 2½ to 3 inches.

Range: Mountain districts of western North America; winters southward to southern California and northern Mexico.

Physical description: A thrush, the male and female plumage differ as follows: The male is a plain, rich turquoise blue, sky blue, or porcelain blue; the head, throat, chest, and sides are paler in color than the upper parts; the abdomen and lower parts are white; the tail and wing feathers are black with longer undertail feathers a pale turquoise or sky blue tipped with white. The female head and back are plain mouse or smoke gray, sometimes tinged with greenish blue; the chin, throat, breast, and sides are a pale brownish gray passing into dull white on the abdomen; the longer undertail feathers are dusky sometimes tinged with blue; the rump, upper tail feathers, tail, and wings are mostly turquoise blue or light sky blue, sometimes nile blue. The adult male in winter turns a duller blue; the adult female's color deepens, especially the buffy grayish underparts.

Behavior: The *Sialia arctica* is now called the *Sialia currucoides* because, unlike previously thought, it is not native to the Arctic region. (Instead, it only summers there.) Mountain bluebirds feed mostly on ants and beetles with a small dietary component of grapes and berries. Flocks of bluebirds may be identified by their strange way of pausing between their deep swooping movements. They build nests in holes in trees, along river banks, in houses, and even in other birds' nesting holes. Bluebird fledglings sometimes fall prey to flickers who have been known to keep parents from feeding their young by blocking the entrance to the nests.

ILLINOIS

The cardinal, *Cardinalis cardinalis,* was designated the state bird of Illinois by the legislature in 1929,[26] after a vote of Illinois school children. The cardinal received 39,226 votes; the next runner-up was the bluebird which received 30,306 votes.[27]

Size: Total length: 7½ to 8 inches; tail length: 4 inches.

Range: Eastern United States, west to the Great Plains, southern Arizona, and northwestern Mexico, and south through Georgia to the Gulf states.

Physical description: A finch, the cardinal is conspicuously crested and thick-billed with the tail longer than the rather short and rounded wing. Adult males are entirely bright red, except for the black patchy band from the eye to the throat on both sides of the bill. The female has a dull grayish patch on the face and throat, is brownish above and dull tawny or pale buffy below; the crest, wings, and tail are a dull reddish color, and the underwing feathers are pinkish red.

Behavior: The cardinal builds its nest in shrubs and bushes, seemingly oblivious to its proximity to people. Eggs are whitish with brown spots incubating over a twelve- to thirteen-day period. Both parents attend to the young with frequent feedings of insects. As the young mature, they become primarily grain and fruit eaters, though insect pests still make up a third of their diet. Cardinals are beautiful birds, popular not only for their striking plumage, but also for their pleasant songs, which are loud, flutelike whistles. The trills last approximately three seconds.

INDIANA

The red bird or cardinal, *Richmondena Cardinalis cardinalis,* was designated the state bird of Indiana by act of legislature in 1933.[28] See the Illinois entry for a description.

IOWA

In 1933, the eastern goldfinch, *Spinus tristis tristis,* was designated the state bird of Iowa by the forty-fifth General Assembly.[29]

Size: Total length: 4½ inches; tail length: 1½ to 2 inches.

Range: United States and southern Canada east of the Rocky Mountains; wintering southward to the Gulf coast.

Physical description: The adult male in the summer is generally pure lemon yellow or canary yellow; the forehead, crown, wings, and tail are black; and white stripes appear near the base of the wings and along the ends of the tail feathers. The adult female and the adult male in the winter are olive brownish or grayish above; the wings and tail are blackish or dusky marked with white; the upper tail feathers are pale grayish or grayish white; and the underparts are dull grayish white tinged with yellow.

Behavior: The eastern goldfinch is a flock bird, often seen in undulating flight, cheerfully singing with his friends. The birds usually sing in choral fashion, whistling their high-pitched tunes which last from two to three seconds. Breeding very late in the season (from July to September), the male and female are constant companions as they build their nests and raise their young. Egg sets average five in number, and the coloration is plain bluish white. Seeds are the mainstay of their diet, supplemented in the winter months by a delicacy, plant lice eggs.

KANSAS

The western meadowlark, *Sturnella neglecta (Audubon),* was designated by the legislature in 1937 as the official state bird of Kansas, as preferred by a vote of school children in the state.[30]

Size: Total length: 8 to 9 inches; tail length: 2½ to 3 inches.

Range: Western United States, southwestern Canada, northwestern Mexico; east to the prairie areas of the Mississippi valley, in Minnesota, Iowa, Missouri, and Texas.

Physical description: The head and back of the neck are a pale dull buffy or white with broad lateral crown stripes of pale grayish brown; the lower sides of the head are largely yellow, topped by a dull grayish white area streaked with gray; mostly buffy or grayish brown above streaked with black; the outermost tail feathers are mostly white; the throat, breast, and abdomen are a deep yellow sometimes with an orangish hue. The yellow area is relieved by a black horseshoe-shaped patch on the chest.

Behavior: An oriole, the western meadowlark feeds mostly on insects with perhaps one third of its diet consisting of grain. Its loud, distinctive song is considered one of its most appealing qualities; the bird sometimes hammers out as many as 200 notes per minute. The young leave their nests early, unable to fly but still under the protection of their parents until they are able to care for themselves. Fledglings are easy prey for weasels, skunks, snakes, owls, and hawks.

KENTUCKY

The native red bird commonly known as the Kentucky cardinal (*Cardinalis cardinalis*) was designated the official state bird by the legislature in 1926.[31] See the Illinois entry for a description.

LOUISIANA

The brown pelican, as it appears on the seal of the state, was designated as the official state bird of Louisiana by the legislature in 1966.[32] This amended a 1958 act naming the pelican, with no further designation, as the official state bird.

Physical description: Mostly grayish brown streaked with brown, the pelican feathers are white tipped, and he has a long brown neck (white in the winter), a white head and white stripe that extends under the bill in a straplike fashion, a yellow forehead that turns to white at the crown followed by a rust-colored tuft at the back of the head, a long bill, and a throat pouch.

Behavior: The *Pelecanus occidentalis occidentalis,* or brown pelican, usually lays three dull white eggs after a solemn courtship culminating on the water's surface. As is the case with many newly hatched birds, the young pelican is fed regurgitated food of a parent. However, it has the unique experience as it grows older of selecting meals smorgasbord-style from the parent's pouch, until it is old enough to capture its own meal from the sea. A hunting expedition is carried out when the pelican dives head first into the water at a downwind angle, making a somersault beneath the surface and emerging against the wind. This remarkable spectacle usually results in catching a supply of fresh fish that is stashed in the pouch for digestion later.

MAINE

The chickadee, *Penthestes atricapillus,* was adopted as official state bird of Maine in 1927.[33]

Size: Total length: 4½ to 5 inches; tail length: 2 to 2½ inches.

Range: Northern United States and Canada.

Physical description: The entire top and back of the head is black; most of the upper back is plain olive gray, passing into buffy gray on the rump and upper tail feathers; the wings and tail are a dusky or blackish slate color; the chin and throat are black; the sides of the head and most of the underparts are white, the sides tinged with buffy. In autumn and winter, this long-tailed small bird is much more deeply colored, contrasting even more strongly with the white abdomen and white wing edgings.

Behavior: The black-capped chickadee is a member of the titmouse family. Beloved by early colonial settlers, the chickadee is friendly and somewhat tame. It has been known to perch fearlessly on fingers and to feed from the hand. One of its songs is calling its own name—"chicka" followed by "dee dee dee."

MARYLAND

The Baltimore oriole, *Icterus galbula,* was designated the official state bird of Maryland by the General Assembly in 1947. The assembly has also made special provision for its protection.[34] The first Lord Baltimore chose orange and black as the colors for his coat of arms because of his fondness for the bird, which he saw often on his estate, that was later named the Baltimore Oriole.[35]

Size: Total length: 6½ to 7 inches; tail length: 2½ to 3 inches.

Range: Eastern United States, west to the Rocky Mountains; winters in Mexico and Central America to Colombia and Venezuela.

Physical description: The male's head, back, and upper chest area are black; the rump, upper tail feathers, and underparts range from cadmium yellow to intense orange; the upper wings are black, broadly tipped with white. The female's head and back are saffron olive, with distinct central spots of black or dusky; the rump and tail feathers are olive saffron; the wings are dusky, narrowly tipped with white or gray; the underparts are saffron yellow or dull orange-yellow, duller on the abdomen and tinged with olive on the sides and flanks.

Behavior: The Baltimore oriole is a talented weaver, building a nest from grapevine bark, plant fibers, and milkweed silk. The nest hangs pouchlike from 30 feet above the ground. Fledglings are strangely quiet until a few days prior to leaving the nest, when they then cry for days in a high-pitched monotonous whine. The oriole feeds heavily on caterpillars and other insects and exhibits a taste for green peas and berries.

MASSACHUSETTS

The chickadee, *Penthestes atricapillus,* was designated the state bird of the Commonwealth of Massachusetts by legislative act in 1941.[36] See the Maine entry for a description.

MICHIGAN

A 1931 House concurrent resolution made the robin the official state bird of Michigan.[37] See the Connecticut entry for a description.

MINNESOTA

The loon, *Gavia immer,* was adopted as the official bird of Minnesota by the legislature in 1961.[38]

Size: Total length: 3 feet; wing span: 5 feet.[39]

Physical description: The head is black with black and white stripes around the head in a vertical zebra pattern; the lower neck is coal black; the upper chest and underparts are white. Above there appears a black and white checkerboard pattern and, along the sides, the same colors give an appearance of polka dots. The winter plumage is grayish brown above, with a brownish head and white underparts.

Behavior: The loon mates for life and returns to the same lake in the spring of every year. After laying two or three eggs, one usually infertile, the loon incubates the eggs for nearly a month. Within two days, the young loons are led into the water by their mother where they exhibit great skill in swimming and diving. They remain in the water, relatively safe from attack, until they are able to fly. Fish eaters, loons capture their prey with great alacrity and strength. Trout are often the objects of their underwater escapades; the loons quickly swallow them before resurfacing. Half running and half flying, the loon puts forth a considerable effort in taking flight, sometimes gliding along the surface for quite a distance before ascending.

MISSISSIPPI

The mockingbird was designated the state bird of Mississippi by the legislature in 1944.[40] See the Arkansas entry for a description.

The state of Mississippi also designated the wood duck, *Aix sponsa,* as the official state waterfowl in 1974.[41]

Range: United States and southern Canada.

Physical description: The crown of the head is metallic green streaked laterally with two white stripes; two white stripes also appear under the chin area; the breast is russet; metallic green, bronze, blue, and purple appear above and buffy to white below; the back, breast, and side regions are separated by white stripes. In July or August, the adult male begins to molt and takes on brownish shades above and yellowish tones below. The female is similar but duller, mostly brownish gray above, brown on the sides, and white below. There is a white ring around the eye.

Behavior: Also called the summer duck because it breeds and summers regularly throughout the South and a tree duck because it nests in tree trunks or branch cavities, the wood duck lays from ten to fifteen eggs per season. After incubating for nearly a month, the whitish eggs hatch and, from then on, the fledglings know little peace until their mother has managed to acclimate them to the water. Sometimes carrying them on her back or in her bill, the mother coaxes and protects her brood as they learn to manage for themselves. The wood duck feeds primarily on vegetable matter such as nuts, weeds, and seeds retrieved by scavenging under leaves and feeding on aquatic plants. The rest of his diet consists of miscellaneous insects, dragonflies, beetles, and locusts, as well as a few small fish, minnows, and frogs. A good swimmer and flyer, the wood duck is usually hunted as he goes from his sheltered roosting spot to his feeding spot along marshy streams.

MISSOURI

The bluebird, *Sialia sialis,* native to Missouri, became that state's official bird by legislative act in 1927.[42]

Size: Total length: 6 inches; tail length: 2½ inches.

Range: United States and southern Canada east of the Rockies; breeds south to Texas, along the Gulf coast and Florida.

Physical description: Above, the male is bright blue, the average hue being between ultramarine and deep blue; the shafts of the wing and tail feathers are black; the sides of the head are light or gray blue; the underparts are mostly a dull cinnamon red or cinnamon chestnut except the abdomen and under the tail feathers, which are white. The female is bluish gray above, tinged with grayish brown; the rump and tail feathers are bright blue; the wings are blue, edged with whitish gray; the underparts are mostly dull cinnamon; the chin, abdomen, and under tail feathers are white.

Behavior: Known as the eastern bluebird, this tiny bird was nicknamed the blue robin by early settlers because it reminded them of the English robin redbreast. Though an amorous and flirtatious suitor, the male loses no time in selecting another companion upon the loss of his mate. The courtship is marked by alluring songs from the male, who attentively pays friendly visits to the female. On such visits he may even feed her by placing food in her mouth. Once egg incubation begins, the singing stops until it is time to begin again with a new nesting (and often a new mate). The majority of the bluebird's diet is insect matter, such as harmful beetles, grasshoppers, crickets, and katydids.

MONTANA

The western meadowlark, *Sturnella neglecta (Audubon),* was declared to be the official state bird of Montana by the legislature in 1931, following a referendum vote of Montana school children.[43]

In 1805 the famous explorer, Meriwether Lewis, entered into his journal the observance of a lark he found similar to the eastern lark. This is believed to be the first recorded mention of what is now known as the western meadowlark. The most notable difference between the two larks is their song.[44]

See the Kansas entry for a description.

NEBRASKA

The western meadowlark was designated the state bird of Nebraska by the legislature in 1929.[45] See the Kansas entry for a description.

NEVADA

The mountain bluebird, *Sialia currucoides,* was designated the official state bird of Nevada by the legislature in 1967.[46] See the Idaho entry for a description.

NEW HAMPSHIRE

The New Hampshire legislature designated the purple finch, *Carpodacus purpureus,* the official state bird in 1957,[47] the year in which a Dartmouth College forester, Robert S. Monahan, along with the Audubon Society of New Hampshire, the New Hampshire Federation of Garden Clubs, and the State Federation of Women's Clubs recommended the designation of the purple finch. Thereupon, Republican Doris M. Spollett, who had previously tried with no success to name the New Hampshire hen as the state bird, began again to campaign for her personal favorite. She lost when, within three months of its introduction, the bill making the purple finch the state bird was signed into law.[48]

Size: Total length: 5½ inches; tail length: 2 inches; wing length: 3 inches.

Range: Eastern North America; winters south to Gulf coast area.

Physical description: The male's top of head and back of the neck are deep wine purple (more crimson in the summer). There is a dusky brownish red spot near the ear and along the side of the head; the rest of the head is pinkish wine purple; the back is reddish brown or wine purplish with dark streaks; the wings and tail are dusky with light brownish red or light brown edgings; the abdomen and under tail feathers are white. The female is olive or olive grayish above streaked with dusky and white; the wings and tail are dusky with light olive or olive grayish edgings; the upper sides of the head are mostly white streaked with olive; the underparts are white, broadly streaked with olive.

Behavior: The purple finch feeds on seeds in the winter and spring, insects in the late spring, and fruit in the summer. Finches are considered generally beneficial by orchard growers, since they prune rather than destroy fruit trees. They also eat such harmful insects as plant lice, cankerworms, and caterpillars. Courtship consists of a wild dance and song by the male, sometimes followed by an equally eccentric response by the female who first ignores the male and then pecks at him before they fly off together to build a nest. The four or five eggs commonly produced by the happy couple are bluish green or pale blue, with black or brown spots mostly located at the large end of each egg.

NEW JERSEY

The eastern goldfinch was designated the state bird of New Jersey by the legislature in 1935.[49] See the Iowa entry for a description.

NEW MEXICO

The chaparral bird, commonly known as the roadrunner, was adopted as the official bird of New Mexico by the legislature in 1949.[50]

Size: Total length: 20 to 21 inches; tail length: 11½ inches.

Range: Southwestern United States; east to Gulf coast of Texas; northern and central Mexico.

Physical description: The roadrunner is a large, long-tailed, long-billed cuckoo. The feathers of the forehead and front of the crown are black, each with a broad lateral spot of russet or light tawny brown; the occipital bushy crest is glossy black or blue-black broken by edgings of tawny brown or pale buffy; above is mostly black broadly edged with light tawny brown passing into dull buffy white on the edges creating a conspicuous streaked effect; the lower back and wing coverts are glossy bronze or bronze greenish and edged with black; the tail feathers are mostly bronzy olive glossed with purplish and margined with dull white; the sides of the head are dull whitish and tawny brown, barred and spotted with black; the chin and throat are mostly dull white; the rest of the underparts are plain grayish white, the neck and chest streaked with black.

Behavior: Many observers have described the roadrunner in unflattering terms such as odd looking and uniquely entertaining. Perhaps because of the barren habitat in which the roadrunner resides, it has had to adapt for survival by exhibiting stealth, speed, ferocity, and strength. This combination of traits and its outward appearance of awkwardness explains why it has attracted such bemused attention. When hungry, the roadrunner runs quickly in pursuit of lizards, scorpions, snakes, tarantulas, mice, insects, and small birds.

NEW YORK

The bluebird, *Sialia sialis,* became the official bird of the state of New York by legislative act in 1970.[51] The robin had been selected initially as the state bird, but, after a vote in 1927 and 1928, the bluebird was determined to be more popular.[52] It was not until 1970, however, that this designation was made official. See the Missouri entry for a description.

NORTH CAROLINA

The cardinal was declared to be the official state bird of North Carolina by the legislature in 1943.[53] See the Illinois entry for a description.

NORTH DAKOTA

The meadowlark, *Sturnella neglecta,* was named the official bird of North Dakota by the legislature in 1947.[54] See the Kansas entry for a description.

OHIO

The cardinal, *Cardinalis cardinalis,* was named the official bird of Ohio by the legislature in 1933.[55] See the Illinois entry for a description.

OKLAHOMA

The scissor-tailed flycatcher, *Muscivora forticata,* was designated the state bird of Oklahoma by joint resolution of the legislature in 1951.[56] The joint resolution notes that the flycatcher's nesting range is centered in Oklahoma, and, because its diet consists of harmful and useless insects, the flycatcher is of great economic value. Furthermore, the scissor-tailed flycatcher has been endorsed as the official state bird by numerous ornithologists, biologists, and wildlife societies.[57]

Size: Total length: 11 to 13 inches; tail length: 6 to 9 inches.

Range: Texas to Kansas, less commonly in Missouri, Arkansas, and Louisiana; migrates to Mexico and Central America.

Physical description: The male's head is clear pale gray with a small concealed orange-red patch on the center of the crown; the back is light gray strongly suffused with a pink wine color; the upper tail feathers are black or dusky, margined with gray; the six middle tail feathers are black; the three outermost tail feathers on each side are white, strongly tinged with salmon pink, terminally black; the tail is deeply forked, especially in the male, the lateral tail feathers more than twice as long as the middle pair and longer than the wing; the cheek, chin, and throat are white, shading into gray on the breast; the sides and flanks are a salmon color to an almost saturn red; there is a large concealed patch of bright orange-red on either side of the breast. The female is similar to the male but duller in color; the breast patches are more restricted and orangish; and the concealed crown spot is often missing.

Behavior: Fondest of open terrain, the flycatcher perches on telephone wires and posts. Its diet is composed mainly of noxious insects such as beetles, wasps, and bees. Favorites are grasshoppers and crickets. Interestingly enough, flycatchers do not seem to care much for flies. An extremely energetic bird when provoked or frightened, it is nonetheless a sloppy nest builder who carelessly leaves strings and twine hanging from the nest. The eggs are a creamy white color spotted with brown and gray.

OREGON

The western meadowlark, *Sturnella neglecta,* was declared the official bird of Oregon by gubernatorial proclamation in 1927, following a vote of the state's school children sponsored by the Oregon Audubon Society.[58] See the Kansas entry for a description.

PENNSYLVANIA

Pennsylvania is the only state that has designated only an official state game bird, the ruffed grouse, *Bonasa umbellus,* which was adopted by the legislature in 1931.[59]

Size: Total length: 15 to 19 inches; tail length: 5 to 6 inches.

Range: Wooded portions of North America.

Physical description: A medium-sized wood grouse, the upperparts are brown and rusty or gray variegated with black; the underparts are buff or whitish, broken by broad bars of brownish; the lower half of the tarsus is nude and scalelike; the tail at approximately 5 inches is nearly as long as the wing and has from eighteen to twenty tail feathers; the tail is gray or rusty with numerous zigzag narrow bars of blackish and a broad subterminal band of black or dark brown; the feathers on the crown are distinctly elongated, forming when erected a conspicuous crest. The male in the summer has a bright orange or red naked space above the eye.

Behavior: The courtship behavior of the ruffed grouse has been the source of much interest throughout the years. The drumming noise made by either the wild flapping of the wings against the sides or by the sheer force of the wings against the air is ear splitting, though no one can seem to agree on the exact noise-making mechanism. The ruffed grouse is primarily a fruit and vegetable eater; insects account for approximately ten percent of his diet. Grouse are remarkably tame by nature and, when allowed, they have become pets. The birds who reside in areas where grouse are hunted are much more wary of humans and take the appropriate evasive actions. A popular game bird, the grouse is called a pheasant in the South and a partridge in the northern states. Its enemies include raccoons, weasels, skunks, and opossum. In addition, disease and parasites take a heavy toll on the grouse population.

RHODE ISLAND

The breed of fowl known commonly as the Rhode Island Red was designated the official state bird of Rhode Island by the legislature in 1954.[60]

Physical description: The Rhode Island Red is a well-known American breed of domesticated fowl. It weighs from 6½ to 8½ pounds, has yellow skin beneath brownish red feathers, and a single rose-colored comb extending from the base of its beak to the upper back of its head. The hen lays brown eggs.

SOUTH CAROLINA

The Carolina wren, a member of the family *Troglodytidae,* was designated the official state bird of South Carolina in 1948 by the state legislature.[61] In 1939, however, the legislature had adopted the mockingbird as the state bird, in spite of the fact that the Carolina wren had been recognized unofficially as the state bird prior to that time. The 1948 act designating the Carolina wren as the official state bird repealed the 1939 act.[62]

Size: Total length: 5 inches; tail length: 2 inches.

Range: Eastern United States.

Physical description: The upperparts of the Carolina wren, *Thryothorus ludovicianus,* are plain rusty brown; the wings and tail are a duller brown than the back, narrowly barred with dusky. There is a sharply defined and conspicuous stripe of white or buffy white on each side from the bill and above the eye to the back of the neck, bordered above in black; beneath the white stripe is a broad area of rufous brown covering the upper half of the auricular region; the underparts are a plain dull buffy white to buff color on the chest, sides, and flanks; the under tail feathers are buffy whitish broadly barred with black. In autumn and winter, the colors are decidedly brighter, and the superciliary stripe is buffy.

Behavior: A sweet and vigorous songster, the wren whistles a variety of loud, cheerful songs. A set of wren eggs usually numbers five, and the eggs are creamy or pinkish white with reddish brown spots encircling the larger end of the egg. The wren is a pest eater; its diet comprises mostly beetles, caterpillars, grasshoppers, crickets, and cockroaches. It is no surprise, then, that the wren is an especially quick and energetic bird able to capture its tiny prey, as well as to escape the perceived danger posed by nosy humans. However, the wren is also a curious creature and will often bravely and swiftly investigate the source of suspicious noises before considering its own safety.

In 1976, the legislature made the South Carolina wild turkey, *Meleagris gallopavo,* the official state wild game bird.[63] See the Alabama entry for a description of the wild turkey.

SOUTH DAKOTA

The ring-necked pheasant, *Phasianus colchicus,* was adopted as the state bird of South Dakota by act of the state legislature in 1943.[64]

Size: Total length: 20 to 27 inches; the tail is proportionally long ranging from 10 inches in the female to 18 inches in the male.

Range: Native to eastern China; now well established in the northern half of the United States, southern Canada, Hawaii, and Europe.

Physical description: The male's head, crown, and neck are of varying shades of glossy green from Roman green to bottle green and dark zinc green; the nape of the neck is tinged with a glossy dark violet-blue that also predominates along the sides of the neck; erectile tufts of iridescent blue-green blackish feathers are located on each side towards the back of the crown. There is a white collar around the neck; the exposed interscapulers are a bright buff yellow with a white triangular space at the base; much of the upperparts are light neutral gray or brown tinged with pale olive buff and broadly edged with russet or black; the lower back region is yellow-green to deep lichen green; the breast is a dark coppery hazel, broadly glossed with magenta purple; the bare skin on the side of the head is bright red; the tail is brown or dark olive buff with black transverse markings. The female is brownish and buffy, variegated with black; the interscapulars are a bright hazel to tawny russet, the central area terminating in a brownish gray or black distally pointed "V"; the scapulars and upper wing feathers are brown to tawny olive, edged and tipped with pale buffy; the back and upper tail feathers are brownish black, broadly edged with pale pinkish buff; the tail feathers are a light pinkish hazel transversely blotched with black; the chin, upper breast, and abdomen are white to buffy.

Behavior: The ring-necked, or Chinese, pheasant was introduced in 1881 in Oregon by Judge O. N. Denny, the American consul general of Shanghai. The muted earth tones of the female's plumage serve as effective camouflage, making it possible for potential intruders to come within a few feet and yet never notice her in her nest. The female has no scent, making her even more secure from attack. The ten to twelve eggs in a set are usually brownish olive. Upon hatching, the newborn chicks follow their mother who helps them scavenge for food and protects them from predators. Though pheasant eat a good many harmful insects, they also attack farm and garden crops such as corn, tomatoes, and beans causing severe damage. Able to escape from danger by a rapid vertical movement if trapped by buildings or trees, the pheasant makes a noisy exit by madly fluttering its wings and croaking loudly in alarm. Very sensitive to earth tremors, caused by explosions or earthquakes, they make their alarm known by crowing loudly.

TENNESSEE

After a popular vote in April 1933, the mockingbird, *Mimus polyglottos,* was selected over the robin, cardinal, bobwhite, and bluebird, among others. In 1933 the General Assembly adopted Senate Joint Resolution 51 naming the mockingbird the official state bird of Tennessee.[65] See the Arkansas entry for a description.

TEXAS

The mockingbird, *Mimus polyglottos,* was adopted as the state bird of Texas by legislative act in 1927, following the recommendation of the Texas Federation of Women's Clubs.[66] See the Arkansas entry for a description.

UTAH

The sea gull, *Larus californicus,* was selected as the state bird of Utah by an act of the legislature in 1955.[67]

Size: Tail length: 6 inches; wing length: 14½ to 16 inches.

Range: Western North America, inland to Nevada, Utah, Kansas, Texas, and Colorado near large lake areas.

Physical description: The head, neck, upper tail feathers, tail, and all underparts are entirely white; the back, scapulars, and wings are between pale and light neutral gray, the wings tipped with white; the eye ring and rictus are vermillion-red; the subterminal third of the bill is red, immediately preceded by a black spot; the legs and feet are a pale grayish green.

Behavior: A faithful friend of the farmer, the California gull eats crickets, grasshoppers, and even mice. This gratitude of the farmer was the primary rationale behind the designation of the gull as the state bird. In 1848 the gulls were credited with saving farmers' crops by consuming the insects endangering them.[68] Aeronautic wizards, gulls are gymnasts of the sky, making the seemingly impossible appear effortless. They can appear motionless in midair by catching wind currents with perfect timing and precision while positioning their bodies at just the right angle. They are quiet birds, considered quite beneficial by agriculturalists, and are usually gentle creatures, exhibiting neither antagonism to nor fondness for man.

VERMONT

The hermit thrush, *Hylocichla guttata faxoni,* became the state bird of Vermont by an act of the legislature in 1941.[69]

Size: Total length: 6½ inches; tail length: 2½ to 3 inches.

Range: Eastern North America; southern migration to Gulf states.

Physical description: The upper parts are a cinnamon brown; the sides and flanks are buffy brown; there is a conspicuous orbital ring of dull white; the ear region is a grayish brown streaked with dull whitish; the underparts are a dull white tinged with a pale cream buff; the throat is streaked along each side in a sooty color; the chest has large triangular spots of dusky grayish brown, broader and more rounded on the lower chest; the tail is a dull cinnamon brown. Spring and summer plumage is brighter.

Behavior: A hardy bird, the hermit thrush arrives in early spring and departs in late fall for its migration southward. Traveling at night, thrushes sometimes become so tired and cold that they lose all natural shyness and feed from the human hand. Hermit thrushes have been observed performing a curious activity known as "anting." The bird catches ants and places them in its feathers beneath the wings. It is thought that either the formic acid in the ants is effective in combating parasitic attacks or the ants are being horded for later consumption during migration. Talented singers, hermit thrushes sometimes sing in unison to form a harmonious chorus. Other times, they are capable of completely fooling the listener into thinking they are farther away or closer than they actually are by calling upon their extraordinary powers of ventriloquism. Protective of their young, thrushes fight so vigorously against predators that they can often fend off attacks.

VIRGINIA

The cardinal was designated the official state bird of Virginia by legislative act in 1950.[70] See the Illinois entry for a description.

WASHINGTON

The willow goldfinch, *Astragalinus tristis salicamans,* was designated the official bird of the state of Washington in 1951 by an act of the legislature.[71]

Size: Total length: 4½ inches; tail length: 1½ to 2 inches.

Range: Pacific coast region.

Physical description: The willow goldfinch is very similar to the eastern goldfinch (see the New Jersey entry), but the wings and tail are shorter and the coloration is darker. The adult male summer plumage of the back is tinged with pale olive green, and the winter adults and the young are decidedly darker or browner than the corresponding eastern goldfinch, with broader markings on the wings.

Behavior: Called the willow goldfinch because of its gravitation to damp areas conducive to the growth of willows, this small bird is a cheery singer and a graceful flyer. Very similar to the eastern goldfinch, this goldfinch begins to nest earlier than its counterparts, usually in April or May. The willow goldfinch is primarily a seed eater, munching mostly on seeds from harmful or neutral plants and occasionally supplementing his diet with harmful insects.

WEST VIRGINIA

The cardinal, *Richmondena cardinalis,* was designated the official bird of West Virginia by legislative act in 1949.[72] See the Illinois entry for a description.

WISCONSIN

The robin, *Turdus migratorius,* was designated the official state bird of Wisconsin by an act of the legislature in 1949.[73] When the school children of Wisconsin voted in 1926–1927 to select a state bird, the robin received twice as many votes as any other bird, but it was not until 1949 that the robin officially became the state bird.[74] See the Connecticut entry for a description.

WYOMING

The meadowlark, genus *Sturnella,* became the state bird of Wyoming by legislative act in 1927.[75] See the Kansas entry for a description.

DISTRICT OF COLUMBIA

Although the wood thrush was first proposed as the District's official bird in 1927, it was not officially designated until January 31, 1967, by the commissioners.[76]

Size: Total length: 8½ inches.

Range: Eastern United States and southeastern Canada; wintering in Central America and Mexico.

Physical description: The plumage of *Hylocichia mustelina* is reddish-cinnamon above becoming olive-brown to tail; auricular region with white, yellowish-brown to tan streaks; underparts are white with large black spots; white ring surrounds eyes.

AMERICAN SAMOA

American Samoa has not designated an official bird.

COMMONWEALTH OF THE NORTHERN MARIANA ISLANDS

The Mariana fruit dove or Paluman tottut was adopted as the official Commonwealth bird in 1989.[77] See entry under Guam for description.

GUAM

The totot (*Ptilinopus*) was named the official territorial bird of Guam in 1969.[78]

Size: Total length: 9 inches.

Range: Mariana Islands.

Physical description: The totot, *Ptilinopus roseicapilla,* is also called the Mariana fruit dove and the love bird. Upper parts are very bright green with gray head, breast, upper back, and tail band; red cap; underparts with purple bar below breast, yellow belly, orange flanks, and pink-orange coverts beneath the tail.

Behavior: Rarely seen, preferring lofty perches and quiet, avoiding populated areas.

PUERTO RICO

Puerto Rico has not designated an official bird.

U.S. VIRGIN ISLANDS

In 1970, the United States Virgin Islands adopted the yellow breast (*Coereba flaveola*) as its official bird.[79]

Size: Total length: 5 inches.

Range: West Indies, Central and South America.

Physical description: Coereba flaveola, commonly called the bananaquit, is black above with white stripes over the eyes and white spots at the base of the wing tips; breast is bright yellow and throat and underparts are white; tail black with white spots; decurved short bill.

Behavior: The bananaquit is a very active honeycreeper that feeds on nectar, fruit, and small insects.

NOTES

1. Ala. Code §1–2–7.
2. Katherine B. Tippetts, "Selecting State Birds," *Nature* 19, no. 4 (1932): 231.
3. *Alabama State Emblems* (Montgomery: Alabama State Department of Archives and History, n.d.), pp. 17–18.
4. Ala. Code §1–2–17.
5. Alaska Stat. §44.09.060.
6. Ariz. Rev. Stat. Ann. §41–854.
7. 1929 Ark. Acts 1536.
8. *Nature* 19, no. 4 (1932): 231.
9. Cal. Gov't. Code §423 (West).
10. *Nature* 19, no. 4 (1932): 231.
11. Colo. Rev. Stat. §24–80–910.
12. *Nature* 19, no. 4 (1932): 231, 234.
13. Conn. Gen. Stat. Ann. §3–109 (West).
14. Del. Code Ann. tit. 29, §304.
15. *Discover Wonderful Delaware: Official Insignia of Delaware* (Dover: Delaware State Development Department, n.d.).
16. 1907 Fla. Laws 1612.
17. *Nature* 19, no. 4 (1932): 234.
18. Ga. Code Ann. §50–3–50.
19. *Georgia's Official State Symbols* (Atlanta: Office of the Secretary of State, n.d.).
20. Ga. Code Ann. §50–3–51.
21. *The State of Georgia and Its Capitol* (Atlanta: State Museum of Science and Industry, Department of Archives and History, n.d.), p. 18.
22. Haw. Rev. Stat. §5–9.
23. *Grzimek's Animal Life* (New York: Van Nostrand Reinhold, 1975), vol. 7, pp. 284, 299.
24. Idaho Code §67–4501.

25. *Nature* 19, no. 4 (1932): 234.
26. Ill. Ann. Stat. ch. 1, §3003 (Smith-Hurd).
27. *Illinois Blue Book, 1983–84,* p. 436.
28. Ind. Code Ann. §1–2–8–1 (West).
29. *1985–1986 Iowa Official Register,* p. 241.
30. Kan. Stat. Ann. §73–901.
31. Ky. Rev. Stat. Ann. §2.080 (Baldwin).
32. La. Rev. Stat. Ann. §49–159 (West).
33. Me. Rev. Stat. tit. 1, §209.
34. Md. Ann. Code §13–302.
35. *Nature* 19, no. 4 (1932): 235.
36. Mass. Gen. Laws ch. 2, §9 (West).
37. Information supplied by the Michigan Department of State.
38. Minn. Stat. Ann. §1.145 (West).
39. *Minnesota Legislative Manual, 1985,* p. 12.
40. Miss. Code Ann. §3–3–11.
41. Ibid., §3–3–25.
42. Mo. Ann. Stat. §10.010 (Vernon).
43. Mont. Rev. Codes Ann. §1–1–504.
44. Rex C. Myers, *Symbols of Montana* (Helena: Montana Historical Society, 1976), p. 16.
45. Neb. Rev. Stat. §90–107.
46. Nev. Rev. Stat. §235.060.
47. N.H. Rev. Stat. Ann. §3:10.
48. *Manual for the General Court, 1981.*
49. N.J. Stat. Ann. §52:9A–1 (West).
50. N.M. Stat. Ann. §12–3–4.
51. N.Y. State Law §78 (McKinney).
52. *Nature* 19, no. 4 (1932): 235.
53. N.C. Gen. Stat. §145–2.
54. N.D. Cent. Code §54–02–06.
55. Ohio Rev. Code Ann. §5.03 (Baldwin).
56. Okla. Stat. Ann. tit. 25, §98.
57. 1951 Okla. Sess. Laws 356.
58. Or. Rev. Stat. §186; *Oregon State Blue Book, 1977–78,* p. 139.
59. Pa. Stat. Ann. tit. 71, §1005 (Purdon).
60. R.I. Gen. Laws §42–4–5.
61. S.C. Code §1–1–630.
62. *1978 South Carolina Legislative Manual,* 59th ed.
63. S.C. Code §1–1–635.
64. S.D. Codified Laws Ann. §1–6–9.
65. *Tennessee Blue Book, 1983–84,* p. 373.
66. Tex. Rev. Civ. Stat. Ann. art. 6143c (Vernon).
67. Utah Code Ann. §63–13–9.
68. *Nature* 19, no. 4 (1932): 235.
69. Vt. Stat. Ann. tit. 1, §497.
70. Va. Code §7.1–39.
71. Wash. Rev. Code Ann. §1.20.040.

72. Information supplied by the West Virginia Department of Culture and History.
73. Wis. Stat. Ann. §1.10 (West).
74. *Wisconsin Blue Book, 1983–84,* p. 948.
75. Wyo. Stat. Ann. §8-3-105.
76. *Symbols of the District of Columbia* (Washington, D.C.: Government of the District of Columbia, Office of the Secretariat, Office of Visual Information Management, n.d.).
77. C.M.C. tit. 1, §233.
78. Guam Code Ann. tit. 1, §1023.
79. V.I. Code Ann. tit. 1, §105.

9 | State and Territory Songs

State songs may celebrate a state's natural beauty and resources, its history and progress, or the hard work of its citizens. Some are quite familiar: "You Are My Sunshine" (Louisiana), "Home On The Range" (Kansas), and "Yankee Doodle" (Connecticut). Although others may be less familiar, forty-eight states have designated songs that express the unique character of the state. Among the states, only New Jersey and New York have never proclaimed state songs. On the other hand, Tennessee has five official songs and West Virginia has three. Furthermore, Georgia also has a state waltz; Kansas and North Dakota, a state march; Massachusetts, a state folk song; New Mexico, a Spanish language song; and Texas, a state flower song.

ALABAMA

The poem "Alabama" was adopted as the state song of Alabama in 1931. The poem was written by Julia S. Tutwiler and gifted to the state. Edna Gockel Gussen put the poem to music.[1] By the time the legislature officially adopted the song, it had already been in use for ten years as the state song. In 1917 the Alabama Federation of Music Clubs endorsed the song and gave it an award at its annual convention.[2]

ALASKA

"Alaska's Flag," composed by Elinor Dusenbury with words by Marie Drake, was adopted as the state song of Alaska in 1955.[3] The poem entitled

"Alaska's Flag" first appeared in the October 1935 *School Bulletin,* published by the state's Department of Education. Marie Drake was an employee of that department for twenty-eight years, having become assistant commissioner of education in 1934 and remaining in that post until her retirement in 1945.[4]

ARIZONA

The Arizona state song or anthem, adopted by the Fourth State Legislature, is entitled "Arizona March Song." The words were written by Margaret Rowe Clifford; the music, by Maurice Blumenthal.[5]

ARKANSAS

In 1987, the Arkansas legislature clarified the state song situation by declaring two state songs, one state historical song, and one state anthem. The songs "Arkansas (You Run Deep in Me)," by Wayland Holyfield, and "Oh, Arkansas," words by Gary Klaff, music by Terry Rose, were both declared to be official state songs. "The Arkansas Traveler," which was composed and approved by the State Song Commission in 1949, was declared to be the official state historical song. The song "Arkansas" by Eva Ware Barnett, first named the state song in 1917, was now declared the official state anthem. However, this 1987 law further instructs the secretary of state to furnish copies of the song "Arkansas" by Eva Ware Barnett when filling requests for the state song.[6]

CALIFORNIA

"I Love You, California," words by F. B. Silverwood and music by A. F. Frankenstein, was first introduced to the public in 1913 by Mary Garden. In 1915, it became the official song of the San Francisco and San Diego Expositions. In 1951 "I Love You, California" was adopted as the official state song by the legislature.[7]

COLORADO

The song "Where the Columbines Grow," words and music by A. J. Flynn, was declared the official state song of Colorado by the legislature in 1915.[8]

CONNECTICUT

"Yankee Doodle" was adopted as the state song of Connecticut in 1978. The composer is unknown.[9]

DELAWARE

In 1925 "Our Delaware" was adopted as Delaware's state song. The words were written by George B. Hynson, and the music by Will M. S. Brown.[10]

FLORIDA

Stephen Foster's well-known song "Old Folks at Home," also known as "The Swanee River," was adopted as Florida's state song in 1935. The song was originally published in 1851.[11]

GEORGIA

"Georgia on My Mind" was designated the official state song of Georgia in 1979. The lyrics were written by Stuart Gorrell, and the music was composed by Hoagy Carmichael.[12] The 1979 act repealed a 1922 resolution designating "Georgia," words by Lottie Bell Wylie and music by Robert Loveman, as the official state song.[13]

Georgia also adopted an official state waltz, "Our Georgia," in 1951. Composed by James B. Burch to depict the glory of the state, this waltz was first played at the Georgia Democratic Convention in 1950.[14]

HAWAII

The song "Hawaii Ponoi" was adopted as the state song of Hawaii in 1967.[15]

IDAHO

In 1931 the Idaho legislature adopted "Here We Have Idaho" as the state song. The music, composed by Sallie Hume Douglas, had been copyrighted under the title "Garden of Paradise" in 1915. In 1930, the state obtained use of the melody forever from the composer. In 1917, McKinley Helm wrote the chorus, and, later, Albert J. Tompkins wrote additional verses to the song. Although other verses to the song had been written for use as an alma mater, the law cites the verses written by Helm and Tompkins as the official text for the state song.[16]

ILLINOIS

The song "Illinois," words by C. H. Chamberlain and music by Archibald Johnston, was established as the Illinois state song in 1925.[17]

INDIANA

In 1913 the song "On the Banks of the Wabash, Far Away" became the state song of Indiana. Paul Dresser wrote both the words and the music.[18]

IOWA

In 1911 the Iowa legislature adopted "The Song of Iowa" as the official state song. Although inspired to write the song while in a Confederate prison in Richmond, Virginia, S.H.M. Byers did not do so until 1897. Byers chose the melody of "O Tannenbaum," the same melody used for "My Maryland," for the song. He thus put "loyal words" to the confederate song "My Maryland," which he had heard in prison.[19]

Although it is not officially designated, the "Iowa Corn Song" is recognized by popular approval as another Iowa song. This marching tune was written by George Hamilton and popularized as early as 1912.[20]

KANSAS

The Kansas legislature designated "Home on the Range," words by Dr. Brewster Higley and music by Dan Kelly, as the official state song in 1947.[21] This was originally titled "My Western Home" when it was penned by Dr. Higley, a pioneer physician in Kansas, in 1871 or 1872.[22]

Kansas also has designated an official state march. In 1935 the legislature named "The Kansas March" by Duff E. Middleton the state's official march.[23]

KENTUCKY

"My Old Kentucky Home" by Stephen Collins Foster was designated the official state song of Kentucky in 1928.[24]

LOUISIANA

Louisiana has two officially designated songs. The first song, "Give Me Louisiana," was written and composed by Doralice Fontane and arranged by John W. Schaum. In 1977 the legislature also designated "You Are My Sunshine" as an official state song. The words and music are by Jimmy H. Davis and Charles Mitchell.

In 1990, Louisiana also designated "The Gifts of Earth," music and lyrics by Frances LeBeau, as its official state environmental song.[25]

MAINE

"State of Maine Song" is the title of the state's official song. The music and lyrics were written by Roger Vinton Snow.[26]

MARYLAND

"Maryland! My Maryland!" was designated the official state song in 1939. The song, a poem written in 1861 by James Ryder Randall, is sung to the tune of "Lauriger Horatius."[27] Randall, a Marylander who lived in the Confederacy during the Civil War, wrote the poem after Union troops went through Baltimore in 1861.[28]

MASSACHUSETTS

In 1981 Massachusetts designated both an official commonwealth song and a folk song. The official commonwealth song is "All Hail to Massachusetts," words and music by Arthur J. Marsh. "Massachusetts," words and music by Arlo Guthrie, is the official commonwealth folk song.

In 1989, the Commonwealth also adopted an official patriotic song, "Massachusetts (Because of You Our Land Is Free)." Bernard Davidson wrote the music and lyrics.[29]

MICHIGAN

"My Michigan," words by Giles Kavanagh and music by H. O'Reilly Clint, was designated an official state song of Michigan in 1937. In 1936 Governor Fitzgerald had designated this song as the official state song, but senate amendments changed a house resolution from designating "My Michigan" as the official song, to designating it as an official state song.[30]

MINNESOTA

"Hail! Minnesota," written in 1904–1905, was adopted as the state song of Minnesota in 1945. The music and the first verse were written by Truman E. Rickard. Arthur E. Upson wrote the words to the second verse. The song had first been used as the song of the University of Minnesota. Thus, the law adopting the song included a change from the original phrase "Hail to thee our college dear" to "Hail to thee our state so dear."[31]

MISSISSIPPI

The Board of Realtors of Jackson, Mississippi, set up an advisory committee to select an appropriate state song. The committee recommended the song "Go, Mississippi," words and music by Houston Davis, to the legislature for adoption. In 1962, the legislature acted positively on this recommendation.[32]

MISSOURI

"Missouri Waltz," arrangement by Frederick Knight Logan, melody by John Valentine Eppel, and lyrics by J. R. Shannon, was designated the Missouri state song in 1949. The song was first published in 1914.[33]

MONTANA

In 1945 the Montana legislature declared the song "Montana," words by Charles C. Cohan and music by Joseph E. Howard, to be the official state song. The legislature had also designated an official state ballad, "Montana Melody," written by Carleen and LeGrande Harvey.[34]

NEBRASKA

"Beautiful Nebraska," words and music by Jim Fras, was adopted as Nebraska's official state song in 1967. The song was copyrighted in 1965.[35]

NEVADA

"Home Means Nevada" was adopted as the official state song of Nevada in 1933. It was written by Mrs. Bertha Raffetto of Reno.[36]

NEW HAMPSHIRE

New Hampshire has designated a state song as well as a second state song. In 1949 the legislature declared "Old New Hampshire," words by Dr. John F. Holmes and music by Maurice Hoffmann, to be the state song. In 1963 "New Hampshire, My New Hampshire," music by Walter P. Smith and words by Julius Richelson, was declared the second state song.[37]

NEW JERSEY

The state of New Jersey does not have a state song. Attempts to make such a designation in 1940, 1954, and 1970 failed. Even an attempt in 1980 to designate "Born to Run" as the state's unofficial rock song failed for lack of legislative action.[38]

NEW MEXICO

In 1917 New Mexico adopted "O, Fair New Mexico," words and music by Elizabeth Garrett, as its official state song. In 1971 the legislature declared "Asi Es Nuevo Mejico," written by Amadeo Lucero, to be the Spanish language state song. Thus New Mexico has both an English language and a Spanish language official song.[39]

New Mexico also designated "Land of Enchantment—New Mexico," lyrics and music by Martin Murphy, Chick Raines, and Don Cook, as its official state ballad in 1989.[40]

NEW YORK

New York has no state songs. All bills to adopt a state song have thus far failed to pass the legislature.[41]

NORTH CAROLINA

The song "The Old North State" was declared the official state song of North Carolina in 1927. Another song, "A Toast" to North Carolina, was declared the official toast in 1957.[42]

NORTH DAKOTA

North Dakota has an official state song and a state march. The state song, "North Dakota Hymn," was written by James W. Foley and composed by Doctor C. S. Putnam. It was declared the state song in 1947.[43] In 1989 the legislature adopted "Flickertail March" by James D. Ployhar as the state march. The state march is to be played at appropriate state functions.[44]

OHIO

"Beautiful Ohio" was designated the official state song of Ohio in 1969. It was written by Ballard MacDonald and composed by Mary Earl.[45] Special lyrics were written by Wilbert B. White. Curiously, this 1918 waltz refers not to the state of Ohio, but to the Ohio River.[46]

OKLAHOMA

"Oklahoma," composed and written by Richard Rogers and Oscar Hammerstein, was declared the Oklahoma state song in 1953.[47] The 1953 act repealed a 1935 act designating "Oklahoma (A Toast)" by Harriet Parker Camden as the state song.

OREGON

"Oregon, My Oregon," words by J. A. Buchanan and music by Henry B. Murtagh, was adopted as the Oregon state song in 1927.[48]

PENNSYLVANIA

In 1990, Pennsylvania adopted the song "Pennsylvania," music and lyrics by Eddie Khoury and Ronnie Bonner, as its official state song.[49]

RHODE ISLAND

"Rhode Island," music and words by T. Clarke Brown, was declared to be the state song of Rhode Island in 1946.[50]

SOUTH CAROLINA

The song "Carolina," words by Henry Timrod and music by Anne Custis Burgess, was declared to be the state song of South Carolina in 1911, when the legislature acted on the memorial of the South Carolina Daughters of the American Revolution. There is, however, another state song. "South Carolina on My Mind" was designated as an official state song in 1984 to promote the image of South Carolina beyond its borders "by further developing tourism and industry through the attraction of vacationers, prospective investors, and new residents."[51]

SOUTH DAKOTA

"Hail! South Dakota," music and words by Deecort Hammitt, was adopted as the official state song of South Dakota in 1943.[52]

TENNESSEE

Tennessee has five official state songs. In designating new official songs, the legislature has not repealed formerly designated songs. The first official song, "My Homeland, Tennessee" by Nell Grayson Taylor and Roy Lamont Smith was adopted in 1925. In 1935 "When It's Iris Time in Tennessee" by Willa Mae Waid became Tennessee's second official song. "My Tennessee" by Francis Hannah Tranum was adopted as the third song in 1955, and "The Tennessee Waltz" by Redd Stewart and Pee Wee King, was designated the fourth in 1965. The fifth official state song, "Rocky Top," by Boudleaux and Felice Bryant, was adopted in 1982.[53]

TEXAS

In 1928 the Texas legislature adopted "Texas, Our Texas" by William J. Marsh and Gladys Yoakum Wright as the official state song. This song was chosen following contests in each senatorial district and a final contest in Dallas, after which a legislative committee chose it twice.[54]

In 1933 the legislature designated a state flower song: "Bluebonnets," words by Julia D. Booth and music by Lora C. Crockett.[55]

UTAH

"Utah We Love Thee" was designated Utah's state song in 1937. It was written by Evan Stephens.[56]

VERMONT

In 1937 a committee was empowered to select an official state song. "Hail, Vermont!" was selected from over 100 songs in 1938, and the governor was informed of the selection. The song was written by Josephine Hovey Perry.[57]

VIRGINIA

"Carry Me Back to Old Virginia" by James B. Bland was declared by the General Assembly to be the official Commonwealth of Virginia song in 1940.[58]

WASHINGTON

"Washington My Home" by Helen Davis was designated the official state song of Washington in 1959. In 1987, Washington also designated an official state folk song, "Roll On Columbia, Roll On," which was composed by Woody Guthrie.[59]

WEST VIRGINIA

West Virginia has adopted three state songs. "This Is My West Virginia" was written and composed by Mrs. Iris Bell of Charleston. "West Virginia My Home Sweet Home," words and music by Colonel Julian G. Hearne, Jr., was designated the official state song in 1947. The third song, "The West Virginia Hills," was written in 1879 by the Reverend David King as a poem for his wife, Ellen King. Mrs. King's name may be found on the music, as this was the request of the poet. H. E. Engle put the poem to music in 1885, and it was designated an official state song in 1961.[60]

WISCONSIN

"On, Wisconsin" was designated the state song of Wisconsin in 1959.[61] The song was composed in 1909 by William T. Purdy as a football fight song. While the song was recognized unofficially as the state song, several lyrics had come into existence in the fifty years before it was officially designated the state song. The 1959 law therefore actually prescribes the words to be used.[62]

WYOMING

In 1955 the march song "Wyoming," words by Charles E. Winter and music by George E. Knapp, was designated Wyoming's official state song.[63]

DISTRICT OF COLUMBIA

The District of Columbia has no official song.

AMERICAN SAMOA

In 1973, "Amerika Samoa" was designated the official song of the territory.[64]

COMMONWEALTH OF THE NORTHERN MARIANA ISLANDS

The Commonwealth has not declared an official song.

GUAM

Guam has both an official territorial hymn and an official territorial march. "Guam Hymn," composed by Dr. Ramon M. Sablan, is the official hymn and "Guam March," composed by Jose Martinez Torres, is the official march.[65]

PUERTO RICO

"La Borinquena" was made the Commonwealth's anthem in 1952. In 1977, the music and lyrics of this *danza* by Don Manuel Fernandez Juncos were adopted as the anthem.[66]

U.S. VIRGIN ISLANDS

"Virgin Islands March," composed by Alton A. Adams, Sr., is the official Virgin Islands anthem. It was adopted in 1982.[67]

NOTES

1. Ala. Code §1–2–16; *Alabama State Emblems* (Montgomery: Alabama State Department of Archives and History, n.d.), pp. 20–21.
2. 1931 Ala. Acts 190.
3. Alaska Stat. §44.09.040.
4. *Alaska Blue Book 1979,* p. 123.
5. *Welcome to Arizona* (Phoenix: Arizona Office of Tourism, n.d.).
6. Ark. Code Ann. (1987) §1–4–116.
7. *California's Legislature, 1984,* p. 203.
8. Colo. Rev. Stat. §24–80–909.
9. Conn. Gen. Stat. Ann. §3–110c (West).
10. *Official Insignia of Delaware* (Dover: Delaware State Development Department, n.d.).
11. 1935 Fla. Laws 1540.
12. Ga. Code Ann. §50–3–60.
13. *The State of Georgia and Its Capitol* (Atlanta: State Museum of Science and Industry, Department of Archives and History, 1979), p. 11.
14. 1951 Ga. Laws 842.
15. Haw. Rev. Stat. §5–10.
16. "Idaho State Song," Idaho Historical Society Reference Series no. 125 (Boise: Idaho Historical Society, December 1984), p. 1.
17. Ill. Ann. Stat. ch. 1, §3008 (Smith-Hurd).
18. Ind. Code Ann. §1–2–6–1 (West).
19. *1985–86 Iowa Official Register,* vol. 61, p. 238.
20. Ibid., p. 239.
21. Kan. Stat. Ann. §73–1301.
22. *Kansas Directory, 1982,* p. 128.
23. Kan. Stat. Ann. §73–801.
24. Ky. Rev. Stat. Ann. §2.100 (Baldwin).
25. *Louisiana Facts* (Baton Rouge: Louisiana Department of State, n.d.); La. Rev. Stat. Ann. §49–155.2 (West).
26. Me. Rev. Stat. tit. 1, §210.
27. Md. Ann. Code §13–307.
28. *Maryland Manual, 1981–1982,* p. 10.
29. Mass. Gen. Laws ch. 2, §19, §20, §31 (West).
30. *Journal of the Michigan House of Representatives, 1937,* pp. 171, 1183.
31. *Minnesota Legislative Manual, 1958,* pp. 16–17; *Official Minnesota Symbols* (St. Paul: Minnesota Historical Society, December 1983), p. 1.
32. *Souvenir of Mississippi* (Jackson: Dick Molpus, n.d.), p. 28.
33. Mo. Ann. Stat. §10.050 (Vernon).
34. Mont. Rev. Codes Ann. §1–1–511; Rex C. Myers, *Symbols of Montana* (Helena: Montana Historical Society, 1976), p. 14.
35. Neb. Rev. Stat. §90–111.
36. Nev. Rev. Stat. §235.030.
37. N.H. Rev. Stat. Ann. §3:7, §3:7-a.
38. *Manual of the Legislature of New Jersey, 1984,* pp. 11–12.

39. N.M. Stat. Ann. §12–3–5, §12–3–6.
40. Ibid., §12–3–10.
41. Information supplied by Maureen Bigness, Director of Information Services, Department of State, Albany, New York.
42. N.C. Gen Stat. §149–1, §149–2.
43. N.D. Cent. Code §54–02–04.
44. Ibid., §54–02–09.
45. Ohio Rev. Code Ann. §5.09 (Baldwin).
46. *Ohio Almanac* (Lorain: Lorain Journal Co., 1977), pp. 46, 60.
47. Okla. Stat. Ann. tit. 25, §94.1, §94.3 (West).
48. *Journals of the Oregon Senate and House of the 34th Legislative Assembly, Regular Session, 1927,* p. 35.
49. Pa. Stat. Ann. tit. 1, §1010.4 (Purdon).
50. R.I. Gen. Laws §42–4–4.
51. S.C. Code §1–1–685; *South Carolina State Symbols and Emblems* (Columbia: House of Representatives, n.d.).
52. *South Dakota Signs and Symbols* (n.p., n.d.).
53. Tenn. Code Ann. §4–1–302.
54. Tex. Rev. Civ. Stat. Ann. art. 6143b (Vernon).
55. Ibid., art. 6143bb (Vernon).
56. Utah Code Ann. §63–13–8.
57. 1937 Vt. Acts 350; *Vermont Legislative Directory and State Manual, 1979–80,* p. 19.
58. Va. Code §7.1–37.
59. Wash. Rev. Code Ann. §1.20.070, §1.20.073.
60. *West Virginia Blue Book, 1980,* p. 924.
61. Wis. Stat. Ann. §1.10 (West).
62. *State of Wisconsin 1983–84 Blue Book,* p. 948.
63. Wyo. Stat. Ann. §8–3–108.
64. A.S. Code tit. 1, §1105.
65. G.C.A., tit. 1, §416.
66. P.R. Laws Ann. tit. 1, §38, §39.
67. V.I. Code Ann. tit. 1, §104.

10 State and Territory Legal Holidays and Observances

Legal holidays are prescribed by law to commemorate important historical events, religious holidays, or people who have made significant contributions to society. Many of the states and territories recognize federal holidays, but they also add to the list of legal holidays their own special celebrations. Robert E. Lee's Birthday, for example, is a holiday in many southern states. Hawaii celebrates King Kamehameha I Day; Illinois celebrates Casimir Pulaski's Birthday; and Guam celebrates Lady Camarin Day.

Observances are not necessarily legal holidays, but days, weeks, or months recognized in the laws of many of the states and territories as worthy of special honor and remembrance. Some state codes may designate a legal holiday also as a special day of observance. Massachusetts sets out some 135 observances in its laws. They include such things as Homeless Unity Day, Armenian Martyrs' Day, Visiting Nurse Association Week, Rose Fitzgerald Kennedy Day, and Commodore John Barry Day. Taken all together, the observances provide an outline of historical, cultural, and social events in the states and territories.

ALABAMA

Legal Holidays

1. Sunday
2. New Year's Day (January 1)

3. Robert E. Lee's Birthday (third Monday in January)
4. Martin Luther King, Jr.'s Birthday (third Monday in January)
5. George Washington's Birthday (third Monday in February)
6. Thomas Jefferson's Birthday (third Monday in February)
7. Confederate Memorial Day (fourth Monday in April)
8. National Memorial Day (last Monday in May)
9. Jefferson Davis' Birthday (first Monday in June)
10. Independence Day (July 4)
11. Labor Day (first Monday in September)
12. Columbus Day (second Monday in October)
13. Fraternal Day (second Monday in October)
14. Veterans' Day (November 11)
15. Christmas Day (December 25)
16. Any day proclaimed by the governor as Thanksgiving

Notes: In Mobile and Baldwin counties, Mardi Gras is a legal holiday. Holidays falling on a Sunday are observed the next day. Holidays falling on a Saturday are observed on the preceding day.[1]

ALASKA

Legal Holidays

1. Sunday
2. New Year's Day (January 1)
3. Martin Luther King, Jr.'s Birthday (third Monday in January)
4. Presidents' Day (third Monday in February)
5. Seward's Day (last Monday in March)
6. Memorial Day (last Monday in May)
7. Independence Day (July 4)
8. Labor Day (first Monday in September)
9. Alaska Day (October 18)
10. Veterans' Day (November 11)
11. Thanksgiving Day (fourth Thursday in November)
12. Christmas Day (December 25)
13. Any day publicly proclaimed by the governor or the president of the United States as a legal holiday[2]

Notes: When a holiday (other than a Sunday itself) falls on a Sunday, both that Sunday and the following Monday are legal holidays. When a holiday falls on a Saturday, both that Saturday and the preceding Friday are both legal holidays.[3]

Observances

Ernest Gruening Day (February 6)[4]
Elizabeth Peratrovich Day (February 16)[5]
Bob Bartlett Day (April 20)[6]
Wickersham Day (August 24)[7]
William A. Egan Day (October 8)[8]
Anthony J. Dimond Day (November 30)[9]

ARIZONA

Legal Holidays

1. Sunday of each week
2. New Year's Day (January 1)
3. Lincoln Day (second Monday in February)
4. Washington Day (third Monday in February)
5. Mother's Day (second Sunday in May)
6. Memorial Day (last Monday in May)
7. Father's Day (third Sunday in June)
8. Independence Day (July 4)
9. American Family Day (first Sunday in August)
10. Labor Day (first Monday in September)
11. Constitution Day (September 17)
12. Columbus Day (second Monday in October)
13. Veterans' Day (November 11)
14. Thanksgiving Day (fourth Thursday in November)
15. Christmas Day (December 25)

Notes: A proposed amendment would combine Lincoln Day and Washington Day into Lincoln/Washington Presidents' Day, to be observed on the third Monday in February, and add Martin Luther King, Jr./Civil Rights Day on the third Monday in January. Except for holidays numbered 1, 5, 7, 9, and 11, when a holiday falls on a Sunday, it is observed on the following Monday. If New Year's Day, Independence Day, Veterans' Day, or Christmas Day falls on a Saturday, it is observed on the preceding Friday. If Constitution Day falls on a day other than Sunday, it is observed on the Sunday preceding September 17.[10]

Observances

Arbor Day (Friday following April 1 in Apache, Coconino, Mohave, Navajo, and Yavapai counties, and the Friday following February 1 in other counties)

Korean War Veterans' Day (July 27)[11]

ARKANSAS

Legal Holidays

1. New Year's Day (January 1)
2. Martin Luther King, Jr.'s Birthday and Robert E. Lee's Birthday (third Monday in January)
3. George Washington's Birthday (third Monday in February)
4. Memorial Day (last Monday in May)
5. Independence Day (July 4)
6. Labor Day (first Monday in September)
7. Veterans' Day (November 11)
8. Thanksgiving Day (fourth Thursday in November)
9. Christmas Eve (December 24)
10. Christmas Day (December 25)

Notes: State employees are granted holidays for their birthdays. Holidays falling on Sunday are observed on the next Monday and holidays falling on Saturday are observed on the preceding Friday.[12]

Observances

General Douglas MacArthur Day (January 26)

Abraham Lincoln's Birthday (February 12)

Arkansas Teachers' Day (first Tuesday in March)

Patriots' Day (April 19)

Arkansas Bird Day (April 26)

Good Friday (Friday preceding Easter)

Jefferson Davis' Birthday (June 3)

Columbus Day (October 12)

Arbor Day (third Monday in March)[13]

In addition, the state of Arkansas has designated three other special days:

Prisoners of War Remembrance Day (April 9)[14]

Confederate Flag Day (Saturday preceding Easter Sunday)[15]

White Cane Safety Day (October 15)[16]

CALIFORNIA

Legal Holidays

1. Every Sunday
2. New Year's Day (January 1)
3. Dr. Martin Luther King, Jr., Day (third Monday in January)
4. Lincoln Day (February 12)
5. Presidents' Day (third Monday in February)
6. Memorial Day (last Monday in May)
7. Labor Day (first Monday in September)
8. Admission Day (September 9)
9. Columbus Day (second Monday in October)
10. Veterans' Day (November 11)
11. Christmas Day (December 25)
12. Good Friday from noon to 3:00 P.M. (Friday preceding Easter)
13. Days proclaimed by the governor or the president of the United States for public fast, thanksgiving, or holiday[17]

Notes: If the holidays of January 1, February 12, July 4, September 9, November 11, or December 25 fall on Sunday, the following Monday is a holiday. If Veterans' Day (November 11) falls on a Saturday, the preceding Friday is a holiday.[18]

Observances

A Day of Remembrance: Japanese American Evacuation (February 19)[19]

Arbor Day (March 7)[20]

John Muir Day (April 21)[21]

California American Indian Day (fourth Friday in September)[22]

Cabrillo Day (September 28)[23]

Stepparents' Day (first Sunday in October)[24]

Pearl Harbor Day (December 7)[25]

COLORADO

Legal Holidays

1. New Year's Day (January 1)
2. Dr. Martin Luther King, Jr.'s Birthday (third Monday in January)
3. Washington-Lincoln Day (third Monday in February)
4. Memorial Day (last Monday in May)
5. Independence Day (July 4)
6. Labor Day (first Monday in September)
7. Columbus Day (second Monday in October)
8. Veterans' Day (November 11)
9. Thanksgiving Day (fourth Thursday in November)
10. Christmas Day (December 25)
11. Any days proclaimed by the governor or the President of the United States for thanksgiving, prayer, or fasting
12. Saturdays from noon until midnight during the months of June, July, and August in cities with a population of 25,000 or more

Note: When holidays fall on Sundays, the following day is considered to be the holiday.[26]

Observances

Susan B. Anthony Day (February 15)

Arbor Day (third Friday in April)

Good Roads Day (second Friday in May)

Colorado Day (first Monday of August)

Leif Erikson Day (October 9)[27]

Alabama

Alaska

Arizona

Arkansas

California

Colorado

Connecticut

Delaware

Florida

Georgia

Hawaii

Idaho

Illinois

Iowa

Indiana

Kansas

Louisiana

Kentucky

Maine

Massachusetts

Maryland

Michigan

Mississippi

Minnesota

Missouri

Montana

Nebraska

Nevada

New Hampshire

New Jersey

New Mexico

New York

North Carolina

North Dakota

Ohio

Oklahoma

Oregon

Pennsylvania

South Carolina

Rhode Island

South Dakota

Texas

Tennessee

Utah

Virginia

Vermont

Washington

Wisconsin

West Virginia

Wyoming

District of Columbia

American Samoa

CNMI

Guam

Puerto Rico

U.S. Virgin Islands

Alaska

Alabama

Arizona

California

Arkansas

Colorado

Delaware

Connecticut

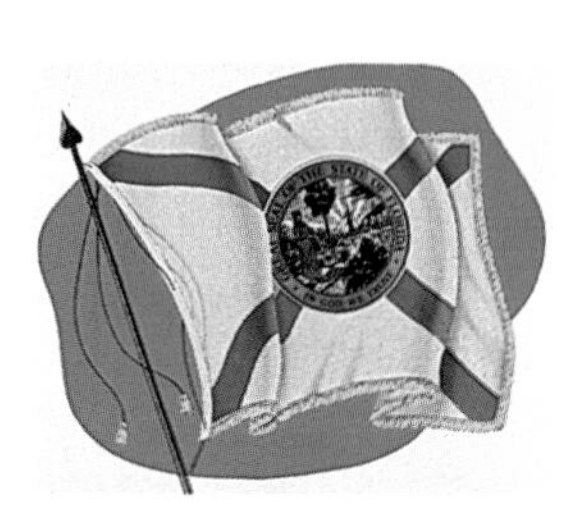

Florida

Hawaii

Georgia

Idaho

Illinois

Iowa

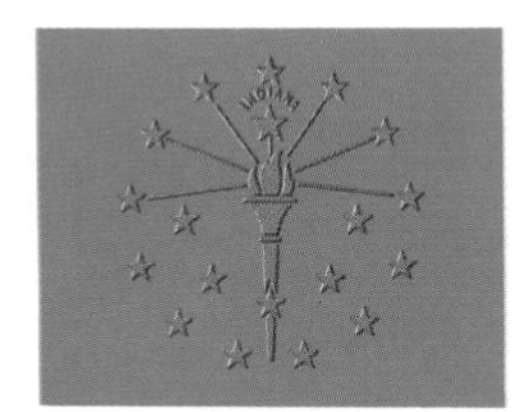

Indiana

Kansas

Louisiana

Kentucky

Maine

Massachusetts

Maryland

Michigan

Mississippi

Minnesota

Missouri

Montana

Nevada

Nebraska

New Hampshire

New Mexico

New Jersey

New York

North Dakota

North Carolina

Ohio

Oregon

Oklahoma

Pennsylvania

Rhode Island

South Carolina

South Dakota

Tennessee

Texas

Utah

Vermont

Virginia

Washington

West Virginia

Wisconsin

Wyoming

District of Columbia
(Insignia)

American Samoa

CNMI

Guam

Puerto Rico

U.S. Virgin Islands

Camellia
Alabama

Forget-Me-Not
Alaska

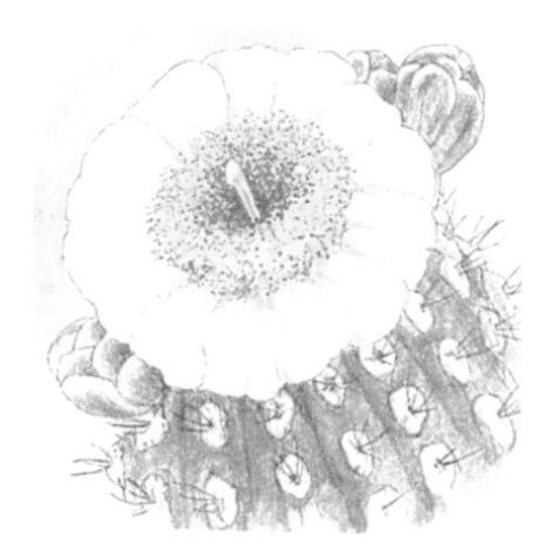

Saguaro
Arizona

Apple Blossom
Arkansas, Michigan

Golden Poppy
California

Columbine
Colorado

Mountain Laurel
Connecticut, Pennsylvania

Peach Blossom
Delaware

Orange Blossom
Florida

Cherokee Rose
Georgia

Hibiscus
Hawaii

Syringa
Idaho

Violet
Illinois, New Jersey, Wisconsin

Peony
Indiana

Wild Rose
Iowa

Wild Native Sunflower
Kansas

Goldenrod
Kentucky, Nebraska

Magnolia
Louisiana, Mississippi

Pine Cone and Tassel
Maine

Black-Eyed Susan
Maryland

Mayflower
Massachusetts

Pink and White Lady Slipper
Minnesota

Red Haw Blossom
Missouri

Bitterroot
Montana

Sagebrush
Nevada

Purple Lilac
New Hampshire

Yucca Flower
New Mexico

Rose
New York

Dogwood
North Carolina, Virginia

Wild Prairie Rose
North Dakota

Scarlet Carnation
Ohio

Mistletoe
Oklahoma

Oregon Grape
Oregon

Wood Violet
Rhode Island

Yellow Jessamine
South Carolina

American Pasque Flower
South Dakota

Iris
Tennessee

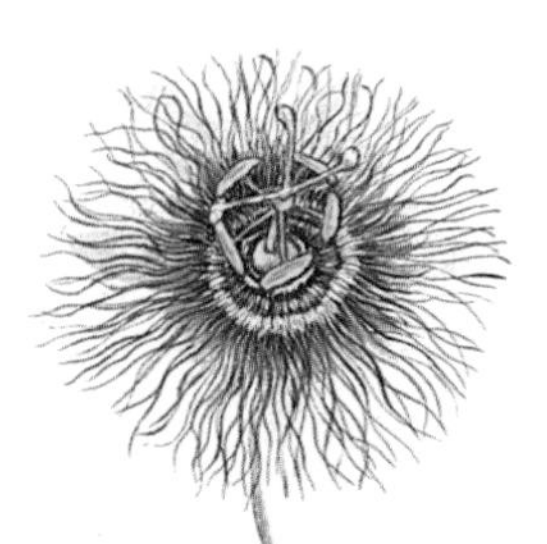

Passion Flower
Tennessee

Bluebonnet
Texas

Segolily
Utah

Red Clover
Vermont

Pink Rhododendron
Washington

Rhododendron Maximum
West Virginia

Indian Paintbrush
Wyoming

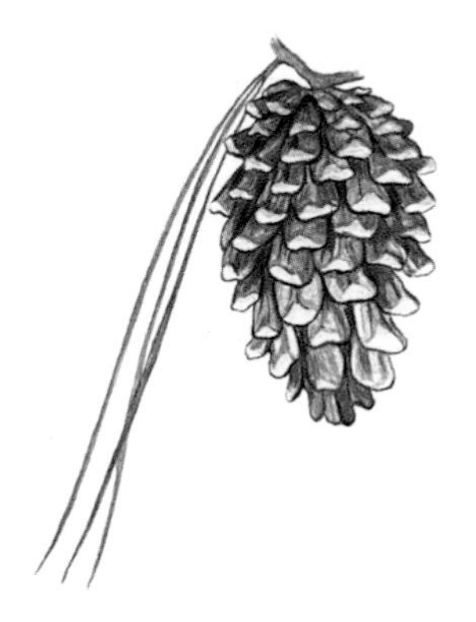

Southern Pine
Alabama, Arkansas, North Carolina

Sitka Spruce
Alaska

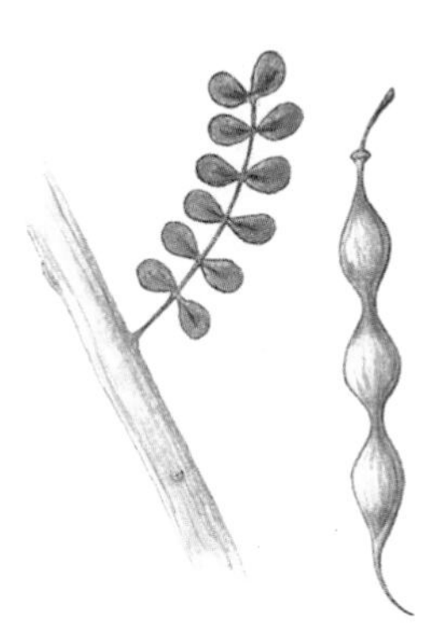

Palo Verde
Arizona

California Redwood
California

Giant Sequoia
California

Blue Spruce
Colorado, Utah

White Oak
Connecticut, Illinois, Iowa, Maryland

American Holly
Delaware

Sabal Palmetto Palm
Florida, South Carolina

Live Oak
Georgia

Kukui Tree
Hawaii

Western White Pine
Idaho

Tulip Tree
Indiana, Tennessee

Cottonwood
Kansas, Nebraska, Wyoming

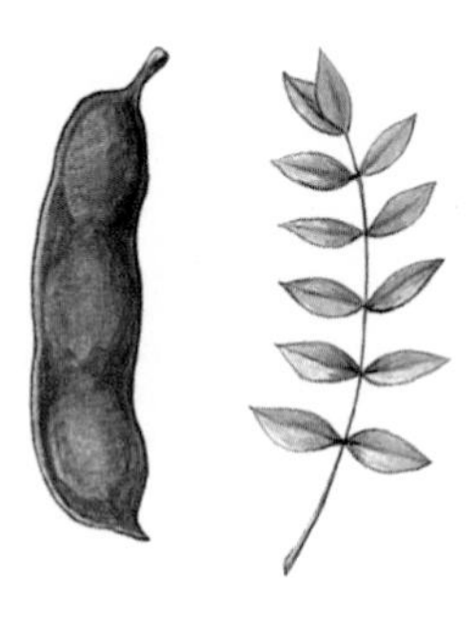

Coffeetree
Kentucky

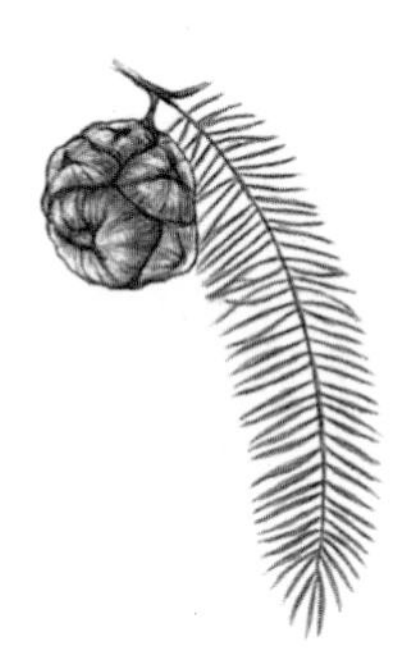

Bald Cypress
Louisiana

Eastern White Pine
Maine, Michigan

American Elm
Massachusetts, North Dakota

Red Pine
Minnesota

Magnolia
Mississippi

Flowering Dogwood
Missouri, Virginia

Ponderosa Pine
Montana

Single-Leaf Pinon
Nevada

White Birch
New Hampshire

Northern Red Oak
New Jersey, Iowa

Nut Pine
New Mexico

Sugar Maple
New York, Vermont, West Virginia, Wisconsin

Buckeye
Ohio

Redbud Tree
Oklahoma

Douglas Fir
Oregon

Hemlock
Pennsylvania

Red Maple
Rhode Island

Black Hills Spruce
South Dakota

Pecan Tree
Texas

Western Hemlock
Washington

Yellow-Hammer
Alabama

Wild Turkey
Alabama, South Carolina

Willow Ptarmigan
Alaska

Cactus Wren
Arizona

Mockingbird
Arkansas, Florida, Mississippi, Tennessee, Texas

California Valley Quail
California

Lark Bunting
Colorado

Robin
Connecticut, Michigan, Wisconsin

Blue Hen Chicken
Delaware

Bobwhite Quail
Georgia

Brown Thrasher
Georgia

Nene
Hawaii

Mountain Bluebird
Idaho, Nevada

Cardinal
Illinois, Indiana, Kentucky, North Carolina, Ohio, Virginia, West Virginia

Eastern Goldfinch
Iowa, New Jersey

Western Meadowlark
Kansas, Montana, Nebraska, North Dakota, Oregon, Wyoming

Brown Pelican
Louisiana

Chickadee
Maine, Massachusetts

Baltimore Oriole
Maryland

Loon
Minnesota

Wood Duck
Mississippi

Bluebird
Missouri, New York

Purple Finch
New Hampshire

Chaparral Bird
New Mexico

Scissor-Tailed Flycatcher
Oklahoma

Ruffed Grouse
Pennsylvania

Rhode Island Red
Rhode Island

Carolina Wren
South Carolina

Ring-Neck Pheasant
South Dakota

Sea Gull
Utah

Hermit Thrush
Vermont

Willow Goldfinch
Washington

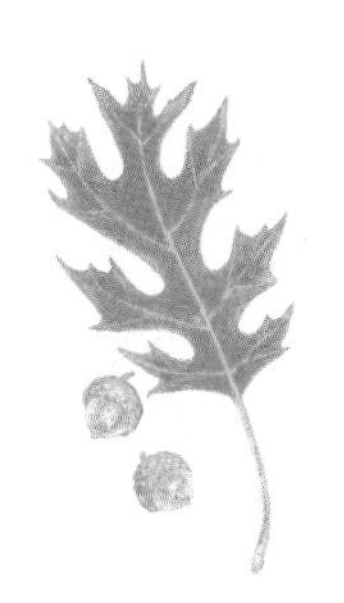

Scarlet Oak Tree
District of Columbia

American Beauty Rose
District of Columbia

Wood Thrush
District of Columbia

Paogo (Pandanus Tree)
American Samoa

Flame Tree
CNMI

Plumeria
CNMI

Ifit Tree
Guam

Puti-tai-nobio (Bougainvillea)
Guam

Red-Capped Fruit Dove
Guam

Yellow Elder
U.S. Virgin Islands

Bananaquit
U.S. Virgin Islands

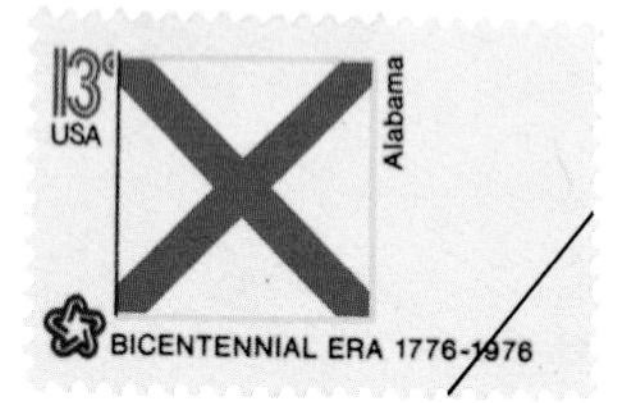

Alabama

Alaska

Arizona

Arkansas

California

Colorado

Connecticut

Delaware*

Florida

Georgia

Hawaii

Idaho

*© U.S. Postal Service

Illinois*

Indiana

Iowa

Kansas

Kentucky

Louisiana

Maine

Maryland

Massachusetts

Michigan

Minnesota

Mississippi

Missouri

Nebraska

Nevada

Montana stamp (same as Washington)

New Hampshire

New Jersey

New Mexico

New York

North Carolina

Ohio

North Dakota stamp (same as Washington)

Oklahoma

Oregon

Pennsylvania*

Rhode Island

South Carolina

South Dakota

Tennessee

Texas

Utah

Vermont

Virginia*

Washington

West Virginia

Wisconsin

Wyoming

District of Columbia

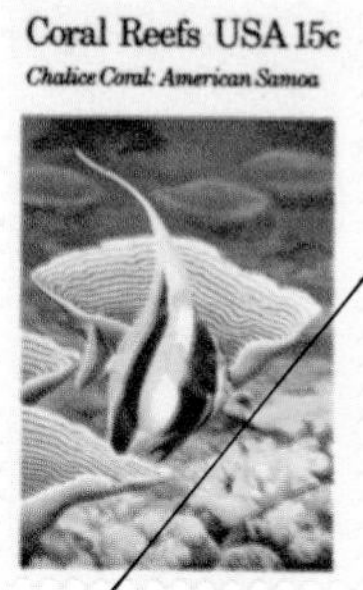

American Samoa*

CNMI*

Puerto Rico

U.S. Virgin Islands

Alabama

Alaska

Arizona

Arkansas

California

Colorado

Connecticut

Delaware

Florida

Georgia

Hawaii

Idaho

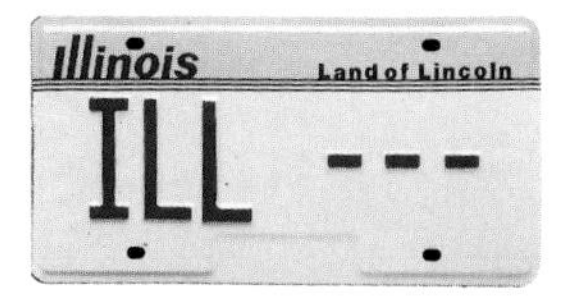

Illinois

Indiana

Iowa

Kansas

Kentucky

Louisiana

Maine

Maryland

Massachusetts

Michigan

Minnesota

Mississippi

Missouri

Montana

Nebraska

NEVADA
123 · ABC
THE SILVER STATE

Nevada

New Hampshire

New Jersey

New Mexico

New York

North Carolina

North Dakota

Ohio

Oklahoma

Oregon

Pennsylvania

Rhode Island

South Carolina

South Dakota

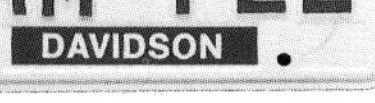

Tennessee

Texas

Utah

Vermont

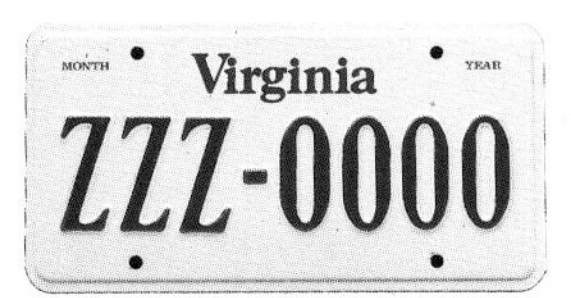

Virginia

Washington

West Virginia

Wisconsin

Wyoming

District of Columbia

American Samoa

CNMI

Puerto Rico

U.S. Virgin Islands

CONNECTICUT

Legal Holidays

1. New Year's Day (January 1)
2. Martin Luther King Day (first Monday after January 15)
3. Lincoln Day (February 12)
4. Washington's Birthday (third Monday in February)
5. Memorial Day (last Monday in May)
6. Independence Day (July 4)
7. Labor Day (first Monday in September)
8. Columbus Day (second Monday in October)
9. Veterans' Day (November 11)
10. Christmas Day (December 25)
11. Any day proclaimed or recommended by the governor or the President of the United States for thanksgiving, fasting, or religious observance

Notes: When holidays fall on a Sunday, the following Monday is a legal holiday; when holidays fall on a Saturday, the preceding Friday is a legal holiday. In the public schools, Presidents' Day may be observed on the third Monday in February in lieu of observing Washington's Birthday and Lincoln Day.[28]

Observances

Martin Luther King Day (first Monday on or after January 15)

Ukrainian-American Day (January 22)

Retired Teachers Day (third Wednesday in February)

St. Patrick's Day (March 17)

Pan American Day (April 14)

Friends Day (fourth Sunday in April)

Workers' Memorial Day (April 28)

Loyalty Day (May 1)

Senior Citizens Day (first Sunday in May)

Arbor Day (last Friday in May)

Flag Day (June 14)

Disability Awareness Day (July 26)

Volunteer Fire Fighter and Volunteer Emergency Medical Services Personnel Day (first Saturday in August)

End of World War II Day (August 14)

911 Day (September 11)

School Safety Patrol Day (second Monday in September)

Nathan Hale Day (last Friday in September)

Indian Day (last Friday in September)

Puerto Rico Day (fourth Sunday in September)

German-American Day (October 6)

Leif Erikson Day (a day within the first nine days of October)

Fire Prevention Day (on or about October 9)

Columbus Day (second Monday in October)

Veterans' Day (November 11)

Lithuanian Day (a date certain in each year)

Powered Flight Day (a date certain in each year)[29]

DELAWARE

Legal Holidays

1. New Year's Day (January 1)
2. Martin Luther King, Jr. Day (third Monday in January)
3. Presidents' Day (third Monday in February)
4. Good Friday (Friday preceding Easter)
5. Memorial Day (last Monday in May)
6. Independence Day (July 4)
7. Labor Day (first Monday in September)
8. Columbus Day (second Monday in October)
9. Veterans' Day (November 11)
10. Thanksgiving Day (fourth Thursday in November)
11. Christmas Day (December 25)
12. Saturdays
13. Day of the biennial election

Notes: Return Day (the second day after the general election) is a legal holiday after noon in Sussex County. If a legal holiday falls on Sunday, the following Monday is a legal holiday. If a legal holiday falls on Saturday, the preceding Friday is a legal holiday.[30]

Observances

Arbor Day (last Friday in April)
Delaware Day (December 7)[31]

FLORIDA

Legal Holidays

1. Sundays
2. New Year's Day (January 1)
3. Martin Luther King, Jr.'s Birthday (January 15)
4. Robert E. Lee's Birthday (January 19)
5. Lincoln's Birthday (February 12)
6. Washington's Birthday (third Monday in February)
7. Good Friday (Friday preceding Easter)
8. Pascua Florida Day (April 2)
9. Confederate Memorial Day (April 26)
10. Memorial Day (last Monday in May)
11. Jefferson Davis' Birthday (June 3)
12. Flag Day (June 14)
13. Independence Day (July 4)
14. Labor Day (first Monday in September)
15. Columbus Day and Farmers' Day (second Monday in October)
16. Veterans' Day (November 11)
17. General Election Day
18. Thanksgiving Day (fourth Thursday in November)
19. Christmas Day (December 25)
20. Days of mourning proclaimed by the President of the United States and the governor

Notes: In counties where carnival organizations exist to celebrate Mardi Gras, Shrove Tuesday is a legal holiday. Chief judges are authorized to designate Rosh Hashanah and Yom Kippur as legal holidays for courts in their judicial circuit. In Hillsborough County, Gasparilla Day and Parade Day of the Hillsborough County Fairs and Plant City Strawberry Festival are legal holidays. Desoto Day, the last Friday of Desoto Week, is a legal holiday in Manatee County. The days following holidays that fall on Sunday are public holidays.[32]

Observances

Arbor Day (third Friday in January)
Save the Florida Panther Day (third Saturday in March)
Pascua Florida Week (March 27 to April 2)
Florida State Day known as Pascua Florida Day (April 2)
Children's Day (second Tuesday in April)
Pan-American Day (April 14)
Patriots' Day (April 19)
Teacher's Day (third Friday in May)
Law Enforcement Appreciation Month (May)
Law Enforcement Memorial Day (May 15)
Juneteenth Day (June 19)
Grandmother's Day (second Sunday in October)
I Am an American Day (third Sunday in October)
Retired Teachers' Day (Sunday beginning the third week of November)[33]

GEORGIA

Legal Holidays

1. New Year's Day (January 1)
2. Martin Luther King, Jr., Day (third Monday in January)
3. Washington's Birthday (third Monday in February)
4. Memorial Day (last Monday in May)
5. Independence Day (July 4)
6. Labor Day (first Monday in September)
7. Columbus Day (second Monday in October)
8. Veterans' Day (November 11)
9. Thanksgiving Day (fourth Thursday in November)
10. Christmas Day (December 25)

Notes: In addition, any days proclaimed by the governor for fasting, prayer, or religious observance are also legal holidays. The governor is obligated by statute to close state offices for twelve days per year and must choose January 19, April 26, or June 3 as one of those legal holidays.[34]

Observances

Sundays (only official religious holidays)
American History Month (February)
Georgia History Month (February)
Girls and Women in Sports Day (first Thursday in February)
Law Enforcement Officer Appreciation Day (second Monday in February)
Wildflower Week (fourth week in March)
Former Prisoners of War Recognition Day (April 9)
Peace Officer Memorial Day (May 15)
Police Week (week in which May 15 falls)
Children's Day (first Sunday in October)
Bird Day (second Thursday in October)[35]

HAWAII

Legal Holidays

1. New Year's Day (January 1)
2. Dr. Martin Luther King, Jr., Day (third Monday in January)
3. Presidents' Day (third Monday in February)
4. Prince Jonah Kuhio Kalanianaole Day (March 26)
5. Good Friday (Friday preceding Easter)
6. Memorial Day (last Monday in May)
7. King Kamehameha I Day (June 11)
8. Independence Day (July 4)
9. Admission Day (third Friday in August)
10. Labor Day (first Monday in September)
11. Veterans' Day (November 11)
12. Thanksgiving Day (fourth Thursday in November)
13. Christmas Day (December 25)
14. Election days other than primaries and special elections in counties where elections are occurring
15. Any days designated as a holiday by the governor or the President of the United States

Notes: When a holiday falls on a Sunday, the following Monday is observed as a holiday. When a holiday falls on a Saturday, the preceding Friday is observed as a holiday.[36]

Observances

Baha'i New Year's Day (March 21)

Buddha Day (April 8)

Father Damien De Veuster Day (April 15)

Discoverers' Day (second Monday in October)

Respect for Our Elders Day (third Sunday in October)

Arbor Day (first Friday in November)

Bodhi Day (December 8)[37]

IDAHO

Legal Holidays

1. Sundays
2. New Year's Day (January 1)
3. Martin Luther King, Jr.–Idaho Human Rights Day (third Monday in January)
4. Washington's Birthday (third Monday in February)
5. Decoration Day (last Monday in May)
6. Independence Day (July 4)
7. Labor Day (first Monday in September)
8. Columbus Day (second Monday in October)
9. Veterans' Day (November 11)
10. Thanksgiving Day (fourth Thursday in November)
11. Christmas Day (December 25)
12. Any day designated by the governor or the President of the United States as a holiday or day of fasting or thanksgiving

Notes: When a holiday other than a Sunday itself falls on a Sunday, the following Monday is a holiday. When a holiday falls on a Saturday, the preceding Friday is a holiday.[38]

Observances

Constitutional Commemorative Day (September 17)[39]

ILLINOIS

Legal Holidays

1. New Year's Day (January 1)
2. Martin Luther King, Jr.'s Birthday (third Monday in January)
3. Abraham Lincoln's Birthday (February 12)
4. Presidents' Day (third Monday in February)
5. Casimir Pulaski's Birthday (first Monday in March)
6. Good Friday (Friday preceding Easter)
7. Memorial Day (May 30)
8. Independence Day (July 4)
9. Labor Day (first Monday in September)
10. Columbus Day (second Monday in October)
11. Veterans' Day (November 11)
12. Thanksgiving Day (fourth Thursday in November)
13. Christmas Day (December 25)
14. Election days (when House of Representatives elections occur)
15. Any days proclaimed as legal holidays by the governor

Note: Saturdays from noon to midnight are half-holidays.[40]

Observances

American History Month (February)
Arbor and Bird Day (last Friday in April)
Mothers' Day (second Sunday in May)
Citizenship Day (third Sunday in May)
Senior Citizens' Day (third Sunday in May)
Retired Teachers' Week (fourth week of May)
Flag Day (June 14)
Fathers' Day (third Sunday in June)
Gold Star Mothers' Day (second Sunday in August)
Prairie Week (third full week of September)

Grandmothers' Day (second Sunday in October)

Coal Miners Memorial Day (November 13)[41]

INDIANA

Legal Holidays

1. Sundays
2. New Year's Day (January 1)
3. Martin Luther King, Jr.'s Birthday (third Monday in January)
4. Abraham Lincoln's Birthday (third Monday in February)
5. Good Friday (Friday preceding Easter)
6. Memorial Day (last Monday in May)
7. Independence Day (July 4)
8. Labor Day (first Monday in September)
9. Columbus Day (second Monday in October)
10. Election Day (any general, municipal, or primary election)
11. Veterans' Day (November 11)
12. Thanksgiving Day (fourth Thursday in November)
13. Christmas Day (December 25)

Notes: When a holiday other than a Sunday itself falls on a Sunday, the following Monday is the legal holiday. When a holiday falls on a Saturday, the preceding Friday is the legal holiday.[42]

Observances

George Rogers Clark Day (February 25)

Casimir Pulaski Day (first Monday in March)

Flag Day (June 14)

Northwest Ordinance Day (July 13)

Indiana Day (December 11)[43]

IOWA

Legal Holidays

1. New Year's Day (January 1)
2. Dr. Martin Luther King, Jr.'s Birthday (third Monday in January)

3. Lincoln's Birthday (February 12)
4. Washington's Birthday (third Monday in February)
5. Memorial Day (last Monday in May)
6. Independence Day (July 4)
7. Labor Day (first Monday in September)
8. Veterans' Day (November 11)
9. Thanksgiving Day (fourth Thursday in November)
10. Christmas Day (December 25)[44]

Observances

Dr. Martin Luther King, Jr., Day (third Monday in January)
Mother's Day (second Sunday in May)
Father's Day (third Sunday in June)
Independence Sunday (Sunday preceding July 4 or July 4 if on a Sunday)
Herbert Hoover Day (August 10)
Columbus Day (October 12)
Youth Honor Day (October 31)
Veterans' Day (November 11)
Note: Veterans' Day is to be observed as a legal holiday.[45]

KANSAS

Legal Holidays

1. New Year's Day (January 1)
2. Lincoln's Birthday (February 12)
3. Washington's Birthday (third Monday in February)
4. Memorial Day (last Monday in May)
5. Independence Day (July 4)
6. Labor Day (first Monday in September)
7. Columbus Day (second Monday in October)
8. Veterans' Day (November 11)
9. Thanksgiving Day (fourth Thursday in November)
10. Christmas Day (December 25)[46]

Observances

Arbor Day (last Friday in March)
Mother's Day (second Sunday in May)
Flag Day (June 14)
American Indian Day (fourth Saturday in September)
General Pulaski's Memorial Day (October 11)
Pearl Harbor Remembrance Day (December 7)[47]

KENTUCKY

Legal Holidays

1. New Year's Day (January 1)
2. Martin Luther King, Jr.'s Birthday (third Monday in January)
3. Robert E. Lee Day (January 19)
4. Franklin D. Roosevelt Day (January 30)
5. Lincoln's Birthday (February 12)
6. Washington's Birthday (third Monday in February)
7. Memorial Day (last Monday in May)
8. Confederate Memorial Day and Jefferson Davis' Birthday (June 3)
9. Independence Day (July 4)
10. Labor Day (first Monday in September)
11. Columbus Day (second Monday in October)
12. Veterans' Day (November 11)
13. Christmas Day (December 25)
14. Any days proclaimed as holidays or days of thanksgiving by the governor or the President of the United States

Note: If a holiday falls on a Sunday, the following Monday is observed as a holiday.[48]

Observances

Barrier Awareness Day (May 7)
Retired Teachers' Week (fourth week of May)
Garden Week (first week of June)
Handicapped Day (August 2)[49]

LOUISIANA

Legal Holidays

1. Sundays
2. New Year's Day (January 1)
3. Battle of New Orleans (January 8)
4. Dr. Martin Luther King, Jr.'s Birthday (third Monday in January)
5. Robert E. Lee Day (January 19)
6. Washington's Birthday (third Monday in February)
7. Good Friday (Friday before Easter)
8. National Memorial Day (last Monday in May)
9. Confederate Memorial Day (June 3)
10. Independence Day (July 4)
11. Huey P. Long Day (August 30)
12. Labor Day (first Monday in September)
13. Columbus Day (second Monday in October)
14. All Saints' Day (November 1)
15. Veterans' Day (November 11)
16. Thanksgiving Day (fourth Thursday in November)
17. Christmas Day (December 25)
18. Any days proclaimed by the governor

Notes: When January 1, July 4, or December 25 falls on a Sunday, the next day is a holiday; when they fall on a Saturday, the preceding Friday is a holiday, if declared by ordinance.

Governing authorities of the parishes may declare Saturdays to be holidays, but if that is not accomplished, Saturdays from noon until midnight are half-holidays. The provision for Saturday half-holidays does not apply to the Parish of Orleans or Baton Rouge. In certain parishes and municipalities, Mardi Gras is a holiday if declared so by local authorities. When the governor declares the Friday following Thanksgiving Day a holiday, that holiday is designated as Acadian Day.[50]

Observances

Arbor Day (third Friday in January)

Doctors' Day (March 30)

Garden Week (first week in June)
My Nationality American Day (December 17)[51]

MAINE

Legal Holidays

1. Sundays
2. New Year's Day (January 1)
3. Martin Luther King, Jr., Day (third Monday in January)
4. Washington's Birthday (third Monday in February)
5. Patriot's Day (third Monday in April)
6. Memorial Day (last Monday in May)
7. Independence Day (July 4)
8. Labor Day (first Monday in September)
9. Columbus Day (second Monday in October)
10. Veterans' Day (November 11)
11. Christmas Day (December 25)

Notes: If the federal government designates May 30 as Memorial Day, it will be celebrated on May 30. When holidays fall on a Sunday, the following Monday is a holiday.[52]

Observances

American History Month (February)
National Women's History Week (week containing March 8)
Maine Cultural Heritage Week (week containing March 15)
Statehood Day (March 15)
Edmund S. Muskie Day (March 28)
Former Prisoner of War Recognition Day (April 9)
Arbor Week (third full week in May)
Maine Clear Water Week (first full week in June)
Garden Week (first full week in June)
Samantha Smith Day (first Monday in June)
Seamen's Memorial Day (second Sunday in June)
Saint Jean-Baptiste Day (June 24)
R. B. Hall Day (last Saturday in June)

Old Home Week (week beginning second Sunday in August)
Alcohol Awareness Week (first full week in September)
Deaf Culture Week (last full week in September)
Poetry Day (October 15)
Maine Business Women's Week (third full week in October)
Margaret Chase Smith Day (December 14)
Chester Greenwood Day (December 21)[53]

MARYLAND

Legal Holidays

1. New Year's Day (January 1)
2. Dr. Martin Luther King, Jr.'s Birthday (January 15)
3. Lincoln's Birthday (February 12)
4. Washington's Birthday (third Monday in February)
5. Maryland Day (March 25)
6. Good Friday (Friday preceding Easter)
7. Memorial Day (last Monday in May)
8. Independence Day (July 4)
9. Labor Day (first Monday in September)
10. Defenders' Day (September 12)
11. Columbus Day (second Monday in October)
12. Veterans' Day (November 11)
13. Thanksgiving Day (fourth Thursday in November)
14. Christmas Day (December 25)
15. General statewide election days
16. Any days designated by the President of the United States or governor for businesses to be closed

Note: Holidays falling on a Sunday are observed on the following Monday.[54]

Observances

John Hanson's Birthday (April 13)
Law Day USA (May 1)
Poetry Day (October 15)[55]

MASSACHUSETTS

Legal Holidays

1. New Year's Day (January 1)
2. Martin Luther King, Jr.'s Birthday (third Monday in January)
3. Presidents' Day (third Monday in February)
4. Patriots' Day (third Monday in April)
5. Memorial Day (last Monday in May)
6. Independence Day (July 4)
7. Labor Day (first Monday in September)
8. Columbus Day (second Monday in October)
9. Veterans' Day (November 11)
10. Thanksgiving Day (fourth Thursday in November)
11. Christmas Day (December 25)

Note: If January 1, July 4, November 11, or December 25 falls on a Sunday, the following Monday is a holiday.[56]

Observances

New Orleans Day (January 8)
Albert Schweitzer's Reverence for Life Day (January 14)
Martin Luther King, Jr. Day (January 15)
Jaycee Week (third week in January)
Jaycee Day (Wednesday of the third week in January)
Child Nutrition Week (last week in January)
American History Month (February)
Tadeusz Kosciuszko Day (first Sunday in February)
USO Appreciation Day (February 4)
Boy Scout Week (first full week of February)
Lincoln Day (February 12)
Spanish War Memorial Day and Maine Memorial Day (February 15)
Lithuanian Independence Day (February 16)
Iwo Jima Day (February 19)
Washington's Day (third Monday in February)
Homeless Unity Day (February 20)

Homeless Awareness Week (last week in February)
Kalevala Day (February 28)
Boston Massacre Anniversary (March 5)
Slovak Independence Day (March 14)
Peter Francisco Day (March 15)
Evacuation Day (March 17)
Employ the Older Worker Week (third week in March)
Practical Nursing Education Week (last full week in March)
Greek Independence Day (March 25)
Italian American War Veterans of the United States, Inc. Day (March 27)
Vietnam Veterans Day (March 29)
Parliamentary Law Month (April)
School Library Media Month (April)
Student Government Day (first Friday in April)
Veterans of World War I Hospital Day (first Sunday in April)
Bataan-Corregidor Day (April 9)
Former Prisoner of War Recognition Day (April 9)
Aunt's and Uncle's Day (second Sunday in April)
Patriots' Day (April 19)
Secretaries Week (last full week in April)
Licensed Practical Nurse Week (last full week in April)
Secretaries Day (Wednesday in the last full week in April)
Armenian Martyrs' Day (April 24)
Arbor and Bird Day (last Friday in April)
School Principals' Recognition Day (April 27)
Exercise Tiger Day (April 28)
Workers' Memorial day (fourth Friday in April)
Earth Week (one week in April, unspecified)
Senior Citizens Month (May)
Keep Massachusetts Beautiful Month (May)
Loyalty Day (May 1)
Polish Constitution Day (May 3)
Horace Mann Day (May 4)
Massachusetts Whale Awareness Day (first Thursday in May)
Mother's Day (second Sunday in May)

Police Officers' Week (week in which May 15 occurs)
Police Memorial Day (May 15)
Visiting Nurse Association Week (third week in May)
National Family Week (third week in May)
American Indian Heritage Week (third week in May)
Massachusetts National Guard Week (week preceding third Saturday in May)
Joshua James Day (third Sunday in May)
Anniversary of the Death of General Marquis de Lafayette (May 20)
Massosoit Day (Wednesday of the third week in May)
Maritime Day (May 22)
Anniversary of the Enlistment of Deborah Samson (May 23)
Massachusetts Art Week (last week in May)
Memorial Day (last Monday in May)
Presidents' Day (May 29)
Teachers' Day (first Sunday in June)
Retired Members of the Armed Forces Day (first Monday in June)
Public Employees Appreciation Day (first Wednesday in June)
Rabies Prevention Week (second week in June)
Children's Day (second Sunday in June)
Fire Fighters Memorial Sunday (second Sunday in June)
State Walking Sunday (second Sunday in June)
Flag Day (June 14)
Anniversary of the Battle of Bunker Hill (June 17)
Father's Day (third Sunday in June)
Destroyer Escort Day (third Saturday in June)
Saint Jean de Baptiste Day (fourth Sunday in June)
John Carver Day (fourth Sunday in June)
Battleship Massachusetts Memorial Day (last Saturday in June)
Reflex Sympathetic Dystrophy Awareness Month (July)
Independence Day (July 4)
Rose Fitzgerald Kennedy Day (July 22)
Korean War Veterans Day (July 27)
Public Employees Week (first week in August)
Jamaican Independence Day (first Monday in August)

Youth in Government Day (first Friday in August)
Purple Heart Day (August 7)
Social Security Day (August 14)
Liberty Tree Day (August 14)
Caribbean Week (last week in August)
Susan B. Anthony Day (August 26)
Sight-saving Month (September)
Literacy Awareness Month (September)
Labor Week (first week in September)
Endangered Species Day (second Saturday in September)
Grandparents' Day (Sunday after the first Monday in September)
Alzheimer's Awareness Week (week after the Sunday after the first Monday)
Commodore John Barry Day (September 13)
Constitution Day (September 17)
Cystic Fibrosis Week (third full week in September)
POW/MIA Day (third Friday in September)
National Hunting and Fishing Day (fourth Saturday in September)
Pro-Life Month (October)
Lupus Awareness Month (October)
Employee Involvement and Employee Ownership Week (first week in October)
Employ Handicapped Persons Week (first full week in October)
Senior Citizens' Day (first Sunday in October)
Independent Living Center Day (first Sunday in October)
Social Justice for Ireland Day (first Saturday in October)
Town Meeting Day (October 8)
Leif Ericson Day (October 8)
Columbus Day (second Monday in October)
Anniversary of the Death of Brigadier General Casimir Pulaski (October 11)
White Cane Safety Day (October 15)
United Nations Day (October 24)
State Constitution Day (October 25)
Statue of Liberty Awareness Day (October 26)
Youth Honor Day (October 31)

American Education Week (an unspecified week in October or November)

Massachusetts Hospice Week (second week in November)

Geographic Education Awareness Week (second week in November)

United States Marine Corps Day (November 10)

Veterans' Day (November 11)

Armistice Day (November 11)

Silver-Haired Legislature Days (third Wednesday, Thursday, and Friday in November)

John F. Kennedy Day (last Sunday in November)

American Education Week (an unspecified week in October or November)

Disabled American Veterans' Hospital Day (first Sunday in December)

Pearl Harbor Day (December 7)

Civil Rights Week (December 8–15)

Human Rights Day (December 10)

Army and Navy Union Day (second Saturday in December)

Samuel Slater Day (December 20)

Traffic Safety Week (unspecified)

Veteran Firemen's Muster Day (unspecified)[57]

MICHIGAN

Legal Holidays

1. New Year's Day (January 1)
2. Martin Luther King, Jr. Day (third Monday in January)
3. Lincoln's Birthday (February 12)
4. Washington's Birthday (third Monday in February)
5. Memorial Day (last Monday in May)
6. Independence Day (July 4)
7. Labor Day (first Monday in September)
8. Columbus Day (second Monday in October)
9. Veterans' Day (November 11)
10. Thanksgiving Day (fourth Thursday in November)
11. Christmas Day (December 25)
12. Saturdays from noon until midnight

Note: When January 1, February 12, July 4, November 11, or December 25 falls on a Sunday, the following Monday is a holiday.[58]

Observances

John Fitzgerald Kennedy Day (May 29)

Michigan Garden Week (first full week in June)

Log Cabin Day (last Sunday in June)

American Family Day (last Sunday in August)

Michigan Indian Day (fourth Friday in September)

Casimir Pulaski Day (October 11)

Arbor Day (unspecified, to be designated by governor)[59]

MINNESOTA

Legal Holidays

1. New Year's Day (January 1)
2. Martin Luther King's Birthday (third Monday in January)
3. Washington's and Lincoln's Birthday (third Monday in February)
4. Memorial Day (last Monday in May)
5. Independence Day (July 4)
6. Labor Day (first Monday in September)
7. Christopher Columbus Day (second Monday in October)
8. Veterans' Day (November 11)
9. Thanksgiving Day (fourth Thursday in November)
10. Christmas Day (December 25)

Note: When New Year's Day, Independence Day, Veterans' Day, or Christmas Day falls on a Sunday, the following day is a holiday. When they fall on a Saturday, the preceding day is a holiday.[60]

Observances

American Family Day (first Sunday in August)[61]

MISSISSIPPI

Legal Holidays

1. New Year's Day (January 1)
2. Robert E. Lee's and Dr. Martin Luther King, Jr's Birthday (third Monday in January)
3. Washington's Birthday (third Monday in February)
4. Confederate Memorial Day (last Monday in April)
5. National Memorial Day and Jefferson Davis' Birthday (last Monday in May)
6. Independence Day (July 4)
7. Labor Day (first Monday in September)
8. Veterans' Day (November 11)
9. Thanksgiving Day (fourth Thursday in November)
10. Christmas Day (December 25)

Note: When a holiday falls on a Sunday, the following Monday is a legal holiday.[62]

Observances

Hernando de Soto Week (first week of May)

Hernando de Soto Day (May 8)

Elvis Aaron Presley Day (August 16)

Retired Teachers Day (Sunday preceding Thanksgiving Day)[63]

MISSOURI

Legal Holidays

1. New Year's Day (January 1)
2. Martin Luther King Day (third Monday in January)
3. Lincoln Day (February 12)
4. Washington's Birthday (third Monday in February)
5. Truman Day (May 8)
6. Memorial Day (last Monday in May)
7. Independence Day (July 4)
8. Labor Day (first Monday in September)

9. Columbus Day (second Monday in October)
10. Veterans' Day (November 11)
11. Christmas Day (December 25)

Note: When holidays fall on a Sunday, the following Monday is considered the holiday.[64]

Observances

Arbor Day (first Friday in April)

Prisoner of War Remembrance Day (April 9)

Jefferson Day (April 13)

Law Day (May 1)

Truman Day (May 8)

Flag Day (June 14)

Korean War Veterans Day (July 27)

Missouri Day (third Wednesday of October)[65]

MONTANA

Legal Holidays

1. Sundays
2. New Year's Day (January 1)
3. Martin Luther King, Jr. Day (third Monday in January)
4. Lincoln's and Washington's Birthdays (third Monday in February)
5. Memorial Day (last Monday in May)
6. Independence Day (July 4)
7. Labor Day (first Monday in September)
8. Columbus Day (second Monday in October)
9. Veterans' Day (November 11)
10. Thanksgiving Day (fourth Thursday in November)
11. Christmas Day (December 25)
12. State general election day

Note: When holidays other than Sundays fall on a Sunday, the following Monday is a holiday.[66]

Observances

Right to Keep and Bear Arms Week (week beginning first Monday in March)

Arbor Day (last Friday in April)

Montana's Hunting Heritage Week (week beginning the third Monday in September)[67]

NEBRASKA

Legal Holidays

1. New Year's Day (January 1)
2. Birthday of Martin Luther King, Jr. (third Monday in January)
3. Presidents' Day (third Monday in February)
4. Arbor Day (last Friday in April)
5. Memorial Day (last Monday in May)
6. Independence Day (July 4)
7. Labor Day (first Monday in September)
8. Columbus Day (second Monday in October)
9. Veterans' Day (November 11)
10. Thanksgiving Day (fourth Thursday in November)
11. Day after Thanksgiving
12. Christmas Day (December 25)

Notes: The following Monday is a holiday when any holiday listed above falls on a Sunday. Except for Veterans' Day, the federal holiday takes precedence over the state-designated day.[68]

Observances

George W. Norris Day (January 5)

Martin Luther King, Jr. Day (January 15)

State Day (March 1. If falling on a weekend, the governor may proclaim either the preceding Friday or the following Monday as State Day.)

Workers Memorial Day (April 28)

Pioneers' Memorial Day (second Sunday in June)

Howard's Day (September 2)

American Indian Day (fourth Monday in September)

White Cane Safety Day (October 15)

Veterans' Day (November 11)

Thanksgiving Day (fourth Thursday in November)[69]

NEVADA

Legal Holidays

1. New Year's Day (January 1)
2. Martin Luther King, Jr.'s Birthday (third Monday in January)
3. Washington's Birthday (third Monday in February)
4. Memorial Day (last Monday in May)
5. Independence Day (July 4)
6. Labor Day (first Monday in September)
7. Nevada Day (October 31)
8. Veterans' Day (November 11)
9. Thanksgiving Day (fourth Thursday in November)
10. Family Day (Friday after Thanksgiving)
11. Christmas Day (December 25)
12. Any day other than the fourth Monday in October, observed as Veterans' Day, appointed by the President of the United States as a legal holiday or a day of public fast or thanksgiving

Notes: If New Year's Day, Independence Day, Nevada Day, Veterans' Day, or Christmas Day falls on a Sunday, the next Monday must be observed as a legal holiday. If any of those holidays falls on a Saturday, the preceding Friday must be observed as a legal holiday. October 12, 1992, was declared a legal holiday to celebrate the 500th anniversary of Christopher Columbus' discovery of the New World.[70]

Observances

Arbor Day (last Friday in April)

Law Day USA (May 1)

Mother's Day (second Sunday in May)

Nevada Mineral Industry Week (first week in June)

Nevada All-Indian Stampede Days (third week in July)

Constitution Day (September 17)

Constitution Week (third week in September)

Nevada Indian Day (fourth Friday in September)
Columbus Day (second Monday in October)[71]

NEW HAMPSHIRE

Legal Holidays

1. New Year's Day (January 1)
2. Civil Rights Day (third Monday of January)
3. Washington's Birthday (third Monday of February)
4. Memorial Day (May 30)
5. Independence Day (July 4)
6. Labor Day (first Monday of September)
7. Columbus Day (second Monday of October)
8. Day on which biennial election is held
9. Veterans' Day (November 11)
10. Thanksgiving Day (whenever appointed)
11. Christmas Day (December 25)

Notes: Civil Rights Day is not an additional paid holiday for state employees. When any of the eleven holidays fall on a Sunday, it is observed the next day.[72]

NEW JERSEY

Legal Holidays

1. Saturdays (after noon)
2. Sundays
3. New Year's Day (January 1)
4. Martin Luther King's Birthday (third Monday in January)
5. Lincoln's Birthday (February 12)
6. Washington's Birthday (third Monday in February)
7. Good Friday (Friday before Easter)
8. Memorial Day (last Monday in May)
9. Independence Day (July 4)
10. Labor Day (first Monday in September)
11. Columbus Day (second Monday in October)

12. Veterans' Day (November 11)
13. Thanksgiving Day (fourth Thursday in November)
14. Christmas Day (December 25)
15. General Election Days
16. Any days declared as holidays, bank holidays, or days of fasting and prayer or other religious observance by the governor or the President of the United States

Notes: When holidays fall on Sundays, the following Mondays are public holidays. When holidays fall on Saturdays, the preceding Fridays are public holidays.[73]

Observances

Volunteer Fireman's Day (second Sunday in January)
Volunteer First Aid and Rescue Squad Day (third Sunday in January)
Crispus Attucks Day (March 5)
Women's History Week (second week in March)
New Jersey Day (April 17)
Law Day (May 1)
Mother's Day (second Sunday in May)
Grandparent's Day (last Sunday in May)
American Flag Week (June 7–14)
Lidice Memorial Day (June 10)
Father's Day (third Sunday in June)
New Jersey P.O.W.–M.I.A. Recognition Day (July 20)
New Jersey Retired Teachers Day (first Sunday in November)[74]

NEW MEXICO

Legal Holidays

1. New Year's Day (January 1)
2. Martin Luther King, Jr.'s Birthday (third Monday in January)
3. Presidents' Day (third Monday in February)
4. Memorial Day (last Monday in May)
5. Independence Day (July 4)
6. Labor Day (first Monday in September)
7. Columbus Day (second Monday in October)

8. Veterans' Day (November 11)
9. Thanksgiving Day (fourth Thursday in November)
10. Christmas Day (December 25)

Note: When a holiday falls on a Sunday, the next Monday is a legal holiday.[75]

Observances

American History Month (February)

American Indian Day (first Tuesday of February)

Bataan Day (April 9)

Onate Day (a day in the month of July)

Ernie Pyle Day (August 3)[76]

NEW YORK

Legal Holidays

1. New Year's Day (January 1)
2. Dr. Martin Luther King, Jr. Day (third Monday in January)
3. Lincoln's Birthday (February 12)
4. Washington's Birthday (third Monday in February)
5. Memorial Day (last Monday in May)
6. Flag Day (second Sunday in June)
7. Independence Day (July 4)
8. Labor Day (first Monday in September)
9. Columbus Day (second Monday in October)
10. Veterans' Day (November 11)
11. Thanksgiving Day (fourth Thursday in November)
12. Christmas Day (December 25)
13. Days following all holidays except Flag Day, if they fall on Sunday
14. General Election Days
15. Any days declared by the governor or the President of the United States as days of general fasting or prayer, thanksgiving, or religious observances
16. Saturdays, from noon until midnight[77]

Observances

Haym Salomon Day (January 6)
Lithuanian Independence Day (February 16)
Pulaski Day (March 4)
Workers' Memorial Day (April 28)
Korean War Veterans' Day (June 25)
John Barry Day (September 13)
Uncle Sam Day in the State of New York (September 13)
Friedrich Wilhelm von Steuben Memorial Day (September 17)
War of 1812 Day (last Saturday in September)
Raoul Wallenberg Day (October 5)
New Netherland Day in the State of New York (October 11)
Theodore Roosevelt Day (October 27)
Pearl Harbor Day (December 7)[78]

NORTH CAROLINA

Legal Holidays

1. New Year's Day (January 1)
2. Martin Luther King, Jr.'s Birthday (third Monday in January)
3. Robert E. Lee's Birthday (January 19)
4. Washington's Birthday (third Monday in February)
5. Greek Independence Day (March 25)
6. Anniversary of Signing of Halifax Resolves (April 12)
7. Good Friday (Friday before Easter)
8. Anniversary of Mecklenburg Declaration of Independence (May 20)
9. Memorial Day (last Monday in May)
10. Confederate Memorial Day (May 10)
11. Independence Day (July 4)
12. Labor Day (first Monday in September)
13. Columbus Day (second Monday in October)
14. Yom Kippur
15. Veterans' Day (November 11)

16. Election Days (Tuesday after the first Monday in November when elections are held)
17. Thanksgiving Day (fourth Thursday in November)
18. Christmas Day (December 25)

Note: When a holiday falls on a Sunday, the following Monday is a public holiday.[79]

Observances

Arbor Week (week in March containing March 15)

Prisoner of War Day (April 9)

American Family Day (first Sunday in August)

Indian Solidarity Week (last full week in September)

National Employ the Physically Handicapped Week (first full week in October)

Pearl Harbor Remembrance Day (December 7)

Indian Day (unspecified day named by governor)[80]

NORTH DAKOTA

Legal Holidays

1. Sundays
2. New Year's Day (January 1)
3. Martin Luther King Day (third Monday in January)
4. George Washington's Birthday (third Monday in February)
5. Good Friday (Friday before Easter)
6. Memorial Day (last Monday in May)
7. Independence Day (July 4)
8. Labor Day (first Monday in September)
9. Veterans' Day (November 11)
10. Thanksgiving Day (fourth Thursday in November)
11. Christmas Day (December 25)
12. Any days declared public holidays by the President of the United States or the governor

Note: If New Year's, Independence, Veterans', or Christmas day falls on a Sunday, the following day is a holiday. If any of these days falls on a Saturday, the preceding Friday is a holiday.[81]

Observances

Temperance Day (third Friday in January)

Bird Day (April 26)

Workers' Memorial Day (April 28)

Arbor Day (first Friday in May)

Mother's Day (second Sunday in May)[82]

OHIO

Legal Holidays

1. New Year's Day (January 1)
2. Martin Luther King Day (third Monday in January)
3. Washington-Lincoln Day (third Monday in February)
4. Memorial Day (last Monday in May)
5. Independence Day (July 4)
6. Labor Day (first Monday in September)
7. Columbus Day (second Monday in October)
8. Veterans' Day (November 11)
9. Thanksgiving Day (fourth Thursday in November)
10. Christmas Day (December 25)
11. Days appointed and recommended by the President of the United States or the governor
12. Saturdays from noon until midnight
13. Election Days from noon to 5:30 P.M.

Note: If a legal holiday falls on a Sunday, the next day is a legal holiday.[83]

Observances

Ohio Statehood Day (March 1)

World War I Day (April 6)

Workers' Memorial Day (April 28)

Arbor Day (last Friday in April)

Native American Indian Day (fourth Saturday in November)

General Pulaski Memorial Day (October 11)[84]

OKLAHOMA

Legal Holidays

1. Sundays
2. New Year's Day (January 1)
3. Martin Luther King, Jr.'s Birthday (third Monday in January)
4. Washington's Birthday (third Monday in February)
5. Memorial Day (last Monday in May)
6. Independence Day (July 4)
7. Labor Day (first Monday in September)
8. Veterans' Day (November 11)
9. Thanksgiving Day (fourth Thursday in November)
10. Christmas Day (December 25)

Note: If any holiday other than a Sunday itself falls on a Sunday, the following Monday is a holiday.[85]

Observances

Arbor Day (Friday after second Monday in February)
Youth Day (third Sunday in March)
Prisoners of War Remembrance Day (April 9)
Jefferson Day (April 13)
Oklahoma Day (April 22)
Bird Day (May 1)
Mother's Day (second Sunday in May)
Shut-In Day (first Sunday in June)
Flag Week (June 8–14)
Senior Citizens Day (June 9)
Indian Day (first Saturday after first full moon in September)
Cherokee Strip Day (September 16)
Oklahoma Historical Day (October 10)
Will Rogers Day (November 4)
Oklahoma Week (November 11–16)
Oklahoma Statehood Day (November 16)
Oklahoma Heritage Week (week in which November 16 falls)

Bill of Rights Day (December 15)

Bill of Responsibilities Day (December 16)

Citizenship Recognition Day (fixed by governor)

Holiday for each Indian tribe in state, chosen by tribes[86]

OREGON

Legal Holidays

1. Sundays
2. New Year's Day (January 1)
3. Martin Luther King, Jr.'s Birthday (third Monday in January)
4. Presidents' Day (third Monday in February)
5. Memorial Day (last Monday in May)
6. Independence Day (July 4)
7. Labor Day (first Monday in September)
8. Veterans' Day (November 11)
9. Thanksgiving Day (fourth Thursday in November)
10. Christmas Day (December 25)
11. Days appointed by the governor or the President of the United States as holidays

Notes: When holidays other than Sundays fall on Sundays, the next Mondays are legal holidays. When holidays fall on Saturdays, the preceding Fridays are holidays.[87]

Observances

Arbor Week (first full week of April)

Garden Week (first full week of June)[88]

PENNSYLVANIA

Legal Holidays

1. New Year's Day (January 1)
2. Dr. Martin Luther King, Jr. Day (third Monday in January)
3. Presidents' Day (third Monday in February)
4. Good Friday (Friday before Easter)

5. Memorial Day (last Monday in May)
6. Flag Day (June 14)
7. Independence Day (July 4)
8. Labor Day (first Monday in September)
9. Columbus Day (second Monday in October)
10. Election Day (first Tuesday after the first Monday in November)
11. Veterans' Day (November 11)
12. Thanksgiving Day (fourth Thursday in November)
13. Christmas Day (December 25)
14. Saturdays, from noon to midnight
15. Days appointed by the governor or the President of the United States as days of fasting, prayer, or thanksgiving

Note: When New Year's Day, July 4, or Christmas Day falls on a Sunday, the next Monday may be a holiday.[89]

Observances

Day of the Disabled (January 30)

Lithuanian Independence Day (February 16)

Charter Day (March 14)

Bird Day (March 21)

Local Government Day (April 15)

Rothrock Memorial Conservation Week (last Friday in April)

Arbor Day (last Friday in April)

American Loyalty Day (May 1)

See Pennsylvania's Covered Bridges Week (from the first Saturday after the first Sunday in May to and including the third Sunday of May)

Hubert H. Humphrey, Jr. Day (May 27)

Rachel Carson Day (May 27)

Pennsylvania German Day (June 28)

Commodore John Barry Day (September 13)

National Anthem Day (September 14)

Shut-In Day (third Sunday in October)

William Penn's Birthday (October 24)[90]

RHODE ISLAND

Legal Holidays

1. Sundays
2. New Year's Day (January 1)
3. Dr. Martin Luther King, Jr.'s Birthday (third Monday in January)
4. Washington's Birthday (third Monday in February)
5. Rhode Island Independence Day (May 4)
6. Memorial Day (last Monday in May)
7. Independence Day (July 4)
8. Labor Day (first Monday in September)
9. Columbus Day (second Monday in October)
10. Veterans' Day (November 11)
11. Christmas Day (December 25)
12. General election days
13. Any days that the governor, general assembly, President, or Congress appoints as holidays for any purpose

Note: When holidays fall on Sundays, the following Mondays are holidays.[91]

Observances

Viet Nam Veterans' Day (January 27)

American History Month (February)

Founders Day of the Italian American War Veterans of the United States, Inc. (February 15)

Lithuanian Independence Day (February 16)

Retired Teachers' Day (first Wednesday of March)

National Women's History Week (week containing March 8)

Rhode Island School Bus Safety Week (second week of March)

Social Workers' Day (second Wednesday of March)

Peter Francisco Day (March 15)

Dauphine Day (April 21)

Motorcycle Safety Awareness Week (fourth week in April)

Workers' Memorial Day (fourth Friday in April)

Arbor Day (last Friday in April)

V.F.W. Loyalty Day (May 1)
Nurses' Day (first Monday in May)
Friendship Day (second Friday in May)
National Police Week (week containing May 15)
National Police Awareness Day (May 15)
Itam-Vets Daisy Day (first Saturday in June)
Destroyer Escort Day (third Saturday in June)
Saint Jean-Baptiste Day (June 24)
Cape Verdian Recognition Week (July 2–9)
Old Home Week (week beginning with the first Sunday in July, or any subsequent week during July, August, or September)
Puerto Rican Recognition Week (July 23–29)
General Casimir Pulaski Day (October 11)
Narragansett Indian Day (last Saturday before second Sunday in August)
White Cane Safety Day (October 15)
Disabled American Veterans Day (December 7)
Veteran Firemen's Muster Day (date not specified)[92]

SOUTH CAROLINA

Legal Holidays

1. New Year's Day (January 1)
2. Martin Luther King's Birthday (January 15)
3. Robert E. Lee's Birthday (January 19)
4. Washington's Birthday (third Monday in February)
5. Confederate Memorial Day (May 10)
6. National Memorial Day (last Monday in May)
7. Jefferson Davis' Birthday (June 3)
8. Independence Day (July 4)
9. Labor Day (first Monday in September)
10. Veterans' Day (November 11)
11. Thanksgiving Day and the following day (fourth Thursday in November and the following day)
12. Christmas Day and the following day (December 25 and December 26)
13. General election days

Notes: Christmas Eve may be declared a holiday by the governor. When holidays fall on Sundays, the next Mondays are holidays. When they fall on Saturdays, the preceding Fridays are holidays.[93]

Observances

Martin Luther King Day (January 15)
South Carolina Day (March 18)
Loyalty Day (May 1)
Mother's Day (second Sunday in May)
Garden Week (week beginning the first Sunday in June)
Family Week (last week in August)
General Pulaski Memorial Day (October 11)
Frances Willard Day (fourth Friday in October)
Arbor Day (first Friday in December)[94]

SOUTH DAKOTA

Legal Holidays

1. Sundays
2. New Year's Day (January 1)
3. Martin Luther King, Jr. Day (third Monday in January)
4. Washington's and Lincoln's Birthdays (third Monday in February)
5. Memorial Day (last Monday in May)
6. Independence Day (July 4)
7. Labor Day (first Monday in September)
8. Native Americans' Day (second Monday in October)
9. Veterans' Day (November 11)
10. Thanksgiving Day (fourth Thursday in November)
11. Christmas Day (December 25)
12. Any day declared by the governor or the President of the United States as a holiday

Notes: When January 1, July 4, November 11, or December 25 falls on a Sunday, the following Monday is a legal holiday. When they fall on a Saturday, the preceding Friday is a legal holiday.[95]

TENNESSEE

Legal Holidays

1. Saturdays from noon until midnight
2. New Year's Day (January 1)
3. Martin Luther King, Jr. Day (third Monday in January)
4. Washington Day (third Monday in February)
5. Good Friday (Friday before Easter)
6. Memorial Day (last Monday in May)
7. Independence Day (July 4)
8. Labor Day (first Monday in September)
9. Columbus Day (second Monday in October)
10. Veterans' Day (November 11)
11. Thanksgiving Day (fourth Thursday in November)
12. Christmas Day (December 25)
13. Any days declared holidays by the governor or the President of the United States
14. Election Days

Notes: The following Monday is substituted for holidays that fall on Sunday. The preceding Friday is substituted for holidays falling on Saturday.[96]

Observances

Robert E. Lee Day (January 19)

Abraham Lincoln Day (February 12)

Andrew Jackson Day (March 15)

Mother's Day (second Sunday in May)

Statehood Day (June 1)

Confederate Memorial Day (June 3)

Nathan Bedford Forrest Day (July 13)

Family Day (last Sunday in August)

Veterans' Day (November 11)

Free Sport Fishing Day (date not specified)[97]

TEXAS

Legal Holidays

1. New Year's Day (January 1)
2. Confederate Heroes Day (January 19)
3. Martin Luther King, Jr. Day (third Monday in January)
4. Washington's Birthday (third Monday in February)
5. Texas Independence Day (March 2)
6. San Jacinto Day (April 21)
7. Memorial Day (last Monday in May)
8. Juneteenth (June 19)
9. Independence Day (July 4)
10. Lyndon B. Johnson's Birthday (August 27)
11. Labor Day (first Monday in September)
12. Veterans' Day (November 11)
13. Thanksgiving Day (fourth Thursday in November)
14. Christmas Day (December 25)
15. Election Days[98]

Observances

Sam Rayburn Day (January 6)
Texas Week (entire week in which March 2 is contained)
Former Prisoners of War Recognition Day (April 9)
Texas Conservation and Beautification Week (April 19–26)
International Trade Awareness Week (May 22–26)
Columbus Day (second Monday in October)[99]

UTAH

Legal Holidays

1. Sundays
2. New Year's Day (January 1)
3. Martin Luther King, Jr.'s Birthday (third Monday in January)
4. Presidents' Day (third Monday in February)

5. Memorial Day (last Monday in May)
6. Independence Day (July 4)
7. Pioneer Day (July 24)
8. Labor Day (first Monday in September)
9. Columbus Day (second Monday in October)
10. Veterans' Day (November 11)
11. Thanksgiving Day (fourth Thursday in November)
12. Christmas Day (December 25)
13. Days of thanksgiving or fasting designated by the governor or the President of the United States

Notes: When a holiday other than a Sunday falls on a Sunday, the following Monday is the holiday. When a holiday falls on a Saturday, the preceding Friday is the holiday.[100]

VERMONT

Legal Holidays

1. New Year's Day (January 1)
2. Martin Luther King, Jr.'s Birthday (third Monday in January)
3. Lincoln's Birthday (February 12)
4. Washington's Birthday (third Monday in February)
5. Town Meeting Day (first Tuesday in March)
6. Memorial Day (May 30)
7. Independence Day (July 4)
8. Bennington Battle Day (August 16)
9. Labor Day (first Monday in September)
10. Columbus Day (second Monday in October)
11. Veterans' Day (November 11)
12. Thanksgiving Day (fourth Thursday in November)
13. Christmas Day (December 25)

Notes: When holidays fall on Sundays, they are observed on the following Mondays. When they fall on Saturdays, they are observed on the preceding Fridays.[101]

Observances

American History Month (February)
Arbor Day (first Friday in May)[102]

VIRGINIA

Legal Holidays

1. New Year's Day (January 1)
2. Lee-Jackson-King Day (third Monday in January)
3. George Washington Day (third Monday in February)
4. Memorial Day (last Monday in May)
5. Independence Day (July 4)
6. Labor Day (first Monday in September)
7. Columbus Day and Yorktown Victory Day (second Monday in October)
8. Veterans' Day (November 11)
9. Thanksgiving Day (fourth Thursday in November)
10. Friday following Thanksgiving Day
11. Christmas Day (December 25)
12. Any day appointed as a legal holiday by the governor or the President of the United States

Notes: When a holiday falls on a Sunday, the following Monday is a legal holiday. When a holiday falls on a Saturday, the preceding Friday is a legal holiday.[103]

Observances

Religious Freedom Week (second full week of January)
Virginia and American History Month (January 19–February 22)
Motherhood and Apple Pie Day (January 26)
Arbor Day (second Friday in March)
Bone Marrow Donor Programs Recognition Day (April 8)
Dogwood Day (third Saturday in April)
Mother's Day (second Sunday in May)
First Lady's Day in Virginia (June 2)
Citizenship Day (September 17)

Constitution Week (September 17–23)

Native American Indian Week (last full week in September)

Yorkstown Day (October 19)

Early Childhood and Day-Care Providers and Professionals Recognition Day (October 22)

Vietnam War Memorial Dedication and Veterans' Recognition Day (second Saturday in November)

Pearl Harbor Remembrance Day (December 7)[104]

WASHINGTON

Legal Holidays

1. Sundays
2. New Year's Day (January 1)
3. Martin Luther King, Jr.'s Birthday (third Monday in January)
4. Presidents' Day (third Monday in February)
5. Memorial Day (last Monday in May)
6. Independence Day (July 4)
7. Labor Day (first Monday in September)
8. Veterans' Day (November 11)
9. Thanksgiving Day (fourth Thursday in November)
10. Friday following Thanksgiving Day
11. Christmas Day (December 25)

Notes: When a holiday other than a Sunday itself falls on a Sunday, the following Monday is the legal holiday. When a holiday falls on a Saturday, the preceding Friday is the legal holiday.[105]

Observances

Washington Army and Air National Guard Day (January 26)

Former Prisoner of War Recognition Day (April 9)

Purple Heart Recipient Recognition Day (August 7)

Columbus Day (October 12)[106]

WEST VIRGINIA

Legal Holidays

1. New Year's Day (January 1)
2. Martin Luther King's Birthday (third Monday in January)
3. Lincoln's Birthday (February 12)
4. Washington's Birthday (third Monday in February)
5. Memorial Day (last Monday in May)
6. West Virginia Day (June 20)
7. Independence Day (July 4)
8. Labor Day (first Monday in September)
9. Columbus Day (second Monday in October)
10. Veterans' Day (November 11)
11. Thanksgiving Day (fourth Thursday in November)
12. Christmas Day (December 25)
13. Election Days
14. Any days appointed as days of thanksgiving or business holidays by the President of the United States or the governor

Note: When a holiday falls on a Sunday, the following Monday is observed as the legal holiday.[107]

Observances

Native American Indian Heritage Week (week beginning the Sunday before Thanksgiving)[108]

WISCONSIN

Legal Holidays

1. New Year's Day (January 1)
2. Martin Luther King, Jr.'s Birthday (January 15)
3. Presidents' Day (third Monday in February)
4. Memorial Day (last Monday in May)
5. Independence Day (July 4)
6. Labor Day (first Monday in September)
7. Veterans' Day (November 11)

8. Thanksgiving Day (fourth Thursday in November)
9. Christmas Day (December 25)
10. September Primary and November General Election Days

Notes: Good Fridays, from 11:00 A.M. to 3:00 P.M., are to be used for worship. When a holiday falls on a Sunday, the legal holiday is the following Monday.[109]

Observances

American History Month (February)
Mother's Day (second Sunday in May)
Citizenship Day (third Sunday in May)
Indian Rights Day (July 4—if it falls on Sunday, the day may be observed on July 3 or July 5)
Labor Day (first Monday in September)
Wonderful Wisconsin Week (third week in September)
Gold Star Mother's Day (last Sunday in September)
Wisconsin Family Month (November)
Wisconsin Family Week (first seven days of November)
Family Sunday (first Sunday of November)
Arbor and Bird Day (unspecified date)[110]

WYOMING

Legal Holidays

1. New Year's Day (January 1)
2. Martin Luther King, Jr., Wyoming Equality Day (third Monday in January)
3. Washington's and Lincoln's Birthdays (third Monday in February)
4. Memorial Day (last Monday in May)
5. Independence Day (July 4)
6. Labor Day (first Monday in September)
7. Veterans' Day (November 11)
8. Thanksgiving Day (fourth Thursday in November)
9. Christmas Day (December 25)
10. Any days appointed by the President of the United States and declared by the governor for rejoicing, mourning, or national emergency

Note: When January 1, July 4, November 11, or December 25 falls on a Sunday, the following Monday is a legal holiday.[111]

Observances

Arbor Day (last Monday in April)

Native American Day (third Friday in September)

Nellie Tayloe Ross's Birthday (November 29)

Pearl Harbor Remembrance Day (December 7)

Wyoming Day (December 10)[112]

DISTRICT OF COLUMBIA

Legal Holidays

1. New Year's Day (January 1)
2. Martin Luther King, Jr.'s Birthday (third Monday in January)
3. Washington's Birthday (third Monday in February)
4. Memorial Day (last Monday in May)
5. Independence Day (July 4)
6. Labor Day (first Monday in September)
7. Columbus Day (second Monday in October)
8. Veterans' Day (November 11)
9. Thanksgiving Day (fourth Thursday in November)
10. Christmas Day (December 25)
11. Saturdays after noon
12. Presidential Inauguration Day every four years
13. Any days appointed by the President of the United States for public fasting or thanksgiving

Notes: When a holiday other than Inauguration Day falls on a Sunday, the next day is a holiday. When a holiday other than Inauguration Day falls on a Saturday, the preceding day is a holiday.[113]

AMERICAN SAMOA

Legal Holidays

1. New Year's Day (January 1)
2. Washington's Birthday (February 22)
3. Good Friday (Friday before Easter)
4. American Samoa Flag Day (April 17)
5. Memorial Day (May 30)
6. Independence Day (July 4)
7. Labor Day (first Monday in September)
8. Veterans' Day (November 11)
9. Thanksgiving Day (fourth Thursday in November)
10. Christmas Day (December 25)[114]

COMMONWEALTH OF THE NORTHERN MARIANA ISLANDS

Legal Holidays

1. New Year's Day (January 1)
2. Commonwealth Day (January 9)
3. Presidents' Day (third Monday in February)
4. Covenant Day (March 25)
5. Good Friday (Friday before Easter)
6. Memorial Day (last Monday in May)
7. Independence Day (July 4)
8. Labor Day (first Monday in September)
9. Columbus Day (second Monday in October)
10. Citizenship Day (November 4)
11. Veterans' Day (November 11)
12. Thanksgiving Day (fourth Thursday in November)
13. Constitution Day (December 9)
14. Christmas Day (December 25)

Observances

Ash Wednesday (varies)

Assumption of Mary (August 1)

All Saints Day (November 1)[115]

GUAM

Legal Holidays

1. Sundays
2. New Year's Day (January 1)
3. Martin Luther King, Jr.'s Birthday (January 18)
4. Presidents' Day (third Monday in February)
5. Guam Discovery Day (first Monday in March)
6. Good Friday (Friday before Easter)
7. Memorial Day (last Monday in May)
8. Independence Day (July 4)
9. Liberation Day (July 21)
10. Labor Day (first Monday in September)
11. Columbus Day (second Monday in October)
12. Veterans' Day (November 11)
13. Thanksgiving Day (fourth Thursday in November)
14. Lady Camarin Day (December 8)
15. Christmas Day (December 25)
16. Election Days
17. Any day proclaimed by the governor or the President of the United States as a holiday or day of fasting or thanksgiving

Notes: If any holiday other than a Sunday falls on a Sunday, the next Monday is a holiday. If any holiday falls on a Saturday, the preceding Friday is a holiday.[116]

Observances

Gubernatorial Inauguration Day (first Monday in January every fourth year)

Chamorro Week (beginning first Monday in March and ending eight days later)

Farmers Appreciation Days (last Saturday in March and the immediately following Sunday)

Guam Youth Month (April)

White Cane Days (second Saturday and Sunday in April)

Earth Week (third week in April)

Children and Youth Sunday (fourth Sunday in April)

Family Sunday (Sunday following Children and Youth Sunday)

Guam Youth Week (a week in April)

Senior Citizens Month (May)

Teacher Appreciation Day (first Saturday in May)

Atbot de Fuego (Flame Tree) and Arbor Day Week (first week in June)

Gold Star Mothers' Day (second Sunday in August)[117]

PUERTO RICO

Legal Holidays

1. Sundays
2. New Year's Day (January 1)
3. Three Kings' Day (January 6)
4. Eugenio Maria de Hostos' Birthday (January 11)
5. Martin Luther King's Birthday (third Monday in January)
6. Washington's Birthday (third Monday in February)
7. Abolition of Slavery (March 22)
8. Good Friday (Friday preceding Easter)
9. Antonio R. Barcelo Day (second Sunday in April)
10. Jose de Diego Day (April 16)
11. Memorial Day (last Monday in May)
12. Independence Day (July 4)
13. Luis Munoz Rivera Day (July 17)
14. Day of the Constitution (July 25)
15. Dr. Jose Celso Barbosa's Birthday (July 27)
16. Labor Day (first Monday in September)
17. Santiago Iglesias Pantin Day (first Monday in September)
18. Columbus Day (October 12)
19. Discovery Day (October 12)

20. Veterans' Day (November 11)
21. Christmas Day (December 25)
22. Election Days
23. Any day appointed by the governor or the President of the United States or the Legislative Assembly for fasting or thanksgiving or as a holiday[118]

Note: When holidays fall on Sundays, the next day is the holiday.

Observances

Educational Week Pro Tourism in Puerto Rico (first week after last Sunday in January)

Birth Date of Armando Sanchez Martinez (January 28)

Day in Commemoration of the Birthday of Don Luis Munoz-Marin (February 18)

Police Day (February 21)

Roman Baldorioty de Castro Day (February 28)

Advent of American Citizenship in Puerto Rico Day (March 2)

International Women's Day (March 8)

Cancer Prevention and Control Month (April)

Ramon Emeterio Betances Commemorative Day (April 8)

Renowned Puerto Rican Statesmen's Day (April 18)

Rafael Martinez Nadal's Birthday (April 22)

Ernesto Ramos Antonini Day (April 24)

Puerto Rican Land Week (last week in April)

Day of the Land (Sunday of last week in April)

Arbor Day (Monday of last week in April)

School Janitors' Day (last Friday in April)

Day in Honor of the Aged (April 30)

Day of Homage to Old Age (a day in April)

Natural Resources and Environmental Quality and Health Educational Term (May 1–June 5)

Teachers Week (first week beginning with first Monday in May)

Teachers Day (Friday of first week beginning with first Monday in May)

Mother's Day (second Sunday in May)

Week of the Puerto Rican Danza (week including May 16)

Juan Morel Campos' Birthday and Day of the Puerto Rican Composer (May 16)

Accountant Week (third week in May)

Recreational Leaders Week (third week in June)

Puerto Rico Youth Organizations Week (week ending in fourth Sunday in June)

Youth Day (fourth Sunday in June)

Press Week (week beginning July 1)

Members of Municipal Assembly Week (first week in July)

Puerto Rican Domino Players Week (first week in July)

Puerto Rican Press Day (first Friday in July)

Day of the Flag, Anthem, and Coat of Arms (July 24)

Day of the Child (second Sunday in August)

Roberto Clemente Day (August 18)

Lola Rodriguez de Tio's Birthday (September 14)

Grito de Lares Day (September 23)

National Guard Week (a week in September proclaimed by governor)

General Casimir Pulaski Day (October 11)

Natural Resources Rangers Corps Week (third week in October)

Quality of Life Week (last week in October)

Ramon Power y Giralt Day (October 27)

Day of Peace (November 1)

Pedrin Zorrilla Memorial Day (November 9)

Day of the Composer (November 22)

Day of No More Violence Against Women (November 25)

Day of the Blind (December 13)

Librarian's Day (Friday of Library Week)

School Lunchroom Employee's Day (Friday of School Lunchroom Week)

Native Industries Week (a week to be proclaimed by governor)[119]

U.S. VIRGIN ISLANDS

Legal Holidays

1. Sundays
2. New Year's Day (January 1)

3. Three Kings' Day (January 6)
4. Martin Luther King, Jr.'s Birthday (third Monday in January)
5. Presidents' Day (third Monday in February)
6. Transfer Day (March 31)
7. Holy Thursday (Thursday before Easter)
8. Good Friday (Friday before Easter)
9. Easter Monday (Monday following Easter)
10. Memorial Day (last Monday in May)
11. Organic Act Day (last Monday in May)
12. Danish West Indies Emancipation Day (July 3)
13. Independence Day (July 4)
14. Supplication Day (fourth Monday in July)
15. Labor Day (first Monday in September)
16. Columbus Day and Puerto Rico Friendship Day (second Monday in October)
17. Local Thanksgiving Day (third Monday in October)
18. D. Hamilton Jackson day (November 1)
19. Veterans' Day (November 11)
20. Thanksgiving Day (fourth Thursday in November)
21. Christmas Day (December 25)
22. Christmas Second Day (December 26)
23. Any days the President of the United States or governor proclaims as holidays

Note: When holidays other than Sundays fall on Sundays, the following Monday is a legal holiday.[120]

Observances

Midwives Week (second week in February)

Cyril Emmanuel King Day (April 7)

Earth Day (April 22)

Secretaries Week (last week in April)

Peace Officers Memorial Day (May 15)

Peace Officers Memorial Week (week in which May 15 occurs)

African Liberation Day (May 25)

Virgin Islands African Heritage Week (third week in May)

French Heritage Week (week in June ending on Father's Day)

Ferry Boat Transportation Day (July 2)

Nicole Robin Day (August 4)

Melvin H. Evans Day (August 7)

Eastern Caribbean–Virgin Islands Friendship Week (August 4 and the following ten days)

Virgin Islands Citizenship Day (a day in August or September)

Support Our Public Schools Month (September)

Rothschild Francis Day (October 5)

Virgin Islands Taxi Week (last week in October)

Human Relations Week (second week in December)

George Scott Day (Monday of Fire Prevention Week)[121]

NOTES

1. Ala. Code §1–3–8.
2. Alaska Stat. §44.12.010.
3. Ibid., §44.12.020, §44.12.025.
4. Alaska Stat. §44.12.050.
5. Ibid., §44.12.065.
6. Ibid., §44.12.055.
7. Ibid., §44.12.030.
8. Ibid., §44.12.060.
9. Ibid., §44.12.040.
10. Ariz. Rev. Stat. Ann. §1–301.
11. Ibid., §1–304, §1–306.
12. Ark. Code Ann. §1–5–101.
13. Ibid., §1–5–106.
14. Ibid., §1–5–109.
15. Ibid., §1–5–107.
16. Ibid., §1–5–108.
17. Cal. Gov't. Code §6700 (West).
18. Ibid., §6701 (West).
19. Ibid., §6711 (West).
20. Ibid., §6710 (West).
21. Ibid., §6714 (West).
22. Ibid., §6712 (West).
23. Ibid., §6708 (West).
24. Ibid., §6713 (West).
25. Ibid., §6716 (West).
26. Colo. Rev. Stat. §24–11–101, §24–11–103.
27. Ibid., §24–11–108, §24–11–104, §24–11–106, §24–11–111, §24–11–109.

28. Conn. Gen. Stat. Ann. §1–4 (West).
29. Ibid., §10–29a (West).
30. Del. Code Ann. tit. 1, §501.
31. Ibid., tit. 1, §601, §602.
32. Fla. Stat. Ann. §683.01, §683.13, §683.19, §683.08, §683.12, §683.09 (West).
33. Ibid., §683.04, §683.18, §683.06, §683.17, §683.05, §683.14, §683.15, §683.11, §683.115, §683.21, §683.21, §683.10, §683.145, §683.16 (West).
34. Ga. Code Ann. §1–4–1.
35. Ibid., §1–4–2, §1–4–3, §1–4–10, §1–4–6, §1–4–4, §1–4–9, §1–4–7, §1–4–8, §1–4–5.
36. Haw. Rev. Stat. §8–1, §8–2.
37. Ibid., §8–4–5, §8–4, §8–8, §8–1.5, §8–9, §8–7, §8–10.
38. Idaho Code §73–108.
39. Ibid., §73–108B.
40. Ill. Stat. Ann. ch. 17, §2201 (Smith-Hurd).
41. Ibid., ch. 1, §3101, §3103, §3107, §3106, §3115, §3142, §3109, §3108, §3110, §3130, §3112, §3161 (Smith-Hurd).
42. Ind. Code Ann. §1–1–9–1 (Burns).
43. Ibid., §1–1–13–1, §1–1–12.5–1, §1–1–11–1, §1–1–14–1, §1–1–10–1 (Burns).
44. Iowa Code Ann. §33.1 (West).
45. Ibid., §31.10, §31.4, §31.5, §31.9, §31.6, §31.8, §31.7 (West).
46. K.S.A. §35–107.
47. Ibid., §35–204, §35–202, §73–705, §35–205, §35–203, §35–206.
48. Ky. Rev. Stat. Ann. §2.110 (Baldwin).
49. Ibid., §2.135, §2.245, §2.250, §2.135.
50. La. Rev. Stat. Ann. §1–55 (West).
51. Ibid., §1–57, §1–56, §49–170.1, §1–58 (West).
52. Me. Rev. Stat. Ann. tit. 30–A, §1051.
53. Ibid., tit. 1, §113, §122, §118, §116, §130, §131, §111–A, §121, §127, §128, §126, §123, §120, §119; tit.30-A, §2902; tit. 1, §125, §132, §112, §124, §129, §117.
54. Md. Ann. Code (1957) art. 1, §27.
55. Md. State Gov't. Code Ann. §13–401, §13–402, §13–403.
56. Mass. Gen. Laws Ann. ch. 7, §7, cl. 18th.
57. Ibid., ch. 6, §12F, §12T, §15S, §15Y, §15X, §15C, §12BB, §12RR, §15H, §13, §14A, §12GG, §12AA, §12T, §12QQ, §15CCC, §15T, §12D, §12II, §12S, §12K, §15GG, §15UU, §15RR, §15J, §15MM, §15QQ, §15AAA, §12M, §12T, §15Z, §12PP, §12T, §12J, §15AA, §15LL, §15AA, §15II, §15, §12UU, §1200, §15KKK, §14C, §15B, §15O, §12O, §12R, §12T, §15ZZ, §12T, §15N, §15JJJ, §12JJ, §15KK, §12I, §15BB, §15XX, §12H, §12I, §12Y, §12FF, §15D, §12Q, §15VV, §12X, §15CC, §15TT, §15EEE, §12U, §15JJ, §15NN, §14, §12C, §12T, §12TT, §15OO, §15HH, §15M, §15OOO, §15DD, §12SS, §12MM, §12CC, §12Z, §15WW, §12T, §12LL, §15I, §15QQQ, §15E, 12W, §15NNN, §12KK, §15EE, §12EE, §15GGG, §12E, §15A, §15K, §15BBB, §15W, §15FF, §15LLL, §15HHH, §15F, §12T, §15III, §15U, §15PP, §15YY, §12V, §12B, §15V, §12N, §14B, §12HH, §15G, §12G, §15SS, §15MMM, §15Q, §12A,

§15R, §15DDD, §15L, §12G, §12T, §12DD, §12P, §12NN, §12T, §15PPP, §15P, §12L.

58. Mich. Stat. Ann. §18.861; §18.862.

59. Ibid., §18.891(11), §18.891(35), §18.891(40), §18.891(30), §18.891(25), §18.891(21), §18.881.

60. Minn. Stat. Ann. §645.44 (West).

61. Ibid., §517.21 (West).

62. Miss. Code Ann. §3–3–7.

63. Ibid., §3–3–8, §3–3–7, §3–3–35.

64. Mo. Stat. Ann. §9.010 (Vernon).

65. Ibid., §9.100, §9.070, §9.030, §9.050, §9.035, §9.060, §9.080, §9.040 (Vernon).

66. Mont. Code Ann. §1–1–216.

67. Ibid., §1–1–224, §1–1–225, §1–1–226.

68. Neb. Rev. Stat. §62–301.

69. Ibid., §84.104.04, §83.104.02, §84.107, §84.104.09, §82–112, §83–454, §84.104.07, §20–130, §84.104.01, §84.104.

70. Nev. Rev. Stat. Ann. §236.015.

71. Ibid., §236.018, §236.030, §236.020, §236.050, §236.040, §236.035, §236.040, §236.025.

72. N.H. Rev. Stat. Ann. §288.1,2.

73. N.J. Stat. Ann. §36: 1–1, 1–1.2 (West).

74. Ibid., §36: 1–8, 1–9, 2–1, 2–4, 2–3, 2–6, 1–5, 1–7, 2–2, 1–11, 1–6, 2–7, 2–9 (West).

75. N.M. Stat. Ann. §12–5–2, §12–5–3.

76. Ibid., §12–5–6, §12–5–9, §12–5–7, §12–5–5, §12–5–4.

77. N.Y. Gen. Constr. Law §24 (McKinney).

78. N.Y. Exec. Law §161–a (McKinney).

79. N.C. Gen. Stat. §103–4.

80. Ibid., §103–6, §103–9, §103–7, §103–8, §143–283.3, 103–10, §147–18.

81. N.D. Cent. Code §1–03–01, §1–03–02, §1–03.02.1.

82. Ibid., §15–38–05, §1–03–08, §1–03–10, §1–03–07, §1–03–06.

83. Ohio Rev. Code Ann. §1.14, §5.30, §5.20 (Page).

84. Ibid., §5.224, §5.221, §5.225, §5.22, §5.223, §5.222 (Page).

85. Okla. Stat. Ann. tit. 25, §82.1 (West).

86. Ibid., tit. 70, §24–107; tit. 25, §82.2, §90.4, §87, §90.3, §83, §88; tit 70, §24–109; tit. 25, §90.1, §90.5, §90.6, §89 (West).

87. Or. Rev. Stat. §187.010, §187.020.

88. Ibid., §336.01, §187.200.

89. Pa. Stat. Ann. tit. 44, §11 (Purdon).

90. Ibid., tit. 44, §40, §40.1, §28, §34, §33, §19.3, §19.2, §30, §35, §39, §40.2, §38, §26, §27, §36, §22 (Purdon).

91. R.I. Gen. Laws §25–1–1.

92. Ibid., §25–2–20, §25–2–16, §25–2–11, §25–2–28, §25–2–26, §25–2–25, §25–2–19, §25–2–34, §25–2–33, §25–2–17, §25–2–22, §25–2–31, §25–2–30, §25–2–9, §25–2–24, §25–2–27, §25–2–12, §25–2–10, §25–2–32, §25–2–29, §25–2–23, §25–2–5, §25–2–21, §25–2–15, §25–2–4, §25–2–14, §25–2–8, §25–2–7.

93. S.C. Code §53–5–10, §53–5–20, §53–5–30.
94. Ibid., §53–3–80, §53–3–60, §53–3–70, §53–3–40, §53–3–110, §53–3–90, §53–3–30, §53–3–20, §53–3–10.
95. S.D. Codified Laws §1–5–1.
96. Tenn. Code Ann. §15–1–101.
97. Ibid., §15–2–101, §15–2–102, §15–2–103, §15–2–10, §70–2–109.
98. Tex. Civ. Code Ann. tit. 72, §4591 (Vernon).
99. Ibid., tit. 72, §4591b–1; tit. 106, §6144a; tit. 72, §4591b–2; tit. 106, §6144d; tit. 72, §4591.5, §4591.6.
100. Utah Code Ann. §63–13–2.
101. Vt. Stat. Ann. tit. 1, §371.
102. Ibid., tit. 1, §373, §372.
103. Va. Code §2.1–21.
104. Ibid., §57–2.01, §2.1–28, §21.2, §25, §27.7, §26, §24, §27, §24.1, §27.4, §21.1, §27.6, §27.3, §27.2.
105. Wash. Rev. Code Ann. §1.16.050.
106. Ibid., §1.16.050.
107. W. Va. Code Ann. §2–2–1.
108. Ibid., §2–2–1a.
109. Wis. Stat. Ann. §895.20 (West).
110. Ibid., §14.16; §895.23, §895.22 (West).
111. Wyo. Stat. §8–4–101.
112. Ibid., §8–4–102, §8–4–105, §8–4–104, §8–4–106, §8–4–103.
113. D.C. Code Ann. §28–2701.
114. A.S. Code tit. 1, §951.
115. C.N.M.I. Public Law 5–21.
116. Guam Code Ann. tit. 1, §1000, §1001.
117. Ibid, tit. 1, §1017, §1025, §1016, §1014, §1027, §1020, §1028, §1029, §1014, §1032, §1015, §1021, §1019.
118. P.R. Laws Ann., tit. 1., §71, §74–84.
119. Ibid., tit. 1, §102, §150n, §150o, §132, §134, §143, §142, §150h, §131a, §150j, §144, §130, §127, §105, §120, §150e, §135, §104, §150k, §150c, §113, §139, §147, §138, §149, §150n, §140, §116, §146, §148, §145, §141, §150b, §501, §137, §133, §150s, §119, §150a, §150q, §136, §150, §150f, §150i, §150p, §122, §150m, §150g, §124.
120. V.I. Code Ann. tit. 1, §171.
121. Ibid., tit. 1, §190, §188, §193, §182, §184, §192, §185, §194, §183, §186, §181, §176, §191, §187, §189, §179, §180.

11 State and Territory License Plates

License plates today are commonplace symbols of a mobile society that are often taken for granted as we go about our daily business. Yet the practice of states' registering vehicles and thereby giving a registration number to a vehicle began less than a century ago in 1901, when New York became the first state to require motor vehicle registration. At first, vehicle owners had to make their own plates because the municipality or state with which they registered did not provide them. Everything from leather to porcelainized iron was used to display registration numbers. But the quick spread of the popularity of motorized cars across the nation led to the need for systematic registration at the state level. Not only did vehicles and their owners need to be identified, but governments recognized at once the taxation opportunities automobiles gave them.

The first state-issued plates were quite simple and came in a variety of shapes, sizes, and colors. Not until 1956 was a nationwide standard for license plates adopted. This brought us the familiar six-inch by twelve-inch plate of today, which will fit on any automobile. But variety remains in the colors and designs of the plates. State flags, seals, nicknames, and symbols adorn many license plates. A buffalo roams the North Dakota plate and a bighorn sheep the Nevada plate. Mount Rainier majestically dominates the state of Washington plate and Mount Rushmore appears on South Dakota's plate. The Wright brothers' first airplane still flies on the North Carolina plate and the Statue of Liberty sends her message of freedom from the New York plate. There are sunsets (Nebraska), canoes on lakes (Minnesota), bisons' skulls (Montana), lobsters (Maine), and farm scenes (Indiana). And Idaho continues to remind us of its "famous potatoes."

The illustrations presented in this book are of standard-issue passenger-car plates. Vanity plates and specialized plates are available now in most states. In addition, the states have numerous special plates, often in colors different from the passenger-car plates, for different kinds of vehicles—trailers, trucks, motorcycles, tractors, and so on. There has never before been such a variety of license plates available to the citizens of all the states and territories.

ALABAMA

The state of Alabama began issuing license plates in 1912. From 1905 until 1912, license plate issues were controlled locally rather than at the state level. The first Alabama plate was white on blue. A host of color combinations have been used throughout the years. In 1955, the slogan "Heart of Dixie" was first used and it appears on the current issue, which began in 1987. The current plate features the slogan "Heart of Dixie" in red with the word "of" encircled by the outline of a heart. This appears at the top center of the plate beneath "Alabama," which is centered at the very top center in blue and highlighted by blue horizontal bars at each side. The numerals are also blue and the background is white.[1]

ALASKA

Alaska issued its first license plate, which had orange lettering on a black background, in 1922. Plates in a variety of color combinations were issued each year up to 1944, when, for the first time, a validation tab was used on the 1943 plate. New plates were again issued annually until 1954, when the use of validation tabs replaced the yearly issue of plates. New plates were issued sporadically thereafter—in 1956, 1958, 1960, 1962, 1966, 1968, 1970, and 1976. The current plate was issued in 1981. The design, mandated by law since 1979, uses blue lettering on a gold background in the colors of the state flag, which is depicted in the center of the plate. "Alaska" appears across the top and the slogan "The Last Frontier" across the bottom.[2] The flag graphic had appeared earlier on the 1962 plate. The 1966 gold-on-blue plate displayed a totem pole graphic and the 1976 red-on-white plate a bear graphic.[3]

ARIZONA

Arizona began issuing passenger license plates when it became a state in 1912. The first plate was actually a four-inch disk made of metal, which was to be placed on the dashboard. The 1913 plate was the type of plate for outside display with which we have become familiar. Like most states, Arizona has used a variety of materials to make the plates, from fiberglass during World War II to the aluminum typical of today's plates. However, during the depression years of 1932–1934, alone among states Arizona issued plates made of copper, which proved too soft, to help its struggling copper industry.[4]

Arizona has remained with a simple two-color plate without graphics because of its low cost and easy identification by law enforcement authorities. The current plate was first issued in 1980. Its color, white lettering on a maroon background, was chosen by the Motor Vehicle Division, which remains responsible for such decisions. This plate replaced the green-on-gold plates that were issued in 1973 and used through 1979.[5]

ARKANSAS

The state of Arkansas began issuing license plates in 1911. During that year, 1,611 of the black-on-white plates were issued. From 1911 to 1949, when the 1948 black-on-aluminum plate was validated for the first time by an aluminum tab, black had been used as one of the two colors in all but nine years. Black was used in combination with white, yellow, light blue, green, silver, orange, aluminum, and light gray. With the white-on-green 1950 plate, white became the most frequently used color.

The 1968 red-on-white plate was the first multiyear, reflectorized plate issued by Arkansas. The current plate retains red and white colors in combination with blue numerals. "Arkansas" appears in white at the center top against a red stripe. "The Natural State" appears in red at the bottom center against the white field of the plate.[6]

CALIFORNIA

On March 22, 1905, the state of California began issuing license plates. The plates for the years 1905 through 1913 are known as prestate plates, because the state only assigned numbers—it did not actually manufacture the plates, which were supposed by law to be simple black on white with the words "State of California" on them. But the design law was not always followed strictly and was largely unenforced.

In 1914, the state began to manufacture the plates as it still does today. Until 1943, new issues were produced annually, except for the years 1916 to 1919. In those years symbols were affixed to the basic blue-on-white plates as year validations. The 1916 plate used a bear symbol; the 1917 plate, a poppy; the 1918 plate, a liberty bell; and the 1919 plate, a star. The 1941 plates were replaced in 1945. New plates were issued in the years 1947, 1951, 1956, 1963, 1970, 1982, and 1991. The current plate, issued in 1991, is a nongraphic, blue-on-white design with the name "California" in red lettering across the top.[7]

COLORADO

The state of Colorado first issued license plates in 1913. Cities had issued numbers before then when vehicles were registered, and motorists, like those in most states at the time, had to make their own plates to display the registration number. The first plate was black on white and had a porcelain coating. Annual license plate issues were made in various colors except for 1920, 1944, 1952, 1961, and 1976. In 1977, the current month-year plate was issued. Since 1959, however, Colorado has used the dark green and white color combinations, the only exception having been the 1975–1976 red, white, and blue U.S. bicentennial plates. The outline of the Rocky Mountains that appears on the current plate was used first in 1960, and then from 1962 through 1972, and again in 1974. Colorado described itself as "colorful" on the plates of 1950 through 1955, 1958, and 1973. A skier sped through the 1958 plate.[8]

CONNECTICUT

In 1903, the first year registration was required, 1,353 Connecticut citizens paid one dollar to register their automobiles with the state. For those first two years, automobile owners had to make their own plates. Motorists would commonly tack metal numerals preceded by the letter "C" onto pieces of leather. Then from 1905 through 1916, the state issued metal plates covered in porcelain. Painted plates were issued from 1917 through 1919, and then in 1920 the familiar stamped plates were issued for the first time. Steel was used in the manufacture of the plates from 1913 until 1937, when aluminum was used for the first time.

Connecticut issued annual plates until 1937. New multiple-year plates were issued in 1937, 1948, 1957, 1974, and 1975. The current Connecticut plate, which was issued first in 1975, uses white lettering on a deep blue background. At the top left in white is a stamped graphic of a solid outline of the map of the state. The name "Connecticut" is centered at the top and Connecticut's official nickname, "Constitution State," appears across the bottom of the plate, as it has since 1978 by law.[9]

DELAWARE

Although Delaware issued its first license plate in 1910, it had required vehicle registration and assigned numbers to automobile registrations as early as 1907. Thus the 431 automobile owners who registered their vehicles in 1908 had to go to harness makers to get the mandated tag of leather with nickel numbers. The first state-issued plate was white with lettering in black porcelain enamel. The state continued to issue new plates annually through 1939, followed by a blue-on-gold plate in 1941, a gold-on-blue plate on March 31, 1942, and a white-on-black plate on June 30, 1942. A new plate was not issued until 1958. This plate, which is the current plate, returned to the gold and blue colors, which had been used interchangeably from 1929 to 1937. This all-scotchlite plate has Delaware's nickname, "The First State," centered across the top and the name of the state across the bottom.[10]

FLORIDA

The state of Florida did not issue statewide license plates until 1918. Although the state required the registration of vehicles as early as 1905, motorists received no plate until 1911, when the law was changed to permit licensing by counties. County plates were used until January 1, 1918, when the state comptroller issued the first white-on-black Florida plate. Orange was used on black for the 1919 plate, thus beginning a long love affair with that color, symbolic of one of the state's best-known products. Orange has been used twenty-three times since 1918 in combination with other colors, frequently with blue. Green and white have been used in combination ten times. The current issue combines these traditions as well as the tradition first established in 1923 of placing the outline of the state on the plate. This multiyear plate depicts the outline of Florida in green with orange numerals and lettering on a white background. The sample illustrated has "DMV" at the bottom center where the name of the county would normally occur.[11]

GEORGIA

The state of Georgia issued its first license plate in 1910. It was gray on black and undated. Dates were not used on plates until 1914. From 1913 through 1928, the state issued both disks and plates. A host of color combinations were used over the years in the annual issues, including the somewhat unusual combinations of black on green in 1918 and peach on green in 1964. In 1971, a five-year plate was issued, which was blue on white. In 1976 and 1983, seven-year plates were issued. The 1976 red-on-white plate celebrated the U.S. Bicentennial. The 1983 plate was green on white. The current plate is a five-year black-on-white plate. Centered at the top of the plate is "Georgia" with a peach graphic as the third letter.[12]

HAWAII

While a 1903 territory-wide law taxed automobiles, four motor vehicles were registered on the main island in 1900. When license plates were first required is a matter of some conjecture, as no certain record exists before 1911. The county of Honolulu did, however, issue a plate in 1914. Plates were issued annually from 1921 to 1942 and again from 1946 to 1952. Multiyear plates were issued thereafter. The current 1991 license plate employs black lettering on a white background. "Hawaii" appears above the license plate number at the center, and "Aloha State," the state's official popular name, appears below the number at the center. A red, yellow, and blue rainbow brightens the plate, stretching from side to side.[13]

IDAHO

The state of Idaho, through the newly created State Highway Commission, issued its first plate, white on blue, to 2,083 people who registered their vehicles in 1913. However, since 1893 Idaho municipalities had had the power to issue local plates, often metal numbers on leather; some cities, like Boise, Twin Falls, Weiser, Hailey, and Payette, issued porcelain-enameled or metal plates. Lewiston actually issued a solid brass engraved plate.

Idaho claims to be the first state to place a slogan on its license plate. The 1928 plate displayed a brown russet potato and the words "Idaho Potatoes." In 1943, the potato again appeared on the Idaho plate and then again in 1948. Since 1957, all Idaho plates have had the slogan "Famous Potatoes." Other slogans also appeared over the years. "Scenic Idaho" was found on the 1941, 1942, 1945, and 1946 plates. "Vacation Wonderland" was proclaimed on 1947 plates. The 1940 plate celebrated "50 Years of Statehood" and an optional plate was issued in 1987 for the 1990 centennial celebration of statehood. The current 1992 issue plate uses a silk-screen graphic in red, white, and blue that depicts a scene of the state's trees and mountains, slightly redesigned from the centennial plate. The slogan "Scenic Idaho" returns on this plate at the top and "Famous Potatoes" remains across the bottom.[14]

ILLINOIS

From 1907, when Illinois adopted its first motor vehicle licensing law, to 1910, motorists were given two-inch round aluminum registration seals rather than plates. Because the registration seal had to be displayed, owners were left to their own devices to have plates made. In 1911, the state issued its first plate, which had black numbers on a white background. Plates were issued annually thereafter until 1978. The blue-on-white 1979 plate was used until 1983, when the current plate was issued. The "Land of Lincoln" slogan on this light blue and white plate with dark blue lettering has been found on Illinois plates since 1954.[15]

INDIANA

From 1905 through 1910, the state of Indiana issued two-inch circular numbered seals to those who registered their automobiles. The vehicle owners were then required to have a plate made with their registration number on it to be placed on the rear of the vehicle. Then in 1911, Indiana issued its first plate, a simple white-on-black design. Plates were issued for most years in a variety of colors until a multiyear license plate program was begun in 1981. Stripes of color have typified these multiyear plates. The design of the current issue employs red, gold, and black stripes of color. The black stripe at the bottom depicts in outline a typical farm—outbuildings, silo and barn, home—that is highlighted against the gold stripe. The words "amber waves of grain" are centered in the black stripe. The raised black lettering straddles the gold and red stripes. "Indiana" is centered at the top in the red stripe.[16]

IOWA

In July 1904, the state of Iowa began registering motor vehicles. In that year 155 citizens registered their vehicles for one dollar each. Until 1911, the secretary of state issued two-inch metal disks that were to be displayed on dashboards. There was also a requirement for a plate on the rear of the vehicle, which the state did not supply. These were often the metal numbers on leather plates used in many states at that time. By 1915, the cost of registration had gone to five dollars and the state realized $1,000,000 in revenues from registrations.

Iowa has remained with a plain and simple plate for most of its history. Between 1941 and 1958, plates were black on white or white on black. Only on the 1953 plate did a slogan ever appear: "The Corn State." The use of multiyear plates began first in 1916, for the three-year period of World War I. During World War II, the 1942 plate was used through 1944. Multiyear plates were issued frequently thereafter. The current blue plate with white lettering was issued in 1986 and bears only the name of the state across the top.[17]

KANSAS

The state of Kansas began issuing license plates in 1913. Previous to that, municipalities registered vehicles and owners had to find their own way to display their registration numbers. The 1913 plate was black on white with the abbreviation "KAN" descending on the right. That first year 38,680 automobiles were registered.

Until 1976, black was a frequently used color in combination most frequently with white, yellow, and orange. In 1976, with the issue of multiyear plates, blue and white became a familiar color combination. Kansans received an ornamental plate with their white-on-red 1925 plate. It had light blue lettering on a white background and featured the slogan "Kansas the Wheat State" with a small shock of wheat. In 1952, two sunflower decals were used on the plates. "The Wheat State" appeared again on the 1949, 1950, and 1951 plates. In 1965, the slogan "Midway USA" was used on Kansas license plates. Today, no slogan appears on the Kansas plate, but golden wheat dominates the center of the current plate, over which blue numerals are superimposed against a white background. "Kansas" appears across the top of the plate, outlined in blue against a cream-yellow stripe.[18]

KENTUCKY

Kentucky issued its first plate, which was undated, in 1914. It was a simple white-on-black plate. For all but ten years since the first plate was issued, white was used either for the numerals or the background in combination with black, red, maroon, green, brown, or blue. Black and yellow combinations were used in 1918, 1935, and 1944. Orange was used as the background for black numerals on the 1922 plate and for numerals against a silver-gray background on the 1948 plate. Black and silver-gray combinations were used on the 1941, 1942, 1946, and 1949 plates. No plates were issued in the years 1943, 1945, 1947, and 1953. Since 1953 up until five-year plates were issued in 1988, blue and white were alternated on the plates. The current plate is a graphic blue-on-white plate that features a horse-racing motif and Kentucky's nickname, "Bluegrass State." Horses run through the numerals under the steeples of Churchill Downs.[19]

LOUISIANA

The state of Louisiana began issuing license plates in 1915. Previous to that time and until 1920, cities authorized plates. The first state plate was white and black. Since the 1930s, the pelican has frequently appeared on the Louisiana plates. The slogan "Sportsman's Paradise" has also frequently been used since the late 1950s.[20] The current Louisiana plate incorporates the patriotic colors of red, white, and blue with the pelican and slogan. The brown pelican, the state bird, appears with her nest of three young both on the upper right and upper left corners of the plate in blue. Numbers are also in blue on the white background and "Louisiana" appears at the bottom center in blue and red letters. The blue letters are the *U, S,* and *A,* and they are in larger print than the red letters.

MAINE

The state of Maine began issuing license plates in 1905. The first iron plates, used until 1911, had white numerals on a red background. Plates were issued annually through 1942. The 1942 plate was validated for 1943 with a windshield decal. Plates were again issued annually for 1944, 1945, and 1946, but validation stickers were used for 1947 and 1949. The 1950 plates were used for five years after the year of issue, which began the pattern now used for multiyear plates. The current Maine license plate has "Maine" in red centered at the top, dark blue lettering, "Vacationland" in red centered at the bottom, and a blue border, all on a white background. Slightly right of center beneath the lettering, an orange Maine lobster can be seen peaking through.[21]

MARYLAND

Although Maryland began to require motor vehicle registration in 1904, Maryland motorists, like many others all over the country, were responsible for making their own plates. These plates, known as "prestates," were made from a variety of materials including stencils. In 1910, the commissioner of motor vehicles issued the first Maryland plate. It was made of tin, painted black on yellow. In 1934, Maryland issued a tercentenary plate and from December 1975 to February 1977, a special U.S. Bicentennial plate. In 1984, Maryland celebrated its 350th anniversary with the issue of an award-winning plate that featured the state shield. The 1986 issue retained the shield at the center of the plate on a simple black-on-white plate. This issue remains current, but Maryland residents may also purchase a special blue heron plate that benefits the Chesapeake Bay Trust. This graphic plate features a blue heron in blue against a blue-to-white background and green numerals. "Maryland" appears in blue across the top and "Treasure the Chesapeake" in blue across the bottom, with the suggestion of green wetlands to the bottom right and left.[22]

MASSACHUSETTS

Automobiles could be found on Massachusetts roads by 1900, but no law governing them was passed until 1902. This law set the speed limit at fifteen miles per hour outside of densely populated areas. By 1903, there were 3,241 automobiles registered with the Massachusetts Highway Commission, and in September of that year it became illegal to operate a vehicle without a license and a registration. So began the issuance of license plates in Massachusetts. Like all the states, Massachusetts has used a variety of colors on its plates. The current issue, however, recalls the importance of this original colony in American history. "Massachusetts" in blue lettering is centered at the top. Beneath the red license plate number, the slogan "The Spirit of America" appears in blue lettering. The background is white, completing the display of patriotic colors.[23]

MICHIGAN

Michigan began registering automobiles in 1906. From 1906 through 1909, vehicle owners received numbered dashboard disks rather than plates to identify their vehicles as registered. Then in 1910 the state issued its first plate, which had black numerals on a white background. Plates issued from 1910 to 1919 included a seal, discontinued with the black-on-orange plate of 1920. For a number of years, Michigan plates bore the slogan "Water-Winter Wonderland." Then the slogan was changed in the late 1960s to "Great Lake State." The current plate bears the slogan "Great Lakes" centered in white at the bottom. "Michigan" is centered at the top in white above the white numerals, all on a field of blue.[24]

MINNESOTA

When Minnesota first began registering motor vehicles in 1903, it was done through the office of the state boiler inspector. License numbers had to be painted on the back of the vehicle. In 1909, the secretary of state was given authority to license vehicles and Minnesota issued its first plate, which had silver lettering on a bright red background. Plates were issued annually until 1912. Three-year plates were issued through 1920. The state went back to annual issues until 1943, when, because of war, multiyear plates were issued. Annual issues occurred again after the war until 1957. Three-year issues were made until 1974 and five-year plates were issued thereafter. The current plate uses a graphic design that depicts Minnesota as the state with "10,000 lakes" and encourages everyone to "explore Minnesota." Above the map of the state that bisects the lettering two persons can be seen canoeing across a blue lake set in the green north woods.[25]

MISSISSIPPI

When the Mississippi legislature passed a bill in 1912 requiring the state auditor to issue annual plates to car owners, the citizens of the state rebelled against it as unfair. Demonstrations ensued in Jackson. When the state supreme court finally declared the 1912 law unconstitutional, car owners were refunded their 1912 and 1913 registration fees, which totalled $28,040. As a consequence, the first black-on-white plate of 1912 was used in 1913, since no plates were issued that year. A new law was passed in 1914, when another black-on-white was issued and used through 1918. Effective January 1, 1919, plates were issued annually. The first annual plate was pea green on black. Over the years, a wide variety of color combinations were used on Mississippi plates, but either black or white frequently appeared with another color. The current Mississippi plate, however, utilizes dark blue lettering and numbers on a field that goes from light blue to white from top to bottom. "Mississippi" appears at the center top of the plate.[26]

MISSOURI

A 1903 state law made automobile owners register their vehicles at local city or county offices. Owners were required to display a license number, but they had to find a way to do it on their own. In 1907 a new motor vehicle registration law was passed that required the secretary of state to provide for a two-inch circular seal to go to all registrants. Plates displaying the license number were usually made of leather with "house numbers" tacked to it. Finally in 1911, the first Missouri license plate, which had white letters on an orange background, was issued. Plates were issued annually until a multiyear plate program was initiated in 1948 and validation tabs were used for annual validations. Multiyear plates were issued also in 1956 and 1962. Annual plates were then issued for the years 1968 through 1978. Then in 1979, the white-on-maroon multiyear plate displaying the state's nickname, "Show-Me State," was issued. This plate remains current.[27]

MONTANA

Montana began taxing motor vehicles in 1913 to raise money for road construction. Registration of vehicles, therefore, also began that year. In 1914, the state issued its first plate, an unpainted steel plate with black lettering, 4¾ inches by 12 inches. Since the issue of that first rather basic plate, Montana has developed one of the country's most colorful license plates. An outline of Montana first appeared on the 1933 plate, and the bison skull first appeared in 1938. The "Big Sky Country" slogan replaced the "Treasure State" slogan of 1950 in 1967. Then in 1976, a red, white, and blue U.S. Bicentennial plate was issued and used until 1991. In 1987, a Montana centennial plate was issued and will be used through 1996. The "new issue" plate of 1991, which is pictured, combines a number of themes from earlier Montana plates—the "Big Sky," the bison's skull, the outline of the state—with a tricolor mountain graphic on a field of light and sky blue.[28]

NEBRASKA

From 1903 to 1915, when the Department of Motor Vehicles first issued plates, license plates of the metal number on leather variety had to be made by the vehicle owners themselves. The 1915 plate was a simple black-on-white plate. Plates were issued annually except for 1920 until 1943. After 1946, revalidation stickers were used in 1947 and 1953. In 1958 a multiyear plate issue program has been used more consistently, with new issues made in 1960, 1962, 1965, 1966, 1969, 1972, 1976, 1984, 1987, 1990, and 1993. The current issue brings together colors and themes from the 1976 red, white, and blue bicentennial plate, the 1987 graphic sunset plate, and the 1990 windmill on the prairie plate. The graphic design of the 1993 plate incorporates the sunset theme on the upper third of the plate over a scene in blue outline of mountains, rivers, farms (the windmill), and a cityscape with "Nebraska" in bold red letters. The lettering in blue is on a white background.[29]

NEVADA

The state of Nevada first required motor vehicle registration in 1913. Between 1913 and 1915, a metal disk for display on the dashboard was issued with plates being optional. Beginning in 1916, the state stopped issuing disks and required a license plate. Since 1936, the only exception having been the gold-on-green plate of 1953, Nevada plates have used combinations of cobalt blue and silver, the state colors. Multiyear plates began to be issued in 1960. The current plate was first issued in 1982. Cobalt blue is used for "Nevada" at the center top of the plate, the license number, and the state's nickname, "The Silver State," at the bottom. Against a white background and covering nearly the entire plate is a graphic in silver, which depicts a Nevada mountain scene replete with state symbols: the desert bighorn sheep to the top left, the single-leaf piñon in the center, and the sagebrush to the bottom right.[30]

NEW HAMPSHIRE

New Hampshire's first motor vehicle registration law became effective on March 10, 1905. In that year, five hundred passenger vehicles were issued a pair of green porcelain plates with white numbers. Except for the years 1945 through 1949, New Hampshire plates have had green and white color combinations. In 1926, the Old Man of the Mountains, the state emblem, first appeared on the license plate. This emblem appears again on the current plate, center left at the top. Numerals and lettering in green are on a white background. New Hampshire's memorable motto, "Live Free or Die," appears in green letters at the center bottom of the plate.[31]

NEW JERSEY

The state of New Jersey began issuing license plates in 1908, although plates had been required since 1906. For those first two years, New Jersey residents, like automobile owners in many other states, had to have plates made themselves. The first plate featured cream numbers on a blue background. Various background colors—black, yellow, blue, white, gray, red, orange, green, brown—were used, predominantly with white numbers, from 1909 until 1932. Plates with black backgrounds were utilized from 1932 through 1943. From 1944 through 1947, the plates had cream backgrounds with either black or light blue numbers. The 1948 plate first used black-on-straw colors and these colors were repeated from 1959 through 1978, after five years of orange-on-black plates. In 1979, the familiar buff-on-blue plate was first issued. The new plate has black lettering and numbers on a buff background that fades to white from top to bottom. The outline of the state is colored in black and separates the numbers. "Garden State," New Jersey's nickname, appears at the bottom center.[32]

NEW MEXICO

When New Mexico became a state in 1912, only 870 automobiles and 60 trucks were registered. Because plates were numbered consecutively until 1927, the actual numbers on these tags marked with "NM" equalled the number of registrations. The 1927 plate featured the Zia, the sun symbol which appears on the state flag, and "New Mexico" rather than the abbreviation used until then. In 1941, the slogan "The Land of Enchantment" appeared on the plates, replacing the 1932 "Sunshine State" slogan that Florida had appropriated. "USA" was added to "New Mexico" on the 1975 plates, dropped in 1976, and added again in 1987. It remains on the current plate to identify clearly the owner's country. In 1991, all license plates were replaced with what is surely one of the nation's most distinctive plates. Against a bright yellow background, the city name centered at the top, the numerals and "New Mexico USA" stand out in red. An Indian design at the top left and right, the yucca flower at the bottom left, and "Land of Enchantment" centered at the bottom are in blue.[33]

NEW YORK

The state of New York was the first to require motor vehicle registration. In 1901, 954 vehicles were registered. By 1903, registrations had reached 6,412. Vehicle owners had to supply their own rear plates with their initials on them for the first two years of registration. Numbers were assigned beginning in 1903, but owners still had to supply their own plates until August 1, 1910, when the secretary of state issued a white-on-blue plate. In 1966, permanent plates began to be issued. Since that orange-on-blue plate was issued, only two other plates have been issued: the 1973 blue-on-gold plate and the current plate, which came out on 1986. This red, white, and blue plate features the Statue of Liberty in red at the center, blue lettering with "New York" across the top, and red borders at top and bottom on a white background.[34]

NORTH CAROLINA

The first car registered in the state of North Carolina was John A. Park's Hudson on July 9, 1909. Mr. Park, like all the other car owners, had to manufacture his own front and rear plates until 1913, when the state began to supply the license plates. The first plate was white on black. Various colors were used in the annual issues thereafter. Slogans and mottoes began appearing on the plates in 1956. "Drive Safely" appeared on plates from 1956 through 1964. From 1975 through 1979, "First in Freedom" appeared on the plates. In 1982, the current plate was issued, the design having been mandated by law. This plate has the slogan "First in Flight" in red at the top over a light blue graphic of the Wright brothers' first plane, which was flown at Kitty Hawk. The license plate number is in deep blue at the center. Below, "North Carolina" in red overlays a scene of sea oats in light blue.[35]

NORTH DAKOTA

The state of North Dakota first required vehicle owners to register their vehicles and display plates, front and rear, in 1911. The first plate had gold letters on a black background. Annual plates in various colors were issued except for 1949 until a four-year plate program was begun in 1958. In 1974, a multiyear plate program was begun. The 1988 centennial plate, celebrating one hundred years of North Dakota statehood in 1989, was replaced with the current 1993 issue. This graphic plate, depicting blue sky over the yellow prairie with bronze mountains in the background and beneath the black license plate number, bids everyone to "Discover the Spirit" across the top. Beneath the number, "North Dakota" is centered in white in a band of black, and beneath the state name in brown is the slogan "The Peace Garden State." A buffalo to the bottom left and wheat to the bottom right complete the theme.[36]

OHIO

The state of Ohio issued 10,649 white-on-blue license plates in 1908, the first year for state-supplied plates. By 1909, the number of registered vehicles had more than doubled to 23,003. The same undated porcelain plate of 1908 was used in 1909. From 1910 until 1974, when multiyear plates came into use, with the exceptions only of the years 1943 and 1952, annually issued plates used a variety of color combinations with no particular pattern. Red and white (1910, 1914, 1930, 1934, 1946, 1959, 1965, 1968, 1976) and blue and white (1908, 1909, 1920, 1922, 1924, 1932, 1936, 1939, 1940, 1944, 1945, 1951, 1955, 1958, 1963, 1967, 1969) were, however, frequently used color combinations. Red, white, and blue come back into use in the current Ohio plate. "Ohio" appears in blue at the top center of the plate with the slogan "The Heart of It All!" beneath it in red script. The numerals are in blue on a white background.[37]

OKLAHOMA

The state of Oklahoma began issuing license plates in 1915. Annual plates were issued until 1943, when the metal shortage caused by the war yielded a window sticker plate. Again in 1947, a metal validation tab replaced a new plate, but annual issues continued until 1980, when multiyear plates began to be issued. The slogan "Oklahoma Is OK" appeared on all plates until the current 1989 issue, when it was changed slightly to "OK!" in buckskin color beneath "Oklahoma" in black at the top. License plates in Oklahoma have not been without controversy. The experiment with using school colors—Oklahoma State's orange and black in 1968 and the University of Oklahoma's red and white in 1969—resulted in a 1970 law that prohibited school colors from ever being used again. Official state colors of green and white became the standard. The current issue, which did not invalidate the two previous issues, employs green lettering on a white background with the emblem that appears on the state flag in the center of the plate between the license plate numerals.[38]

OREGON

Oregon began issuing license plates in 1911. The first plate featured black numerals on a yellow background. That same color combination was used again in 1915, 1922, 1925, and finally in 1939, when the color was actually light yellow, but never again. Plates in various color combinations were issued annually with the exceptions of 1930, 1943, 1944, and 1945, until five-year permanent plates began to be issued in 1950. Permanent plates, validated with tabs or stickers, were issued in 1956, 1964, and 1974. Since the 1974 blue-on-gold plates, Oregon changed to graphic plates. The first had a light green fir tree at the center with small gray fir trees below on a tan background. The current issue is much the same as the first graphic except that the fir tree through the center of the plate and "Oregon" at the top are dark green; a white outline silhouettes the mountains beneath the light blue sky, and the small forested peaks at the bottom of the plate are, like the numerals, dark blue.[39]

PENNSYLVANIA

Pennsylvania first issued license plates statewide in 1906. The first plate had white lettering on a deep blue background. It was made of porcelain as were all the annual issues through 1915. While the state used a number of color combinations at first, in 1924 yellow and deep blue were chosen, and those colors have been used in alternating combinations ever since. The current plate is yellow on deep blue, although a deep blue–on-yellow plate remains valid also. Pennsylvania's nickname, "Keystone State," appears across the top, and the keystone emblem lies in the middle of the plate bisecting the license plate number. The word "Pennsylvania" appears across the bottom.[40]

RHODE ISLAND

In 1904, Rhode Island issued its first plate, which was white on black. This began a series of black and white combination issues that continued uninterrupted until the current issue except for the 1946 black and aluminum plate.[41] The current plate is blue on white with the slogan "Ocean State" at the top center and an anchor to its left. This slogan first appeared on the 1973 plate, but the anchor is a familiar Rhode Island symbol, having been used on colonial and state seals since 1647. The words "Rhode Island" appear at the bottom center.

SOUTH CAROLINA

When the State Highway Department was created in 1917, it issued license plates for statewide use. Previous to that, counties issued plates that were made either of wood or metal. The 1917 plate had black numbers on a white background. Combinations of black, white, green, and yellow were used frequently for the annual issues up to 1943. The 1942 plate was used for 1943 and 1944 to save metal for the war effort. From 1930 through 1933, the slogan "Iodine State" or "Iodine Products State" was found on South Carolina plates. Plates were issued yearly from 1945 until a five-year plate program was begun in 1976. All the South Carolina plates issued since the program started have had graphic designs. The 1976 red, white, and blue bicentennial plate featured a blue cannon and a red palmetto tree. The blue-on-white 1981 plate featured the state in outline and the state seal. The 1986 plate was again blue on white with "South Carolina" in red. But the current plate, issued in 1990, brings back the green, yellow, white, and black colors used so often in earlier plates in a graphic design that features the state flower, yellow jasmine, across the top of the plate and the state bird, the Carolina wren, centered in the jasmine's branches.[42]

SOUTH DAKOTA

James F. Biglow of Flandreau received the small disk stamped "No. 1" when he registered his Oldsmobile in 1905. Following this first vehicle registration, 17,692 South Dakota citizens received stamped disks up until

1912, when they registered their vehicles. In 1913, two license plates were issued for each vehicle and annual issues began. Perhaps the most enduring feature of South Dakota license plates is the depiction of Mount Rushmore on them. It first appeared on the 1939 plate and then in 1952 it became a permanent feature with legislative authorization. On the current graphic plate, the figures carved into Mount Rushmore—Washington, Jefferson, Theodore Roosevelt, and Lincoln—peer out over the green numerals in the upper right quadrant. "South Dakota" appears in red script at the bottom right center; at the bottom right appears the slogan "Great Faces. Great Places." The background is a tan color that deepens from bottom to top.[43]

TENNESSEE

Although the state of Tennessee first required motor vehicle registration in 1905, it was not until 1915 that the state supplied license plates. Owners had to make their own plates, usually out of leather or enamel. The 1915 plate had white numerals on a blue background. Annual issues of plates occurred until 1943, when a corner tab was used on the 1942 plate. Plates were then issued annually until 1962. Between 1956 and 1976, the plates were either black on white or white on black, colors which in either combination had appeared on Tennessee plates in 1917, 1926, 1932, 1935, 1941, 1942, 1944, 1947, and 1952. From 1977 through 1987, Tennessee used a white plate with blue numerals. The current plate, first issued in 1988, has the name of the state in blue at the top, the name of the county in white on a blue background strip on the bottom, and numerals in red. The tri-star symbol that bisects the license plate number in the center reproduces the emblem on the state flag, which was designed in 1905.[44]

TEXAS

Although the state of Texas required vehicle registration by county clerks beginning in 1907, it did not issue plates statewide until 1917, when the Highway Department was created. These first plates were good for as long as the vehicle was in operation, but the state also issued radiator seals, in different colors for different years, that validated the registration annually. The 1917 plate was white on black and the round seal was white on red. When new plates were issued in 1920, again white on black but smaller in size than the first plate, the validation disk changed to a seal. Another white on black was issued in 1923 and the last validation plate in 1924. Thus in 1925 began the practice of annual plate issues except for 1943 and 1944 until multiyear plates were introduced in 1975. While a number of color combinations were used over the years, black-gold combinations were frequent (1941–1945, 1948–1956), as were black-white combinations (1917, 1920, 1923, 1931, 1947, 1957–1968), and silver-black combinations

(1969, 1971, 1973, 1975, 1977, 1978, 1983). The current Texas plate is red, white, and blue. The state flag is displayed at the top next to "Texas." At the bottom is the state's nickname, "The Lone Star State." All lettering is in blue against a white background. An outline of Texas in red divides the license plate number.[45]

UTAH

Utah did not issue plates statewide until 1915. Previous to that time, motorists had to make their own plates. The first plate was dark green and white. Over the years, various color combinations have been utilized along with various slogans: "Center Scenic America" in the mid-1940s, "This Is the Place" in 1947, and "The Friendly State" in 1948. In the 1970s, a beehive was depicted on Utah plates.[46] The current plates, issued first in 1986, have blue and red lettering on a field of white. "Utah!" appears in red at the upper right as part of the slogan "Ski Utah!" A skier in blue heads down a slope to the left of the slogan. The numerals are in blue and also in blue at the bottom of the plate is another slogan, "Greatest Snow on Earth."

VERMONT

By a law enacted in December 1904, Vermont citizens had until May 1, 1905, to register their automobiles. Through 1906, motorists received a single plate for two dollars, which was made of enameled iron bearing white lettering on a blue background. Black-on-white plates were issued from 1907 until 1916. Various colors, including the University of Vermont's yellow and green in 1918 and Norwich University's maroon and tan in 1929, were used until 1949. Dark blue and white were used from 1931 through 1942 and black and white from 1944 through 1947. But in 1949, the familiar white and green colors of Vermont were used and they have been used ever since, reversing colors from issue to issue. The current license plate, issued in 1986, depicts a maple tree in white at the upper left and "Vermont" in white at the top center. The license plate numbers in white are surrounded by a white rectangle. The nickname "Green Mountain State" appears in white at the bottom. All of these are against a solid green background.[47]

VIRGINIA

Carl Leroy Armentrout of Staunton was the first Virginian to register his car on June 1, 1906. He received a black and white enamel plate. Over the years, the state experimented with various materials for the manufacture of plates, including fiberplate in 1925 and fiberboard in 1944. Both of these plates were said to be appealing to goats, who happily ate them. Metal plates became the standard, aluminum having been used since 1973. The current regular plate (illustrated) is a simple blue-on-white plate with "Virginia" at the top center in lighter blue than the blue used in the license plate number. However, a host of other plates, including "Heritage" and "Scenic" graphic plates, are available as current issues. The "Heritage" plates depict a cardinal, the state bird, perched on a branch of a flowering dogwood, the state tree, all in a light background with deep blue numerals and "Virginia" in red across the bottom. The "Scenic" plates show an ocean scene—blue water, shore, green land, and blue mountains—on a light blue background with lettering in dark blue.[48]

WASHINGTON

When S. A. Perkins of Tacoma became the first citizen of Washington to register his Pope-Toledo touring car on May 2, 1905, he did not receive a license plate for his two-dollar fee. Motorists had to make their own plates or stencil their numbers on the back and front of their vehicles. Finally in 1916, Washington issued its first plate, which was white on blue. Blue and white were used in 1923–1925 and 1936–1937; green and white were used in 1926–1927, 1929–1934, 1938, 1940–1946, and 1950–1986. In 1987 Washington celebrated its centennial as a state, and the multiyear plate issued that year used patriotic colors: blue numerals on a white background, with "Washington" in red letters at the top and "Centennial Celebration" in red at the bottom, all overlaying a light blue graphic of Mount Rainier. Plates issued in 1990 keep the same design and colors but eliminated the centennial designation.[49]

WEST VIRGINIA

The 1906 white-on-blue West Virginia license plate was the state's first issue. Various color combinations, usually including white, were used until 1931, when yellow and black became the color combination of all West Virginia plates until the 1956 issue. New plates were not issued, however, for 1943 and 1944 owing to wartime shortages. A black and white metal tab was used to validate the 1942 plate for 1943, and a windshield sticker was used for 1944. Between 1956 and 1962, various color combinations were used, green and white being used in 1956, 1958, and 1959. In 1963, a series of blue and yellow combinations began. The current issue retains those colors on a field of white. The outline of West Virginia in yellow dominates the left side of the plate. Numerals in blue are superimposed over it and through the right side. In blue slightly off center at the bottom is the name "West Virginia."[50]

WISCONSIN

The cities of Madison and Milwaukee began registering automobiles in 1904, but the state began furnishing license plates only on July 1, 1905. The first plate was undated with aluminum numbers riveted on a black zinc base. These plates were used until 1912 except by new registrants between July 1 and the end of 1911, who were issued aluminum-on-green plates. The new 1912 annual plates were aluminum on red. The 1913 plates were aluminum on blue. Beginning with the black-on-white 1914 plates, aluminum never was used again as a color on Wisconsin plates. A variety of colors was used over the years from olive drab (1917) to polaris maroon (1965) and jonquil yellow (1961). The slogan "America's Dairyland" first appeared on the red-on-white plate of 1940 and remains today. The first graphic plates were issued in 1986. The current issue continues the use of the graphic plate. "Wisconsin" appears in blue letters at the upper left top of the plate. Green and blue lines cross the plate below the name of the state and define the graphic in the upper right of the plate. The blue line becomes water on which a sailboat is defined sailing against an orange sun. Geese fly toward the sun from a farm scene in the extreme upper right of the plate. The numerals are in red.[51]

WYOMING

The first Wyoming license plate was issued in 1913. It had red letters on a white background and was undated. Not until the white-on-brown plate of 1918 were dates used on the plates. Various color combinations were used in the annual issues that continued each year until 1975, when multiyear plates came into use. Plates were then issued in 1978 (brown on white), 1983 (brown on gold), and 1988 (red, white, and blue bicentennial design). The current 1993 plate is a graphic plate that pictures a green-and-sand-colored prairie at the bottom, which runs up to blue foothills and mountains. "Wyoming" appears in dark blue lettering at the top right. The numerals in dark blue are separated by a cowboy on a bucking horse. The bucking horse first was used on the black-on-white 1936 license plate.[52]

DISTRICT OF COLUMBIA

Black and white and yellow and black have been frequently used color combinations for District license plates. The very first District plate was white on black in 1907. The first yellow and black plate was the 1915 plate. In 1975, however, red, white, and blue became the colors used on the license plates for the nation's capital city.[53] The current license plate highlights the blue numerals between horizontal red stripes on a white background. The license plate number is divided by the "stars and bars" in red. "Washington, D.C." is in blue below the second horizontal stripe, and also in blue above the first stripe is the slogan "Celebrate & Discover" or "A Capital City."

AMERICAN SAMOA

There is no record of when the registration of motor vehicles began in American Samoa. The earliest extant plate dates back to 1933.[54] The current license plate is red on white with a palm tree swaying in the breeze depicted to the left. The words "Motu o Fiafiaga," or "Land of Happiness," are in red across the top of the plate, and "American Samoa" is across the bottom.

COMMONWEALTH OF THE NORTHERN MARIANA ISLANDS

Since the Commonwealth was only recently created, its first license plate was issued in 1978. The first issue was blue on white with "Commonwealth" at the top and "Northern Marianas" at the bottom. A latte stone and a star were depicted to the left of the plate number. In 1988, however, with the redesign of the flag, a new multiyear plate was issued. This plate features the latte stone, on which a star is centered, and surrounding the latte stone is a white, light blue, yellow, and medium orange MarMar. "Hafa Adai," or "hello," is centered in light blue at the top of the plate and "CNMI–USA," also in light blue, is at the bottom center. The license plate numbers are in navy blue and the background is white.[55]

GUAM

In 1924, Guam began to issue license plates every year. Various color combinations were used. In 1965, multiyear plates began to be issued and with these issues came messages. The plates first issued in 1965, 1974, and 1980 contained the message "HAFA ADAI," meaning "hello." The plate issued in 1970 had the words "America's Day Begins in" at the top and "Guam USA" at the bottom. The plate used from 1983 to 1986 displayed the slogan "Hub of the Pacific."[56] The current license plate is not illustrated.

PUERTO RICO

Motor vehicle registrations in Puerto Rico began in 1908, when 188 vehicles were registered. By 1992 that number had grown to 1,650,709. Multiyear plates have been issued since 1959. The current plate, issued since 1985, is black on white with a silk-screen reproduction of a sentry box in the center. These sentry boxes are found in the sixteenth-century

Spanish fortresses on the island. "Garita del Diablo" at San Felipe del Morro is the most famous of the sentry boxes. In black lettering at the top appears "Puerto Rico" and at the bottom, the slogan "Isla del Encanto," or "Island of Enchantment."[57]

U.S. VIRGIN ISLANDS

The 1928 license plate of the U.S. Virgin Islands was probably the first plate issued, even though vehicle registrations may have occurred earlier. For ten years beginning in 1952, the slogan "Tropical Playground" appeared on the plates. From 1963 to 1967, the slogan "Vacation Adventure" appeared. In 1968, the multiyear plates carried the new slogan "American Paradise," which remains on the current issue.[58] The current multiyear plates, which were issued first in 1988, employ red lettering and numerals on a white background. "American Paradise" is centered across the top and "US Virgin Islands 88" across the bottom.

NOTES

1. Unpublished information provided by State of Alabama, Department of Revenue, Motor Vehicle Division.
2. Alaska Stat. §28.10.161.
3. *Brief History of Alaska License Plates* (Anchorage: State of Alaska, Department of Public Safety, Division of Motor Vehicles, n.d.); information supplied by Alaska Division of Motor Vehicles.
4. Justin Herman, *This Week on Arizona Highways* (Phoenix: Arizona Highway Department, 1968); supplied by Arizona Department of Transportation, Motor Vehicle Division.
5. Unpublished information supplied by Arizona Department of Transportation, Motor Vehicle Division.
6. "Arkansas Office of Motor Vehicle [sic]." (Unpublished information provided by the Arkansas State Library.)
7. *California License Plates and Proof of Current Registration, 1991/92* (State of California, Department of Motor Vehicles, 1991), pp. 2–5.
8. *Colorado License Plate History* (n.p., n.d.); information provided by State of Colorado, Department of Revenue.
9. *Historical Notes about Connecticut's Automobile Registration Plates* (Wethersfield: Commissioner, State Motor Vehicle Department, n.d.); information supplied by the Connecticut Department of Motor Vehicles.
10. *Motor Vehicle History* (Dover: State of Delaware, Department of Public Safety, Division of Motor Vehicles, n.d.); information supplied by Delaware Division of Motor Vehicles.
11. "From file located in the Div. of Motor Vehicles Bureau of Registration; Kirtman Bldg., Rm. A-114, Ms. Cindy Britt." (Provided by Florida Department of State, Division of Library and Information Services.)
12. *Georgia Motor Vehicle License Plate Colors, 1910–1994* (Atlanta: Georgia

Department of Revenue, Motor Vehicle Division, n.d.); information supplied by Georgia Department of Revenue, Motor Vehicle Division, Correspondence Section.

13. Gerald Boone, "Hawaii Car Plates," *The New Pacific Magazine* 5 (September/October 1981): 37.

14. *History of Idaho License Plates* (n.p., n.d.); supplied by the Idaho Transportation Department.

15. George H. Ryan, Secretary of State, *Time Marches On . . . As Seen in Illinois License Plates* (n.p., n.d.); supplied by Illinois Office of the Secretary of State.

16. *History of Indiana License Plates* (n.p., 1985); information supplied by the Indiana Bureau of Motor Vehicles.

17. Charles C. Sinclair, Director, *History of Motor Vehicle Registration* (Des Moines: Motor Vehicle Registration Division, Iowa Department of Public Safety, January 17, 1972); information supplied by the Iowa Department of Transportation, Office of Vehicle Registration.

18. *Brief History of License Plates* (n.p., n.d.); information provided by Kansas Department of Revenue, Division of Vehicles.

19. *Kentucky Motor Vehicle Registration Plates* (n.p., n.d.); information provided by the Commonwealth of Kentucky, Transportation Cabinet.

20. Neil Parker, *Registration Plates of the World,* 2d ed. (Somerset, Great Britain: Europlate, 1987), pp. 465, 467.

21. *Color Combinations of Plates Issued by Maine* (n.p., n.d.); information supplied by Maine Motor Vehicle Division.

22. *History of Maryland License Plates* (n.p., revised June 18, 1988); information provided by Maryland Department of Transportation, Motor Vehicle Administration.

23. *Registry of Motor Vehicles, Agency Outline, History of the Registry of Motor Vehicles* (n.p., n.d.); information supplied by the Massachusetts Registry of Motor Vehicles.

24. *The Story of Michigan License Plates* (Lansing: Michigan Department of State, 1967); information provided by the Library of Michigan.

25. *History of Minnesota License Plate* (n.p., n.d.); *State of Minnesota Passenger Car Plate Colors* (n.p., n.d.); information supplied by Minnesota Department of Public Safety, Driver and Vehicle Services Division.

26. Unpublished information supplied by the Mississippi Commission.

27. *License Plate History on Passenger Vehicles* (n.p., n.d.); information supplied by Missouri Department of Revenue, Division of Motor Vehicle and Drivers Licensing.

28. *The Montana License Plate* (n.p., n.d.); information supplied by State of Montana, Department of Justice, Title and Registration Bureau.

29. *License Plate Information* (Lincoln: State of Nebraska, Department of Motor Vehicles, n.d.); *History of Nebraska License Plates* (Lincoln: State of Nebraska, Department of Motor Vehicles, n.d.); information supplied by Nebraska Department of Motor Vehicles.

30. *The Story of the Nevada License Plate* (n.p., n.d.); information supplied by the Nevada Department of Motor Vehicles and Public Safety.

31. Stanley A. Hamel, *A Brief History of New Hampshire License Plates, 1905–1907* (Seabrook: Stanley A. Hamel, published in cooperation with the New Hampshire Automobile Dealers Association, 1977), pp. 2–4, 15.

32. *The New Jersey License Plate Story* (Trenton: Division of Motor Vehicles, n.d.); information supplied by the State of New Jersey, Motor Vehicle Services.

33. Charlotte S. Valdez, *Highlights of New Mexico Motor Vehicle History* (Santa Fe: State of New Mexico, Motor Vehicle Division, n.d.); information supplied by New Mexico Taxation and Revenue Department, Motor Vehicle Division.

34. *Motor Vehicle and Driver Regulation in New York State* (Albany: State of New York, Department of Motor Vehicles, 1986); information supplied by New York Department of Motor Vehicles.

35. *North Carolina License Plate History* (n.p., n.d.); information supplied by State of North Carolina, Division of Motor Vehicles.

36. *North Dakota License Plates (Passenger)* (Bismarck: North Dakota Department of Transportation, Vehicle Services Division, n.d.); information provided by North Dakota Department of Transportation, Motor Vehicle Division.

37. *1980 Ohio License Plates* (Columbus: Bureau of Motor Vehicles, 1980); information supplied by the State of Ohio.

38. *A Brief History of Oklahoma Passenger Plates* (n.p., n.d.); information provided by Oklahoma Tax Commission, Motor Vehicle License Division.

39. *Color of Oregon Passenger License Plates and Tabs* (Salem: Motor Vehicle Division, Department of Transportation, n.d.); information supplied by the Oregon State Library.

40. Commonwealth of Pennsylvania, Department of Transportation, personal letter.

41. Parker, *Registration Plates,* pp. 503–4, 507–8.

42. *Brief Outline History of License Plates* (n.p.: South Carolina Department of Highways and Public Transportation, n.d.); information provided by South Carolina Department of Highways and Public Transportation, Division of Motor Vehicles, Registration-Reciprocity.

43. Bill Farnham, comp., *85 Years of History: A History of Motor Vehicle Registration and Licensing Activities in the State of South Dakota from 1905 until 1990* (Pierre: South Dakota, Department of Revenue, Division of Motor Vehicles, July 1990); information provided by South Dakota Division of Motor Vehicles.

44. *Motor Vehicle History* (n.p., n.d.); *Color Combinations Used on Plates for Passenger Cars, 1915–1991* (n.p., n.d.); information provided by Tennessee Department of Revenue, Motor Vehicle Division.

45. *The History of Texas License Plates* (Austin: Texas Department of Transportation, Motor Vehicle Division, n.d.); information provided by Texas State Department of Highways and Public Transportation, Division of Motor Vehicles.

46. Parker, *Registration Plates,* pp. 503, 517–18.

47. *Vermont Automobile License Plate History* (n.p., n.d.); information provided by State of Vermont, Agency of Transportation, Department of Motor Vehicles.

48. *The Evolution of Virginia's License Plate* (n.p.: Department of Motor Vehicles, February 1991); information provided by Virginia Department of Motor Vehicles.

49. *License Plate History* (Olympia: State of Washington, Department of Licensing, n.d.); information provided by State of Washington, Department of Licensing.

50. Unpublished information provided by the West Virginia State Museum.

51. *Wisconsin Automobile License Plate History* (Madison: Wisconsin Depart-

ment of Transportation, n.d.); information supplied by the State of Wisconsin, Legislative Reference Bureau.

52. *Wyoming License Plates* (n.p., 1993); information provided by the Wyoming Department of Transportation.

53. Parker, *Registration Plates,* p. 22.

54. Parker, *Registration Plates,* pp. 436, 446.

55. Letter to License Plate Collectors from Gregorio M. Camacho, Director of Public Safety, Commonwealth of the Northern Mariana Islands, Department of Public Safety, n.d.; provided by Pete Torres, Office of the United States Representative of the Commonwealth of the Northern Mariana Islands.

56. Parker, *Registration Plates,* p. 195.

57. Information provided by the Departamento de Transportacion y Obras Publicas, Area Vehiculos de Motor and Directoriade Servicios al Conductor, Division de Servicios Tecnicos.

58. Parker, *Registration Plates,* p. 536.

12 State and Territory Postage Stamps

The United States Postal Service has chronicled and commemorated significant events in state and territorial history through its issuance of postage stamps. Anniversaries of statehood have provided the occasion for numerous issues of stamps. Some stamps, like the 1935 Connecticut and 1934 Maryland commemorative issues, celebrated three hundred years of settlement. A 1933 issue commemorates the founding of the colony of Georgia by James Oglethorpe. State flags, birds, flowers, seals, and trees are often found in these stamp designs. There are also depictions of cityscapes, landscapes, mountains—from Mount Rushmore to the Old Man of the Mountains—seascapes, and coral reefs. U.S. postage stamps are interesting and colorful reminders of our history. One stamp for each state and territory has been selected for illustrative purposes in this book.

ALABAMA

A series of fifty 13-cent stamps depicting the state flags was issued in Washington, D.C., on February 23, 1976. The stamps went on sale in each state capital on the same day. The series was designed by Walt Reed and Peter Cocci. A. Saavedra was the engraver. Of these stamps, 436,005,000 were printed.

ALASKA

Alaska became a state on January 3, 1959. On that date in Juneau, the Postal Service issued the special 7-cent airmail stamp called the Alaska Statehood Commemorative. The stamp, designed by Richard C. Lockwood and V. S. McCloskey, Jr., pictures the shape of Alaska in dark blue, over which is superimposed the Big Dipper capped by the North Star, as depicted also on the state flag. The wooded hills and snow-capped mountains in the background are meant to show the terrain and vastness of the state of Alaska as well as its wealth. A total of 90,055,200 of these stamps were issued. C. A. Brooks engraved the vignette and R. J. Jones the lettering.

ARIZONA

The Arizona Statehood Commemorative was issued in Phoenix on February 14, 1962, in celebration of fifty years of statehood for Arizona. This 4-cent stamp was designed by Jimmie E. Ihms, James M. Chemi, and C. R. Chickering. The vignette was engraved by A. W. Dintaman. The lettering was engraved by G. A. Payne. A total of 121,820,000 stamps were issued.

The stamp is dominated by the saguaro cactus in both the foreground and background. A flowering saguaro in the foreground shows off Arizona's state flower, while the outline of a full-grown saguaro in the background enhances the beauty of a moonlit desert night.

ARKANSAS

The Postal Service issued the Arkansas Centennial Commemorative on June 15, 1936, in Little Rock. A. R. Meissner designed this 3-cent stamp, which was engraved by C. T. Arlt, W. B. Wells, and E. M. Hall. A total of 72,992,650 stamps were printed.

A circular shield depicting the portico of the old state house is centered on the stamp, with the "new" capitol to its right and Arkansas' first settlement to its left. At the top left "Arkansas 1836" is lettered and on the top right "Centennial 1936." The stamp was printed in purple.

CALIFORNIA

The 3-cent California Statehood Commemorative celebrates that state's centennial of statehood, 1850–1950. Issued on September 9, 1950, in Sacramento, this stamp was designed by V. S. McCloskey and engraved by M. D. Fenton and A. W. Christensen. A total of 121,120,000 stamps were printed in yellow.

The design of this stamp includes both symbols of modern California—oil derricks in the right background and citrus fruits on the left—and historical scenes. At the center is a man panning gold. To the right, a pioneer couple stands before their covered wagon, which is pulled by a yoke of oxen. To the bottom left, beneath the citrus fruits, is the *Oregon*, the steamship that carried the news of California's statehood to the territory.

COLORADO

Colorado attained statehood in 1876, which was the one hundredth year of U.S. independence. Colorado is known, therefore, as the Centennial State. The Colorado Statehood Centennial that bears this appellation beneath a depiction of the state flower, the columbine, is a 13-cent gravure stamp issued in Denver on May 21, 1977. The green, wooded hills and snow-capped Rocky Mountains of Colorado rise behind the columbine. A total of 189,750,000 of these stamps, designed by V. Jack Ruther, were printed.

CONNECTICUT

The Connecticut Tercentenary Commemorative was issued in Hartford on April 26, 1935. Designed by V. S. McCloskey, Jr., and engraved by J. C. Benzing and W. B. Wells, this 3-cent stamp, printed in lilac, depicts the Charter Oak tree and three hundred years of settlement in Connecticut, from 1635 to 1935. A total of 70,726,800 stamps were issued.

DELAWARE

The U.S. Postal Service issued thirteen stamps, one for each of the original thirteen states, to commemorate the bicentennial of the ratification of the Constitution. The Delaware stamp was issued first, on July 4, 1987, because it had been the first state to ratify the Constitution. This 22-cent stamp, designed by Richard D. Sheaff, is based on the state seal. A farmer with hoe and a frontiersman with rifle hold a banner dominated by an ox. Sheaves of wheat decorate the area above the ox and a banner inscribed with the words "Liberty and Independence" is on the border beneath it. The farmer is also holding aloft a model of a sailing ship. Below this depiction is the date on which Delaware ratified the Constitution: December 7, 1787.

FLORIDA

The Florida Statehood Commemorative stamp was first sold on March 3, 1945, in Tallahassee. This purple 3-cent stamp commemorates one hundred years of statehood for Florida—1845 to 1945. The stamp was designed by William A. Roach. C. A. Brooks engraved the vignette and A.

W. Christensen engraved the lettering. A total of 61,617,350 of the stamps were printed.

The stamp is dominated by the circular state seal in the center. This seal remains the same today except for the substitution of the sabal palmetto for the cocoa tree. The gates of St. Augustine are pictured to the left of the seal and the Florida capitol building to its right.

GEORGIA

General James Oglethorpe founded the colony of Georgia in 1733 with a charter from King George II. The 3-cent General Oglethorpe Commemorative, which commemorates Georgia's founding, was first sold in Savannah on February 12, 1933. C. A. Huston designed the stamp, which pictures a bust of General Oglethorpe in armor. J. Eissler, E. M. Hall, and W. B. Wells did the engravings. A total of 61,719,200 stamps were printed in purple.

HAWAII

On August 21, 1959, President Eisenhower welcomed Hawaii into the Union. On that same date, the Hawaii Statehood Commemorative airmail stamp was issued in Honolulu. A Hawaiian warrior welcomes the star symbolizing statehood by offering a lei in his left hand. A map of the islands runs from the bottom right to the top left. This 7-cent stamp was designed by Joseph Feher. The engravers were C. A. Brooks, W. R. Burnell, and G. A. Payne. A total of 84,815,000 stamps were printed.

IDAHO

In 1940, Idaho celebrated fifty years as a state. The U.S. Postal Service issued the 3-cent Idaho Statehood Commemorative stamp in Boise on July 3, 1940, to commemorate this event. This purple stamp depicts the Idaho capitol, which was completed in 1920 and fashioned after the U.S. Capitol building in Washington. A total of 50,618,150 stamps were printed. The designer was William K. Schrage. J. R. Lowe engraved the vignette and J. S. Edmondson the lettering.

ILLINOIS

The 15-cent windmill series was printed in unlimited numbers of booklets of five. The booklet was issued first in Lubbock, Texas. Depicted in this series designed by Ronald C. Sharp are historic windmills in Virginia, Rhode Island, Massachusetts, Illinois, and the Southwest. The Illinois stamp features the Dutch Mill near Batavia, Illinois. All stamps in the series are printed in brown on an intaglio press.

INDIANA

The Indiana Statehood Commemorative was issued on April 16, 1966, in Corydon, Indiana, the first capital. The design for this 5-cent stamp was made by V. S. McCloskey, Jr., and was based on a commemorative seal designed by Paul Wehr. J. S. Creamer engraved the vignette and K. C. Wiram the lettering. A total of 123,770,000 stamps were printed.

The stamp announces Indiana's sesquicentennial, 1816 to 1966, with an outline in white of the first statehouse and a map of Indiana in blue on which nineteen stars are emblazoned. Indiana was the nineteenth state to enter the Union.

IOWA

Iowa celebrated one hundred years of statehood in 1946. The 3-cent Iowa Statehood Commemorative was issued for the centennial on August 3, 1946, in Iowa City. On each side are stalks of corn. The center of the stamp is a map of Iowa with the state flag upon it. V. S. McCloskey, Jr., designed the stamp. M. D. Fenton and J. S. Edmondson were the engravers. A total of 132,430,000 stamps were printed in blue.

KANSAS

The distinctive 4-cent Kansas Statehood Commemorative stamp, printed on yellow paper, is dominated at the left center by a sunflower, the state flower. Behind a pioneer couple at the lower right are a covered wagon and a wooden fort, all symbols of the settlement of Kansas.

This stamp was occasioned by the centennial of Kansas statehood in 1961. The stamp was issued at Council Grove, Kansas, on May 10, 1961. It was designed by C. R. Chickering. The engravers were R. M. Bower and R. J. Jones. A total of 106,210,000 stamps were issued.

KENTUCKY

The U.S. Postal Service celebrated Kentucky's sesquicentennial by issuing the Kentucky Statehood Commemorative stamp in Frankfort on June 1, 1942. The 3-cent purple stamp was designed by William A. Roach and engraved by C. A. Brooks and A. W. Christensen. The semicircular vignette reproduces a mural by Gilbert White, which is in the Kentucky capitol building. Daniel Boone and three other frontiersmen are looking over the Kentucky River where Frankfort is now located. Beneath this centerpiece are the dates 1792 and 1942, separated by the words "Sesquicentennial of the Statehood of Kentucky." A total of 63,558,400 stamps were printed.

LOUISIANA

The Battle of New Orleans assured Andrew Jackson of the status of a military hero. The Battle of New Orleans 5-cent Commemorative stamp pictures Jackson charging forward with his troops. To the lower right and left, the Battle of New Orleans Sesquicentennial Medal, sculpted by Angela Gregory, is depicted in this Robert J. Jones design. The engravers were C. A. Brooks, H. F. Sharpless, and K. C. Wiram. The stamp was issued in New Orleans on January 8, 1965. A total of 115,695,000 were printed in red, blue, and black.

MAINE

A total of 436,005,000 of the fifty-state flag series were printed (see entry for Alabama in this chapter). The first were issued simultaneously in Washington, D.C., at the occasion of the National Governors' Conference, and in each state capital. Walt Reed and Peter Cocci designed the stamps. They were engraved by A. Saavedra.

MARYLAND

Maryland celebrated three-hundred years of settlement in 1934. The 3-cent Maryland Tercentenary Commemorative stamp recalls the founding of the colony by depicting the *Ark* and the *Dove,* the two ships that first brought European settlers to Maryland in 1634. Designer A. R. Meissner also placed the coat of arms on the right.

This stamp was issued in St. Mary's City, the first settlement in the state, on March 23, 1934. The engravers were J. C. Benzing and E. M. Hall. A total of 46,258,300 stamps were printed.

MASSACHUSETTS

The Massachusetts Bay Colony stamp was issued on April 10, 1930. This rose-colored 2-cent stamp celebrated the three hundredth anniversary of the colony's founding. The seal of the colony is depicted. A total of 32,680,900 stamps were issued.

MICHIGAN

The Michigan Centennial Commemorative stamp was issued on November 1, 1935, in Lansing. A. R. Meissner designed this light-purple 3-cent stamp around the circular state seal in the center with the U.S. flag to its left and the Michigan state flag to the right. At the lower left, a forest and lake are depicted and at the lower right, a scene representing industry and commerce. L. C. Kauffmann engraved the vignette. E. M. Hall engraved the lettering. A total of 75,823,900 stamps were printed.

MINNESOTA

The Minnesota Statehood Commemorative stamp was issued in St. Paul on May 11, 1958, to celebrate one hundred years of statehood, from 1858 to 1958. Designers Homer Hill and C. R. Chickering created a scene in green depicting the beauty of Minnesota's lakes, islands, hills, and trees of the northern woods. A branch of the state tree, the red pine, dominates the left side of this 3-cent stamp. M. D. Fenton engraved the vignette and G. A. Payne the lettering. A total of 120,805,200 stamps were printed.

MISSISSIPPI

The Mississippi Territory Commemorative was first sold in Natchez on April 7, 1948. This maroon 3-cent stamp commemorates the sesquicentennial anniversary of the creation of the Mississippi Territory and depicts the growth of the territory from establishment in 1798 to 1804 and to 1812. The original territorial seal is imposed over the map of the territory. Winthrop Sargent, first territorial governor, is depicted at the upper right. William Schrage designed the stamp. M. D. Fenton engraved the vignette and A. W. Christensen the lettering. A total of 122,650,500 stamps were printed.

MISSOURI

The purple 3-cent Gateway to the West-Midwest Centenary Commemorative stamp first went on sale in Kansas City, Missouri, on June 3, 1950. This design of V. S. McCloskey, Jr., divides a depiction of the Kansas City skyline of 1950 at the top and a depiction of the 1850 settlement of Westport Landing with the words "Kansas City, Missouri, Centennial." R. M. Bower and A. W. Christensen were engravers of this stamp. A total of 122,170,000 were printed.

MONTANA

See description of stamp under state of Washington.

NEBRASKA

First placed on sale May 7, 1954, in Nebraska City, the purple 3-cent Nebraska Territorial Commemorative celebrates the passage of a century since the establishment of the Nebraska Territory. "The Sower," which stands atop the dome of the Nebraska capitol building, is depicted against a background of Mitchell Pass with Scotts Bluff to the right. The stamp was designed by C. R. Chickering and engraved by C. A. Brooks and J. S. Edmondson. A total of 115,810,000 were printed.

NEVADA

The 5-cent Nevada Statehood Commemorative stamp was issued in Carson City on July 22, 1964, the anniversary of the adoption of the state seal one hundred years earlier. The design by William K. Schrage is of the ghost town Virginia City, now a tourist attraction. A map of the state with the centennial dates 1864–1964 is on the right side. M. D. Fenton and G. A. Payne were the engravers. A total of 122,825,000 stamps were printed.

NEW HAMPSHIRE

Dartmouth College is one of New Hampshire's premier colleges and the Dartmouth College Case is one of the country's most famous early cases. The 6-cent stamp that commemorates the 150th anniversary of Daniel Webster's successful argument of the case before the Supreme Court was issued in Hanover on September 22, 1969. John Scotford, Jr.'s design is based on the John Pope portrait of Webster, which hangs in Parkhurst Hall. Dartmouth Hall is sketched in the background. A total of 129,540,000 of these green and white stamps were printed.

NEW JERSEY

The issue of the 3-cent Nassau Hall Commemorative stamp at Princeton on September 22, 1956, commemorated the two hundredth anniversary of that building, the first at what was to become Princeton University. V. S. McCloskey, Jr., based his design of the stamp on a 1764 Dawkins engraving of the building. A total of 122,100,000 stamps were printed.

NEW MEXICO

New Mexico celebrated fifty years as a state in 1962. The 4-cent New Mexico Statehood Commemorative stamp was issued in Santa Fe on January 6, 1962, to commemorate this event. The simple design by Robert J. Jones pictures the sacred Navajo mountain, Shiprock. R. M. Bowever and

H. F. Sharpless were the engravers. A total of 112,870,000 stamps were printed.

NEW YORK

The 1964 World's Fair was held in New York City. The Postal Service issued this 5-cent stamp, designed by Robert J. Jones, at the World's Fair post office on April 22, 1964. The central mall of the fair is depicted. The Unisphere, which is to the center left, is the only remaining monument to the fair. A. W. Dintaman and H. F. Sharpless were the engravers. A total of 145,700,000 stamps were printed.

NORTH CAROLINA

The Postal Service issued a series of 13-cent stamps depicting the state flags of each state for the U.S. Bicentennial in 1976. Designed by Walt Reed and Peter Cocci from flags provided by the governors, the first-day ceremony of issuing the stamps was held on February 23, 1976, in Washington, D.C., at a meeting of the National Governors' Conference. The stamps were issued in order of admission to statehood. North Carolina was the twelfth colony to become a state.

NORTH DAKOTA

See description of stamp under state of Washington.

OHIO

The 3-cent brown Ohio sesquicentennial stamp was issued on March 2, 1953, in Ohio's first capital city, Chillicothe. A map of Ohio on which is printed the state seal is surrounded going out from the center first by the sesquicentennial dates, 1803–1953, and then by rows of eight stars on each side. The sixteen stars represent the sixteen states that preceded Ohio into the Union. The lone star above the map of Ohio represents the seventeenth state. To the bottom left is a leaf from the Ohio state tree, the buckeye. The stamp was engraved by M. D. Fenton and G. A. Payne. A total of 118,706,000 were issued.

OKLAHOMA

"Arrows to Atoms" is the theme of the 3-cent stamp that was issued in Oklahoma City on June 14, 1957, to commemorate the fiftieth anniversary of Oklahoma statehood. This progressive theme is depicted symbolically by the arrow that pierces the orbital emblem above the deep blue outline of the Oklahoma map. This stamp was designed by William K. Schrage and engraved by M. D. Fenton and G. L. Huber. A total of 102,219,500 stamps were printed.

OREGON

The lone covered wagon, many of which were used by early settlers headed over the Oregon Trail, dominates the foreground of the green 4-cent Oregon Statehood Centennial Commemorative stamp. Mt. Hood is depicted in the background to the right. From the right, the terrain slopes gently to the ocean. This stamp was designed by Robert Hallock and engraved by C. A. Brooks and J. S. Edmondson. It went on sale February 14, 1959, in Astoria, Oregon. Astoria claims to be the oldest settlement west of the Rocky Mountains. A total of 120,740,200 stamps were printed.

PENNSYLVANIA

The U.S. Postal Service issued thirteen stamps, one for each of the original thirteen states, to commemorate the bicentennial of the ratification of the Constitution. The Pennsylvania stamp was the second of the series to be issued because Pennsylvania was the second state that ratified the Constitution. The stamp was issued on August 26, 1987. Designed by Richard D. Sheaff, this 22-cent stamp depicts Independence Hall in Philadelphia, where American independence was formally born. Beneath the vignette is the date on which Pennsylvania ratified the Constitution: December 12, 1787.

RHODE ISLAND

On May 4, 1936, the Rhode Island Tercentenary Commemorative was issued in Providence. The design by A. R. Meissner is based on a statue of Roger Williams, founder of Rhode Island, which stands in Roger Williams Park in Providence. The tercentenary dates 1636–1936 appear at each side toward the top. Beneath to the left is the state seal and to the right the 3-cent denomination in a circular shield. L. C. Kauffmann, F. Pauling, and C. T. Arlt engraved the vignette. W. B. Wells and D. R. McLeod engraved the lettering. A total of 67,127,650 stamps were printed.

SOUTH CAROLINA

This interesting design by George Samerjau appears to be a series of black line drawings on a pine plank. The line drawings were engraved by E. P. Archer. H. F. Sharpless engraved the lettering, which consists of the words "South Carolina" across the top, the tricentennial dates "1670–

1970," "U.S. Postage," and the denomination, "6 cents." The drawings depict symbols and scenes of South Carolina's commerce and history: a couple in colonial dress, the state capitol, St. Phillip's church, Carolina Jessamine, the state flag, a palmetto, cannon at Fort Sumter, barrels, tobacco, and cotton. A total of 135,805,000 stamps were printed.

SOUTH DAKOTA

In 1952, the Mount Rushmore National Memorial became twenty-five years old. The Postal Service issued a 3-cent stamp to commemorate this event. William K. Schrage designed this green stamp dominated by Washington, Jefferson, Theodore Roosevelt, and Lincoln. At the lower right, a woman and child are seated looking up the mountain. The sign in front of them reads "Mount Rushmore National Memorial 1927–1952." The words "Black Hills South Dakota" appear at the lower left. A total of 116,255,000 stamps were printed.

TENNESSEE

The purple 3-cent Tennessee Statehood Commemorative stamp was issued in Nashville on June 1, 1946. Designed by V. S. McCloskey, Jr., the state capitol, reminiscent of an Ionic temple, is depicted at the center. A portrait of Andrew Jackson is on an oval panel to the upper left. On the upper right is a portrait on a symmetrical panel of John Sevier, an early governor and founding father of the state. This stamp commemorates the 150th anniversary of Tennessee statehood and identifies Tennessee as the Volunteer State. The engravers were C. A. Brooks, C. T. Arlt, and A. W. Christensen. A total of 132,274,500 stamps were printed.

TEXAS

The flags of the United States and Texas are featured on the blue 3-cent Texas Statehood stamp, which was issued in Austin on December 29, 1945, to commemorate the centennial anniversary of the admission of Texas to the Union. In this stamp designed by James B. Winn, a ray of light coming from the twenty-eighth star of the U.S. flag illuminates the star on the flag of the Lone Star State. Texas was the twenty-eighth state to join the Union. Beneath the U.S. flag are the centennial dates 1845–1945. E. R. Grove and E. H. Helmuth did the engraving. A total of 170,640,000 stamps were printed.

UTAH

This purple 3-cent stamp was issued on July 24, 1947, in Salt Lake City to commemorate the anniversary of one hundred years of settlement in

Utah. Designed by E. R. Chickering and engraved by M. D. Fenton and E. H. Helmuth, the scene, dominated by a covered wagon, is of the first settlers arriving at the valley of the Great Salt Lake. The words "This is the place," attributed to Brigham Young, who led his Mormon followers to Utah, are found to the upper right. A scroll beneath this scene announces the Utah centennial and its dates, 1847–1947. A total of 131,968,000 stamps were printed.

VERMONT

Vermont was the fourteenth state to enter the Union. On March 4, 1941, the purple 3-cent Vermont Statehood Commemorative was issued in Montpelier for that 150th anniversary occasion. The stamp's design by A. R. Meissner pictures the Vermont capitol. A shield to the lower right contains thirteen stars representing the first thirteen states. The star above the shield represents the fourteenth state, Vermont. C. T. Arlt and J. T. Vail did the engraving. A total of 54,574,550 stamps were issued.

VIRGINIA

On February 7, 1980, in Lubbock, Texas, the Postal Service issued a booklet of 15-cent stamps depicting five historic windmills of the United States. An unlimited number of these booklets were printed. Windmills located in Rhode Island, Illinois, Massachusetts, Virginia, and the southwestern United States were depicted on the stamps. The Virginia stamp pictures the Robertson Windmill in Williamsburg. This and the other windmill stamps were designed by Ronald C. Sharpe and engraved by K. Kipperman and A. Saavedra.

WASHINGTON

In 1939, four states—North Dakota, South Dakota, Montana, and Washington—commemorated their fifty-year anniversaries of statehood. The Postal Service issued a purple 3-cent stamp to celebrate these anniversaries with issue dates in each state capital corresponding to the anniversary date for that state's entry to the Union. Thus, for the state of Washington, the stamp was issued on November 11, 1939, in Olympia. In Bismarck, North Dakota, the stamp went on sale on November 2, 1939. And in Helena, Montana, it went on sale on November 8, 1939. A. R. Meissner designed this stamp, which features the four states highlighted on a map of the northwestern United States and the names of the capitals of each state. M. D. Fenton and W. B. Wells were the engravers. A total of 66,835,000 stamps were printed.

WEST VIRGINIA

The series of fifty stamps, all in 13-cent denominations, depicting the state flags went on sale simultaneously in Washington, D.C., and each state capital on February 23, 1976. Walt Reed and Peter Cocci were the designers. A. Saavedra was the engraver. A total of 436,005,000 stamps were printed.

WISCONSIN

On May 29, 1948, the Wisconsin Statehood Commemorative stamp was issued on the one hundredth anniversary of Wisconsin's entrance to the Union. This purple 3-cent stamp, designed by V. S. McCloskey, Jr., and engraved by R. M. Bower and C. A. Smith, has two main features. To the left, a scroll unrolls with the state of Wisconsin in dark outline and the centennial dates 1848–1948. To the right is the state capitol, above which is the word "Forward," which is the state motto. A total of 115,250,000 stamps were printed.

WYOMING

A. R. Meissner designed the Wyoming Statehood Commemorative stamp, which reproduces the state seal in purple. It was issued in Cheyenne on July 10, 1940, the anniversary of fifty years of statehood. C. A. Brooks designed the vignette and E. H. Helmuth the lettering. A total of 50,034,400 stamps were printed.

DISTRICT OF COLUMBIA

The year 1950 marked the sesquicentennial of the nation's capital city. It also marked the issue of four stamps by the Postal Service to commemorate the 150-year anniversary. The themes of the stamps were freedom, executive, judicial, and legislative. The executive stamp, designed by W. K. Shrage, is illustrated. This green 3-cent stamp was issued in Washington, D.C., on June 12, 1950. Above the depiction of the White House is a panel with the sesquicentennial dates 1800–1950, separated by the city's name, "Washington." Below is another panel with the words "National Capital Sesquicentennial." M. D. Fenton and E. H. Helmuth were the engravers. A total of 130,050,000 stamps were printed.

AMERICAN SAMOA

This stamp was issued on August 26, 1980, as a block of four stamps featuring coral reefs in the Virgin Islands, Florida, Hawaii, and American

Samoa. The block of stamps was issued in Charlotte Amalie, St. Thomas, the capital of the U.S. Virgin Islands. Elkhorn coral (*Acropora palmata*) is depicted with two porkfish (*Anisotremus virginicus*) swimming through it. Chuck Ripper designed the stamp, of which 205,165,000 were printed.

COMMONWEALTH OF THE NORTHERN MARIANA ISLANDS

The Commonwealth of the Northern Mariana Islands (CNMI) was honored for the first time by the U.S. Postal Service in November 1993, when a 29-cent commemorative went on sale in post offices. In the foreground to the left, a local inhabitant in native dress sits in the green grass by two latte stones, a palm tree swaying in the breeze to her left. Latte stones, thought to have been used originally by early settlers to support the houses of chieftains or perhaps even to support boat houses, have become important symbols that stand for the strength of the family and the enduring culture of the islands. The flag of the Commonwealth is depicted in the background to the right. Appropriate to the islands, the depictions on the stamp are printed on a surrounding sea of light blue.

GUAM

The U.S. Postal Service has not issued a postage stamp dealing specifically with Guam.

PUERTO RICO

The city of San Juan celebrated its 450-year anniversary in 1971. Founded in 1521, it is the oldest of any city in the United States or its possessions. Designer Walter Brooks depicts the El Morro castle on this 8-cent stamp. The stamp was issued on September 12, 1971, in San Juan. The engraving was done by J. S. Creamer and A. Saavedra. A total of 148,755,000 stamps were printed.

U.S. VIRGIN ISLANDS

The Postal Service issued a series of four 3-cent stamps in 1937 to honor outlying U.S. possessions. They included at the time Hawaii, Alaska, Puerto Rico, and the Virgin Islands. The Virgin Islands stamp was issued on December 15, 1937, in Charlotte Amalie, the city depicted on the stamp with a view of its harbor and surrounding islands. V. S. McCloskey, Jr., designed the stamp. C. T. Arlt engraved the vignette and J. T. Vail the lettering. A total of 76,474,550 stamps were printed.

13 Miscellaneous Official State and Territory Designations

Every state in the union has found it desirable to recognize officially some special symbols that have a unique importance. These legislative actions have largely been phenomena of the past thirty years. Often such official designations recognize the importance of an industry to a particular state. Florida, for example, designated orange juice as its official beverage. Tomato juice is Ohio's state beverage and cranberry juice, Massachusetts'. Wisconsin's official domestic animal is the dairy cow. On the other hand, an official designation may also bring with it special protection for an endangered species. Georgia's and Massachusetts' right whale, California's gray whale, Alaska's bowhead whale, and Florida's manatee received protection as officially designated state marine mammals.

Some designated symbols recall the early history of a state. Gold is the state mineral of California and Alaska. Dog mushing is Alaska's state sport. The American buffalo is the state animal of Kansas, and Plymouth Rock is Massachusetts' historical rock. Other symbols cannot be considered without recalling the state with which they have become identified: Alaskan king salmon, the California grizzly bear, Indiana limestone, Louisiana's crawfish, and Maine's moose.

Whether animals, vegetables, or minerals or even reptiles, mammals, or neckwear, each state expresses its unique character through the symbols it chooses.

ALABAMA

Barbecue championship (1991)	Demopolis Christmas on the River Barbecue Cook-Off
Butterfly and mascot (1989)	Easter Tiger Swallowtail
Championship horse show (1988)	Alabama State Championship Horse Show
Dance (1981)	Square dance
Fossil (1984)	Species *Basilosaurus cetoides*
Freshwater fish (1975)	Largemouth bass, *Micropterus punctulatus*
Gemstone (1990)	Star blue quartz
Horse (1975)	Rocking horse
Insect (1989)	Monarch butterfly
Mineral (1967)	Hematite
Nut (1982)	Pecan
Reptile (1990)	Red-bellied turtle, *Pseudemys alabamensis* of the family *Emydidae* of the order *Testudines*
Rock (1969)	Marble
Saltwater fish (1959)	Tarpon
Shell (1990)	*Scaphella junonia johnstoneae*[1]

ALASKA

Fish (1963)	King salmon, *Oncorhynchus tshawytscha*
Fossil (1986)	Woolly mammoth, *Mammuthus primigenius*
Gem (1968)	Jade
Marine mammal (1983)	Bowhead whale
Mineral (1968)	Gold
Sport (1972)	Dog mushing[2]

ARIZONA

Amphibian (1986)	Arizona tree frog, *Hyla eximia*
Fish (1986)	Arizona trout, *Salmo apache*

Fossil (1986)	Petrified wood, *Araucarioxylon arizonicum*
Gem (1974)	Turquoise
Mammal (1986)	Ringtail, *Bassariscus astutus*
Neckwear (1973)	Bola tie
Reptile (1986)	Arizona ridgenose rattlesnake, *Crotalus willardi*[3]

ARKANSAS

Beverage (1985)	Milk
Folk dance (1991)	Square dance
Fruit and vegetable (1987)	South Arkansas vine ripe pink tomato
Gem (1967)	Diamond
Insect (1973)	Honeybee
Language (1987)	English
Mineral (1967)	Quartz crystal
Musical instrument (1985)	Fiddle
Rock (1967)	Bauxite[4]

CALIFORNIA

Animal (1953)	California grizzly bear, *Ursus californicus*[5]
Dance (1988)	West Coast swing dance
Fish (1947)	Golden trout, *Salmo aqua-bonita*[6]
Folk dance (1988)	Square dance
Fossil (1973)	Saber-toothed cat, *Smilodon californicus*
Gemstone (1985)	Benitoite
Insect (1972)	California dog-face butterfly, *Zerene eurydice*
Marine mammal (1975)	California gray whale, *Eschrichtus robustus*
Mineral (1965)	Native gold
Prehistoric artifact (1991)	Chipped stone bear

Reptile (1972)	California desert tortoise, *Gopherus agassizi*
Rock (1965)	Serpentine[7]

COLORADO

Animal (1961)	Rocky Mountain bighorn sheep, *Ovis canadensis*
Gem (1971)	Aquamarine[8]

CONNECTICUT

Animal (1975)	Sperm whale, *Physeter catadon*
Composer (1991)	Charles Edward Ives
Fossil (1991)	*Eubrontes giganteus*
Hero (1985)	Nathan Hale
Insect (1977)	Praying mantis, *Mantis religiosa*
Mineral (1977)	Garnet
Shellfish (1989)	Eastern oyster, *Crassotrea virginica*[9]
Ship (1983)	USS. *Nautilus*[10]

DELAWARE

Beverage (1983)	Milk
Bug (1973)	Ladybug
Fish (1981)	Weakfish, genus *Cynoscion*
Mineral (1975)	Sillimanite[11]

FLORIDA

Animal (1982)	Florida panther
Band (1990)	St. Johns River City Band
Beverage (1967)	Juice from the mature oranges of the species *Citrus sinensis* and hybrids of that species
Fiddle contest (1989)	Annual contest held by the Florida State Fiddlers' Association at the Stephen Foster State Folk Culture Center

Freshwater fish (1975)	Florida largemouth bass, *Micropterus salmoides floridanus*
Gem (1970)	Moonstone
Litter control symbol (1978)	"Glenn Glitter," the litter control trademark of the Florida Federation of Garden Clubs, Inc.
Marine mammal (1975)	Manatee, commonly called the sea cow
Moving image center and archive (1989)	Louis Wolfson II Media History Center, Inc., in Miami
Opera program (1983)	Greater Miami Opera Association, Orlando Opera Company, Florida State University School of Music
Railroad museums (1984)	Orange Blossom Special Railroad Museum; Gold Coast Railroad Museum, Inc., and Gold Coast Railroad, Inc.; Florida Gulf Coast Railroad Museum
Reptile (1987)	American alligator
Saltwater fish (1975)	Atlantic sailfish, *Istiophorus platypterus*
Saltwater mammal (1975)	Porpoise, commonly called the dolphin
Shell (1969)	Horse conch, *Pleuroploca gigantea,* also known as the giant band shell
Soil (1989)	Myakka fine sand
Stone (1979)	Agatized coral
Transportation museum (1985)	Florida Museum of Transportation and History in Fernandina Beach[12]

GEORGIA

Atlas (1985)	*The Atlas of Georgia*[13]
Butterfly (1988)	Tiger swallowtail
Fish (1970)	Largemouth bass
Fossil (1976)	Shark tooth
Gem (1976)	Quartz
Historic drama (1990)	"The Reach of Song"
Insect (1975)	Honeybee[14]
Marine mammal (1985)	Right whale[15]
Mineral (1976)	Staurolite

Reptile (1989)	Gopher tortoise
Seashell (1987)	Knobbed whelk
Vegetable (1990)	Vidalia sweet onion[16]

HAWAII

Colors (by island):	
Hawaii	Red
Maui	Pink
Molokai	Green
Kahoolawe	Gray
Lanai	Yellow
Oahu	Yellow
Kauai	Purple
Niihau	White
Gem (1987)	Black coral
Team sport (1986)	Outrigger canoe paddling[17]

IDAHO

Fish (1990)	Cutthroat trout
Gem (1967)	Star garnet
Horse (1975)	Appaloosa[18]

ILLINOIS

Animal (1982)	White-tailed deer
Fish (1987)	Bluegill, *Lepomis macrochirus*
Folk dance (1990)	Square dance
Fossil (1990)	*Tullimonstrum gregarium*
Insect (1975)	Monarch butterfly, *Danaus plexippus*
Language (1969)	English
Mineral (1965)	Fluorite
Prairie grass (1989)	Big bluestem[19]

INDIANA

Language (1984)	English
Poem (1963)	"Indiana" by Arthur Franklin Mapes
Stone (1971)	Limestone[20]

IOWA

Rock (1967)	Geode[21]

KANSAS

Animal (1955)	American buffalo, *Bison americanus*
Insect (1976)	Honeybee
Reptile (1986)	Ornate box turtle, *Terrapene ornata, Agassiz*[22]

KENTUCKY

Language (1984)	English
Tug-of-war championship (1984)	Nelson County Fair Tug-of-War Championship Contest
Wild game animal species (1968)	Gray squirrel[23]

LOUISIANA

"Christmas in the Country" (1990)	"Christmas in the Country" in Elizabeth, La.
Crustacean (1983)	Crawfish
Dog (1979)	Louisiana Catahoula leopard dog
Doughnut (1986)	Beignet
Drink (1983)	Milk
Fossil (1976)	Petrified palmwood
Gem (1976)	Agate
Insect (1977)	Honeybee

Musical instrument (1990)	Diatonic ("Cajun") accordion
Reptile (1983)	Alligator[24]

MAINE

Animal (1979)	Moose
Berry (1991)	Wild blueberry
Cat (1985)	Maine coon cat
Fish (1969)	Landlocked salmon, *Salmo salar sebago*
Fossil (1985)	*Pertica quadrifaria*
Insect (1975)	Honeybee
Language of the Deaf Community (1991)	American Sign Language
Mineral (1971)	Tourmaline
Vessel (1987)	Schooner *Bowdoin*[25]

MARYLAND

Boat (1985)	Skipjack
Crustacean (1989)	Maryland blue crab, *Callinectes sapidus*
Dog (1964)	Chesapeake Bay retriever
Fish (1965)	Striped bass
Fossil shell (1984)	*Ecphora quadricostata*
Insect (1973)	Baltimore checkerspot butterfly, *Euphydryas phaeton*
Sport (1962)	Jousting
Summer theater (1978)	Olney Theatre in Montgomery County
Theater (1978)	Center Stage in Baltimore[26]

MASSACHUSETTS

Beverage (1970)	Cranberry juice
Building and monument stone (1983)	Granite
Cat (1988)	Tabby cat
Ceremonial march (1985)	"The Road to Boston"

Designation of citizens (1990)	Bay Staters
Dog (1979)	Boston terrier
Explorer rock (1983)	Dighton Rock
Fish (1974)	Cod
Folk dance (1989)	Square dancing
Fossil (1980)	Dinosaur track
Gem (1979)	Rhodonite
Heroine (1983)	Deborah Samson
Historical rock (1983)	Plymouth Rock
Horse (1970)	Morgan horse
Insect (1974)	Ladybug
Marine mammal (1980)	Right whale, *Eubalaena glacialis*
Memorial to honor Vietnam War veterans (1990)	Memorial in Worcester
Mineral (1981)	Babingtonite
Muffin (1986)	Corn muffin
Poem (1981)	"Blue Hills of Massachusetts" by Katherine E. Mullen
Rock (1983)	Roxbury pudding stone
Shell (1987)	New England neptune, *Neptunea lyrata decemcostata*
Soil (1990)	Paxton soil series[27]

MICHIGAN

Fish (1988)	Brook trout
Gem (1973)	Chlorastrolite, or greenstone
Soil (1990)	Kalkaska soil series
Stone (1966)	Petoskey Stone[28]

MINNESOTA

Drink (1984)	Milk
Fish (1965)	Walleye, *Stizostedion v. vitreum*
Gem (1969)	Lake Superior agate
Grain (1977)	Wild rice, *Zizania aquatica*

Muffin (1988)	Blueberry muffin
Mushroom (1984)	Morel[29]

MISSISSIPPI

Beverage (1984)	Milk
Butterfly (1991)	Spicebush swallowtail, *Pterourus troilus*
Fish (1974)	Largemouth bass, *Micropterus salmoides*[30]
Fossil (1981)	Prehistoric whale[31]
Insect (1980)	Honeybee
Land mammal (1974)	White-tailed deer, *Odocoileus virginianus*
Language (1987)	English
Shell (1974)	Oyster shell
Water mammal (1974)	Bottle-nosed dolphin, *Tursiops truncatus*[32]

MISSOURI

Fossil (1989)	Crinoidea, *Delocrinus missouriensis*
Insect (1985)	Honeybee
Mineral (1967)	Galena
Musical instrument (1987)	Fiddle
Rock (1967)	Mozarkite
Tree nut (1990)	Black walnut, *Juglans nigra*[33]

MONTANA

Animal (1983)	Grizzly bear, *Ursus arctos horribilis*
Arboretum (1991)	University of Montana, Missoula campus
Fish (1977)	Blackspotted cutthroat trout, *Salmo clarki*
Fossil (1985)	Duck-billed dinosaur, *Maiasaura peeblesorum*
Gem (1969)	Sapphire and Montana agate

Grass (1973)	Bluebunch grass, *Agropyron spicatum (pursh)*
Vietnam veterans' memorial (1987)	Memorial in Rose Park, Missoula[34]

NEBRASKA

Fossil (1967)	Mammoth
Gem (1967)	Blue agate
Grass (1969)	Little bluestem grass
Insect (1975)	Honeybee[35]
Mammal (1981)	White-tailed deer[36]
Rock (1967)	Prairie agate
Soil (1979)	Holdrege series, *Typic Argiustolls*[37]

NEVADA

Animal (1973)	Desert bighorn sheep, *Oviscanadensis nelsoni*
Colors (1983)	Silver and blue
Fish (1981)	Lohonton cutthroat trout, *Salmo clarki henshawi*
Fossil (1977)	Ichthyosaur
Grass (1977)	Indian rice grass, *Oryzopsis hymenoides*
Metal (1977)	Silver
Precious gemstone (1987)	Virgin Valley black fire opal
Reptile (1989)	Desert tortoise, *Gopherus agassizii*
Rock (1987)	Sandstone
Semiprecious gemstone (1987)	Nevada turquoise[38]

NEW HAMPSHIRE

Amphibian (1985)	Spotted newt, *Notophthalmus viridescens*
Animal (1983)	White-tailed deer
Gem (1985)	Smoky quartz

Insect (1974)	Honeybee
Mineral (1985)	Beryl
Rock (1985)	Granite[39]

NEW JERSEY

Animal (1977)	Horse
Dinosaur (1991)	*Hadrosaurus foulki*
Fish (1991)	Brook trout
Insect (1974)	Honeybee[40]

NEW MEXICO

Animal (1963)	New Mexico black bear
Cookie (1989)	Bizochito
Fish (1955)	New Mexico cutthroat trout
Fossil (1981)	*Coelophysis*
Gem (1967)	Turquoise
Grass (1973)	Blue grama grass, *Boutelova gracillis*
Insect (1989)	Tarantula hawk wasp, *Pepsis formosa*
Poem (1991)	"A Nuevo Mexico" by Luis Tafoya
Vegetable (1965)	Pinto bean and the chili[41]

NEW YORK

Animal (1975)	American beaver, *Castor canadensis*
Beverage (1981)	Milk
Fish (1975)	Brook or speckled trout, *Salvelinus fontinalis*
Fossil (1984)	*Eurypterus remipes*
Fruit (1976)	Apple
Gem (1969)	Garnet
Insect (1989)	Ladybug, *Coccinella novemnotata*
Muffin (1987)	Apple muffin
Shell (1988)	Bay scallops, *Argopecten irradians*[42]

NORTH CAROLINA

Colors (1945)	Red and blue
Insect (1973)	Honeybee
Mammal (1969)	Gray squirrel, *Sciurus carolinensis*
Military academy (1991)	Oak Ridge Military Academy
Reptile (1979)	Turtle (the eastern box turtle is the emblem representing turtles that inhabit North Carolina)
Rock (1979)	Granite
Saltwater fish (1971)	Channel bass or red drum
Shell (1965)	Scotch bonnet
Stone (1973)	Emerald
Tartan (1991)	Carolina tartan[43]

NORTH DAKOTA

Art gallery (1981)	University of North Dakota Art Gallery on the campus in Grand Forks
Beverage (1983)	Milk
Fossil (1967)	Teredo petrified wood
Grass (1977)	Western wheat grass, *Agropyron smithii*
Language (1987)	English
Railroad museum (1989)	Mandan Railroad Museum[44]

OHIO

Animal (1988)	White-tailed deer, *Odocoileus virginianus*
Beverage (1965)	Tomato juice
Gem (1965)	Ohio flint
Invertebrate fossil (1985)	*Isotelus*[45]

OKLAHOMA

Animal (1972)	American buffalo[46]
Colors (1915)	Green and white

Fish (1974)	White bass, *Morone chrysops*[47]
Grass (1972)	Indian grass, *Sorghastrum nutans*
Poem (1973)	"Howdy Folks" by David Randolph Milsten[48]
Reptile (1969)	Collared lizard, *Crotophytus*[49]
Rock (1968)	Barite rose[50]

OREGON

Animal (1969)	Beaver
Fish (1961)	Chinook salmon
Hostess (1969)	Miss Oregon
Insect (1979)	Swallowtail butterfly
Rock (1965)	Thunderegg[51]

PENNSYLVANIA

Animal (1959)	White-tailed deer
Beautification and conservation plant (1982)	Penngift crownvetch, *Coronilla varia L. penngift*
Beverage (1982)	Milk
Dog (1965)	Great Dane
Fish (1970)	Brook trout, *Salvelinus fontinalis*
Fossil (1988)	*Phacops rana*
Insect (1974)	Firefly, *Lampyridae*[52]

RHODE ISLAND

American folk art symbol (1985)	Charles I. D. Looff Carousel
Fruit (1991)	Rhode Island greening apple[53]
Mineral (1966)	Bowenite
Rock (1966)	Cumberlandite[54]
Shell (1987)	Quahaug, *Mercenaria mercenaria*[55]

SOUTH CAROLINA

Animal (1972)	White-tailed deer, *Odocoileus virginianus*
Beverage (1984)	Milk
Dance (1984)	The shag
Dog (1985)	Boykin spaniel
Fish (1972)	Striped bass, or rockfish
Fruit (1984)	Peach
Gem (1969)	Amethyst
Insect (1988)	Carolina mantid, or praying mantis
Language (1987)	English
Reptile (1988)	Loggerhead turtle, *Caretta caretta*
Shell (1984)	Lettered olive
Stone (1969)	Blue granite[56]

SOUTH DAKOTA

Animal (1949)	Coyote
Drink (1986)	Milk
Fish (1982)	Walleye, *Stizostedion vitreum*
Fossil (1988)	*Triceratops*
Gem (1966)	Fairburn agate
Grass (1970)	Western wheat grass, *Agropyron smithii*
Insect (1978)	Honeybee
Jewelry (1988)	Black Hills gold
Mineral (1966)	Rose quartz
Musical instrument (1989)	Fiddle
Soil (1990)	Houdek soil[57]

TENNESSEE

Agricultural insect (1990)	Honeybee
Commercial fish (1988)	Channel catfish
Fine art (1981)	Porcelain painting

Folk dance (1980)	Square dance
Game bird (1988)	Bobwhite quail
Gem (1979)	Tennessee pearl
Insects (1975)	Firefly and ladybug
Language (1984)	English
Poem (1973)	"Oh Tennessee, My Tennessee" by Admiral William Lawrence
Railroad museum (1978)	Tennessee Valley Railroad Museum in Hamilton County
Rock (1979)	Limestone
Sport fish (1988)	Largemouth bass[58]
Wild animal (1972)	Raccoon[59]

TEXAS

Plays (1979)	*The Lone Star,* presented in Galveston Island State Park; *Texas,* presented in Palo Duro Canyon State Park; *Beyond the Sundown,* presented at the Alabama-Coushatta Indian Reservation; and *Fandangle,* presented in Shackleford County[60]

UTAH

Animal (1971)	Elk
Emblem (1959)	Beehive
Fish (1971)	Rainbow trout
Fossil (1988)	*Allosaurus*
Gem (1969)	Topaz
Insect (1983)	Honeybee
Railroad museum (1988)	Ogden Union Station[61]

VERMONT

Animal (1961)	Morgan horse
Beverage (1983)	Milk

Butterfly (1987)	Monarch
Gem (1991)	Grossular garnet
Insect (1977)	Honeybee
Mineral (1991)	Talc
Rocks (1991)	Marble, granite, and slate
Soil (1985)	Tunbridge soil series[62]

VIRGINIA

Beverage (1982)	Milk
Boat (1988)	*Chesapeake Bay Deadrise*
Dog (1966)	American foxhound
Folk dance (1991)	Square dancing
Folklore center (1986)	Blue Ridge Institute in Ferrum
Insect (1991)	Tiger swallowtail butterfly, *Papilio glaucus Linne*
Shell (1974)	Oyster shell, *Crassoostraea virginica*[63]

WASHINGTON

Dance (1979)	Square dance
Fish (1969)	Steelhead trout, *Salmo gairdnerii*
Fruit (1989)	Apple
Gem (1975)	Petrified wood
Grass (1989)	Bluebunch wheat grass, *Agropyron spicatum*
Tartan (1991)	Asett made up of a green background with blue, white, yellow, red, and black stripes[64]

WEST VIRGINIA

Animal (1973)	Black bear, *Euarctos americanus*
Fish (1973)	Brook trout
Fruit (1972)	Apple[65]

WISCONSIN

Animal (1957)	Badger, *Taxidea taxus*
Beverage (1986)	Milk
Dog (1986)	American water spaniel
Domestic animal (1971)	Dairy cow
Fish (1955)	Muskellunge, *Esox masquinongy masquinongy* Mitchell
Fossil (1988)	Trilobite, *Calymene celebra*
Grain (1991)	Corn, *Zea mays*
Insect (1977)	Honeybee
Mineral (1971)	Galena
Rock (1971)	Red granite
Soil (1983)	Antigo silt loam
Symbol of peace (1971)	Mourning dove
Wildlife animal (1957)	White-tailed deer, *Odocoileus virginianus*[66]

WYOMING

Fish (1987)	Cutthoat trout, *Salmo clarki*
Fossil (1987)	Fossilized fish *Knightia*
Gem (1967)	Jade
Mammal (1985)	American bison, *Bison bison*[67]

AMERICAN SAMOA

Plant (1973)	Kava[68]

COMMONWEALTH OF THE NORTHERN MARIANA ISLANDS

Languages (1985)	Chamorro, Carolinian, English[69]

GUAM

Languages	Chamorro, English[70]

PUERTO RICO

Emblematic Mother's Day flower (1915)	Honeysuckle
Languages (1902)	English and Spanish[71]

NOTES

1. Ala. Code §1–2–29, §1–2–23, §1–2–22, §1–2–18, §1–2–20, §1–2–9, §1–2–26, §1–2–10, §1–2–24, §1–2–13, §1–2–19, §1–2–25, §1–2–14, §1–2–8, §1–2–27.
2. Alaska Stat. §44.09.080, §44.09.120, §44.09.100, §44.09.075, §44.09.110, §44.09.085.
3. Ariz. Rev. Stat. Ann. §41–859, §41–853, §41–858, §41–857.
4. Ark. Rev. Stat. Ann. §41–858, §41–857. Ark. Code Ann. (1987) §1–4–120, §1–4–115, §1–4–117.
5. Cal. Gov't. Code §425, §421.5 (West).
6. *California's Legislature 1984,* p. 201.
7. Cal. Gov't. Code §421.5, §425.7, §425.3, §424.5, §425.5, §425.1, §425.8, §422.5, §425.2 (West).
8. Colo. Rev. Stat. §24–80–911, §24–80–912.
9. Conn. Gen. Stat. Ann. §3–109a, §3–109b, §3–110b, §3–109c; *State of Connecticut: Sites, Seals, Symbols* (Hartford: Secretary of the State, n.d.).
10. *State of Connecticut Register and Manual 1983,* p. 904.
11. Del. Code Ann. tit. 29, §312, §309, §311, §310.
12. Fla. Stat. Ann. §15.0353, §15.049, §15.032, §15.048, §15.036, §15.034, §15.041, §15.038, §15.0396, §15.044, §15.045, §15.0385, §15.037, §15.038, §15.033, §15.047, §15.0336, §15.046 (West).
13. 1985 Ga. Laws 562.
14. Ga. Code Ann. §50–3–62, §50–3–52, §50–3–56, §50–3–57, §50–3–64, §50–3–58.
15. 1985 Ga. Laws 747; *Georgia's Official Symbols* (Atlanta: Secretary of State, n.d.).
16. Ga. Code Ann. §50–3–59, §50–3–63, §50–3–65.
17. *Hawaii, the Aloha State* (Honolulu: State of Hawaii, Hawaii Visitors Bureau, Chamber of Commerce of Hawaii, n.d.); Haw. Rev. Stat. §5–15, §5–14.
18. Idaho Code §67–4505, §67–4508, §67–4506.
19. Ill. Stat. Ann. ch. 1, §3020, §3031, §3051, §3048, §3004, §3005, §3006, §3041 (Smith-Hurd).
20. Ind. Code Ann. §1–2–10–1, §1–2–5–1, §1–2–9–1 (West).
21. *1985–86 Iowa Official Register,* vol. 61, p. 244.
22. Kan. Stat. Ann. §73–1401, §73–1601, §73–1901.
23. Ky. Rev. Stat. Ann. §2.013, §2.260, §2.085 (Baldwin).
24. La. Rev. Stat. Ann. §49–170.2, §49–168, §49–165, note preceding §49–151, §49–170, §49–162, §49–163, §49–164, §49–155.3, §49–169 (West).

25. Me. Rev. Stat. tit. 1, §215, §219, §216, §212, §216, §214, §219, §213, §218.
26. Md. Ann. Code §13–312, §13–301, §13–303, §13–304, §13–311, §13–301, §13–308, §13–309.
27. Mass. Gen. Laws Ann. ch. 2, §10, §25, §30, §27, §35, §14, §24, §13, §32, §17, §15, §26, §23, §11, §12, §16, §34, §18, §28, §21, §22, §29, §33 (West).
28. Mich. Comp. Laws Ann. §2.15, §2.17, §2.61, §2.16.
29. Minn. Stat. Ann. §1.1495, §1.146, §1.147, §1.148, §1.1496, §1.149 (West).
30. Miss. Code Ann. §3–3–29, §3–3–33, §3–3–21.
31. *Souvenir of Mississippi* (Jackson: Dick Molpus, n.d.), p. 27.
32. Miss. Code Ann. §3–3–27, §3–3–17, §3–3–31, §3–3–23, §3–3–19.
33. Mo. Ann. Stat. §10–090, §10.070, §10.047, §10.080, §10.045, §10.100 (Vernon).
34. Mont. Rev. Codes Ann. §1–1–508, §1–1–513, §1–1–507, §1–1–509, §1–1–505, §1–1–506, §1–1–512.
35. Neb. Rev. Stat. §90–109, §90–108, §90–112, §90–114.
36. *Nebraska Blue Book, 1982–1983,* p. 14.
37. Neb. Rev. Stat. §90–110, §90–116.
38. Nev. Rev. Stat. §235.070, §235.025, §235.075, §235.080, §235.055, §235.090, §235.100, §235.065, §235.120, §235.110.
39. N.H. Rev. Stat. Ann. §3:16, §3:12, §3:15, §3:11, §3:14, §3:13.
40. N.J. Stat. Ann. §52:9AAAA–1, §52:9AAAAA–1, §52:9AAAAAA–1, §52:9AAA–1 (West).
41. N.M. Stat. Ann. §12–3–4, §12–3–11.
42. N.Y. State Law §79, §82, §80, §83, §81, §77, §86, §84, §85 (McKinney).
43. N.C. Gen. Stat. §144–6, §145–7, §145–5, §145–14, §145–9, §145–10, §145–6, §145–4, §145–8, §145–15.
44. N.D. Cent. Code §54–02–11, §54–02–12, §54–02–08, §54–02–10, §54–02–13, §54–02–14.
45. Ohio Rev. Code Ann. §5.032, §5.08, §5.07, §5.071 (Baldwin).
46. *Directory of Oklahoma 1981,* p. 20.
47. Okla. Stat. Ann. tit. 25, §93, §98.2.
48. *Directory of Oklahoma 1981,* pp. 18, 19.
49. Ibid., p. 20.
50. Okla. Stat. Ann. tit. 25, §98.1.
51. Or. Rev. Stat. §186.
52. Pa. Stat. Ann. tit. 71, §1007, §1010.2, §1010.1, §1008, §1009, §1010.3, §1010 (Purdon).
53. R.I. Gen. Laws §42–4–11, §42–4–13.
54. *The State of Rhode Island and Providence Plantations, 1983–84 Manual.*
55. R.I. Gen. Laws §42–4–12.
56. S.C. Code §1–1–650, §1–1–690, §1–1–665, §1–1–655, §1–1–640, §1–1–680, §1–1–610, §1–1–645, §1–1–696, §1–1–625, §1–1–695, §1–1–620.
57. S.D. Codified Laws Ann. §1–6–8, §1–6–16, §1–6–15, §1–6–16.1, §1–6–12, §1–6–13, §1–6–14, §1–6–16.2, §1–6–12, §1–6–16.3, §1–6–16.4.
58. Tenn. Code Ann. §4–1–308, §4–1–316, §4–1–313, §4–1–312, §4–1–318, §4–1–310, §4–1–308, §4–1–404, §4–1–303, §4–1–311, §4–1–309, §4–1–317.
59. *Tennessee Blue Book, 1983–84,* pp. 373–74.

60. Tex. Rev. Civ. Stat. Ann. art. 6143d (Vernon).
61. Utah Code Ann. §63–13–7.2, §63–13–10, §63–13–7.3, §63–13–11.7, §63–13–7.1, §63–13–11.5, §63–13–11.9.
62. Vt. Stat. Ann. tit. 1, §500, §503, §505, §506, §502, §508, §507, §504.
63. Va. Code §7.1–40, §7.1–40.3, §7.1–39, §7.1–40.4, §7.1–40.2, §7.1–40.5, §7.1–40.
64. Wash. Rev. Code Ann. §1.20.075, §1.20.045, §1.20.035, §1.20.090, §1.20.025, §1.20.110.
65. *West Virginia Blue Book,* 1980, p. 925.
66. Wis. Stat. Ann. §1.10.
67. Wyo. Stat. Ann. §8–3–113, §8–3–112, §8–3–109, §8–3–111.
68. A.S. Code tit. 1, §1104.
69. *Amendments to the Constitution of the Northern Mariana Islands* (Saipan: Marianas Printing Service, Inc., 1986).
70. *Guam USA Fact Sheet* (Agana: Guam Visitors Bureau, n.d.).
71. P.R. Laws Ann. tit. 1, §114, §115, §52.

14 State and Territory Fairs and Festivals

There is probably a festival or fair going on every day in the United States. They have many purposes. Famous people and native sons are remembered and honored. Art, music, and literature of all sorts are celebrated. Ethnic diversity is recognized and appreciated. History and heritage come alive. The fruits of many harvests are consumed in thanksgiving. Workers from lumberjacks to coals miners are feted. And sometimes, a fair or festival has no other purpose than an escape from everyday life and a good time.

The fairs and festivals enumerated below do not represent exhaustive lists by any means. Rather, fairs and festivals in each state and territory have been chosen to illustrate the special character of those areas. State tourism and travel offices should be contacted for exact dates of events, which change slightly from year to year.

ALABAMA

From March through September is pilgrimage time in Alabama, a time to experience the old South in Alabama from Mobile in the south to Athens in the north and everything in between, including the capital city of Montgomery. There the Civil Rights Memorial is located, along with the state capitol building, where Jefferson Davis declared the Confederacy. The festival season kicks off with Mardi Gras in Mobile. In fact, Mobile rather than New Orleans claims to be the birthplace of Mardi Gras in America. The Helen Keller Festival takes place in Tuscumbia during the last week of June. The highlight of the festival is the annual production of the play *The Miracle Worker* at Ivy Green, Helen Keller's place of birth. W. C. Handy's birthplace of Florence is the site of the W. C. Handy Music Festival, a week-long event held in early August to celebrate the man known as the father of the blues. The Alabama Shakespeare Festival in Montgomery has performances from November through July, and the Alabama Renaissance Faire takes place in Florence in October. This is the official Renaissance Faire of the state. For those who enjoy the pleasures of the sea, there is the Dauphin Island Race in April, the Sea Oats Jamboree in May at Gulf Shores, the Blessing of the Shrimp Fleet at Bayou la Batre in June, and the National Shrimp Festival at Gulf Shores in October.[1]

ALASKA

Alaska's calendar of events seems to be dominated by dogsled races, skiing competitions, and snowmobile races. The Iditarod, a dogsled race of eleven to fifteen days from Anchorage to Nome is the most famous of these events. It occurs in early March. But already in mid-January, Seward is celebrating the Annual Seward Polar Bear Jump-Off Festival with a traditional seafood dinner, tall tales contest, a bachelor auction, and the main event, a plunge into the icy waters of Resurrection Bay by a number of costumed citizens. The Anchorage Fur Rendezvous is scheduled for mid-February. The largest winter festival in Alaska, it features dog and car racing, a snowshoe softball tournament, a downhill canoe race, carnival, and fur auction. The year 1994 marks the twenty-first Festival of Native Arts at the end of February in Fairbanks, with arts, crafts, dancing, and displays. The Bering Sea Ice Golf Classic—huskies pulling sleds or snow machines are the caddies—takes place in Nome toward the end of March and, finally, after the Kittiwake sea gulls return to Whittier in early April, the Annual Alaska Folk Festival takes place in Juneau about a week later. There are performances, workshops, dances and informal jams throughout the city by folk musicians from the Yukon, the Northwest, and Alaska.

In June, Nome celebrates the summer solstice and twenty-two hours of daylight with the Midnight Sun Festival, which includes everything from an Eskimo dance to a raft race and a baby contest. Then in the second week of July another distinctive Alaska festival takes place in Talkeetna—the Annual Moose Dropping Festival. While the festival includes a parade, music, crafts, food, a Mountain Mother contest, and a softball tournament, the premier event is surely the moose nugget toss. The Alaska State Fair, featuring giant vegetables grown in Alaska, runs from late August into the first week of September. In mid-October, the city of Sitka reenacts the transfer of Alaska from Russian to U.S. ownership during its Alaska Day Festival. And finally, in the second week of November, Fairbanks hosts the Athabascan Fiddling Festival, whose purpose is to preserve the tradition of Athabascan fiddling, guitar playing, and dancing.[2]

ARIZONA

Arizona celebrates its Native American and Hispanic heritage in the spirit of the West. The National Festival of the West, held in Scottsdale around the third week of March, is dedicated to keeping the reality and lore of the old West alive. It includes a Western Film Festival, cowboy poetry, gunfights, and cattle shows, among other things. Tombstone helps to keep the old West alive with its Annual Wyatt Earp Days in late May and Vigilante Days in early August. Sedona holds its Wild West Days in late June and Prescott hosts its Annual Arizona Cowboy Poets Gathering in mid-August. The Pioneer Folk Festival is held around July 4 in Flagstaff.

Rodeos are a staple of western entertainment and Arizona has no shortage of them. There is the Lake Powell Rodeo in Page in mid-May, the Annual Senior Pro Rodeo in Payson late in May, the Annual Rodeo in Alpine the second week in June, the Pine Country Pro Rodeo in Flagstaff a week later, Prescott's Frontier Days and World's Oldest Rodeo in late June and early July, Payson's Annual Oldest Continuous Rodeo in the third week of August, and the Andy Devine Days in Kingman during the third week of September. Likewise, western dancing is another staple of entertainment. Prescott hosts the Annual Square and Round Dance Festival the third weekend in May. The Annual Square and Round Dance "Dance-A-Rama" is in mid-July in Show Low/Linden. Square and round dance festivals are also held in Flagstaff in early August and in Payson in the third week of August. Chili seems a staple of western cuisine and the best of it can be found at the Annual Bushvalley May Fair and Chili Cook-Off in Alpine in late May and at the Annual Pine Country Chili Cook-Off in Flagstaff in mid-June.

The Annual Native American Festival takes place in Prescott in mid-August. The All Indian Inter-Tribal Pow-Wow is also in Prescott in June. Pow-wows are also held in Flagstaff in late June and in Camp Verde in early July. Flagstaff is the site of the Festival of Native American Arts from late June through early August. Hopi arts shows are held in Sedona in mid-May and in Flagstaff from late June through early July. Flagstaff also hosts the Annual Zuni Artists Exhibition in late May and early June and the Navajo Artists Exhibition the last week of July. The Central Navajo Fair goes on in August in Chinle and the Annual Navajo Nation Fair in the second week of September in Window Rock. Tuscon hosts its Annual Hispanic Cultural Arts Event at the end of May. In the second week of September, Wickenburg is the site of the Septiembre Fiesta, and in the third week of September in Globle/Miami, the Latinos' Fiesta is held.[3]

ARKANSAS

Ducks, turkeys, and eagles . . . crawfish, mosquitos, and toads . . . oil, bricks, and diamonds . . . armadillos, bream, and pigs . . . grapes, peaches, and spinach—these are just some of the causes for celebration in Arkansas fairs and festivals throughout the year. The year 1994 marks the fifty-ninth World's Championship Duck Calling Contest, which is held in conjunction with the Wings over the Prairie Festival in Stuttgart in late November. The forty-ninth Annual National Wild Turkey Calling Contest and Turkey Trot Festival also occurs in 1994 in early October in Yellville. Annual Eagle Awareness Days at Petit Jean State Park in early February includes field trips to see the eagles that winter there. On the last weekend of April Hamburg holds its Annual Armadillo Festival, which includes armadillo races, and Conway holds its Annual Toad Suck Daze that not only features a "tour de toad" but also a melodrama and a dinosaur dig. In mid-August at Crowley's Ridge State Park the world championship mosquito calling contest is featured at the Annual Great Mosquito Assault. Downtown Dermott is the scene of the Annual Crawfish Festival on the third weekend in May, when over 5,000 pounds of crawfish are consumed. Fish lovers will want to hit the Annual Bream Festival in Felsenthal on the last weekend in May to eat their fill of bream and see the crowning of little Mr. and Mrs. Bream. Lovers of all kinds of food from spaghetti to hot dogs will want to catch the pig chase and hog calling festivals at the Annual Great Arkansas Pig-Out in Morrilton in early August. Fruit and vegetable enthusiasts can catch a glimpse of Popeye at the Annual Spinach Festival in Alma in mid-April, stomp grapes and taste wine at the Annual Grape Festival in mid-July at Altus, and square off in a peach eating contest at the Johnson County Peach Festival in Clarksville. This weeklong mid-July festival is the oldest outdoor festival in the state.

Fortune hunters can dig for diamonds at the Annual Diamond Festival in Murfreesboro early in June. Arkansas is the only state in the United States where diamonds can be found. The Annual Oil Town Festival in mid-June celebrates the oil industry in the town of Smackover. Malvern claims to be the brick capital of the world. Thus, in late June the city hosts the annual Brickfest that among other events includes a best-dressed brick contest and a brick toss.

The state of Arkansas also, of course, celebrates its history and heritage in its festivals. Ouachita Indian Pow-Wows take place at Mount Ida in mid-March and mid-June. Early craft skills like soap making and basket weaving are demonstrated in the Annual Pioneer Craft Festival at Rison the third weekend of March, in the Annual Crafts and Folk Music Festival at Little Rock in early May, and in the Annual Original Ozark Festival at Ozark in early June. In late March, Arkansas' first governor, James Sevier Conway, is memorialized at Bradley in the Annual Governor Conway Days with the biggest parade in the county and numerous other events. And the city of Mena holds the Annual Lum 'n Abner Days celebration in early June to celebrate Chester Lauck and Norris Goff, who grew up in Mena and became popular stars of radio in the 1940s.[4]

CALIFORNIA

California celebrates its tremendous diversity with nearly a thousand scheduled fairs and festivals each year, from the Tournament of Roses Parade in Pasadena on New Year's Day to the Annual Hollywood Christmas Parade. Whale watching and film watching are, of course, famous in California. Whale observations begin at Big Sur on January 2 and continue for the entire month. Among California's film festivals are the Palm Springs International Film Festival in early January, the Native American Film Festival in Los Angeles in mid-January, the Santa Barbara International Film Festival in the second week of March, and the two-week San Francisco International Film Festival in late April and early May, which is the oldest such festival in the Western Hemisphere.

Ethnic festivals abound. In late January, San Francisco's Chinese Chamber of Commerce kicks off the new year with the Chinese New Year Festival and Parade, a two-week event with music, street fairs, cultural shows, and the crowning of Miss Chinatown USA. The year 1994 marks the 114th-year celebration in Marysville of the Chinese water god, Bok Kai, with the Bok Kai Festival in late February. Late in March, the Agua Caliente Heritage Fiesta celebrates the heritage of that culture with Native American dances, music, arts, crafts, food, and storytellers. The Northern California Cherry Blossom Festival in San Francisco showcases traditional Japanese culture and customs in mid-April, as does the Nisei Week Japanese Festival in Los Angeles in August. The Cinco de Mayo Fiesta in Delano is the oldest ongoing Cinco de Mayo festival in the country. It features Mexican musicians, folk dancing, food, and arts and crafts in late April. During the third weekend in September, Roseville celebrates California Indian Days, when 4,000 Native Americans share in Indian dances, arts, crafts, food, and cultural events. California also celebrates its heritage with the Death Valley 49ers Encampment in November, which includes a trek through Death Valley commemorating the passage of the 49ers through the valley on their way to find California gold. And the William Saroyan Festival, late April into early May, celebrates the contribution to literature of this Fresno native.

California's geography and climate are also cause for celebration. The Snowfest in Tahoe City during the second week of March is the biggest winter festival in the West, with more than one hundred unique events. The California State Fair in Sacramento is one of the largest agricultural fairs in the United States. It takes place from mid-August through the first week in September. The same accident of climate and geography that makes California so productive agriculturally also makes it one of the most famous wine-producing regions in the world. The Valley of the Moon Vintage Festival in Sonoma in the last part of September is California's oldest wine festival; it features historic reenactments, a parade, entertainment, and both the stomping and blessing of grapes.

Finally, two unique California festivals are of special note. Since 1928, the Calaveras County Fair and Jumping Frog Jubilee, which takes place in mid-May at Angels Camp, has featured the frog-jumping contest made famous by Samuel Clemens. And then late in November in Pasadena is the annual Doo Dah Parade, an event with no judges and no theme. Its only purpose is to have fun and celebrate the free spirit alive in California.[5]

COLORADO

From hang gliding to cannibal trials and from Shakespeare to mine-drilling competitions, Colorado fairs and festivals truly have something for everyone. Whooping and sandhill cranes can be observed in March at the Monte Vista Crane Festival. The Telluride Mountain Film Festival late in May celebrates films about mountain life and adventure. The Pony Express rides again in mid-June in Julesburg at the Pony Express Re-Run. From mid-June through July Larkspur hosts the Renaissance Festival. Boulder hosts the Colorado Dance Festival, which occupies most of July, the Colorado Music Festival from the third week of June to the first week of August, and the Colorado Shakespeare Festival from June to August. Later in July, there are two choices: digging for dinosaur bones at Dinosaur Days in Grand Junction or seeing llama and pack burro races at Burro Days in Fairplay. The curious may wish to attend a performance of the Alfred Packer Trial in Lake City during July or August. The adventurous may wish to visit the Telluride Hang Gliding Festival in mid-September.

The Rendezvous of Cultures in Fort Garland late in May recalls the Native American, Hispanic, and military influences that came together in the San Luis Valley during the nineteenth century. Other ethnic and cultural festivals include Vinotok, a Slavic festival in Crested Butte the third week of September; the Annual Scottish-Irish Highland Festival at Estes Park in early September; the Native American Lifeways Festival at Montrose in mid-September; and Pueblo's Oktoberfest, also in mid-September. The Bill Pickett Invitational Rodeo on the second weekend in August at Denver celebrates African-American cowboys and is named for the father of bulldogging.

There are, of course, other rodeos too in this western state, including the National Western Stock Show and Rodeo in Denver for two weeks in mid-January; the Annual Music and Blossom Festival and Royal George Rodeo, one of Colorado's oldest rodeos, in Canon City early in May; Evergreen

Rodeo Weekend in late June; the Brush Rodeo in early July; and the Pikes Peak or Bust Rodeo in Colorado Springs early in August. The cultural contributions of cowboys are featured at the Chuchara Valley Cowboy Arts Festival at the end of May. Fur trappers are also remembered in Platteville at the end of May at the Fort Vasquez Fur Trappers Rendezvous and in La Junta in early July at Bent's Old Fort Fur Trade Encampment. Mountain Man rendezvous takes place toward the end of April in Kit Carson and in late July at Crested Butte.

The lure of gold brought many to Colorado, and mining remains an important industry. There's still gold in those hills and fair goers can look for it at Gold Digging Days in Yuma in early June and at Gold Rush Days in Idaho Springs in mid-July. A mine drilling competition is featured at Leadville's Annual Boom Days Celebration in early August. Old-fashioned hand-mucking is offered at Silverton's Hardrocker's Holiday and Mining Celebration, also in early August.[6]

CONNECTICUT

Connecticut celebrates its heritage in numerous festivals, including the early June International Folk Festival in Bridgeport and the mid-July High Ridge Folk Festival in Stamford. In Danbury, the Assumption Greek Orthodox Church puts on the Greek Experience in mid-July. In New Haven, the Connecticut Irish Festival or "Feis" in late June is three days of continuous Irish music with dancing competition and cultural exhibits. Italians celebrate their cultural contributions in early July in Westport at the Festival Italiano and later in the month in New Britain at the Italian-American Feast. New Preston hosts the Bagpipe Festival and Scottish Dancing around August 1 and Goshen the Connecticut Scottish Festival early in October. Native American culture is celebrated at the Strawberry Moon Pow Wow in Rocky Hill in late June; the Connecticut River Pow Wow in Farmington in late August; and the Paucatuck Eastern Pequot Harvest Moon Pow Wow in North Stonington the second week of October.

The sea is, of course, a major theme of Connecticut history and life, and it is not forgotten in festival events. The U.S. Navy Submarine Base at Groton is home of the Subfest over the July 4 holiday. New London's waterfront is the scene of the Sailfest a week later. Old marine engines are on display in Mystic at the Antique Marine Engine Exposition in the third week of August. Mystic also remembers the musical heritage of the sea in mid-June at the Sea Music Festival. Seafood is perhaps the sea's greatest bounty. The Lobsterfest in Mystic late in May and the Lobster Fest and Arts and Crafts Show in Niantic around July 4 celebrate a favored crustacean. Clinton's town dock is the site of the Bluefish Festival in August. Milford has its Oyster Festival in August and Norwalk has its version the second week of September. Mystic has a Chowderfest the second weekend of October.

But what about dessert? Strawberry festivals are held in Brookfield late in May, in Cheshire in mid-June, and in Monroe also in mid-June. Apple harvest festivals are held in Southington and in Glastonbury during the first three weekends in October. But those wanting to sample a bit of everything in the Connecticut culinary tradition can go to downtown Mystic around the second weekend of September to experience the Taste of Connecticut Food Festival.[7]

DELAWARE

Although Delaware is a small state geographically, it is quite diverse ethnically. The city of Wilmington celebrates its Greek culture at the Holy Trinity Greek Festival in early June and its Italian culture at the St. Anthony's Italian Festival the next week. Then during the second week of July, African-American culture is celebrated at the African American Festival and Parade. Polish Day at Fort Delaware (Delaware City) is held in mid-June. And at Millsboro near mid-September, the Nanticoke Indian Pow-Wow occurs.

The winds of spring have people in Delaware up in the air. At Cape Henlopen State Park in early April, the Great Delaware Kite Festival gets under way. Later in May in Milton, the Delmarva Hot Air Balloon Festival takes off. As summer warms up, people cool down at Wilmington's Old-Fashioned Ice Cream Festival the second weekend of July. The Delaware State Fair in Harrington occupies the last week of the month. As fall approaches, the Willey Farm Autumn Celebration and Craft Festival takes place in Townsend. On that same weekend of early September, the city of Odessa hosts the Delaware Decoy Festival and Carving Championship.[8]

FLORIDA

In a state with seemingly endless coastline, it is not surprising that Florida seafood is the center of numerous festivals. The Grant Seafood Festival in February, the Port Canaveral Seafood Festival in March, the Pompano Beach Seafood Festival in April, and the John's Pass Seafood Festival at Madeira Beach in October are but a few. The Sanibel Shell Fair in March gives tribute to Sanibel Island, a renowned shelling island. And surfing and sailing competitions can be found year-round.

Florida also pays homage to its famous sons, native and adopted. The Edison Festival of Light is a two-week event that remembers Fort Myers' famous winter resident, Thomas Edison. In May, at White Springs, crafts and foods of early Florida are remembered at the Stephen Foster Folk Festival at Stephen Foster State Park. In July, Key West celebrates the Hemingway Days Festival with an Ernest Hemingway look-alike contest, literary contests, and walking tours.

Coconut Grove is the site in June of the biggest African-American heritage festival in the country. The Miami/Goombay Festival celebrates the culture and significance of Miami's early Bahamian settlers. The Carnaval Miami/Calle Ocho is the biggest Hispanic celebration in the country. After Carnaval night at the Orange Bowl, the streets of Little Havana come alive with dancing, top Latin entertainment, food, and revelers in costume. Florida's biggest Civil War battle is reenacted and celebrated at the Olustee Battle Festival in Lake City in February. During the second weekend of October, the first settlers and native inhabitants of Florida are remembered in the Seminole Indian and Florida Pioneer Festival.

Florida also offers some excellent air shows, including the Florida International Airshow, usually held in late March or April in Punta Gorda, and the Florida State Air Fair in Kissimmee in November. Music lovers in St. Petersburg will enjoy the Festival of States, which began in 1921, and during which bands from all over the nation compete. And visitors to the oldest city in the United States, St. Augustine, may wish to see *Cross and Sword,* the Florida state play by Paul Green. The play, which depicts the first two years of the settlement of St. Augustine by the Spanish, is performed from mid-June until the end of August.[9]

GEORGIA

Peaches, peanuts, and pine trees—of course are the cause for celebration in Georgia. The official Georgia Peach Festival takes place in Fort Valley/Byron for a week in mid-June. The historical site of Possum Poke is the scene of the Georgia Peanut Festival in the first week of October. And at the end of October, Sparta hosts the Pinetree Festival. But Georgia marble is celebrated too at Jasper in early October, and rattlesnakes are rounded up each year in Whigham on a late January day and in Claxton in mid-March.

Georgia is famous also for the beauty of its flora. Festivals celebrating these flora are, therefore, diverse and numerous throughout the year. Each year begins with the annual Camellia Festival at Fort Valley in early February. The Azalea Festival at Callaway Gardens gets under way at the end of March. Thomasville hosts the Annual Rose Festival during the third week in April. At the end of April the Enchanted Valleys Rhododendron Festival begins in Hiawassee. In mid-June, Newnan celebrates the Magnolia Blossom Festival, and then later in June, Winterville holds its Marigold Festival. In mid-September, Stone Mountain is the site of the Annual Yellow Daisy Festival. Pine Mountain is the site of the Chrysanthemum Festival in mid-October.

Georgia's rich cultural heritage is also the subject of much celebration throughout the year. The Georgia National Fairgrounds in Perry is where the state's official folk festival takes place the third weekend in March. It celebrates all the traditional folk arts. Native American culture is celebrated in many festivals, including Native American Days in Warm Springs early in May, the Chehaw National Indian Festival in Albany in mid-May, the Annual Lower Muscogee Creek Tribe Pow-Wow over the July 4 weekend, the Nacoochee Valley Native American Indian Festival and Pow Wow in Helen late in August, and the Annual Indian Cultural Festival at Columbus College in October. The Annual Pioneer Rendezvous at Elijah Clark State Park takes place in the second week of October. African-American cultural contributions are celebrated around the Martin Luther King Birthday observance in Atlanta and also at the Black History Festival during the last two weeks of February and at Sautee-Nacoochee at the National Black Arts Festival in Atlanta for a week in early August. Scottish culture is celebrated at Scottish Days at Indian Springs in early April and at the Savannah Scottish Highland Games in early May. German culture comes alive in Helen at the Fasching Karnival late in January and Oktoberfest in September and October. Atlanta's Greek Orthodox Church puts on the Greek Festival late in September and Savannah's Greek Festival occurs in mid-October.[10]

HAWAII

While the Aloha Festivals of mid-September through October and the June 11 King Kamehameha Day celebrations are common to all the main islands, each major island also puts on festivals unique to that island. Oahu's January Cherry Blossom Festival coincides with the blooming of cherry blossoms in Japan. The Narcissus Festival, beginning with the first new moon of the Chinese lunar calendar, is a festival that celebrates Chinese culture in Hawaii with pageants, lion dances, banquets, and traditional dances. The May Day or, in Hawaii, Lei Day celebration is a festival of flowers, whose biggest event takes place in Waikiki with music, dances, ethnic food, and lei-making competitions. Festivals on the island of Hawaii celebrate nuts, coffee, and the hula. October brings the Hilo Macadamia Nut Festival. November brings the Kona Coffee Festival, a weeklong event featuring Hawaii's famous coffee and numerous events. During the week after Easter begins the Merrie Monarch Hula Festival, which features a three-day hula competition among other cultural events. This festival is a tribute to King David Kalakaua, who ruled from 1874 to 1891 and was responsible for bringing back many ancient Hawaiian traditions.

On Maui, the three-day Na Mele o Maui gets underway in January. There is a Keiki song competition and the Emma Farden Sharpe Hula Festival amid an art and crafts fair. In July, Mr. and Mrs. Maui Onion are crowned in the pageant at the Maui Onion Festival, which celebrates the island's sweet onion. The island of Kauai has the state's largest Prince Kuhio Festival. Prince Jonah Kuhio Kalaniana'ole was Hawaii's first congressman. The weeklong festival of Polynesian shows, canoe races, songfests, hula competitions, and historical exhibits centers around March 26, the state holiday honoring the prince, a Kauai native. And on Molokai in May is the Molokai Ka Hula Piko. Hula dances, cultural events, lectures, and visits to sacred areas highlight this festival on the island said to be where the hula was born.[11]

IDAHO

Idaho's seven regions each provide unique public events. North Idaho has everything from the ten-day Sandpoint Winter Carnival the third week of January, to the Idaho State Draft Horse International in early October, also in Sandpoint. In between, there is music—the Great Northern Bluegrass Festival late in July and the Festival at Sandpoint, in the beginning of August—and the opportunity to see the Coeur d'Alene Indians' Coming of the Black Robes ceremony at the Coeur d'Alene Indian Pilgrimage at Cataldo in mid-August. Moscow in North Central Idaho presents the Lionel Hampton/Chevron Jazz Festival for five days in February for jazz lovers, and the Rendezvous in the Park in mid-July for lovers of all kinds of music. Moscow's Renaissance Faire takes place in the first part of May. Chief Lookingglass Days in Kamiah in mid-August is a traditional pow-wow during which the Nez Perce Indian Tribe presents cultural ceremonies and dancing. Lumberjacks from all over the world gather in Orofino for competition at the Clearwater County Fair and Lumberjack Days the third weekend of September, and rodeo fans have their choices of the Riggins Rodeo in early May, the Grangeville Border Days Rodeo over the Independence Day holidays, and the Lewiston Roundup in September. Southwestern Idaho also has its share of rodeos: the Caldwell Night Rodeo in mid-August and the Snake River Stampede in July in Nampa, one of the country's top rodeos. While South Central Idaho has rodeos too—in Burley the Cassia County Fair and Rodeo in mid-August and the Twin Falls County Fair and Rodeo early in September—Twin Falls also celebrates the railroad with the Iron Horse Roundup, the third weekend of June, and western culture with Western Days at the end of May. In mid-July in Gooding is the Gooding Basque Association Picnic. Idaho has the country's largest Basque population.

Southeastern Idaho celebrates the famous Idaho potato in Shelley in mid-September with Idaho Spud Day and Idaho history in Lava Hot Springs with the Mountain Man Rendezvous-Pioneer Days at the end of July. Indian culture is celebrated at the Shoshone-Bannock Indian Festival in August at Fort Hall. This festival features an all-Indian old timers' rodeo. Horse and pig racing are just part of the entertainment during the Eastern Idaho State Fair in Blackfoot, which runs from the last week of August through the first week of September. Big-time country-western entertainment and tales of the West are featured at the High Country Cowboy Festival in Driggs in mid-July. Rexburg, also in Eastern Idaho, is the site for the Idaho International Folk Dance Festival during the first week of August. Sun Valley in Central Idaho begins the year with the Winter Sports Week the third week of January, and continues with the Sun Valley Music Festival from mid-July through the end of August, among other events. The Ketchum Wagon Days Celebration celebrates Idaho's mining history and the importance of mining to Idaho's economy.[12]

ILLINOIS

Illinois celebrates its early history in mid-April at the Shoal Creek Muzzleloaders Rendezvous in Hillsboro and in early June at the Ft. de Chartres Summer Rendezvous in Prairie du Rocher. The Annual Native American Pow Wow in Peoria and the Argyle Civil War Rendezvous in Colchester take place in mid-June. The *City of Joseph,* performed in an outdoor theater, traces the history of the Mormon settlement in Nauvoo in late July and early August. Ottawa celebrates Lincoln and Douglas debates at its Lincoln Douglas Days the last weekend of August. Ellis Grove hosts the French and Indian War Assemblage at the beginning of October. Old settlers and threshers are remembered from July in Freeport and Rockton and August in Hamilton to Old Settlers Days in Kampsville on the second weekend of October. And Illinois rails and rivers are celebrated at the mid-June Railroad Days in Galesburg and Steamboat Days in Peoria.

Famous sons are recognized around the state in a variety of events. Galesburg celebrates the birthday of Carl Sandburg, its most famous native son, on January 6. Lewistown celebrates Edgar Lee Masters Day on June 5 in recognition of the famous author of the *Spoon River Anthology* with a dance, poetry contest, and epitaph readings in the Oak Hill cemetery. In May and October, Oak Park and Glencoe, respectively, host tours of homes designed by Frank Lloyd Wright. Wyatt Earp is remembered often in Monmouth: in March to celebrate his birthday, in early August at an OK Corral reenactment, and in September at the Wyatt Earp Prime Beef Days. Oak Park celebrates Ernest Hemingway at its mid-July Fiesta de Hemingway. And the most famous citizen of Illinois is remembered at the annual Abraham Lincoln National Railsplitting Contest and Crafts Festival in Lincoln in mid-September.

Illinois expresses appreciation for its rich agricultural bounty at many festivals throughout the year. Strawberries are celebrated in Monticello at the Strawberry Festival in June. Collinsville celebrates its claim as the Horseradish Capital of the World at the early May International Horseradish Festival, where visitors join in a root toss and horseradish eating contest. Pumpkin festivals, held from mid-September into November in

Morton, Carlinville, Sycamore, and Rossville, offer tastes of pumpkin ice cream, pancakes, and even pumpkin chili. Corn is an Illinois staple, celebrated at the mid-August Annual Downtown Urbana Sweetcorn Festival, the National Sweetcorn Festival in September in Hoopeston, the Grundy County Corn Fest in Morris toward the end of September, the DeKalb Corn Fest in DeKalb at the end of August, the Southern Illinois Sweetcorn and Watermelon Festival in Mt. Vernon in mid-August, and the Annual Popcorn Festival in Manito and the Casey Popcorn Festival, both in September. And a "Wedding of the Wine and Cheese" is held at the Nauvoo Grape Festival in early September. Hogs are king at the Hog Capital of the World Festival in Kewanee early in September. Peoria hosts the Heart of Illinois Fair beginning in mid-July, and the Illinois State Fair is held in August in Springfield. Jordbruksdagarna (Agriculture Days) are celebrated in Bishop Hill toward the end of September.

From boating to Shakespeare, there are many ways to celebrate life in Illinois. The many ethnic celebrations include Oktoberfests in Tinley Park, Libertyville, Rochelle, Steeleville, Maeystown and Troy; the Annual Swedish Days Festival in Geneva in the latter half of June; and the Rockford Fiesta Hispana the first part of July. There is Chinese Dragon Boat Racing in Oquawka late in May and, in early June, the Annual Miller Grand Prix of Karting in Quincy. The World Freefall Convention is also held in Quincy early in August. The Annual Superman Celebration takes place around mid-June in Metropolis, of course; the Knox/Rootabaga Jam Jazz Fest is in Galesburg toward the middle of March; and the Illinois Shakespeare Festival is in Bloomington at the end of July.[13]

INDIANA

The Indianapolis 500 on the Sunday of Memorial Day weekend is perhaps Indiana's single most famous event, but Indy racing is only one event among hundreds every year. Of course, there's the Indiana State Fair, also in Indianapolis, in mid-August, which attracts tens of thousands and showcases national entertainment. But Indiana also celebrates its rich heritage, diversity, and native sons.

The Amish Spring Expo takes place in mid-April in Montgomery. Displays of Amish handiwork, food, and buggy rides are part of the celebration. The Volksfest in Portland in early June celebrates the German heritage of East Central Indiana and West Central Ohio with performances, art exhibits, and workshops that focus on German cultural traditions. The Germanfest of Vincennes in mid-August celebrates German culture with German food, music, and dance. Puerto Rican culture is celebrated at a real island festival in East Chicago at the Puerto Rican Festival in mid-July. Berne celebrates its Swiss heritage in late July with the Berne Swiss Days Festival, which includes yodelers and polka bands. Scottish heritage is celebrated with pipe band competitions and entertainment in mid-August at the Columbus Scottish Festival. But before European settlers arrived, Native Americans occupied the territory and made their contributions to the local culture. These contributions are recognized at the early September Kee-Boon-Mein-Kaa Festival in South Bend, a Potawatami pow-wow that ends the huckleberry season. Angel Mounds State Historic Site presents Native American artists and demonstrations of crafts during Native American Days later in September. And in early October, the Feast of the Hunters' Moon at Fort Ouiatenon Historic Park re-creates the mid-eighteenth-century gathering of French and Indians at Fort Ouiatenon with authentic crafts, period clothing, and Indian culture.

Movie star James Dean is remembered on February 7 at the James Dean Birthday Celebration in his hometown of Fairmont. Abraham Lincoln's Indiana roots are remembered in Lincoln City at the Lincoln Boyhood National Memorial toward mid-June with an outdoor drama and historical exhibits. Poet James Whitcomb Riley is remembered in a festival bearing his name by the citizens of Greenfield, his place of birth, in early October.

While Indiana limestone, celebrated in Bedford in late June at the Limestone Heritage Festival, is a well-known product of the state, agriculture is perhaps the driving economic force. Numerous festivals celebrate Indiana's diverse agricultural products. Maple Sugarin' Days take place in Terre Haute for most of February. Herb festivals are held in Newburgh in April, Warsaw in May, and Hartford City in July. The Sassafras Tea Festival occurs in mid-April in Vernon. The North Judson Mint Festival in mid-June includes tours of peppermint and spearmint farms. The Batesville Raspberry Festival in late July features raspberries for breakfast, lunch, and dinner, and a raspberry queen. The Tipton County Pork Festival in early September features pork chops barbecued by the ton. Rising Sun even has a Navy Bean Festival in October. From late September through October, apple festivals are held in Batesville, Nappanee, Hobart, Kendallville, Frankton, Covington, and Chrisney.[14]

IOWA

Iowa has a little something for everyone in its fairs and festivals throughout the year. The Irish are celebrating in Emmetsburg in mid-March at the St. Patrick's Day Celebration. Tulips are the cause for celebration at Pella's Tulip Time Festival early in May and at the Orange City Tulip Festival in mid-May. At the beginning of June, Frontier Days get under way in Dodge City; Story City celebrates Scandinavian Days, and Waterloo has its My Waterloo Days. Toward mid-June, Iowa City hosts the Iowa Festival; Clarinda hosts the Glenn Miller Festival; and the Lewis and Clark Festival begins at the Lewis and Clark State Park at Onawa. Arts and music are also part of mid-June celebrations. The Donna Reed Festival for the Performing Arts is in Denison; the Grant Wood Art Festival is in Anamosa/Stone City; and Burlington has its Steamboat Days/American Music Festival. Around July 4, the Annual Leon Rodeo is held in Leon and the Quad City Air Show goes on a week later in Davenport. In mid-July, Waukee is the site of the Central Hawkeye Old-Time Power and Machinery Show and Sioux City celebrates its Rivercade. The Bix Beiderbecke Jazz Festival is in late July in Davenport, and Decorah hosts its Nordic Fest also in late July.

The Mesquakie Indian Pow Wow is held in Tama, and the National Hobo Convention in Britt in mid-August. The Iowa State Fair in Des Moines runs the last part of August. Early September brings the Midwest Old Threshers Reunion to Mount Pleasant and the Great Iowa Balloon Race to Storm Lake. Boone celebrates Pufferbilly Days the second weekend of September. Amana has its Farm Progress Show toward the end of September, and Winterset celebrates the Madison County Covered Bridge Festival the second weekend of October. The National Farm Toy Show in Dyersville takes place in early November and Santa's Village is open from late November to December 24 in Storm Lake.[15]

KANSAS

nsas celebrates its Native American heritage at the Haskell Indian Pow Wow in Lawrence in mid-May, the Pawnee Rendezvous in Republic the second weekend of September, and the American Indian Weekend and Mountain Man Rendezvous in Fort Scott the last weekend of September. Pioneer days are recalled during Prairie Days in Canton early in June, Pioneer Days celebrations in Hays and Highland in mid-September, and Chisholm Trail Days in Abilene early in October. Swedish pioneers are remembered during the Svensk Hyllningsfest a few days later in Lindsborg. Goodland holds its Annual Windwagon Races toward the end of September, where prairie schooners race powered by the Kansas wind. Santa Fe Trail Days in Larned at the end of May and Dalton Days in Meade early in June recall the days of the wild West.

Ethnic diversity is celebrated in Lawrence after mid-April at the Celebration of Cultures. The Hillsboro Folk Festival later in May and the German Fest in Marysville in early June recall Kansas' German settlers and their culture. The Sand Creek Folk Life Festival takes place toward the end of April in Newton, and the Annual Ninnescah Valley Folk Festival takes place in Kingman in mid-August. Mexican culture is featured at the Fiesta Mexicana in Topeka in mid-July, the Annual Mexican Fiesta in Chanute the second weekend of September, the Fiesta and Mexican/American Festival in Emporia also on the second weekend of September, and the Newton Fiesta a week later.

Oil, coal, and railroads have been vital to the development of Kansas. Hugoton holds its Oil and Gas Appreciation Weekend the first weekend of

April. The Little Balkans Days/PAACA Little Balkans Folklife Festival celebrates the importance of coal mining to Pittsburg and the surrounding area. It is held in early September, as is Topeka's Railroad Days Festival. But agriculture and cattle are perhaps the best-known features of Kansas life.

Mankato is the site of the Jewell County Threshing Bee in mid-July. Goessel holds its Country Threshing Days early in August. The Barnes Old Home Days and Threshing Bee is in mid-August. The Sumner County Wheat Festival is held the second week of July in Wellington. Beef is on the table during the Beef Empire Days toward mid-June in Garden City. Scott City holds its Beefiesta later in July. Emporia's Beef Fest is on the third weekend of August. Rodeos are, of course, a feature of cattle country and Kansas has many. Among them are Ft. Wallace Memorial Rodeo in Wallace at the end of May; the Annual Elk County Rodeo in Moline centered around Independence Day; the Annual NCK Rodeo in Concordia in mid-July; the PRCA Rodeo in Dodge City, the largest in Kansas, at the beginning of August; Kansas' Biggest Rodeo in Phillipsburg also in early August; and the Central Kansas Free Fair and Wild Bill Hickok Rodeo in Abilene in mid-August.

Finally, Kansas' most famous fictional citizens are cause for celebration too. Oakley holds its Yellow Brick Road Festival in mid-September. It features, among other activities, a Dorothy look-alike contest. Liberal holds its Oztoberfest in mid-October. It features original Munchkins from the movie and Oz exhibits.[16]

KENTUCKY

Kentucky is horse country. Everyone has heard of the Kentucky Derby and the celebrations of the Kentucky Derby Festival held around this Louisville event in late April. Lexington puts on the Kentucky Horse Fair in late July and the Equi Festival of Kentucky during the second week of October, both celebrating Kentucky's horse industry. Georgetown is the scene of the Festival of the Horse in mid-September. But horses are only one element in Kentucky's history and economy.

Coal Digger Days in Hardy in mid-May honors coal miners and railroaders. Hazard's Black Gold Festival in mid-September simply honors coal and its importance to Kentucky. Kentucky is also the home of the bourbon that goes into the mint juleps drunk on Derby Day. It is celebrated in Bardstown at the Kentucky Bourbon Festival in mid-September. And Kentucky is also a major tobacco producer. Tobacco's importance to the economy is celebrated in numerous festivals, among them the Black Patch Tobacco Festival in Princetown the second week of September, the Logan County Tobacco Festival in Russellville the first week of October, the Bloomfield Tobacco Festival in mid-October, and the Hart County Tobacco Festival the third week of October. Last, but not least, the World Chicken Festival, at the site of Colonel Sanders' first establishment in London at the end of September, celebrates Kentucky's primary contribution to American cookery.

Kentucky also celebrates the diversity of its heritage and culture. Appalachian crafts and culture are celebrated at Hillbilly Days in Pikesville in mid-April, Appalachian Family Folk Week at the Hindman Settlement School the second week of June, the Appalachian Celebration in Morehead during the third week of June, the Appalachian Humor Festival in Berea in mid-July, and the Cumberland Mountain Fall Festival in Middlesboro in mid-October. The last western Shaker settlement was Shakertown at South Union, founded in 1807 and lasting until 1922. The Shaker Festival is held there in June. Native American culture is celebrated at Manchester's Native American Pow Wow at the end of April, the Trail of Tears Indian Pow Wow in Hopkinsville toward the middle of September, the Red Crow Indian Council Pow Wow in Clermont in the beginning of October, and the Native American Games Weekend at Wickliffe Mounds at the end of October. Bagpipes sound the celebration of Scot heritage at the Kentucky Scottish Weekend at General Butler State Resort Park. Germans celebrate their heritage in Covington at Maifest in mid-May, in Louisville at the Strassenfest in mid-August, and again in Covington at the Oktoberfest toward mid-September. The Newport Italian Festival in early June celebrates Italian culture.

Kentucky's famous sons and daughters are obviously cause for celebration too. Jefferson Davis' birthplace in Todd County is the site of the Jefferson Davis Birthday Celebration on June 5–6. W. C. Handy came to Henderson to play at a barbecue in 1893 and left ten years later. "The Father of the Blues" is celebrated during a week in mid-June in Henderson's W. C. Handy Blues and Barbecue Festival. Daniel Boone is remembered at the log cabin he and his wife occupied at Carlisle in mid-August at the Daniel Boone Cabin Open House. He is also celebrated at the Daniel Boone Pioneer Festival in Winchester in early September and Barbourville's early October Daniel Boone Festival. Kentucky poet laureate Jesse Stuart is remembered at the Greenbo Lake State Resort Park's Jesse Stuart Weekend in late September. The founder of the Frontier Nursing Service is honored in Hyden at the Mary Breckinridge Festival held at the end of September. The Jenny Wiley Festival, held in Prestonsburg the first week of October, honors the pioneer who escaped from the Indians.[17]

LOUISIANA

Even though Mardi Gras lasts officially only from January 6 until the first day of Lent, it seems that Louisiana is in a constant state of satisfied celebration. Oil City has its Gusher Days Festival at the end of April, and

Morgan City hosts the Louisiana Shrimp and Petroleum Festival early in September to celebrate the state's biggest cash "crop." Tennessee Williams is remembered at the Tennessee Williams Literary Festival late in March in New Orleans, and Jim Bowie at the Jim Bowie Festival in early October in Vidalia. But the mix of cultures that makes up Louisiana has become almost legendary and certainly unique in America. Creole festivals are held in Jeanerette and Houma in late April. New Orleans is the site of the Annual Greek Festival in May, the Carnaval Latino in June, and the Festa D'Italia in October. African-American culture is celebrated in Hammond at the Tangipahoa Black Heritage Festival in late August. Native American culture is honored at the United Houma Indian Festival in early September. Cajun culture is feted at the Cajun Heritage Festival at Cut Off and the Festivals Acadiens at Lafayette, both in September.

Louisiana's cultural diversity has translated into a fabulous cuisine that can be sampled in Lake Providence at the Louisiana Soul Food and Heritage Festival in June, in Chalmette at the Louisiana Creole Food Festival in September, and in Lake Charles at the Annual Cajun Music and Food Festival in July. Aficionados may wish, however, to embark on a gustatory pilgrimage to sample the ingredients of these cuisines one by one. The journey might begin at the oyster festivals in Amite in March or in Cut Off in July. Then on to the Annual Poke Salad Festival at Blanchard in May. Crawfish festivals are held at Meraux and Sorrento in April and at Breaux Bridge early in May. Catfish is served at the Franklin Parish Catfish Festival in May in Winnsboro. The Zachary Sausage Festival takes place in late April. The Great French Market Tomato Festival is in early June, and the Louisiana Corn Festival is in Bunkie in mid-June. Sorrento hosts the Jambalaya Festival, also in mid-June, and then later in the month the Bayou Lacombe Crab Festival is celebrated. In August, the Blessing of the Fleet Festival at Grand Isle kicks off the shrimp season and Delcambre holds its Shrimp Festival. In October, Crowley hosts the International Rice Festival and Chackbay, the Louisiana Gumbo Festival. The Sauce Piquante Festival in Raceland ends the main courses.

For dessert, there is the Ponchatoula Strawberry Festival in April, the Louisiana Peach Festival at Ruston in June, and Mansfield's Louisiana Blueberry Festival, also in June. The Louisiana Watermelon Festival takes place at Farmersville in July. But those with a sweet tooth will want to visit the Louisiana Sugar Cane Festival and Fair in September in New Iberia and the St. Gregory Louisiana Praline Festival at Houma in early May. After dessert, there's music and dancing. Breaux Bridge hosts Mulate's Accordion Festival in July. Lafayette hosts the Cajun French Music Association "Le Cajun" Music Awards and Festival in August. And in October, La Cajun Zydeco and Music Festival takes place in Kaplan.[18]

MAINE

Maine celebrates the culture of its native inhabitants during the Indian Day Celebration at Pleasant Point Reservation in early August. French-American culture is celebrated in late June at the Acadian Festival in Madawaska and at La Kermesse–Franco Americaine Festival in Biddeford. In New Sweden, the Midsummer Celebration in June is a Swedish event on the longest day, with dance and maypole decoration.

The sea and its bounty are a vital part of Maine's history and culture. At Village Cove on Moosehead Lake, the International Seaplane Fly-In Weekend takes place in September. Schooner Days in Rockland in early July includes the Annual Great Schooner Race along with music, art and crafts displays, and harbor cruises. Rockland is also the site in early August of what may be Maine's best-known festival, the Maine Lobster Festival. Thousands of lobster dinners are prepared and eaten each day amid such events as the Great Lobster Crate Race, the Maine Seafood Cooking contest, and a lobster eating contest. In July, festival goers can also get their fill of oysters at the Damariscotta River Oyster Festival and of clams at the Yarmouth Clam Festival. The Festival of Traditional Sea Music is held in Bath at the end of May or beginning of June. Workshops and concerts that feature forebidders and sea chanties are held during the festival.

In about the third week of March, maple sugarhouses open their doors to the public on Maine Maple Sunday. Late in June, strawberries come in and can be sampled at the Strawberry Festival in South Berwick. For a week in mid-July, Fort Fairfield hosts the long-running Maine Potato Blossom Festival. And in August, blueberry festivals are held in Wilton, Machias, and Rangeley. In July and August, music helps to brighten the festivities. The Annual Bar Harbor Music Festival presents series of classical and popular concerts. The Arcady Music Festival goes from mid-July into early September. The Annual Bluegrass Festival features three days of famous Blue Grass artists in early August in Brunswick.[19]

MARYLAND

Maryland's state sport is jousting. The Maryland Renaissance Festival, which runs from late August to mid-October, features real combat jousting. The Old St. Joseph's Jousting Tournament takes place in August and the Oxon Hill Jousting Tournament in September. In October, the Cowtown Rodeo and Maryland State Jousting Championship goes on in Bel Air.

Maryland celebrates its cultural heritage in numerous festivals. The American Indian Pow Wow takes place in early June at McHenry. In late July, Baltimore celebrates its Italian Festival and its Uruguay Ethnic Festival, while Ocean City holds its Greek Festival. Snow Hill's African American Heritage Festival goes on in the second week of September. German heritage is celebrated at Baltimore's German Ethnic Festival late in August, Rockville's Oktoberfest in September, and the Germantown Oktoberfest in mid-October. Annapolis holds the Scottish Highland Games and Adelphi its Hispanic Festival in the second week of October.

Seafood is the cause of many celebrations in Maryland. There are the early August Harford County Seafood Festival in Havre de Grace, the Seafood Fest-i-val in Cambridge, and Crab Day in St. Michaels. In September, Annapolis hosts the Maryland Seafood Festival and Crisfield hosts the National Hard Crab Derby and Fair, which features not only a Miss Crustacean Pageant and a Crab Picking Contest, but also the Governor's Cup Race, with crabs representing the fifty states racing for the cup, and the Crab Derby, first won by "Scobie" in 1948. In November, oysters are on the plate at Oyster Day in St. Michaels and at the Fell's Point Oyster Festival in Baltimore. The Maryland Wine Festival, a mid-September celebration of Maryland wines at Westminster, can provide a beverage always appropriate to seafood.

Maryland's Eastern Shore in November is the scene of the annual Waterfowl Festival. Held at Easton, this festival celebrates the Chesapeake Bay, its wildlife, food, and art. Wildlife artists showcase their work at the festival. There are paintings, photos, decoys, and sculptures. There are also duck-calling contests and goose-calling contests. Since the Waterfowl Festival began in 1971, over $2.5 million has been raised for wildlife conservation on the Atlantic Flyway.[20]

MASSACHUSETTS

Massachusetts is the place to experience early American colonial and revolutionary history. The First Muster Reenactment in Salem toward the latter part of June re-creates seventeenth-century military and domestic life. The Indian House Memorial 1704 Weekend in Old Deerfield in late February re-creates the early New England cultures represented by Native Americans, French marines, and English Puritans. In Boston, the Annual Lantern Service on April 18 at the Old North Church recalls Paul Revere's signal to ride. On the next day, Paul Revere's ride is reenacted, as is the Battle of Lexington and Concord. Bunker Hill Day Weekend, a military encampment, takes place in mid-June in Charlestown. The Boston Tea Party is reenacted on December 13.

When the sap rises in late February and early March, maple sugaring goes on at Old Sturbridge Village as well as at many other sites. The Longfellow Birthday Anniversary Celebration takes place at the Longfellow National Historical Site on February 27. Then with spring in bloom, Nantucket Island celebrates its Daffodil Festival toward the end of April, and Heritage Plantation Dexter Rhododendron Festival in Sandwich occurs later in May. The summer is filled with events around the water. There are the Annual Salem Seaport Festival at the end of May, the Annual Blessing of the Fleet at Provincetown near the end of June, the Boston Harborfest and the Harborfest at the Navy Yard in Charlestown around Independence Day, waterfront festivals in Gloucester the third weekend of August and Newburyport the first week of September, and the Boston Seaport Festival for a week at the end of August, among many others. Boston also holds an Annual Chowderfest early in July and Plymouth holds its Lobster Festival the third weekend in August. Nathanial Hawthorne's Birthday on July 4 is among the summer celebrations at Salem, and the Annual Festival of the Blessed Sacrament, in its eightieth year in 1994, is the biggest Portuguese festival held in the United States.[21]

MICHIGAN

Michigan's ethnic diversity is celebrated in numerous fairs and festivals throughout the year. Indian pow-wows take place in Escanaba the first part of February, in Lainsburg the third week of June, in Baraga toward the end of July, and in St. Ignace at the beginning of September. Clare is the site of the Irish Festival in mid-March as well as the Amish Arts and Crafts Show at the beginning of May and September. German culture is celebrated in Frankenmuth at Maifest in mid-May and at the Bavarian Festival for a week in mid-June. Wyandotte hosts the German-American Festival in early June. The Benton Harbor German-American Summerfest is later in June and the Polish Festival is held near the end of July. The Mexican Festival in Wyandotte at the end of May and the Mexicantown Fiesta in Detroit in mid-June celebrate Mexican culture. Greeks celebrate at Kalamazoo's Greek Fest the first weekend in June and at Saginaw's Greek Festival toward the end of June. Wyandotte hosts both the Czechoslovak Festival and the Hungarian Festival in the first part of June. African-American Heritage is celebrated in Flint on June 19. Caspian hosts Scandinavian Midsummer Day late in June, Croatian Day in mid-July, Italian Day in early August, and St. Lucia Swedish Day in early December.

Michigan's maritime heritage is honored at Maritime Days in Marine City in early August and at the White Lake Maritime Festival in Whitehall a little later in August. Lumberjacks can test their mettle at the Lumberjack Festival in Wolverine at the end of June, at Lumberjack Days in Baraga over July 4, and in Newberry in late August. Negaunie hosts the Iron Heritage Fest in early August and Mackinaw City honors those who work with iron at the Ironworkers Festival at the end of August. Farmers are honored at the Farmers Festival in Pigeon toward the end of July and at Hilldale's Farm Festival in August.

Michigan also has a festival celebrating just about any fish that can be found in Michigan waters. There is the Perch Festival in Caseville for a week beginning in mid-April, the National Trout Festival in Kalkaska, also in April, the Bass Festival in Mancelona from the end of May into the beginning of June, the Salmon and Trout Derby in Manistee early in June, Crappiethon USA at Houghton Lake from early June to early August, the Carp Rodeo in Union City in mid-June, the Pickerel Tournament in Algonac at the beginning of July, the Bass Festival in Crystal Falls in mid-July, the Bluegill Festival in St. Helen at the end of July, the Salmon Derby Festival in Sault Ste. Marie from the end of August into September, and the National Coho Festival in Honor at the beginning of September. There is even a Fish Sandwich Festival in Bay Port in early August.

Flowers and food are also features of many festivals. Holland hosts the Tulip Time Festival in the first part of May and Muskegon the Trillium Festival. Lilac festivals are held in Barryton at the end of May and on Mackinac Island the first part of June. The National Strawberry Festival is in Belleville the third weekend of June. The National Cherry Festival is in Traverse City the first week of July. And where there are cherries there are pits. The International Cherry Pit–Spitting Championship is held in early July in Eau Claire. The National Asparagus Festival is in Hart in mid-June. Maple syrup festivals take place in Mason, Shepard, and Vermontsville from mid-February through the third week of April. Mesick has its Mushroom Festival early in May and Boyne City has its in mid-May. Battle Creek hosts the Cereal Festival the second weekend in June. The Michigan Peach Festival is held in Romeo in early September and the Bologna Festival is held toward the end of July in Yale. Blueberry festivals are held in Imlay City the first week of August and South Haven a week later. Fremont hosts the National Baby Food Festival in the latter part of July. And for something a little different, there is a Buzzard Festival in May in Hell.[22]

MINNESOTA

Minnesota remembers its early fur-trading history at the Eagle Creek Rendezvous in Shakopee late in May. But mining, logging, and agriculture became the backbone of the state's economy. Leonidas Merritt Days at Iron Mountain on the second weekend of August celebrates the local discovery of iron ore. Jasper celebrates its Quarry Festival in mid-June. The annual Buena Vista Logging Days in Bemidji near the end of February includes the induction of lumberjacks into the Hall of Fame. Agriculture is the focus of numerous festivals, including Dairy Days in Adams and Pine Island's Cheese Fest, both in June. Wild rice festivals are held at Deer River toward the end of June and at Kelliher in the first part of July, where the Wild Rice Queen is crowned. Corn is featured in Olivia at the end of July at Corn Capital Days. In August, there is the Corn Carnival at Cokato, the Corn Festival at Ortonville, the Corn on the Cob Festival at Plainview, and Buttered Corn Day at Sleepy Eye. Potatoes are picked, peeled, and consumed at the Barnesville Potato Days Festival at the end of August. Hanley Falls hosts the Pioneer Power Threshing Show in mid-August, one of many such shows across the state.

Minnesota celebrates its famous at the Judy Garland Festival the second week of June in her hometown of Grand Rapids and at Sinclair Lewis Days at Sauk Centre in mid-July. The state bird is celebrated in Nisswa in July at the Minnesota Loon Festival. Rodeos get under way in June at Hawley and Buffalo. But perhaps Minnesota's biggest cause for celebration is its ethnic diversity.

St. Paul's Festival of Nations, held at the end of April or early May, celebrates eighty-five different ethnic groups. Chisholm hosts Minnesota Ethnic Days in July and August, which includes the Festival Italiana, All-Slav Day, the Bavarian Summerfest, U.K. Day, and a Finnish culture celebration. Scandinavian culture is celebrated at the Midsummer Scandinavian Festival in Mora in mid-June, Scandinavian Days in Fergus Falls a little later in June, and the Scandinavian Hjemkomst Festival in Moorhead toward the end of June. Laskiainen is a Finnish sliding festival held in Aurora in early February. Finns also celebrate in Finland on St. Urho's Day in March and in Embarrass at the Summer Finnish Festival in June. Syttende Mai celebrations of Norwegian independence are held in mid-May at Benson, Spring Grove, and Hendricks. Swedes celebrate at the Swedish Festival in Cambridge in mid-June. Midsommer Dag in Scandia and Svenskarnas Dag in Minneapolis in late June present Swedish singing, dancing and other features. Aebleskiver Day in Tyler on June 26 is a Danish heritage celebration.

German culture is celebrated in mid-July in New Ulm at the Heritagefest and late in August in Young America at the Stiftungsfest. Swiss culture is celebrated in West Concord at the Annual Berne Swissfest in August. Scots have the Scottish Country Fair in St. Paul at the beginning of May and the Irish have an Irish Celebration in mid-March. Poles celebrate in Ivanhoe in mid-August at Polska Kielbasa Days and Greeks celebrate in Rochester in August at the Greek Festival. Tribes from the United States and Canada gather at the Grand Celebration Pow Wow in Hinckley toward the end of June.

The Festival of Ethnic Music and Dance, held in St. Paul the last week of February, features music and dance from all over the world. But in Minnesota, one is never far from a polka festival. There are the International Polkafest toward the end of June and the Range Polka Fest in mid-July in Chisholm, Polka Days in Seaforth, also in mid-July, and Polka Days in Gibbon toward the end of July.[23]

MISSISSIPPI

Mississippi recalls its early history on the last weekend in April with the reenactment of d'Iberville's landing in 1699 at Ocean Springs. On the fourth Saturday in October, the 1830 Treaty of Dancing Rabbit Creek is recalled in Macon at the Dancing Rabbit Festival. This treaty opened Choctaw lands to white settlers. Beauvoir, Jefferson Davis' last home in Biloxi, is the scene of the Fall Muster in mid-October, in which Mississippi's role in preparing for the Civil War is emphasized. Antebellum architecture remains resplendent in Natchez. The homes are opened to the public during the Spring Pilgrimage in March and April and the Fall Pilgrimage in October. Folk life is celebrated at the Bear Creek Folklife Festival in Dennis on the first Saturday in June, the Folklife Festival in Jackson on the first Saturday in July, and the Folk Life Festival in Columbus in August. Native American heritage is remembered in Natchez at the Natchez Pow-Wow at the Grand Village of the Natchez Indians at the end of March, the Choctaw Indian Fair in Philadelphia in July, and the Pioneer and Indian Heritage Festival in Ridgeland at the end of October.

Music is one of Mississippi's enduring legacies. The Jimmie Rodgers Country Music Festival takes place in Meridian during the last full week of May. Grand Ole Opry star Rod Brasfield is honored at the festival that bears his name in Smithville in late August. Bluegrass fans can hit the Annual Magnolia State Bluegrass Festival on the first weekend of June in Wiggins and the Sandy Ridge Fall Bluegrass Festival in Meridian in August. Meridian also hosts the Chunky Rhythm and Blues Festival on the third Saturday of July. On the third Saturday of September, Greenville gives tribute to the birthplace of the blues with the Delta Blues Festival. And on August 8, Elvis Presley Commemoration Day takes place on the grounds of his birthplace in Tupelo.

Music and food are natural allies, and Mississippi has its share of food extravaganzas. Jackson celebrates the International Beans and Rice Festival in late October. Belzoni, the "Catfish Capital of the World," is the site of the World Catfish Festival on the first Saturday of April. The Delta Jubilee in Clarksville on the first weekend of June includes the state's championship barbecue cook-off and festival. Chicken cooking contests and the crowning of the Miss Broiler Festival Queen are featured at the Mississippi Broiler Festival in Forest in June.

Seafood from the Mississippi Gulf Coast is always cause for celebration. There is the Oyster Festival at Biloxi and the Ron Meyers Crawfish Festival at Gulfport in April. On the first weekend of May there is the Biloxi Shrimp Festival and Blessing of the Fleet. Biloxi has its Annual Seafood Festival later in September. Bay St. Louis holds a Fourth of July Crab Festival. And when the fruits ripen, they are the subject of festivals too. Poplarville holds a Blueberry Jubilee in June. Mize holds its Watermelon Festival on the next to last Saturday of July. Gulfport holds a Banana Festival in September, and on the second Saturday of September, Pelahatchie celebrates its Muscadine Jubilee, when muscadine grapes are stomped, baked, and eaten.[24]

MISSOURI

Missouri celebrates its history and heritage by remembering its days as the gateway to the West with Santa-Cali-Gon Days in Independence early in September, which celebrates the Santa Fe, California, and Oregon trails. Western Weekend in Cape Girardeau in the latter part of May and Wild West Days in Springfield near mid-September recall its western tradition. And rodeos remain a feature of Missouri life. Licking's PRCA Rodeo, Auxasse's PRCA Championship Rodeo, and the Butler Rodeo are all in June. Fredericktown's International Pro Rodeo is in mid-July. Hartville's Annual Rodeo is in late August and Steelville's Harvest Festival and Rodeo takes place the second week of September. Folklife is featured at the Big Muddy Folk Festival in Boonville in mid-April, the Missouri Heritage Fair in St. Louis the third weekend of April, Hillbilly Days in Lebanon in mid-June, and the Salt River Folklife Festival in Florida and Stoutsville in mid-August.

Native American culture is celebrated at the beginning of May at Native American Days in Jackson, American Indian Days in St. Louis the third week of May, the Osage Indian Heritage and Crafts Festival in Gravois Mills at the end of July, Monroe City's Native American Pow Wow in early August, the Peace Pipe Indians Pow Wow in Hannibal in mid-August, and the Clear Creek Indian Pow Wow in Milo the third week of August. Missouri's rivers played a vital role in its settlement and continue to influence daily life. Cape Girardeau celebrates its Riverfest, as does New Madrid, around mid-June. The Blessing of the Fleet takes place in mid-July in St. Louis. The rivers brought French colonists, who are remembered during French Colonial Heritage Days in Ste. Genevieve in mid-June. French colonists and the German settlers who came later are celebrated in Ste. Genevieve in mid-August at the Jour de Fete. German culture is featured in Hermann at the Maifest in mid-May and the Octoberfest on all October weekends.

Mining was an early Missouri industry and is celebrated at Coal Miner Days in late May in Novinger and at Old Miner's Days in early October in Viburnum. The Fine Art and Winefest in Washington in mid-May recalls the time when Missouri was the nation's largest wine producer. Of course, many of Missouri's agricultural products are reason for celebration. Morels are featured at Richmond's Mushroom Festival at the beginning of May. Mexico holds its Soybean Festival in mid-September and Stockton holds its Black Walnut Festival toward the end of September. As October begins, Versailles holds its Annual Old Tyme Apple Festival. Then a week later Apple Butter Makin' Days gets under way in Mt. Vernon, and at the end of October Kimmswick holds its Apple Butter Festival. And at the Clark County Mule Festival in Kohoka in mid-September, festival goers can find out just how stubborn a Missouri mule can be.

Famous names grace several Missouri festivals. Houston celebrates the

Emmett Kelly Clown Festival early in May. Grandview's Harry's Hay Days in mid-May honor Harry Truman. Samuel Clemens' hometown of Hannibal is the site of National Tom Sawyer Days from the end of June into early August. Kearney celebrates Missouri's most famous outlaw in mid-September with its Jesse James Festival. Grant City, boyhood home of Glenn Miller, celebrates Glenn Miller Day on June 13. The Scott Joplin Ragtime Festival takes place in Sedalia early in June. Carthage has its Ragtime Music Festival at the end of September into October, and the St. Louis Blues Festival is in early September.[25]

MONTANA

Other than the Montana Pro Rodeo Circuit Finals in Great Falls and the Perch Festival in Townsend in mid-January, Montana's winter months are taken up for the most part by winter festivals. Among them are the Frost Fever/Winterfest in Missoula from late January into the first week of February, the Whitefish Winter Carnival early in February, and the Winter Carnival at Red Lodge Mountain in early March. At the end of March and into May, the Annual International Wildlife Film Festival takes place in Missoula. It is one of only two such festivals in the world.

With the approach of spring, Native American celebrations, rodeos, and traditional festivals get under way. Bozeman's Indian Powwow is in early April. The Buffalo Feast and Powwow in St. Ignatius is in mid-May. Conrad hosts the Whoop-Up Parade and Rodeo in mid-May, and the Big Timber Rodeo is held toward the end of June. Bigfork and Polson hold cherry blossom festivals at the beginning of May, and Billings holds its Strawberry Festival near the middle of June. The old West is celebrated during Sidney's Western Days, Culbertson's Frontier Days, Pioneer Days in Ennis, Western Days in Stevensville, and Pioneer Days in Scobey, all of which are in June. Great Falls honors explorers Lewis and Clark at its Lewis and Clark Festival toward the end of June, and Cut Bank holds its Lewis and Clark Days toward the end of July.

Rodeos continue throughout the summer with the Home of Champions Rodeo at Red Lodge and the Livingston Roundup Rodeo in early July, the Harlowton Rodeo around July 4, and the Calamity Jane Rodeo among them. Likewise, Native American festivities continue with the Badlands Indian Celebration later in June, North American Indian Days in Browning in the first part of July, the Iron Ring Indian Celebration in Poplar and the Standing Arrow Powwow in Elmo in mid-July, the Central Montana Horse Show, Fair, and Rodeo in Lewiston at the end of July, Rocky Boy's Annual Powwow at the end of July, and the Crow Indian Fair and Rodeo at the Crow Agency the third weekend of August.

Montana celebrates its mining industry at the Troy Mining Festival and 4th of July and its oil industry at the Oil Discovery Celebration in Poplar the third week of August. Huckleberries are ripe in August and are celebrated at huckleberry festivals in Swan Lake the first weekend of August and in Trout Creek on the next weekend. Early in September, the wagon trains are in gear again at the Annual Milk River Wagon Train in Malta. Lewiston is the site of the Montana State Chokecherry Festival a bit later in the month. And from mid-November to mid-December, the Eagle Watch in Helena provides the opportunity to see bald eagles flock to the Missouri River to catch salmon.[26]

NEBRASKA

Nebraska is proud of its early settlers, and many of the festivals and fairs celebrated throughout the year feature some aspect of early life in the state. These include a wide range and number of ethnic events, rodeos, and pioneer days, along with pow-wows and other celebrations of the Native American heritage of the state. Of course, the cuisine is enjoyed at many of the festivals and chili cook-offs abound. But the first events of the year focus on nature with the early February Groundhog Day Parade and Wild Game Feed at Unadilla, the Groundhog Capital of Nebraska, and the mid-March Wings Over the Platte gathering in Grand Island, where naturalists celebrate the largest migration of sandhill cranes.

The first rodeo of the year is the World's Toughest Rodeo held at Lincoln in mid-February, followed by over fifty others throughout the year. For example, Nebraska's Big Rodeo and Parade in Burwell in late July boasts a professional rodeo as well as chuck wagon races, a dinner bell derby, and clown bullfighting. Although part of other western heritage events, chili cooking is the only focus of one event, the Annual Chili Cook-Off held in mid-March at Arnold.

The culture of the West is captured in several festivals. Early in June, Wagons West Celebrations annually remember the wagon trains that passed through Kearney before winter snowfall made mountains west of Kearney impassible. Pawnee City hosts the Pawnee Pioneer Panorama in mid-June, and in mid-July the Oregon Trail Days celebration at Gering gets under way. Trenton celebrates the last major battle between two Indian tribes, the Sioux and the Pawnee, at the Massacre Canyon Pow Wow in early August. Scottsbluff hosts the Nebraska American Indian Days Celebration with speakers, displays, a pow-wow dance, costumes, and food toward the end of September, and in Valentine cowboys celebrate western heritage with melodrama, cowboy poetry, songs, and a mountain man rendezvous at the Annual Nebraska Cowboy Poetry Gathering and Old West Days at the start of October.

Among Nebraska's many ethnic festivals are the Omaha Czech Cultural Club Czech Festival on a mid-April day, the Czech Festival held in Lincoln at the beginning of May, and the Clarkson Czech Festival toward the end of June. The Grundlovsfest (Danish Days) is held in Dannebrog and the Swedish Festival in Oakland in early June. Kolach Days in Verdigre follow the next week. Nebraskaland Days Mexican Fiesta in North Platte runs around the second weekend of June as does Wurst Tag in Eustis. Midsommarfest (Swedish Days) in Holdrege and the Stromsburg Swedish Festival are on the third weekend in June. Norwegian Days in Newman Grove follows a week later. Omaha's St. Stanislaus Polish Festival is in mid-August. The Annual Germanfest is held in mid-September in Fairbury, and there are annual Oktoberfests in Sidney at the beginning of October and in Grand Island toward the end of October.

Rounding out Nebraska's selection of festivals and fairs are the Annual Arbor Day Festival at the end of April in Nebraska City, where the founder of Arbor Day, J. Sterling Morton, lived. Red Cloud celebrates another famous Nebraskan at the Willa Cather Annual Spring Conference in early May. Cinco de Mayo is celebrated in early May in Scottsbluff, Norfolk, and Lexington, and the state tree is celebrated at the Cottonwood Prairie Festival in Hastings on the first weekend of June. Railroad Days in Omaha celebrates railroading with games, rides, and model train displays toward the end of September, and the Days of Swine and Roses in Madison around July 4 features hog calling, husband calling, and smelly boot contests, along with a pork barbecue, a women's chore outfit fashion show, and a farm olympics.[27]

NEVADA

Nevada's fairs, festivals, and events reflect its history as part of the American West. In late January events get under way with the Cowboy Poetry Gathering in Elko. In early March, there is the Hoover Dam Square Dance and the Snowfest in North Lake Tahoe. In April, Elko hosts the International Collegiate Mining Competition. May finds a Chili Cook-Off and Cinco de Mayo celebration in Virginia City. On the first weekend of June, the Winnemucca Mule Show and Races are off and running and the Winnemucca Basque Festival takes place the next weekend. The Kit Carson Rendezvous takes place in mid-June in Carson City, and one week later Carson City is also the site of the Stewart Indian Museum Pow Wow. At the same time, the Red Mountain Powwow takes place in McDermitt. The Reno Rodeo runs during the third week of June.

Nevada remembers its heritage in early July at Minden/Gardnerville with Carson Valley Heritage Days and then later in July at Panaca Pioneer Day and Pioche Heritage Days. July rodeos include the Silver State International Rodeo in Fallon, the Twin States Stampede in McDermitt, the Lincoln County Rodeo Series in Caliente, and the All-Indian Stampede and Rodeo in Fallon. Jackpot hosts the Carl Hayden Daze and National Hollerin' Contest over Independence Day celebrations. Mid-August brings the Nevada State Fair in Reno and the Reno Basque Festival.

In early September Reno hosts the Numaga Indian Days Celebration Powwow. Sparks has the Best in the West Nugget Rib Cook-Off and Fallon celebrates the Hearts of Gold Cantaloupe Festival. Not to be missed is the Virginia City International Camel Races the second weekend of September. Early October brings another Chili Cook-Off in Carson City, and two weeks later the North Las Vegas Fairshow and Hot Air Balloon Races take place. Late in November, Hawthorne is the site of the Walker Lake Fishing Derby. In early December, the rodeo season comes to an end with the National Finals Rodeo in Las Vegas.[28]

NEW HAMPSHIRE

New Hampshire is premier ski country in the winter months. Besides ski events too numerous to mention, New London holds its Frost Bite Follies and the King Pine Ski Area its Winter Carnival. When the sap begins flowing in early March, Maple Sugaring at Pinkham Notch gets under way. Finally at the end of March, it's time for the Annual Beach Party at Bretton Woods.

Lilacs are planted in mid-May at the Annual Marjorie Field Lilac Festival in Bristol. The Chowder Festival, part of the Prescott Park Arts Fest in Plymouth, is held at the end of May. June begins with the Annual Monadnock Balloon and Aviation Festival, the Festival of Shaker Crafts and Herbs at Enfield, and Bethlehem's Wildflower Festival. A clambake is just part of the festivities at the Annual Market Square Day Weekend in Portsmouth in mid-June. The Annual Portsmouth Jazz Festival takes place at the end of June. Maritime history and song is celebrated in Portsmouth at the Annual Boat Builder's Day in mid-July. Later in July, the Shaker Revels in Enfield feature Shaker life in words and music. America's oldest craft fair, the Annual Craftsman's Fair at Mt. Sunapee State Park, is held at the beginning of August, and in mid-August, Attitash holds its Equine Festival. The Annual New Hampshire Highland games at Loon Mountain are held in mid-September, and the Annual Ciderfest at New Boston goes on the second weekend in October.

Agricultural fairs are held throughout the state from the end of July to mid-October. These fairs highlight the importance of agriculture to the economy of the state and the state's diversity. Fairs are held in Stratham, Cheshire, and North Haverhill in July. August fairs include the Cornish Fair, the Belknap County 4-H Fair in Belmont, and the Plymouth State Fair. The Hopkinton Fair, the Lancaster Fair, the Hillsboro County Fair, the Rochester Fair, and the Deerfield Fair are in September. The Sandwich Fair takes place in October.[29]

NEW JERSEY

The warmth of spring takes citizens of the Garden State outside to celebrate. Spring flowers and Dutch lifestyle are celebrated toward the end of April at the Tulip Festival in Cape May. At the same time, Morris Township holds the Annual New Jersey Daffodil Show. Ocean City hosts the Annual Ocean City Flower Show, and Annual Rose Day is celebrated in Somerset the first weekend in June. June Strawberry festivals are numerous: there is a festival in Bridgeton on the first weekend, in Belvidere and Montclair on the second weekend, and in Lyndhurst on the third. New Jersey's claim that it is the second highest producer of cultivated blueberries in the country is reason enough for the annual Whitesbog Blueberry Festival held on the second Saturday in July. New Jersey wineries host the early June Garden State Winegrowers Association Annual Spring Festival at Cream Ridge, where wine is tasted and grapes stomped by wine connoisseurs. The sea's bounty is enjoyed at several festivals: the Lambertville Shad Festival toward the end of April, the Annual New Jersey Fresh Seafood Festival at Atlantic City and the New Jersey Seafood Festival at Belmar on the second weekend of June, and Seafood at Seaside, held in Seaside Heights on the third weekend of June.

Summer begins early when, in mid-June, the Annual Baseball Day in Hoboken celebrates the first organized baseball game, played in Elysian Field in 1846. Other June events include the New Jersey Renaissance Festival, held every weekend in June at Somerset. Holmdel hosts the Polish Festival, the Festa Italiana, the Ukrainian Festival USA, and the Irish Festival on succeeding June weekends. There is a Revolutionary War Reenactment in mid-June in River Edge. The Bridgeton Folk Festival is held annually on June 19 and the Riverfest at Red Bank toward the end of June. The Battle of Monmouth re-creation in Freehold takes place toward the end of June too. The New Jersey Festival of Ballooning in Readington is held at the end of July, and during the latter part of June the JVC Jazz Weekend is held in Stanhope. Peaches are celebrated in Bridgeton in early August and also at the Bluegrass and Peach Festival later in the month in Belvidere.

The Jewish Renaissance Fair is in Morristown on the Sunday of Labor Day weekend in September. Labor Day is the date also for the Victorian Faire in Bridgeton and the Revolutionary War Military Encampment in Port Monmouth. A variety of festive occasions, large and small, are held in September and October. Progressing through the month of September there are the Monarch Butterfly Migration at Chatham, the African-American Festival in Holmdel, the state-sponsored New Jersey Ethnic Festival at Jersey City, an Irish Festival in North Wildwood, the Waterloo Oktoberfest in Stanhope, and the Slovak Festival at Holmdel. The Clownfest in Seaside Heights is scheduled for the third weekend in September, and the Barnegat Bay Duck and Decoy Show in Tuckerton is also scheduled during the last weekend in the month. At the beginning of October, Somerville is the site of the Annual Sommerville International Crafts Festival, where there are 250 exhibitors of crafts and art as well as food and entertainment. On the second weekend of October, the annual Juried American Indian Arts Festival, held in Westampton at the Rankokus Indian Reservation, features one hundred American Indian artists and entertainers. The Chatsworth Cranberry Festival is held during the third weekend in October. Of note are two historical events commemorative of New Jersey's role in the Revolutionary War: the 18th Century Encampment at Fort Lee, held on the third weekend in November, and the Re-enactment of Washington Crossing the Delaware held on Christmas Day in Titusville.[30]

NEW MEXICO

New Mexico offers enormous numbers of arts and crafts fairs and special events. It celebrates the importance of mining in the state in Silver City's Mining Days in early September. Its western heritage is celebrated in numerous events, including the Western Week Celebration in July in Carlsbad, the Cowboy Camp Meeting in Tucumari at the end of July, and the Cowboy Poetry Gathering in Silver City in August. And Albuquerque's International Balloon Festival in October is not to be missed. But New Mexico also offers unique opportunities to learn about and observe Native American culture.

During American Indian Week in Albuquerque at the end of April, there is the Gathering of Nations Powwow. In mid-May near Carlsbad, the Living Desert State Park Mescal Roast features Mescalero Apache ceremonies, dances, and food. Cuba celebrates Navajo Days in mid-June and Albuquerque hosts eleven days of Aztec Dances at the beginning of July. Perhaps one of the most interesting ways to observe Native American cultural events, however, is to visit the pueblos themselves on the special feast days of the saints. On these feast days, various dances—harvest, elk, buffalo, corn, Comanche—may take place depending on the occasion.

These special feast days begin at most pueblos on January 1, with dances and the Transfer of Canes. On January 23, the San Ildefonso Pueblo Feast Day is celebrated. Laguna Pueblo holds its San Jose Day Festival on March 19. The San Felipe Feast Day at the Cochiti Pueblo takes place on May 1. Two days later, the Taos Pueblo has its Santa Cruz Corn Dance and Field Blessing. The Santa Clara, San Ildefonso, and San Juan pueblos hold their St. Anthony's Feast Day Comanche Dance on June 13. On June 29, corn dances are held at the San Felipe, Santa Ana, and Santo Domingo pueblos for the San Pedro Feast Day. The Santa Ana Pueblo celebrates Santa Ana Feast Day on July 26 with a corn dance.

In August, the Laguna Rublo Pueblo celebrates the San Lorenzo Festival on the tenth and the San Antonio Feast Day on the fifteenth. Harvest dances are held at the Isleta Pueblo for the San Augustin Feast Day on September 4 and for the San Geronimo Feast Day at the San Juan Pueblo on September 30. Corn, buffalo, and eagle dances are held at the Laguna Pueblo on September 19 during the Festival of San Jose de Los Lagunas and Arts and Crafts Fair. On October 4, the Nambe Pueblo celebrates St. Francis Feast Day. The Tesuque and Jemez pueblos celebrate San Diego Feast Day on November 12 and the Pojoaque Pueblo celebrates the Guadalupe Feast Day on December 12.[31]

NEW YORK

Once all the winter festivals and carnivals play out in March, the maple sap begins to run. In early April, Marathon holds its Annual Central New York Maple Festival and Andover its Maple Festival. Then the Annual Arbor Day Festival in Adams honors the founder of that day and native son, J. Sterling Morton. This April festival sets the tone for a number of other festivals later in the year. In May, Rochester and Burke celebrate lilac festivals. At the end of July, Paul Smiths is the site of the Adirondack Wildflower Festival. Apple festivals begin toward the end of September with the Johnny Appleseed Festival in Olean and the Apple Festival in Busti. Forestville's Apple Festival kicks off October, and the Annual Falling Leaves Apple Festival at Long Lake follows the next week. The Greig Farm Pumpkin Festival at Red Hook goes on for most of October. But from May through September, New York's wine industry is celebrating. Kenka Lake holds its Annual Barrel Tasting in mid-May. Hammondsport holds its Vintage Days Weekend in mid-June. On the second weekend of July, the Cheese and Wine Festival in held at Kenka Lake. When the grapes come in around the second weekend of September, Forestville is the site of the Septemberfest and Hammondsport of the Vintage Harvest Weekend. Silver Creek holds its Festival of Grapes and Naples holds its Great Grape and Wine Festival in mid-September.

New York celebrates its heritage in several festivals throughout the state. Massena hosts the Festival of North Country Folklife in mid-August. The Indian–Mountain Man Rendezvous takes place in Hunter at the end of May. Native American culture is celebrated at the Iroquois Indian Festival in Howes Cave the first weekend of September, the Annual July Pow Wow in Barryville the second week of July, the Mountain Eagle Indian Festival in Hunter in early September, the Otsiningo Pow Wow and Indian Craft Fair in Apalachin early in June, and the Annual Shinnecock Powwow in Southampton early in September. As May begins, Fishkill celebrates Dutch Spring Weekend. A week later, the Dutch legacy of tulips is featured at Holland's Tulip Festival and at the Annual Tulip Festival in Albany. Celtic heritage is celebrated in Hunter at the International Celtic Festival in mid-August, the Central New York Scottish Games and Celtic Festival in Liverpool, also in mid-August, and the Celtic Fair at Hunter in the beginning of October. Rockaway's Irish Festival is on the third weekend of July. German culture is celebrated in Hunter the first half of July at the German Alps Festival and International Beer Festival, as well as at Oktoberfests in North Creek and Cherry Creek on the last weekend of September. Toward the middle of July, Cape Vincent features French culture at its French Festival. African-American culture is featured at Juneteenth in Buffalo in June and Japanese culture at Sakura Matsuri (cherry blossom festival) in Brooklyn near the end of April. The Friendship Festival, with events in Buffalo and Fort Erie, Ontario, celebrates Canadian-American friendship over the July 4 holidays.[32]

NORTH CAROLINA

Kites and cotton, mules and molasses, hang gliding and fictional TV characters—all are causes for celebration in North Carolina. The Wright Kite Festival takes place in Nags Head in mid-July and the Carolina Kite Festival in Atlantic Beach late in October. Dallas hosts Cotton Ginning Days and Laurinburg hosts the John Blue Cotton Festival on the second weekend of October. Benson Mule Days are at the end of September. Molasses festivals are held at Granite Falls in early October and at Snow Camp early in November. Francis Rogallo, a pioneer of hang gliding, is honored at the Annual Festival of Rogallo Wing Invention at Nags Head in mid-August. Mayberry Days in Mt. Airy at the end of September remember fondly the fictional lives of Aunt Bee, Andy, Barney and Opie.

The Biltmore Estate Festival in mid-September in Asheville shows off one of America's premier homes and estates. The North Carolina International Folk Festival, Folkmoot USA, runs in various locations during the last week of July. The Smoky Mountain Folk Festival is at Lake Junaluska in early September, and the International Festival of Raleigh takes place in early October. Native American celebrations include Grandma's Annual Pow Wow in Concord (mid-August), the Catawba Indian Pottery Festival at Gastonia (early September), the Lumbee Pow Wow in Pembroke (second weekend of September), and Kituwah—the American Indian National Arts Exposition in Asheville (late September). The Annual Statewide American Indian Cultural Festival is held in Fayetteville early in October. Greek culture is celebrated during the Annual Yiason Greek Festival in mid-September. Germans celebrate at Oktoberfests in Maggie Valley, Little Switzerland, and Asheville. The Grandfather Mountain Highland Games and Gathering of the Clans bring Scots together at Linville in July.

Farmers play an integral role in North Carolina's economy. Farm life is celebrated at the Southeast Old Threshers' Reunion in Denton (early July) and at the Caldwell Agricultural Fair in Lenoir and the Old Fashion Farmer's Days in Silk Hope (early September). North Carolina has rodeos too.

There are the Mid-Atlantic Pro Rodeo in Woodley early in July, the Governor's Rodeo in Love Valley, Munro Mid-Atlantic Pro Rodeo, the Lake Myers World Championship Rodeo in Mocksville over the Labor Day weekend, and the Mid-Atlantic Rodeo Championship Finals in Raleigh at the end of November.

Food festivals abound. The North Carolina Seafood Festival takes place early in October in Morehead City. The Winterville Watermelon Festival is in late August. Hendersonville hosts the North Carolina Apple Festival early in September and Raeford hosts the North Carolina Turkey Festival in mid-September. The North Carolina Chili Championship is in Clemmons in mid-September. Early October brings the Annual Spring Hope National Pumpkin Festival and Mt. Airy's Sonker Festival (a sonker is a deep-dish pie).[33]

NORTH DAKOTA

North Dakota has over forty rodeos between May 1 and the end of October. The NDRA Finals Rodeo in Dickinson is held in early September. Cowboy life is also celebrated at the Dakota Cowboy Poetry Gathering in Medora at the end of May. But farming is also a mainstay of North Dakota life. It is celebrated at the Wyndmere Annual Crop Show early in February, at the North Dakota Winter Show in Valley City early in March, and Sodbuster Days in Fort Ransom in July and September. Threshing Shows bring big crowds too. There are the Threshing Show (mid-June) and the Divide County Historical Society Threshing Bee (mid-July) in Crosby, the Park River Threshing Bee (end of August), the Drake Threshing Show (mid-September), and the Makoti Threshing Show in early October, among others.

Pioneer days are recalled in Cavalier at Pioneer Heritage Days the third weekend of June and at Pioneer Days in Fargo in mid-August. Elgin celebrates Carson to Almont Wagon Train Week in early September. Frontier Army Days takes place in Mandan at the end of June. Folk festivals include Fargo's Folk Arts Fest in July and Bismarck's Folkfest in late August and early September. Pioneer Days and Northern Pines Ethnic Festival in Dickinson the first weekend of September celebrates North Dakota's ethnic heritage. Scandinavians celebrate at Fargo's Scandinavian Hjemkomst Festival toward the end of June and at the Norsk Hostfest in Minot in mid-October. Germans celebrate at Fargo's German Folkfest at the end of July and at Oktoberfests in New Leipzig, Jamestown, Beulah, Ashley, and Hope. Ukrainians celebrate at Dickinson's Ukrainian Cultural Institute Festival on the July 4 weekend.

With the heavy population of German and Scandinavian descendants, polka festivals can be found throughout the state. They include the Eagles Polkafest in Dickinson in late April, the Annual Polka Festival in Lankin in mid-June, the Trinity Polka Fest in Dickinson in mid-September, and Bismarck's Polkafest in early October. Sauerkraut and goose go well with polkas. Wishek Sauerkraut Days and Kenmare's Annual Goosefest are in October.

Native Americans were, of course, North Dakota's first ethnic group and their presence remains strong and vibrant. Celebrations of Native American heritage run from late March to mid-October all over the state. Native American Days is held in Grand Forks from the end of March into April. Pow-wows include the All Nations Pow-Wow in Bismarck a week into May, the White Shield Pow-Wow toward mid-July, the Indian Cultural Celebration in Mandan in mid-August, the Nemewin Turtle Mountain Pow-Wow in Belcourt, and the Williston Indian Culture Club Pow-Wow in mid-October.[34]

OHIO

Ohio bills itself as "the heart of it all." Indeed, Ohio's geographical location has made it both a crossroad for travelers and commerce as well as a place of settlement for numerous ethnic groups. America's first great highway, old Route 40, is celebrated at National Pike Festivals in Bridgeport and Morristown on the first weekend of June and in Norwich a week later. The canals are celebrated at the Olde Canal Days Festival in Canal Fulton early in July and at Coshocton's Canal Festival in mid-August. The Dennison depot is the site of the Railroad Festival in May. Marietta's Ohio River Sternwheel Festival in mid-September recalls the riverboat days.

The Old Fort Steuben Festival in Steubenville on the first weekend of June, the Hocking Hills Indian Pow-Wow and Rendezvous in Rockbridge a week later, and the Great Mohican Indian Pow-Wow and Rendezvous in Loudonville in mid-July all honor the heritage of Native Americans. German culture is featured at Englewood's German-American Festival Days on the second weekend of July as well as at Oktoberfest celebrations in Painesville, Dayton, Bremen, Canton, Aurora, and Columbus in September, and in Lowell, Minster, and Galion in October. The Ohio Swiss Festival is held in early October in Sugarcreek. Celtic heritage is celebrated at the Celtic Festival in Rio Grande early in June, the Celtic Heritage Fair in Warren in mid-July, and the Celtic Feis in Geneva-on-the-Lake the third weekend of August. The Ohio Scottish Games Weekend takes place in Oberlin toward the end of June and the Scot's Settlement Festival in early September. Huron hosts the Irish Festival on the Green in mid-August and Berea the Irish Cultural Festival toward the end of July. Czech Days is celebrated in Dillonvale the second weekend of August and the Grecian Festival in Canton the next weekend. Italians celebrate their heritage during the Italian-American Heritage Festival in Warren in mid-August, the Italian-American Festival in Tallmadge early in July, and the Italian Festival in Columbus in mid-September. Celebrations of African-American heritage include the African-American Achievers Festival in Warren the first weekend of June and the African-American Festival in Lorain the second week of July.

Ohio festivals also celebrate state-designated symbols—the Tomato Festival in Reynoldburg early in September and the Buckeye Tree Festival in Utica in mid-September. And they celebrate famous native sons. Portsmouth, boyhood home of Roy Rogers, hosts the Roy Rogers Festival at the beginning of June, and New Rumley hosts Custer Day on June 5, celebrating the birth of General George Custer there in 1839. But Ohio festivals also celebrate the unusual. There is, for example, the Moonshine Festival in New Straitsville at the end of May. Adelphi has a Bologna Festival to get June under way. Ulrichsville celebrates National Clay Week in mid-June at "the Clay Center of the World." Radish bobbing contests are a feature of McClure's Radish Festival in June. Twinsburg appropriately hosts the Twin Days Festival in early August, during which pairs of twins flock into town and have everyone seeing double. The Zucchinifest in Obetz toward the end of August features zucchini fudge. The Ohio Tobacco Festival in Ripley, held at the end of August, includes a tobacco worm race among its festivities. The Mantua Potato Festival on the second weekend of September has food and games with a potato theme. And finally, Piqua's Great Outdoor Underwear Festival in early October features the running of the "Undy 500."[35]

OKLAHOMA

Oklahoma celebrates its history and Native American heritage with a variety of gatherings and competitions, from tribal pow-wows to international rodeos. The Fort Washita Fur Trade Rendezvous is held in Durant at the beginning of April, and the Eighty-Niner Celebration and Parade, recalling the 1889 Oklahoma Land Run, is held in Guthrie toward the end of April. Pioneer Days is held at the end of April in Guymon and the Gilcrease Rendezvous Fair at the beginning of May in Tulsa. The Cimarron Territory Celebration and Cow Chip Throw is held toward the end of April in Beaver, where "pasture patties" are flung for the championship title.

The International Finals Rodeo runs in Oklahoma City during the third week of January and offers over $225,000 in prize money. Other rodeos include the Longhorn World Championship Rodeo in Tulsa in early February, the Bullnanza for the PRCA's top bull riders held in Guthrie, also in early February, the Timed Event Championship in Guthrie in March, the Annual Rodeo and Old Cowhand Reunion in Freedom in mid-August, and the All-Indian Rodeo, golf tournament, parade and pow-wow held during the Cherokee National Holiday in Tahlequah in early September. For the truly devoted tamers of the wild, there are several rattlesnake roundups—the Rattlesnake Hunt held on the first weekend of April in Waurika draws over 20,000 visitors. Other Rattlesnake hunts are held in Apache, where awards are given for the longest, shortest, and heaviest rattlers captured, and in Waynoka on the next week of April.

There are many large and small celebrations of the Native American heritage, held primarily during the summer months. In June, the Annual Tulsa Powwow, held on the first of the month, is followed by the Iowa Tribal Powwow in Perkins and the Potawatomi Powwow in Shawnee. The Red Earth Festival, held on the second weekend of June in Oklahoma City, features the culture of over one hundred Native American tribes as represented in paintings, sculpture, jewelry, pottery, costume, and storytelling. July pow-wows include the Pawnee Indian Veterans Homecoming and Powwow, the Tonkawa Powwow, the Quapaw Tribal Powwow, the Sac and Fox Nation Annual Powwow and Parade in Stroud, and the Cheyenne Homecoming Powwow in Clinton. Mid-August brings the American Indian Exposition held in Anadarko. At the end of September, the Chickasaw Nation Annual Festival is held in Tishomingo, and in mid-October the Tahlequah Indian Territory Festival is celebrated in Tahlequah.

Food is the focal point of many Oklahoma festivals. The Whole Hawg Day Festival in Eufaula at the end of July, where entire hogs are roasted as prizes and there are free barbecue sandwiches and watermelon for all, takes place after the World Championship Hog Calling Contest in Weatherford late in February. There is also the Chocolate Festival in early February in Norman, the Strawberry Festival in early May in Stilwell, and the Pecan Festival in mid-June in Okmulgee. Guthrie hosts a Sand Plum Festival, Jay has a Huckleberry Festival, and Stratford a Peach Festival. The State Championship Chili Cookoff is in mid-July in Oklahoma City. The Lavitsef Festival is in Marlow in mid-September, where the peanut is celebrated with a Goober Gallop and peanut butter whistling contest. But the largest food and livestock show is the State Fair of Oklahoma in Oklahoma City, which occupies the second half of September.

The state rock of Oklahoma, the barite rose, is honored at the Rose Rock Festival in Noble in early May. Oklahoma oil field days are recalled at the Gusher Days Festival on the first weekend of June in Seminole. Will Rogers is remembered during the Will Rogers Days and Parade in Claremore on the first weekend of November. A variety of ethnic festivals include the Kolache Festival in Prague at the beginning of May, the Italian Festival in McAlester at the end of May, the early September Ethnic Festival in Krebs, the Czech Festival in Yukon in early October, and the Oktoberfest held in Tulsa toward the end of October.[36]

OREGON

In Oregon you can hear Shakespeare from February through October at the Oregon Shakespeare Festival in Ashland, or hear crowing at the National Rooster Crowing Contest on Rogue River toward the end of June. You can even hear square dances called at the Oregon State Summer Square and Round Dance Festival in Coos Bay toward the middle of June. There is something for the whimsical—the Annual Kite Festival at Rockaway Beach in mid-May, the Stunt Kite Festival in Lincoln City in July, and the Asian Kite Festival in Eugene in September—and there is a lot for those who love to eat and drink.

There are cherries at the Annual Northwest Cherry Festival in Dalles the third week of April, blueberries at the Oregon Blueberry Festival in Cornelius the third weekend of July, blackberries at the Wild Blackberry Festival in Cave Junction in mid-August and the Blackberry Festival in Nehalem a week later, melons at the Winston/Dillard Melon Festival the second weekend of September, nuts at the Springfield Filbert Festival the first weekend of September, and cranberries at Brandon's Annual Cranberry Festival at the end of September. But the main course in Oregon is seafood. North Bend holds the Annual Governor's Cook-Off Challenge–Oregon Seafood Festival the third weekend of March. Charleston is home to the World of Oysters Feast in mid-April, and Astoria hosts its Crab and Seafood Festival the next week. The Clam Chowder Cook-Off takes place at Gold Beach the beginning of May. Reedsport's Ocean Festival toward the end of July features a barbecued salmon feed, and Tualatin holds its Crawfish Festival in mid-August. Seafood and wine being naturally complementary, North Bend hosts its South Coast Shrimp and Wine Festival the third weekend of April, and in late August the Charleston Seafood and Wine Festival gets under way. Proud of its wine and brewing industry, Oregon also celebrates its Annual Southern Wine Festival at Cave Junction on the second weekend of June and the Oregon Annual Brewer's Festival in Portland at the end of July.

Oregon also celebrates its important timber industry, as well as its natural beauty, at the World Championship Timber Festival in Albany early in July and at the Timber Festival of Champions in Estacada in mid-July. Irises are on display at the Silverton Iris Jubilee and the Keiger Iris Festival in May. The year 1994 was the eighty-seventh year of the Rhododendron Festival in Florence, held in mid-May. Brookings-Harbor holds its Azalea Festival at the end of May. Against this background, ethnic diversity is also celebrated. There is Irish Day in Lakeview in mid-March. Cinco de Mayo celebrations take place early in May in Klamath Falls, Dayton, Hillsboro, Portland, and Eugene. Scandinavian festivals are held in Astoria the third weekend of June and Junction City in mid-August. German culture is celebrated at Oktoberfests in Mt. Angel and Portland in mid-September. Corvallis is the site of the Oregon Folklife Festival later in June. Native American celebrations include the Native American Salmon Bake and Pow Wow in Bandon toward the end of June, the Scappoose Pow Wow in mid-July, the Wallowa Band Nez Perce Descendants Pow Wow and Friendship

Feast in mid-July, and the Tribal Treaty Days Pow Wow and Rodeo in Chiloquin the third weekend of August.[37]

PENNSYLVANIA

On February 2, about two weeks after White Haven's Ice Carving Festival, Punxsutawney Phil, the Great Seer of Seers revered for his age and his ability to forecast the coming of spring, emerges from his official home on Gobbler's Knob. It's Groundhog Day. Phil can be seen also at the Punxsutawney Groundhog Festival during the last week in June, when he resides at the Groundhog Zoo. The legend of groundhog prognostication on Candlemas Day was brought to Pennsylvania by early German settlers.

Pennsylvania was a stopping point for many early settlers whose heritage and culture are still celebrated today. Ambridge has its Nationality Days in mid-May. The Pittsburgh Folk Festival and New Holland's Spring Gulch Folk Festival are both held the third weekend of May. The Monessen Cultural Heritage Festival is in mid-June. Philadelphia's Folk Festival takes place in late August. Festivals with a Pennsylvania Dutch flavor include the Kutztown Folk Festival from late June into early July, the Hanover Dutch Festival at the end of July, and the Goschenhoppen Folk Festival in East Greenville in mid-August. Pennsylvania's many ethnic celebrations also include the Mid-Winter Scottish and Irish Festival and Fair in Willow Grove in early February, the Pittsburgh Irish Festival the second weekend of September, and the Pocono's Greatest Irish Festival in Blakeslee at the end of May. Pittsburgh has its Greek Food Festival in early May, its Ukrainian Festival toward the end of September, and its Polishfest in mid-November. Mt. Jewett hosts the Swedish Festival in early August and Philadelphia holds its Puerto Rican Week Festival Parade toward the end of September. Philadelphia is also the site of the Africamericas Festival from the end of April into May and the Hispanic Fiesta at Penn's Landing at the end of August. Italian heritage is celebrated at Stroudsmoor's Italian Festival early in August, the San Rocco Festa in Aliquippa in mid-August, La Festa Italiana in Scranton early in September, and the Fayette Italina Heritage Festival in Uniontown in mid-August. Native American culture is highlighted at the Settlers Day American Indian Pow Wow in Bedford in July and at the American Indian Pow Wow in Kelletville in mid-August.

Pennsylvania's natural beauty and resources are celebrated throughout the year in many festivals. The Philadelphia Flower Show goes for a week in early April. It is the biggest indoor flower show in the world. Meyersdale hosts the Pennsylvania Maple Festival in late March and early April. Troy has its Maple Syrup Festival toward the end of April. The Western Pennsylvania Laurel Festival in Brookville, the Pennsylvania State Laurel Festival in Wellsboro, and the Laurel Blossom Festival in Jim Thorpe are held in mid-June. With its extensive forests, it is not surprising to find Pennsylvania the home of the Sawmill Woodcarving Show and All-Wood Festival in Cooksburg toward the middle of July and the Shawnee Mountain Lumberjack Festival in the second week of October. The importance of coal mining is celebrated at the Scottsdale Coke and Coal Heritage Festival in mid-September. The Oil Festival the second week of August celebrates 135 years since Edwin L. Drake drilled the first oil well in Titusville. Oil City also celebrates Oil Heritage Week in mid-June.

In Pennsylvania, American history comes to life. French Alliance Day is celebrated at Valley Forge Historical Park early in May. On Christmas Day at Washington Crossing, the Reenactment of Washington Crossing the Delaware takes place. Gettysburg Civil War Heritage Days run from the end of June to July 4, and then on November 19 the Anniversary Celebration of the Gettysburg Address honors Abraham Lincoln.[38]

RHODE ISLAND

Rhode Island has a long and rich history and heritage that is celebrated in its fairs and festivals. Gaspee Days in Cranston and Warwick remembers June 9, 1772, when Rhode Island patriots burned the HMS *Gaspee,* a British revenue ship. Rhode Island Navy Day in East Greenwich commemorates the founding of the Rhode Island Navy on June 12, 1775. Providence holds its Festival of Historic Houses early in June. And Elephant Day in Chepachet and Glocester on May 22 celebrates the first visit to Rhode Island in 1826 of Little Bett, an elephant.

Celebrations of heritage include the Woonsocket Heritage Festival in mid-May, the Annual East Providence Heritage Festival in mid-July, the Annual Narragansett Heritage Days at the end of July, and the Rhode Island Labor and Ethnic Heritage Festival in Pawtucket early in September. Native American culture is featured at the Pow Wow of the Pequot and Narragansett Indian Nations in Westerly in June, the American Indian Federation of Rhode Island Pow Wow in Richmond at the beginning of August, and the Annual Pow Wow held at Charleston in mid-August. The year 1994 marked the 318th year for this event. The Black Ships Festival in Newport toward the end of July is a Japanese celebration commemorating Rhode Island son Admiral Perry and the Treaty of Kanagawa. Cranston holds the Armenian Food Festival and Bazaar in mid-November.

Music, art, and crafts are featured in numerous fairs and festivals, such as the Annual Newport Outdoor Art Festival in mid-June, the Newport Music Festival during the middle two weeks of July, the Wickford Art Festival on the second weekend of July, and Newport's Folk Art Craft Festival late in August. The Annual Hopkinton Colonial Crafts Festival is in mid-September. But perhaps the most notable element of Rhode Island culture is the influence of the sea. Providence celebrates its Waterfront Festival after Labor Day. Narragansett holds its Blessing of the Fleet ceremonies toward the end of July and its annual Lobstermen's Festival toward the end of June. The Sail Newport Sailing Festival takes place toward the end of May. Seafood is on the plate or in the bowl at the Block Island Seafood Festival and the Great Chowder Cook-Off in Newport in mid-June. Narragansett's Annual Seafood Festival is held at the end of July and the Charleston Chamber Seafood Festival is held early in August. Foster's Annual Clambake is in early September, and in early October the Annual International Quahog Festival in Wickford gives tribute to the official Rhode Island shellfish.[39]

SOUTH CAROLINA

South Carolinians celebrate everything from grits and collard greens to the opera and chamber music. Indeed, perhaps the most well-known event is the annual Spoleto Festival USA held in Charleston from the end of May into June, where visitors can soak in the arts for two weeks. Over one hundred events are offered in opera, chamber music, symphonic concerts, theater, dance, and art. The arts are also focal points of the Southeastern Wildlife Exposition in Charleston in mid-February; the Carolina Craftsmen's Summer Classic, where over two hundred artists and craftsmen exhibit their creations in Myrtle Beach in early August; the Moja Arts Festival late in September, where the African-American and Caribbean cultures of the Low Country are highlighted through exhibits, performances, and historical tours in Charleston; and the Fall Fiesta of the Arts, an outdoor festival of the visual and performing arts, held in Sumter in mid-October.

South Carolina has much to offer food enthusiasts too. There is the mid-March Gizzard Festival in Columbia, the Possum Creep Festival in Barnwell toward the end of March, and the World Grits Festival in St. George in mid-April. Seafood lovers will enjoy the Lobster Race and Oyster Fest in Aiken and the Lowcountry Shrimp Festival in McClellanville in early May as well as the mid-May Blue Crab Festival in Little River. The South Carolina Peach Festival is in Gaffney beginning in mid-July, and Pageland's Watermelon Festival occurs toward the end of July. The South Carolina Peanut Party in Pelion in mid-August features tons of boiled peanuts. There is also the Okra Strut in Irmo the first weekend of October, the Collard Festival in Gaston the next weekend, and the Chitlin' Strut in Salley at the end of November. South Carolina industry is celebrated at the National Timber Festival in Saluda on the second weekend of April and the South Carolina Tobacco Festival in Lake City toward the end of July.

South Carolina's natural beauty is celebrated during Clemson's Daffodil Festival in mid-March and the Dogwood Festival in Denmark in early April. The Southern Plant and Flower Festival is held in Florence in mid-April. Orangeburg hosts the South Carolina Festival of Roses toward the end of April. The Iris Festival is in Sumter on the third weekend of May, and the South Carolina Festival of Flowers in Greenwood is in late June. Too numerous to mention are the many historical tours in Charleston, Beaufort, Georgetown, and Pendleton, where homes, gardens, and plantations are toured throughout the spring and fall.

Cultural and ethnic events celebrating African-American, Appalachian, and German heritage go on throughout the year. Marketplace, which celebrates African-American theater, dance, music, art, and food in Georgetown, is held in mid-February. The Africa Alive festival in Rock Hill, also in mid-February, features African art, dance, and drama. The Gullah Festival in Beaufort at the end of May and the Juneteenth Festival in Greenville from June 17–19 also celebrate African-American culture. Appalachian cultural heritage is celebrated at the Ildewilde at Clemson in mid-October.[40]

SOUTH DAKOTA

South Dakota celebrates its first residents at Mammoth Days in Hot Springs in mid-July. Buffalo still roam the plains and are rounded up each year at the Buffalo Roundup early in October at Custer State Park. Powwows are many in South Dakota, including the Annual Wacipi at Agency Village, in its 127th year in 1994, held early in July. Other July Powwows include the Iron Lightning Powwow, the Black Hills Powwow and Indian Art Market in Rapid City, and the Flandreau Santee Sioux Powwow. The Oglala Nation Powwow takes place in early August in Pine Ridge, and the Great Plains Powwow on the second weekend of October in Sioux Falls.

The discovery of gold in the Black Hills, remembered during Gold Discovery Days toward the end of July in Custer, hurried the settlement of the state. Early pioneers and settlers are celebrated at the West Whitlock Recreation Area late in July during Pioneer Days, the Sodbuster Fest in Webster on the second weekend of June, and Sodbusting Days at Lone Tree toward the end of June. The Black Hills Threshing Bee in Sturgis the third weekend of August and the Prairie Village Threshing Jamboree at Madison at the end of August also recall those early days. The Fort Sisseton Historical Festival in early June includes infantry drill reenactments, living history demonstrations, a medicine show, and Native American cultural demonstrations. One of South Dakota's best-known authors, Laura Ingalls Wilder, is remembered in the pageant bearing her name, which takes place in DeSmet in late June and early July.

The Germans who settled South Dakota celebrate their heritage at the Schmeckfest in Freeman in late March, the German Schmeckfest in Eureka in late September, and Oktoberfest in Yankton toward the end of October. Czech Days takes place in mid-June in Tabor. Canton holds its Scandinavian Folk Festival in August. But in South Dakota, one is never too far from a rodeo. Among the many are the Rough Riders Rodeo in St. Onge on the third weekend of June, the Crystal Springs Rodeo at Clear Lake on the fourth weekend of June, Wild West Days in Faulkton, the Sitting Bull Stampede in Mobridge, the Black Hills Roundup in Belle Fourche, the Ft. Pierre Rodeo, the Gary Championship Rodeo around July 4, the Burke Stampede Rodeo on the second weekend of July, the Corn Palace Stampede Rodeo in Mitchell and the Great Plains Indian Rodeo in Rapid City on the next July weekend, and the SDRA Championship Finals Rodeo in Sioux Falls at the beginning of October.[41]

TENNESSEE

From the beginning of December until mid-March visitors to Reelfoot Lake State Park can go on Reelfoot Eagle Watch tours. When things begin to thaw out in late March, Clarksville hosts the Tennessee Old-Time Fiddlers Championship. Mountain and country arts and crafts are shown early in April in Gatlinburg at the Great Smoky Arts and Crafts Community Spring Show. The Tennessee Crafts Fair takes place in Nashville in early May. The Gatlinburg Scottish Festival and Games are held in the middle of May.

Rhododendrons are in full bloom at the Annual Rhododendron Festival at Roan Mountain on the third weekend of June. A bit earlier Elizabethton holds its Annual Covered Bridge Celebration around the city's old covered bridge. Music is in full sway too. Nashville is the scene of the International Country Music Fan Fair the second week of June. The Tennessee River Bluegrass Festival in Savannah goes from mid-June to July 4, and Chattanooga's Riverbend Festival runs from mid-June to almost the end of the month.

Tennessee's oldest city celebrates its past in early July during Historic Jonesborough Days. Brownsville is the site of the Tennessee Peach Festival in the second week of July. Gatlinburg's Annual Summer Craftmen's Fair begins the last week of July and runs until August. Red Boiling Springs hosts the Folk Medicine Festival at the end of July. August is dominated by famous Tennessee products: walking horses and Elvis. Murfreesboro hosts the International Grand Championship Walking Horse Show the first week of August. Shelbyville hosts the Tennessee Walking Horse National Celebration from the end of August into early September. Elvis Week in Memphis, the second week of August, features an Elvis Tribute Concert, a "Rock-a-Hula" Party, a candlelight vigil, and an Elvis trivia contest, among other events, all sponsored by Graceland.

The Tennessee State Fair is in Nashville during the third week of September. In early October, Jonesborough hosts the National Storytelling Festival, and in Lebanon the Alliance for Native American Indian Rights Pow Wow takes place. After Oktoberfests in Clarksville and Memphis in the first part of October, Winterfest begins in mid-November in Gatlinburg, Pigeon Forge, and Sevierville and runs until the last day of February.[42]

TEXAS

It seems that Texans love to round 'em up year round beginning with the Southwestern Exposition Fat Stock Show in Fort Worth from late January through the first week of February and continuing throughout the year at numerous county and livestock shows. Some of these roundups and rodeos include the Southwestern Livestock Show and Rodeo, held the first week in February in El Paso; the San Antonio Livestock Show and Rodeo, held for the middle two weeks of February; the Livestock Show and Rodeo held from mid-February through the first week of March in Houston; the Livestock Show and Rodeo held in San Angelo in early March; the Rio Grande Valley Livestock Show and Rodeo, held in Mercedes in mid-March; the Chisholm Trail Roundup, celebrated in Fort Worth on the second weekend in June; the West of the Pecos Rodeo, held in Pecos in early July; and the mid-September Four-States Fair and Rodeo, held in Texarkana. Though individual events vary, common activities include country-western entertainment, chili and barbecue cook-offs, parades, trail rides, and, of course, roping competitions and bronc riding. Texans don't stop with cattle, however, rounding up over 12,000 pounds of live western diamondback rattlesnakes annually at the World's Largest Rattlesnake Roundup, held in Sweetwater during the second weekend in March. Festivities at this event include snake handling, snake milking, a rattlesnake-meat eating contest, performance of the Rattlesnake Dance, and the Miss Snake Charmer Queen contest.

The sea bordering the abundant Texas coastline offers many opportunities for celebration. Fulton hosts the annual Oysterfest, which includes oyster-shucking and eating contests. Crabs are celebrated during Mother's Day weekend, Friday through Sunday, in Crystal Beach at the Texas Crab Festival, where Miss Crab Legs and her subjects enjoy fresh gulf seafood and crab. For two days in mid-October, seafood is served continually at the Seafair, held in Rockport. But Austin claims that it hosts the "largest beach party in the state" over three weekends in August at the Aqua Festival, where wild water and land events are joined by over sixty musical groups in providing entertainment to the 300,000 people who attend.

Texas offers a broad range of rich culinary experiences celebrated throughout the year at fiestas, festivals, and cook-offs. The Texas Citrus Fiesta held the last week of January in Mission features the ruby red grapefruit along with other citrus fruits. Strawberries are celebrated at the early April Strawberry Festival held in Poteet and at the San Jacinto Strawberry Festival held in Pasadena later in April. Peaches and melons are celebrated at the Peach and Melon Festival, held usually during the first full week in August in De Leon. In fact, a number of festivals feature watermelons as part of larger events and as the focus of events. Two such events are the Watermelon Thump in Luling, usually held during the last weekend in

June, and the late July Watermelon Festival and Rodeo in Naples. The East Texas rice harvest is celebrated at the Texas Rice Festival at Winnie from Wednesday through Saturday, including the first Saturday in October. As the weather turns cool, the theme warms up as Texas celebrates chili: the CASI (Chili Appreciation Society, International) sanctions the Republic of Texas Chilympiad, held in San Marcos in mid-September. This event is followed by the CASI International Chili Championship on the first Saturday in November, when the state chili champ is selected, and also in Terlingua by the Tolbert International Championship Chili Cookoff held on the first Friday and Saturday in November. New Braunfels hosts the Wurstfest (Sausage Festival) at the end of October through the first week of November, where revelers celebrate sausage making and enjoy German dancing, food, and music.

History and heroes are honored in several events. Texas' independence from Mexico is celebrated February 27–28 in Washington at the Texas Independence Day Celebration. Huntsville hosts the General Sam Houston Folk Festival in mid-April, and the Battle of San Jacinto is commemorated at the Fiesta San Antonio in that city the second week of April. Early history is re-created at the Buccaneer Days in Corpus Christi at the end of April, and Cinco de Mayo celebrations are held in San Marcos, Goliad, and San Antonio in early May. Texas Panhandle history is told at the "Texas" Historical Musical Drama in Canyon from early June through the third week of August, where 100,000 people enjoy the outdoor drama written by Pulitzer Prize winner Paul Green. Ethnic diversity and pioneer heritage are themes at the Texas Folklife Festival held at the fifteen-acre HemisFair Plaza in San Antonio early in August. Dozens of tribes attend the National Championship Powwow in Grand Prairie, generally held the first weekend after Labor Day, when Texas salutes its Native American heritage. Caldwell invites visitors to "Czech it out" at the Kolache Festival, usually held on the second Saturday in September. Polka, the official dance of ancient Czechoslovakia, is the theme of the National Polka Festival, held in Ennis on the first Saturday and Sunday in May. On the fourth weekend of September, Fort Worth hosts one of the largest historical events in the state: the Pioneer Days Celebration and Rodeo. Gunfights and rodeos join activities centering around the music, dance, and the local cuisine.

A miscellany of other festivals round out the big way Texans celebrate their history, cuisine, music, sports, flora, and leisure activities. The state flower of Texas is celebrated in Austin at the Highland Lakes Bluebonnet Trail, usually held during the first two weekends in April. The Scarborough Faire in Waxahachie on weekends from late April to mid-June is one of two large Renaissance festivals, the other being the Texas Renaissance Festival, held on weekends from early October through mid-November. The Sweet Onion Festival held in Noonday on the second Saturday in June includes a tearjerker contest. The Great Texas Mosquito Festival features a mosquito legs look-alike contest, a mosquito calling contest, and a mosquito chase. It is held in Clute, usually on the last Thursday, Friday, and Saturday in July. The State Fair of Texas in Dallas, attended by over three million people, runs the first three weeks of October. And, finally, there is the East Texas Fire Ant Festival in Marshall on the second weekend in October, where a chili cook-off includes at least one fire ant as an ingredient in each chili pot.[43]

UTAH

Utah begins the year with the perfect remedy for cabin fever: the Sundance Film Festival, held annually in Park City at the end of January. Sponsored by the Sundance Institute, the festival offers an opportunity for independent filmmakers to develop and showcase their work and at the same time provides rich entertainment to thousands of filmgoers. Winter sporting events and celebrations dominate the winter months, from snowmobiling and skiing to the January Hof Winter Carnival in Ogden and the Snow-Shine Festival in Park City from mid-March into early April, which features spring skiing events.

Celebrations of the arts and western and international cultures begin with the Annual Music in the Mountains in March festival in Park City the third week of March, followed by the Art Festival in St. George the second weekend of April and Art City Days in Springville the second week of June. The Westfest International Celebration takes place in West Valley City toward the end of June, the World Folkfest in Springville for a week in mid-July, and the Western Heritage Art Show in Salt Lake City the next week. Pioneer Days are celebrated in Ogden, Enterprise, and Washington toward the end of July. The Festival of the American West is held in Logan from the end of July into August. There are Greek Festival Days at Price in July, Swiss Days at Midway in early September, and the Folklife Festival at Springdale a week later. In addition to festivals, the wild West is celebrated at rodeos held in June in Price (Black Diamond Stampede PRCA Rodeo), toward the end of July in Enterprise (American Legion Rodeo), and on the second weekend of September at St. George (Dixie Round-Up PRCA Rodeo). Perhaps the most famous artistic celebration is the summer-long Utah Shakespearean Festival, held from the end of June through early September in Cedar City. Here, six Shakespearean dramas are performed in rotation to over 100,000 visitors annually.

Harvest festivals begin with the Corn Festival at the end of August in Enterprise, followed by the state's celebration at the mid-September Utah State Fair in Salt Lake City. The Peach Days Celebration is held in Ferron the second weekend of September and the Melon Days Celebration in Green River a little later in the month. Orangeville hosts the Castle Valley Pageant in early August as it celebrates the settling of the valley with a pageant and nightly lamb fry. And finally, chili is the featured cuisine at the Utah State Chili Competition held in St. George in early October.[44]

VERMONT

Vermont celebrates and luxuriates in its great natural beauty year round. Winter festivals and carnivals, dog sled races, skiing events, "sugar on snow" celebrations in the spring, summer festivals, and fall foliage pilgrimages provide ample opportunities to enjoy Vermont's natural heritage. Stowe hosts the Winter Carnival beginning in mid-January, followed by the early February Winter Carnival in Killington, the mid-February Annual Snowflake Festival in East Burke, and the Winter Carnival in Brattleboro. One is likely to find snow sculptures, sleigh rallies, skating, crafts, torchlight parades, and samples of Vermont foods at one or more of these celebrations. Lake Elmore, Norwich, and East Burke all host dogsled races in January and March, and skiing events are continuous.

Arts and crafts events are numerous throughout the year. The Annual Snowflake Festival Art Show is in East Burke for the whole month of February and the first week of March, and the Essex Junction Annual Vermont Festival of Ceramics and Crafts begins the month of May. There are the Annual Champlain Valley Quilt Contest held in Shelburne at the end of May, the Annual Summer Festival and Craft Fair in Woodstock in early July, the Annual Vermont Quilt Festival in Northfield and the Annual Summer Festival on the Green in Middlebury in mid-July, the Village Days Festival in Brattleboro toward the end of July, the Annual Art in the Round Barn in Waitsfield from the end of September into October, and the Annual Wildlife Art Show in Woodstock from the end of September until mid-October. These are just a few of the many events held annually throughout the state to further the appreciation of a variety of art and craft forms practiced in Vermont.

Trees provide much beauty and enjoyment to Vermont visitors and residents alike. From maple sugar festivals in the spring to tours and events in appreciation of the fall foliage, nature has provided many reasons to celebrate. In mid-March, Woodstock hosts the Annual Maple Festival, followed by the Annual Vermont Maple Festival, held in St. Albans in mid-April. In addition, there are local Sugar-on-Snow Suppers in Cavendish and Waterbury Center in late March. Fall foliage fairs and festivals are held throughout the fall. The Northeast Kingdom–Fall Foliage Festival beginning at the end of September is celebrated in a variety of ways by each of the participating towns: Walden, Cabot, Plainfield, Peacham, Barnet, Groton, and Marshfield. Apples are celebrated at several festivals from the Apple Days Festival, held in late September in Brattleboro, to the mid-October Annual Vermont Apple Festival and Craft Show in Springfield and the Annual Apples and Crafts Fair, held in Woodstock.

The Bennington Battle Day Celebration commemorates Vermont's participation in key Revolutionary War events. Held in mid-August, festivities include a drum and bugle competition. June finds two events highlighting the state's strong participation in the dairy industry: the Annual Vermont Dairy Festival in early June in Enosburg Falls and the Annual Cow Appreciation Day and Hand Milking Contest in Woodstock later in the month. Jazz is rediscovered and enjoyed annually at the Discover Jazz Festival, held in Burlington in early June, and the Pico Mountain Jazz Festival in Killington at the end of July.[45]

VIRGINIA

Virginia's history comes alive at the Jamestown Weekend during the second weekend in May. Landing Day reenacts the landing of the first colonists. Civil War Life at Chantilly is in early April, and the Civil War Reenactment and Living History Encampment at Haymarket is at the end of August. Virginia is also, of course, the birthplace of presidents. George Washington's birthday is celebrated at Mount Vernon on February 17. The day before, in Montpelier, James Madison's is celebrated. April 13 is Thomas Jefferson's birthday, commemorated at Monticello. James Monroe's birthday is celebrated on April 26 at the James Monroe Museum in Fredericksburg. On June 30 at Arlington National Cemetery, the wedding anniversary of General and Mrs. Robert E. Lee is commemorated. And even though Theodore Roosevelt was not a Virginian, his birthday is celebrated at the end of October at the Theodore Roosevelt Island and Reserve in Arlington.

The natural beauty of Virginia is celebrated as spring arrives at the Honacker Redbud Festival during the month of April, the Pear Blossom Festival in Fredericksburg on the second weekend of April, and the International Azalea Festival in Norfolk on the third weekend in April. Winchester's Shenandoah Apple Blossom Festival is at the end of April. The famous Chincoteague ponies swim the channel between Assateague and Chincoteague on the Wednesday of the last week of July. The Virginia Horse Center in Lexington hosts the Annual Virginia Horse Festival in mid-April.

Virginia's mountain heritage is featured during the first two weeks of August at the Virginia Highlands Festival in Arlington. Native American culture is celebrated at the Virginia Indian Heritage Festival in Williamsburg in mid-June and at the Virginia Indian Heritage Festival and Pow-Wow in Martinsville on the second weekend in September. At the end of April, Norfolk is the site of the Annual Guinness Import Company British and Irish Festival. Germans celebrate at Mayfest in Strasburg in mid-May and at Norfolk's annual Oktoberfest in mid-October. Richmond holds its Greek Festival at the very end of May.

The riches of the sea are enjoyed at Chincoteague's Seafood Festival in early May and its Annual Oyster Festival in October. Urbanna also has its own Annual Oyster Festival in early November. The riches of the land are enjoyed at Chilhowie's Apple Festival at the end of September and Syria's Apple Harvest Festival on the middle two weekends of October. Clifford hosts the Sorghum Molasses Festival in early October and Lynchburg the Virginia Garlic Festival a bit later in the month. The Suffolk Peanut Fest runs during the second weekend in October. The Virginia Poultry Festival is held in mid-May in Harrisonburg and the Annual Virginia Chicken Festival in Crewe in mid-June. Montpelier celebrates its Wine Festival in mid-May and The Plains celebrates its Virginia Wine Festival the last week in August.[46]

WASHINGTON

Washington fairs and festivals get under way with the Columbia River Circuit Rodeo in Yakima on the second week of January. The Ellensburg Rodeo at the Kittitas County Fair over Labor Day is Washington's largest rodeo. In mid-January, the Great Bavarian Ice Fest goes on in Leavenworth. On the last two weekends of January, the Upper Skagit Bald Eagle Festival features guided eagle watching float trips. Late in April, the Washington State Apple Blossom Festival commences in Wenatchee and goes on for eleven days. Meanwhile, Spring Barrel Tasting goes on in Yakima Valley. In early May, Spokane celebrates its Lilac Festival and Walla Walla has its Hot-Air Balloon Stampede. Paulsbo celebrates Scandinavian culture during its Viking Fest later in May and Seattle holds the Northwest Folklife Festival, also in May. From mid-July to the beginning of August, Seattle is also the site of the Seafair, which includes ethnic events and an air show. In July, exotic food lovers can sample bear meat and bear stew at the McCleary Bear Festival and buffalo at the Kalispel Salish Fair and Buffalo Barbecue in Usk. Other July events include the Pacific Northwest Arts and Crafts Fair in Bellevue and the Pacific Northwest Scottish Highland Games in Enumclaw.

Lumberjack contests are part of the Logger's Jubilee in Morton early in August. Then in mid-August, the Washington State International Kite Festival at Long Beach features kite flying competitions. September is a busy month with the Spokane Interstate Fair and the Western Washington Fair in Puyallup, as well as the World Boat Festival in Townsend and the Odessa Deutschesfest. The Annual Indian Days Celebration and Pow Wow at White Swan and the National Lentil Festival are also in September. Early in October, spawning salmon return during Issaquah Salmon Days. In mid-October, the cranberry bogs may be toured in Long Beach and Ilwaco. It's harvest time in early November in Pasco, where the Northwest Wine Festival is celebrated. December brings St. Nicholas to Anacortes and Sinterklaas to Lynden.[47]

WEST VIRGINIA

On the third weekend in March, Pickens is the site of the West Virginia Maple Festival, which celebrates the state's long history of sugar making, learned by settlers from Native Americans. In late April, the West Virginia Dance Festival in Charleston includes jazz, ballet, and modern dance. The strawberry harvest is celebrated in Buckhannon around the third week of May at the West Virginia Strawberry Festival, marking its fifty-third year in 1994. On Memorial Day weekend, the West Virginia Dandelion Festival in White Sulphur Springs features arts and crafts and the greens and wine of dandelions. The West Virginia Bass Festival at St. Mary's on the second full weekend in June includes an Ohio River bass catching tournament, crafts, and nightly musical entertainment. The Pearl S. Buck Birthday Celebration in mid to late June honors the state's best-known author.

Glenville is filled with old-time music on the third weekend of June during the West Virginia State Folk Festival. In late July, Hinton hosts the West Virginia State Water Festival. In mid-August, the State Fair of West Virginia is under way in Lewisburg. This fair's origin dates back to 1858, when General Robert E. Lee's warhorse, Traveller, was exhibited as a yearling. The West Virginia Honey Festival takes place on the second weekend in September in Parkersburg. The West Virginia Oil and Gas Festival in Sistersville in early to mid-September celebrates antique engines of the 1890s as well as rides on the Ohio River's last ferry.

With the approach of fall, the sorghum cane, pumpkins, walnuts, and apples are ready for harvest. With a harvest comes celebration. Arnoldsburg hosts the West Virginia Molasses Festival on the third weekend in September. The West Virginia Pumpkin Festival is held at Milton on the first full weekend in October. Spencer is the site of the West Virginia Black Walnut Festival on the second full weekend in October, and the Mountain State Apple Harvest Festival takes place in Martinsburg on the third full weekend in October.[48]

WISCONSIN

It gets cold in Wisconsin and that is reason enough for celebration. Winterfests are held in Greendale, Eau Claire, Beloit, and Sister Bay in mid-January and continue in February in Cedarburg. There's the North Woods Ice Festival in Phillips the second week in January, Golf on Ice at Iron River in the first week in February, and Sheboygan's Annual Indoor Ice Bowling Classic later in March. Ice does not inhibit what might be called Wisconsin's favorite pastime, fishing. Right after New Year's Day, Friendship holds its Annual Ice Fisheree. Burlingame Lake and Medford have ice fishing contests at the end of January. "Fisherees" go on all year, with or without ice.

Port Washington celebrates the smelt run in late April at its Smelt Fry and Festival. There's a Walleye Challenge in Hayward in early May, the High Falls Walleye Tournament in Crivitz in mid-May, and the Walleye Fishing Tournament in Land O'Lakes in October. Sunfish Days takes place at the end of May in Onalaska, and the Annual Bluegill Festival is in Birchwood in mid-July. Eagle River hosts the National Championship Musky Open in mid-August. The world's largest one-day outdoor fish fry is in mid-July in Port Washington on Fish Day.

Wisconsin has a rich ethnic heritage. The Northland Folk Festival is held early in May in Ashland. Germans celebrate Maifest at Germantown in mid-May. Milwaukee holds its Bavarian Volksfest at the end of June and its German Fest toward the end of July. The Sausage Festival in Johnsonville and Bratwurst Days in Sheboygan are July celebrations. In August, West Bend and Manitowoc hold German fests. Oktoberfests are too numerous to mention. Scandinavians celebrate their heritage at Fyr Bal in Ephraim in mid-June. There is a Danish Breakfast in Kenosha in mid-January, a Syttende Mai celebration in Woodville, and the Syttende Mai Folk Festival in Stoughton, which is the biggest Norwegian celebration of this mid-May event outside of Norway. Czech culture is celebrated at Cesky Den in Hillsboro in the second week of June and at the Czechoslovakian Community in Phillips a week later. Waupin's Klompenfest in June and Cedar Grove's Holland Fest at the end of July feature Dutch heritage. Belgian Days in Brussels in mid-July and Green Bay's Belgian Farm Days at the end of August feature Belgian culture. Poles celebrate their culture at the Otto Grunski Polski Festyn in Menasha the second weekend in May and at the Polish Fest in Wisconsin Dells in September. Serbian Days are held in the third week of August in Milwaukee and Croatian Days in Ashland in early September. The polka is a favored dance of these ethnic groups. Wisconsin Dells hosts the Spring Polka Fest in early April. In mid-May, Concord holds the Wisconsin Polkafest and Boulder Junction the Swiss Polkafest. Merrill's Central Wisconsin Polka Festival and Birchwood's Polka Celebration Festival occur in June. Pulaski's Polka Days are at the end of July and Hartford's Polkafest is in early August.

Native American culture is featured at the Ojibway School Contest Pow-Wow in Hayward early in June and at Ojibway Craft Days in La Pointe later in the month. The Fourth of July holiday brings the Annual Red Cliff Traditional Pow-Wow and the Oneida Pow-Wow and Festival of Performing Arts. A bit later in July, there is the Annual Bear River Pow-Wow in Lac du Flambeau and the Honor the Earth Pow-Wow in Hayward. Milwaukee hosts its Fiesta de la Comunidad in June, the Puerto Rican Parade and Festival at the beginning of August, and its Mexican Fiesta in the third week of August. Milwaukee's Festa Italiana and Bastille Days Festival are in mid-July. Its African World Festival is in the first part of August and its Irish Fest in mid-August. Racine holds its Greek Festival at the end of June.

Timber, an important industry in Wisconsin, is celebrated at Woodruff's Timberfest and Lumberjack Tournament of Champions and Catawba's Annual Lumberman's Day in mid-June. Wausau holds its Log Jam and Butternut its Lumberjack Day at the end of June. But Wisconsin farmers have made Wisconsin cheese famous. June dairy fests are held in Marshfield, West Salem, Elroy, Cadott, Spring Valley, West Bend, and Wauzeka. The Annual Great Wisconsin Cheese Festival, which features cheese carving among other activities, is held at Little Chute in early June. In mid-June, the Cheese Derby is held in Hilbert. In mid-September, Blair holds its Cheese Festival and Cheese Days get under way in Monroe. Reedsburg is the site of the Butter Festival in the third week in June.[49]

WYOMING

Wyoming's top events kick off with the Wyoming State Winter Fair late in January. In mid-February, Riverton holds its Wild West Winter Carnival and Encampment and its Winter Carnival and Dog Sled Races. The Championship Snowmobile Hill Climb is in early April and Old West Days in late May in Jackson. The rodeo season gets under way in early June with the Hulett Rodeo. July rodeos include the Cody Stampede Rodeo, the Sheridan WYO Rodeo, the Old Timers Rodeo in Gillette, and the Red Desert Rodeo. The Fair and Rodeo Klondike Rush in Buffalo is in August, and rodeos of early September include Evanston's Cowboy Days Rodeo, Meeteetse's Labor Day Rodeo, and the Wright Roundup and Rodeo.

The old days of the West come to life during Cody's Frontier Festival and Greybull's Days of '49 in early June. Later in June, there is Ft. Washakie's Indian Days, Lovell's Mustang Days Celebration, and Ft. Fetterman Days in Douglas. Lander celebrates Pioneer Days in early July. In late July, Powell holds its Homesteader Days, Cheyenne holds its Frontier Days, and Kemmerer its Turn of the Century Days. Fossil discovery day is also held in Kemmerer late in July.[50]

DISTRICT OF COLUMBIA

Many visitors to the District of Columbia will visit the museums and national landmarks, but the District is much more than famous institutions. It is also home to a diverse population of people who celebrate their diversity in fairs and festivals throughout the year. The Chinese Lunar New Year Celebration gets under way on the third weekend of January. Two weeks after the St. Patrick's Day Parade on March 17, the Cherry Blossom Festival begins and runs into April.

May 1 marks the Asian Pacific American Heritage Festival. Malcolm X Day is celebrated on May 16. June 5 is the Philippine Independence Day Parade. The annual Festival of American Folklife runs from late June to early July. The Latin-American Festival takes place on the Washington Monument grounds in late July. The African-American Family Day Summerfest is in early August, the Thai Heritage Festival is in mid-August, and the African Cultural Festival and Black Family Reunion are in September after Labor Day. October 2 is the United Nations Celebration.

The District swings when Duke Ellington's Birthday is celebrated on April 24. Dance Africa, D.C., is in mid-June, and the D.C. Free Jazz Festival is held around July 4. The Mambo USA Festival takes place in early August and the D.C. Blues Festival in early September.[51]

AMERICAN SAMOA

April 17 is Flag Day in American Samoa, celebrating the first day that the flag of the United States was raised over the Samoan Islands in 1900. The celebration features singing, dancing, and longboat races as well as basket weaving, coconut husking, spear throwing, and fire making contests. The Annual Arts Festival is also part of the celebration. Tourism Week is in May and features cultural awareness programs along with various other activities. White Sunday occurs on the second Sunday in October. A children's celebration introduced by English missionaries, White Sunday is quite a special day for the children of American Samoa. They lead church services and receive special foods and clothing. The Swarm of the Palolo takes place in October and November, when the tides and lunar conditions are just right. Sometimes called the Caviar of the Pacific, palolo are marine worms that emerge from the reefs annually to reproduce. Thousands of people wade out to the reef to scoop them up and often eat them raw. Christmas Week is a special time in American Samoa, with festivities that go on the full week before Christmas.[52]

COMMONWEALTH OF THE NORTHERN MARIANA ISLANDS

Free Chamorro food—coconut crab, lobster, fish, taro and sweet potatoes, fruit bat, roast pig, deer kelaquin, breadfruit—is a main attraction at Commonwealth fiestas. The fiestas are held around feast days of the saints and the church calendar. On the island of Rota, San Francisco De Borja is honored on October 11. On the island of Tinian, St. Joseph is honored on May 1. Saipan, the largest of the islands, honors St. Joseph the Worker on May 1, St. Anthony of Padua on June 13, San Roque on August 18, Santos Remedios on October 11, Christ the King on November 25, and the Immaculada Concepcion on December 8.[53]

GUAM

Festivals are a way of life on Guam. Many of them are centered around the church calendar and village celebrations of patron saints. In January, there is a nationwide novena for the Celebration of the Holy Family. Village fiestas for patron saints are held in Asan, Chalon Pago, Yigo, Agat, Barrigada, Agana, Talafofo, Yona, Mangilao, Sinajana, Agana Heights, and Dededo.

Cultural festivals include Chamorro Week and the Guam Visual Arts "Kaleidoscope" in February and the Chamorro Arts Festival in March. The Guam Micronesia Island Fair takes place in April. Three weeks of carnival celebrating liberation from the Japanese culminate in July with the Independence Day Parade in Agana. The Merizo Water Festival, usually held in August, features various water sport competitions and carnival activities.[54]

PUERTO RICO

Fiestas seem to occur daily somewhere in Puerto Rico. Each town celebrates the *fiestas patronales* in honor of its patron saint in a ten-day festival that often mixes local and African elements in a series of processions, games, dances, and music around the town plaza. These festivals are held in the evening during the week and all day on weekends. In the month of June alone, for example, there are nine such festivals, including three festivals on June 18–27 honoring St. John the Baptist in Maricao, Orocovis, and San Juan. Carnival festivities, which include the traditional coastal burial of the sardine, are also celebrated in many towns.

The Casals Festival, founded by cellist Pablo Casals in 1957, is a highly respected international music festival. It is held from early to mid-June. Other festivals of interest include the Festival of Land Crabs in Guanica during the second week of June and the Aibonito Flower Festival, held from late June into July. One of Puerto Rico's most colorful traditions, however, is the July Saint James Festival in Loiza. The "Vejigante," the popular character of this festival, wears a mask carved from dried coconuts resembling bats in a devil-shaped human form. The dance and music of this festival are very much influenced by African tradition.[55]

U.S. VIRGIN ISLANDS

Regattas feature prominently on the calendar of events for the Virgin Islands, from the Rolex Cup Regatta in early April to the Mumm's Cup Regatta in October, to the Boxing Day Race on December 26 at the St. Croix Yacht Club. But the Islands also celebrate their heritage in such events as French Heritage Week in Frenchtown on St. Thomas, held the third week of June. The St. John Festival and Cultural Celebration goes from mid-June into early July. Puerto Rico Friendship Celebration Activities on St. Croix occur early in October. Then during the middle of October, the St. Croix Jazz and Caribbean Music and Arts Festival features an ongoing arts and cultural exhibition.

The celebrations of special historical events are recurring reminders of the past. Organic Act Day on June 21 commemorates the Organic Act of 1936 that granted local government to the Islands. The Slaves Rebellion of 1733 is remembered on St. John at the end of June. In the first mass resistance ever displayed in the Islands' history, slaves took control of St. John for six months before the revolt was crushed. July 3 is Virgin Islands Emancipation Day, marking the end of slavery in the former Dutch West Indies in 1848. Fireburn recalls an 1878 revolt in Frederiksted led by a slave named Queen Mary of St. Croix, who led women and children in the razing of homes and stores in a protest against slavery. D. Hamilton Jackson Day on November 1 commemorates the man who won the right to a free press and other reforms from Denmark on a 1915 mission there.[56]

NOTES

1. *Alabama: The State of Surprises, 1992–93* (Montgomery: Alabama Bureau of Tourism and Travel, 1992).
2. *Alaska 1993 Calendar of Events* (n.p., n.d.); information provided by the Alaska Division of Tourism.
3. *Arizona Calendar of Events and Activities, October–November–December 1992* (Phoenix: Arizona Office of Tourism, 1992); *Arizona Summer Scene 93: 1993 Calendar of Events* (Phoenix: Arizona Office of Tourism, 1993).
4. *Arkansas Calendar of Events* (Little Rock: Arkansas Department of Parks and Tourism, 1992, 1993).
5. *California Special Events 1993* (Sacramento: State of California Trade and Commerce Agency, Office of Tourism, 1993).
6. *Colorado Official State Vacation Guide* (Denver: Colorado Tourism Board, 1993).
7. *Connecticut Vacation guide, 1993–1994* (Rocky Hill: Connecticut Department of Economic Development, Tourism Division, 1993).
8. *1993 Delaware Calendar of Events* (Dover: Delaware Tourism Office, Delaware Development Office, 1993).
9. *Florida's Space Coast Vacation Planner* (Cocoa, Florida: Florida's Space Coast Office of Tourism, n.d.); *Florida Vacation Guide 1992–93* (Tallahassee: Florida Department of Commerce, Division of Tourism, 1992).
10. *Georgia Days, January–June 1993, July–December 1992* (Atlanta: Georgia Department of Industry, Trade, and Tourism, 1992, 1993).
11. *The Islands of Aloha: The Official Travel Guide of the Hawaiian Visitors Bureau* (Honolulu: Davick Publications, Inc., 1992), p. 140.
12. *Idaho: Official Idaho State Travel Guide* (Boise: Idaho Department of Commerce/Idaho Division of Tourism Development, 1992).
13. *Western Illinois 1993 Official Visitors Guide* (Macomb: Western Illinois Tourism Council, n.d.); *Northern Illinois 1993 Official Visitors Guide* (Rockford: Northern Illinois Tourism Council, n.d.); *Southern Illinois 1993 Official Visitors*

Guide (Whittington: Southern Illinois Tourism Council, n.d.); *Central Illinois 1992 Fairs and Festivals and Special Events* (Springfield: Central Illinois Tourism Council, n.d.).

14. *Indiana Festivals 1993* (Indianapolis: Indiana Department of Commerce, Tourism Development Division, 1993).

15. *Passport to Iowa: 1993 Visitors Guide* (Des Moines: Division of Tourism, Department of Economic Development, 1993), pp. 106–9.

16. *Kansas 1993 Calendar of Events* (Topeka: Kansas Department of Commerce and Housing, Travel and Tourism Division, 1993).

17. *Kentucky Calendar of Events* (Frankfort: Kentucky Department of Travel Development, 1993).

18. *Louisiana Fairs and Festivals 1992* (Baton Rouge: Louisiana Office of Tourism, 1992).

19. *Exploring Mid-Coast Maine* (Rockland: Rockland-Thomaston Area Chamber of Commerce, 1992); *Maine Invites You* (Hallowell: Maine Publicity Bureau, Inc., 1992).

20. *Maryland 1992 Calendar of Events* (Baltimore: Maryland Office of Tourism Development, 1992); information provided by the Waterfowl Festival and the National Hard Crab Derby.

21. *Massachusetts Winter Events and Ski Guide* (Boston: Massachusetts Office of Travel and Tourism, 1992); *Massachusetts Summer Getaway Guide* (Boston: Massachusetts Office of Travel and Tourism, 1993).

22. *Michigan Winter Travel Guide and Calendar of Events* (Lansing: Michigan Travel Bureau, 1992); *Michigan Summer Travel, 1993 Calendar of Events* (Lansing: Michigan Travel Bureau, n.d.).

23. *Minnesota Explorer* (St. Paul: Minnesota Office of Tourism, Winter 1992–1993, Spring/Summer 1993).

24. *1992 Mississippi Calendar of Annual Events* (Jackson: Mississippi Division of Tourism Services, 1992).

25. *Missouri Calendar of Events, November 1992–April 1993* (Jefferson City: Missouri Division of Tourism, 1992); *The Missouri Calendar of Fairs, Festivals and Fun Things to Do, May–October 1993* (Jefferson City: Missouri Division of Tourism, 1993).

26. *Montana Calendar of Events* (Helena: Travel Montana, Department of Commerce, 1992, 1993).

27. *1993 Nebraska Catalog of Events* (Lincoln: Nebraska Department of Economic Development, Travel and Tourism Division, 1993); *Nebraska Visitor Guide* (Lincoln: Nebraska Department of Economic Development, Travel and Tourism Division, n.d.); *Annual Nebraska Festivals* (n.p, n.d); information provided by the Nebraska Department of Economic Development, Travel and Tourism Division.

28. *1993 Nevada Events* (n.p., n.d.); information provided by the Nevada Commission on Tourism.

29. *The Official New Hampshire Guidebook* (Concord: State of New Hampshire, Office of Travel and Tourism Development; Glen Graphics of Jackson, N.H.; and Hospitality Promotions, Inc., of Concord, N.H., 1992).

30. *New Jersey: Garden State Facts and Fun* (Trenton: Department of Commerce and Economic Development, Division of Travel and Tourism, 1992); *New Jersey Travel Guide* (Pleasantville: South Jersey Publishing Company for New Jersey Di-

vision of Travel and Tourism, 1993); *New Jersey Calendar of Events: October '92–March '93* (Trenton: Department of Commerce and Economic Development, Division of Travel and Tourism, 1992); *New Jersey Calendar of Events: April '93–September '93* (Trenton: Department of Commerce and Economic Development, Division of Travel and Tourism, 1993); *New Jersey Fall and Winter Guide* (Trenton: Department of Commerce and Economic Development, Division of Travel and Tourism, 1992).

31. *New Mexico 1993 Vacation Guide* (Santa Fe: New Mexico Department of Tourism, 1993).

32. *I Love New York 1993 Events* (Albany: New York State Department of Economic Development, Bureau of Media Services, October 1992).

33. *North Carolina Traveler's Almanac* (Raleigh: North Carolina Travel and Tourism Division, Department of Economic and Community Development, 1992).

34. *North Dakota Calendar of Events, April 1992–March 1993* (Bismarck: North Dakota Tourism Promotion, 1992).

35. *Ohio, the Heart of It All! Calendar of Events* (Columbus: Division of Travel and Tourism, 1992, 1993).

36. *1993 Oklahoma Calendar of Major Events* (Oklahoma City: Oklahoma Tourism and Recreation Department, Travel and Tourism Division, n.d.).

37. *Oregon Events Calendar* (Salem: Oregon Tourism Division, 1993).

38. *1993 Pennsylvania Calendar of Events: Advance Copy* (Harrisburg: Pennsylvania Department of Commerce, Bureau of Travel Marketing, September 1992).

39. *Rhode Island Visitor's Guide 1993* (Providence: Rhode Island Tourism Division, Department of Economic Development, 1993).

40. *South Carolina: Smiling Faces. Beautiful Places* (Columbia: South Carolina Division of Tourism, 1993).

41. *South Dakota 1993 Calendar of Events* (Pierre: South Dakota Department of Tourism, 1992).

42. *Travel Tennessee: The Official 1993 Vacation Guide* (Brentwood, Tenn.: Journal Communications, Inc., in cooperation with the Tennessee Department of Tourist Development, 1993).

43. *1993 Texas Events* (Austin: Texas Department of Commerce, Tourism Division, 1993).

44. *Utah! Calendar of Events: May, 1992 through December, 1993* (Salt Lake City: Utah Travel Council, n.d.); *Sundance Film Festival '93: Film Guide* (Salt Lake City: The Festival, 1993).

45. *Vermont Annual Events, 1993* (Montpelier: Vermont Department of Travel and Tourism, 1993); *Vermont in Brief* (Montpelier: Vermont Department of Travel and Tourism, n.d.).

46. *Virginia Is for Lovers: 1992 Travel Guide* (Richmond: Virginia Department of Economic Development, Tourism Development Group, 1992).

47. *Washington State Field Guide, Winter '92–'93* (Olympia: State of Washington, Tourism Division, 1992); *Destination Washington* (Bothell, Wash.: GTE Discovery Publications, Inc., 1992); *1993 Washington State Calendar of Events, July–September* (Olympia: Department of Trade and Economic Development, Tourism Development Division, 1993).

48. *West Virginia—It's You* (n.p.: The State of West Virginia, C & P Telephone,

Bell Atlantic, n.d.); *History of the State Fair of West Virginia* (n.p., n.d.); informtion provided by the State Fair of West Virginia.

49. *Wisconsin Calendar of Events* (Madison: Wisconsin Department of Development, Wisconsin Division of Tourism, 1992).

50. *Wyoming Vacation Guide* (Cheyenne: Wyoming Division of Tourism, n.d.).

51. *Washington, D.C. 1993 Weekends* (Washington, D.C.: D.C. Committee to Promote Washington, 1993).

52. *American Samoa* (n.p., n.d.); pamphlet provided by the Office of Eni Faleomavaega, Member of Congress from American Samoa.

53. *Mariana Islands Visitor's Guide* (n.p., n.d.); information supplied by Pete Torres, Office of the United States Representative of the Commonwealth of the Northern Mariana Islands.

54. *Guam and Micronesia* (Agana: Guam Visitors Bureau, 1989), p. 25.

55. *Que Pasa* 45 (April–June 1993): 4–8; " 'Vejigante Mask' " (San Juan: Tourism Company, n.d.).

56. *United States Virgin Islands Visitors' Guide* (n.p.: United States Virgin Islands, Division of Tourism, 1993), pp. 8, 25.

Selected Bibliography of State and Territory Histories

ALABAMA

Du Bose, Joel C. *Alabama History.* Richmond: B. F. Johnson, 1908.
Griffith, Lucille B. *Alabama: A Documentary History.* Rev. and enl. ed. University: University of Alabama Press, 1972.
Hamilton, Virginia V. *Alabama, A History.* New York: Norton; Nashville: American Association for State and Local History, 1984.
Moore, Albert B. *History of Alabama and Her People.* 3 vols. Chicago: American Historical Society, 1927.
Owen, Marie B. *The Story of Alabama; A History of the State.* 5 vols. New York: Lewis Historical Publishing Company, 1949.
Owen, Thomas M. *History of Alabama and Dictionary of Alabama Biography.* 4 vols. Chicago: S. J. Clarke, 1921.

ALASKA

Andrews, Clarence L. *The Story of Alaska.* Seattle: Lowman & Hanford, 1931.
Gruening, Ernest H. *The State of Alaska.* New York: Random House, 1968.
Naske, Claus-M., and Herman E. Slotnick. *Alaska, a History of the 49th State.* 2d ed. Norman: University of Oklahoma Press, 1987.
Nichols, Jeannette P. *Alaska.* New York: Russell & Russell, 1963.
Ritter, Harry. *Alaska's History: The People, Land, and Events of the North Country.* Anchorage: Alaska Northwest Books, 1993.
Wold, Jo Anne. *The Way It Was: Of People, Places, and Things in Pioneer Interior Alaska.* Anchorage: Alaska Northwest Publishing Company, 1988.

ARIZONA

Farish, Thomas E. *History of Arizona.* 8 vols. Phoenix: State of Arizona, 1915–1918.

Goff, John S. *Arizona, An Illustrated History of the Grand Canyon State.* Northridge, Calif.: Windsor Publications, 1988.

Leshy, John D. *The Arizona State Constitution: A Reference Guide.* Westport, Conn.: Greenwood Press, 1993.

Miller, Joseph. *Arizona; The Grand Canyon State; A State Guide.* 4th completely rev. ed. New York: Hastings House, 1966.

Officer, James E. *Hispanic Arizona, 1536–1856.* Tucson: University of Arizona Press, 1987.

Peplow, Edward H. *History of Arizona.* 3 vols. New York: Lewis Historical Publishing Company, 1958.

Sloan, Richard E., and Ward R. Adams. *History of Arizona.* 4 vols. Phoenix: Record Publishing Company, 1930.

Walker, Henry P., and Don Bufkin. *Historical Atlas of Arizona.* 2d ed. Norman and London: University of Oklahoma Press, 1986.

Wyllys, Rufus K. *Arizona: The History of a Frontier State.* Phoenix: Hobson & Herr, 1950.

ARKANSAS

Ashmore, Harry S. *Arkansas, A History.* New York: Norton; Nashville: American Association for State and Local History, 1984.

Berry, Fred, and John Novak. *The History of Arkansas.* Little Rock: Rose Publishing Company, 1987.

Fletcher, John G. *Arkansas.* Chapel Hill: University of North Carolina Press, 1947.

Goss, Kay Collett. *The Arkansas State Constitution: A Reference Guide.* Westport, Conn.: Greenwood Press, 1993.

Hanson, Gerald T., and Carl H. Moneyhon. *Historical Atlas of Arkansas.* Norman and London: University of Oklahoma Press, 1989.

Herndon, Dallas T. *Centennial History of Arkansas.* Easley, S.C.: Southern Historical Press, 1984; originally published in 1922.

McNutt, Walter S., et al. *A History of Arkansas.* Little Rock: Democrat Printing and Lithographing, 1932.

Thomas, David Y. *Arkansas and Its People, A History, 1541–1930.* 4 vols. New York: American Historical Society, 1930.

Williams, C. Fred, and Starr Mitchell. *Arkansas, An Illustrated History of the Land of Opportunity.* Northridge, Calif.: Windsor Publications, 1986.

CALIFORNIA

Bancroft, Hubert H. *California.* 7 vols. San Francisco: A. L. Bancroft, 1884–1890.

Bean, Walton, and James J. Rawls. *California, An Interpretive History.* 4th ed. New York: McGraw-Hill, 1983.

Boule, Mary Null. *The Missions: California's Heritage.* 21 vols. Vashon, Wash.: Merryant Publishers, 1988.
Chapman, Charles E. *A History of California: The Spanish Period.* New York: Macmillan, 1921.
Cleland, Robert G. *A History of California: The American Period.* Westport, Conn.: Greenwood Press, 1975; reprint of 1922 edition.
Fehrenbacher, Don E. *A Basic History of California.* Princeton, N.J.: Van Nostrand, 1964.
Grodin, Joseph R., Calvin R. Massey, and Richard B. Cunningham. *The California State Constitution: A Reference Guide.* Westport, Conn.: Greenwood Press, 1993.
Hutchinson, William H. *California; Two Centuries of Man, Land, and Growth in the Golden State.* Palo Alto: American West Publishing Company, 1969.
Lavender, David S. *California, a History.* New York: Norton; Nashville: American Association for State and Local History, 1985.
Rice, Richard B., et al. *The Elusive Eden: A New History of California.* New York: McGraw-Hill, 1988.
Rolle, Andrew F. *California: A History.* 4th ed. Arlington Heights, Ill.: H. Davidson, 1987.
Wheeler, B. Gordon. *Black California: The History of African-Americans in the Golden State.* New York: Hippocrene Books, 1992.

COLORADO

Abbott, Carl. *Colorado: A History of the Centennial State.* Boulder: Colorado Associated University Press, 1976.
Echevarria, Evelio, and Jose Otero, eds. *Hispanic Colorado: Four Centuries of History and Heritage.* Fort Collins, Colo.: Centennial Publications, 1976.
Ellis, Richard N., and Duane A. Smith. *Colorado: A History in Photographs.* Niwot, Colo.: University Press of Colorado, 1991.
Hafen, LeRoy R., ed. *Colorado and Its People; A Narrative and Topical History of the Centennial State.* 4 vols. New York: Lewis Historical Publishing Company, 1948.
Hall, Frank. *History of the State of Colorado . . .* 4 vols. Chicago: Blakely Printing Company, 1889–1895.
May, Stephen. *Pilgrimage: A Journey through Colorado's History and Culture.* Athens: Swallow Press/Ohio University Press, 1987.
Schmidt, Cynthia. *Colorado: Grassroots.* Phoenix: Cloud Publishing, 1984.
Sprague, Marshall. *Colorado: A Bicentennial History.* New York: Norton, 1976.
———. *Colorado, A History.* New York: Norton; Nashville: American Association for State and Local History, 1984.
Stone, Wilbur F. *History of Colorado.* 6 vols. Chicago: S. J. Clarke, 1918–1919.
Ubbelohde, Carl, et al. *A Colorado History.* 6th ed. Boulder: Pruett Publishing Company, 1988.

CONNECTICUT

Bingham, Harold J. *History of Connecticut.* 4 vols. New York: Lewis Historical Publishing Company, 1962.

Grant, Ellsworth S., and Oliver O. Jensen. *The Miracle of Connecticut.* Hartford: Connecticut Historical Society and Fenwick Productions, 1992.

Horton, Wesley W. *The Connecticut State Constitution: A Reference Guide.* Westport, Conn.: Greenwood Press, 1993.

Morgan, Forrest, ed. *Connecticut As a Colony and As a State, or One of the Original Thirteen.* 4 vols. Hartford: Publishing Society of Connecticut, 1904.

Osborn, Norris G. *History of Connecticut in Monographic Form.* 5 vols. New York: The States History Company, 1925.

Roth, David M. *Connecticut, a History.* New York: Norton; Nashville: American Association for State and Local History, 1985.

Sherer, Thomas E. *The Connecticut Atlas.* 2d ed. Old Lyme, Conn.: Kilderatlas Publishing Company, 1992.

Trumbull, Benjamin. *A Complete History of Connecticut.* New York: Arno Press, 1972; reprint of 1818 edition.

DELAWARE

Conrad, Henry C. *History of the State of Delaware.* 3 vols. Wilmington: The Author, 1908.

Eckman, Jeannette, et al., eds. *Delaware: A Guide to the First State.* New and rev. ed. St. Clair Shores, Mich.: Scholarly Press, 1976; reprint of 1955 edition.

Munroe, John A. *History of Delaware.* 3d ed. Newark: University of Delaware Press; London: Associated University Presses, 1993.

Reed, H. C. Roy, ed. *Delaware: A History of the First State.* 3 vols. New York: Lewis Historical Publishing Company, 1947.

Scharf, John T. *History of Delaware, 1609–1888.* 2 vols. Philadelphia: L. J. Richards, 1888.

FLORIDA

Brevard, Caroline M., and James A. Robertson. *A History of Florida from the Treaty of 1763 to Our Own Times.* 2 vols. Deland, Fla.: Florida State Historical Society, 1924–1925.

Coker, William S., et al. *Florida: From the Beginning to 1992: A Columbus Jubilee Commemorative.* Houston: Pioneer Publications, 1991.

D'Alemberte, Talbot. *The Florida State Constitution: A Reference Guide.* Westport, Conn.: Greenwood Press, 1991.

Dovell, Junius E. *Florida: Historic, Dramatic, Contemporary.* 4 vols. New York: Lewis Historical Publishing Company, 1952.

Gannon, Michael V. *Florida: A Short History.* Gainesville: University Press of Florida, 1993.

George, Paul S., ed. *A Guide to the History of Florida.* Westport, Conn.: Greenwood Press, 1989.

Jahoda, Gloria. *Florida, a History.* New York: Norton; Nashville: American Association for State and Local History, 1984.

Keuchel, Edward F., and Judy Moore. *Florida, Enterprise under the Sun: An Illustrated History.* Chatsworth, Calif.: Windsor Publications, 1990.

Patrick, Rembert W., and Allen Morris. *Florida under Five Flags*. 4th ed. Gainesville: University of Florida Press, 1967.

GEORGIA

Bonner, James C., and Lucien E. Roberts. *Georgia History and Government*. Spartanburg, S.C.: Reprint Company, 1974; reprint of 1940 edition.
Clements, John. *Georgia Facts: A Comprehensive Look at Georgia Today, County by County*. Dallas: Clements Research, Inc., 1989.
Coleman, Kenneth, ed. *A History of Georgia*. 2d ed. Athens: University of Georgia Press, 1991.
Coulter, E. Merton. *Georgia; A Short History*. Chapel Hill: University of North Carolina Press, 1947.
Jones, Charles C. *The History of Georgia*. 2 vols. Boston: Houghton, Mifflin, 1883.
Lane, Mills. *The People of Georgia: An Illustrated History*. 2d ed. Savannah: Library of Georgia, 1992.
London, Bonnie. *A History of Georgia*. Montgomery, Ala.: Clairmont Press, 1992.
Rice, Bradley R., and Harvey H. Jackson. *Georgia: Empire State of the South*. Northridge, Calif.: Windsor Publications, 1988.

HAWAII

Day, A. Grove. *Hawaii and Its People*. Rev. ed. New York: Meredith Press, 1968.
Kuykendall, Ralph S. *The Hawaiian Kingdom*. 3 vols. Honolulu: University of Hawaii, 1966–1968.
Kuykendall, Ralph S., and A. Grove Day. *Hawaii: A History, From Polynesian Kingdom to American State*. Rev. ed. Englewood Cliffs, N.J.: Prentice-Hall, 1961.
Lee, Anne Feder. *The Hawaii State Constitution: A Reference Guide*. Westport, Conn.: Greenwood Press, 1993.
Tabrah, Ruth M. *Hawaii, a History*. New York: Norton; Nashville: American Association for State and Local History, 1984.
Withington, Antoinette. *The Golden Cloak: An Informal History of Hawaiian Royalty and of the Development of the Government during each Reign under Steadily Increasing Foreign Influence*. Honolulu: Mutual Publishing, 1986.

IDAHO

Arrington, Leonard J. *History of Idaho*. Moscow: University of Idaho Press; Boise: Idaho State Historical Society, 1993.
Beal, Merrill D., and Merle W. Wells. *History of Idaho*. 3 vols. New York: Lewis Historical Publishing Company, 1959.
Crowley, Donald, and Florence Heffron. *The Idaho State Constitution: A Reference Guide*. Westport, Conn.: Greenwood Press, 1994.
Hailey, John. *The History of Idaho*. Boise: Press of Syms-York Company, 1910.
Hawley, James H. *History of Idaho, The Gem of the Mountains*. 4 vols. Chicago: S. J. Clarke, 1920.

Schwantes, Carlos A. *In Mountain Shadows: A History of Idaho.* Lincoln: University of Nebraska Press, 1991.
Wells, Merle W., and Arthur A. Hart. *Idaho, Gem of the Mountains.* Northridge, Calif.: Windsor Publications, 1985.

ILLINOIS

Alvord, Clarence W., ed. *Centennial History of Illinois.* 5 vols. Chicago: A. C. McClurg, 1922, c 1918–1920.
Bridges, Roger D., and Rodney O. Davis. *Illinois, Its History and Legacy.* St. Louis: River City Publishers, 1984.
Carrier, Lois. *Illinois: Crossroads of a Continent.* Urbana: University of Illinois Press, 1993.
Clements, John. *Illinois Facts: A Comprehensive Look at Illinois Today, County by County.* Dallas: Clements Research, Inc., 1989.
Hoffmann, John, ed. *A Guide to the History of Illinois.* Westport, Conn.: Greenwood Press, 1991.
Pease, Theodore C. *The Story of Illinois.* 3d ed., rev. by Marguerite J. Pease. Chicago: University of Chicago Press, 1965.

INDIANA

Barnhart, John D., and Donald Carmony. *Indiana from Frontier to Industrial Commonwealth.* 4 vols. New York: Lewis Historical Publishing Company, 1954.
Esarey, Logan. *A History of Indiana.* 2 vols. in one. Indianapolis: Hoosier Heritage Press, 1970; reprint of 1915 and 1918 editions.
Madison, James H. *The Indiana Way: A State History.* Bloomington: Indiana University Press; Indianapolis: Indiana Historical Society, 1990.
Taylor, Robert M., ed. *Indiana: A New Historical Guide.* Indianapolis: Indiana Historical Society, 1989.
Wilson, William E. *Indiana: A History.* Bloomington: Indiana University Press, 1966.

IOWA

Bennett, Mary. *An Iowa Album: A Photographic History, 1860–1920.* Iowa City: University of Iowa Press, 1990.
Brigham, Johnson. *Iowa: Its History and Its Foremost Citizens.* 3 vols. Chicago: S. J. Clarke, 1915.
Cole, Cyrenus. *A History of the People of Iowa.* Cedar Rapids: Torch Press, 1921.
———. *Iowa through the Years.* Iowa City: State Historical Society of Iowa, 1940.
Gue, Benjamin T. *History of Iowa from the Earliest Times to the Beginning of the Twentieth Century.* 4 vols. New York: Century History Company, 1903.
Harlan, Edgar R. *A Narrative History of the People of Iowa.* 5 vols. Chicago: American Historical Society, 1931.
Kimball, Donald L. *A History of Iowa.* 2 vols. Fayette, Iowa: Historic Publications (division of the Trends and Events Publishing Company), 1987.

Sabin, Henry, and Edwin L. Sabin. *The Making of Iowa.* Chicago: A. Flanagan, 1916.

Sage, Leland L. *A History of Iowa.* Ames: Iowa State University Press, 1987.

KANSAS

Blackmar, Frank W., ed. *Kansas: A Cyclopedia of State History . . .* 3 vols. in four. Chicago: Standard Publishing Company, 1912.

Bright, John D., ed. *Kansas: The First Century.* 4 vols. New York: Lewis Publishing Company, 1956.

Clements, John. *Kansas Facts: A Comprehensive Look at Kansas Today, County by County.* Dallas: Clements Research, Inc., 1990.

Connelley, William E. *History of Kansas, State and People.* 5 vols. Chicago: American Historical Society, 1928.

Davis, Kenneth S. *Kansas, a History.* New York: Norton; Nashville: American Association for State and Local History, 1984.

Heller, Francis H. *The Kansas State Constitution: A Reference Guide.* Westport, Conn.: Greenwood Press, 1992.

Isern, Thomas D., and Raymond Wilson. *Kansas Land.* 2d ed. Salt Lake City: Peregrine Smith Books, 1992.

Richmond, Robert W. *Kansas, a Land of Contrasts.* 3d ed. Arlington Heights, Ill.: Forum Press, 1989.

———. *Kansas, a Pictorial History.* Rev. ed. Lawrence: University Press of Kansas, 1992.

KENTUCKY

Clark, Thoms D. *A History of Kentucky.* Revised edition, 6th printing. Lexington: John Bradford Press, 1977.

Connelley, William E., and E. Merton Coulter. *History of Kentucky.* 5 vols. Chicago: American Historical Society, 1922.

Schmidt, Martin F., ed. *Kentucky Illustrated: The First Hundred Years.* Lexington: University Press of Kentucky, 1992.

Smith, Zachariah F. *History of Kentucky, From its Earliest Discovery and Settlement, to the Present Date.* Louisville: Prentice Press, 1895.

Wallis, Frederick A., and Hambleton Tapp. *A Sesqui-Centennial History of Kentucky.* 4 vols. Hopkinsville: Historical Record Association, 1945.

LOUISIANA

Castle, Joseph D. *Louisiana: Exploration and Early Settlement, 1584–1803.* New Orleans: Louisiana State Museum, 1989.

Chambers, Henry E. *A History of Louisiana, Wilderness-Colony-Province-Territory-State-People.* 3 vols. Chicago: American Historical Society, 1925.

Cummins, Light Townsend, and Glen Jeansonne, eds. *A Guide to the History of Louisiana.* Westport, Conn.: Greenwood Press, 1982.

Davis, Edwin A. *The Story of Louisiana.* 4 vols. New Orleans: Hyer, 1960–1963.

Davis, Edwin A., et al. *Louisiana, the Pelican State.* Rev. ed. Baton Rouge: Louisiana State University Press, 1985.
Dethloff, Henry C., and Allen E. Begnaud. *Louisiana, a Study in Diversity.* Austin, Tex.: Steck-Vaughn Company, 1992.
Eakin, Sue L., et al. *Louisiana: The Land and Its People.* 3d ed. Gretna, La.: Pelican, 1991.
Fortier, Alcee. *Louisiana.* 2 vols. Atlanta: Southern Historical Association, 1933.
Gayarre, Charles. *History of Louisiana.* 4 vols. 4th ed. New Orleans: Pelican, 1965; reprint of 1903 edition.
Giraud, Marcel. *A History of French Louisiana.* Trans. Joseph C. Lambert. Baton Rouge: Louisiana State University Press, 1974–.
Hargrave, Lee. *The Louisiana State Constitution: A Reference Guide.* Westport, Conn.: Greenwood Press, 1991.
Taylor, Joe Gray. *Louisiana, a History.* New York: Norton; Nashville: American Association for State and Local History, 1984.
Wall, Bennett H., and Light Townsend Cummins, eds. *Louisiana, a History.* Arlington Heights, Ill.: Forum Press, 1990.

MAINE

Abbott, John S. *The History of Maine.* Boston: B. B. Russell, 1875.
Clark, Charles E. *Maine, a History.* New York: Norton; Nashville: American Association for State and Local History, 1985.
Hatch, Louis C. *Maine: A History.* 5 vols. New York: American Historical Society, 1919.
Rich, Louise Dickinson. *State o' Maine.* Camden, Me.: Down East Books, 1987.
Rolde, Neil. *Maine: A Narrative History.* Gardiner, Me.: Harpswell Press, 1990.
Smith, David C., and Edward O. Schriver. *Maine: A History through Selected Readings.* Dubuque: Kendall/Hunt, 1985.
Smith, Marion J. *A History of Maine from Wilderness to Statehood.* Portland: Falmouth Publishing House, 1949.
Tinkle, Marshall J. *The Maine State Constitution: A Reference Guide.* Westport, Conn.: Greenwood Press, 1992.
Williamson, William D. *The History of the State of Maine.* 2 vols. Freeport, Maine: Cumberland Press, 1966; reprint of 1832 edition.

MARYLAND

Andrews, Matthew P. *History of Maryland: Province and State.* Hatboro, Pa.: Tradition Press, 1965; reprint of 1929 edition.
Bozman, John L. *The History of Maryland: From the Settlement in 1633, to Restoration, in 1660.* 3 vols. Bowie, Md.: Heritage Books, 1990; published originally in 1837.
Brugger, Robert J. *Maryland: A Middle Temperament, 1634–1980.* Baltimore and London: Johns Hopkins University Press in association with the Maryland Historical Society, 1988.
Richardson, Hester D. *Side-lights on Maryland History, with Sketches of Early*

Maryland Families. 2 vols. in one. Cambridge, Md.: Tidewater Publishers, 1967; reprint of 1913 edition.
Rollo, Vera A. Foster. *Your Maryland: A History.* 5th rev. ed. Lanham: Maryland Historical Press, 1993.
Russo, Jean B., ed. *Unlocking the Secrets of Time: Maryland's Hidden Heritage.* Baltimore: Maryland Historical Society, 1991.
Scharf, John T. *History of Maryland from the Earliest Period to the Present Day.* 3 vols. Hatboro, Pa.: Tradition Press, 1967; reprint of 1879 edition.
Walsh, Richard, and William L. Fox. *Maryland, a History.* Annapolis: Hall of Records Commission, Department of General Services, 1983.

MASSACHUSETTS

Clark, Judith Freeman, and David Horn. *Massachusetts from Colony to Commonwealth: An Illustrated History.* Northridge, Calif.: Windsor Publications, 1987.
Clements, John. *Massachusetts Facts: A Comprehensive Look at Massachusetts Today, County by County.* Dallas: Clements Research, 1987.
Hart, Albert B., ed., *Commonwealth History of Massachusetts.* 5 vols. New York: Russell & Russell, 1966; reprint of 1930 edition.
Kaufman, Martin, et al., eds. *A Guide to the History of Massachusetts.* Westport, Conn.: Greenwood Press, 1988.
Marsh, Daniel L., and William H. Clark. *The Story of Massachusetts.* 4 vols. New York: American Historical Society, 1938.
Wilkie, Richard W., et al., eds. *Historical Atlas of Massachusetts.* Amherst: University of Massachusetts Press, 1991.

MICHIGAN

Bald, F. Clever. *Michigan in Four Centuries.* Rev. and enl. ed. New York: Harper & Row, 1961.
Catton, Bruce. *Michigan, a History.* New York: Norton; Nashville: American Association for State and Local History, 1984.
Deur, Lynne, and Sara Michel. *The Making of Michigan.* Spring Lake, Mich.: River Road Publications, 1989.
Dunbar, Willis F. *Michigan, a History of the Wolverine State.* Rev. ed. by George S. May. Grand Rapids: Eerdman, 1980.
Fuller, George N. *Michigan: A Centennial History of the State and Its People . . .* 5 vols. Chicago: Lewis Publishing Company, 1939.
Grimm, Joe, ed. *Michigan Voices: Our State's History in the Words of the People Who Lived It.* Detroit: Detroit Free Press and Wayne State University Press, 1987.
Hathaway, Richard J., ed. *Michigan: Visions of Our Past.* East Lansing: Michigan State University Press, 1989.
Quaife, Milo M., and Sidney Glazer. *Michigan: From Primitive Wilderness to Industrial Commonwealth.* New York: Prentice-Hall, 1948.

Utley, Henry M., and Byron M. Cutcheon. *Michigan As a Province, Territory and State*. 4 vols. New York: Publishing Society of Michigan, 1906.

MINNESOTA

Blegen, Theodore C. *Minnesota: A History of the State*. Minneapolis: University of Minnesota Press, 1975.

Clark, Clifford E., ed. *Minnesota in a Century of Change: The State and Its People since 1900*. St. Paul: Minnesota Historical Society Press, 1989.

Folwell, William W. *A History of Minnesota*. 4 vols. St. Paul: Minnesota Historical Society, 1921–1930.

Hubbard, Lucius F., et al. *Minnesota in Three Centuries, 1655–1908*. 4 vols. New York: Publishing Society of Minnesota, 1908.

Lass, William E. *Minnesota, a History*. New York: Norton; Nashville: American Association for State and Local History, 1983.

MISSISSIPPI

Akin, Edward N., and Roger Walker. *Mississippi, an Illustrated History*. Northridge, Calif.: Windsor Publications, produced in cooperation with Mississippi Historical Society, 1987.

Banks, Sarah J., et al., ed. *Mississippi's Spanish Heritage: Selected Writings, 1492–1798*. Jackson: Mississippi State Department of Education and Mississippi Institutions of Higher Learning, 1992.

Buzhardt, Gail A., and Margaret Hawthorne, eds. *Mississippi's French Heritage: Selected Writings, 1682–1763*. Jackson: Mississippi State Department of Education and Mississippi Institutions of Higher Learning, 1992.

Carpenter, Barbara, ed. *Ethnic Heritage in Mississippi*. Jackson: Published for the Mississippi Humanities Council by the University Press of Mississippi, 1992.

Lowry, Robert, and W. H. McCardle. *A History of Mississippi*. Spartanburg, S.C.: Reprint Company, 1978; reprint of 1891 edition.

Rowland, Dunbar. *Encyclopedia of Mississippi History*. 2 vols. Madison, Wis.: S. A. Brant, 1907.

———. *History of Mississippi, the Heart of the South*. 2 vols. Spartanburg, S.C.: Reprint Company, 1978; reprint of Chicago: S. J. Clarke, 1925.

Skates, John R. *Mississippi, a History*. New York: Norton; Nashville: American Association for State and Local History, 1985.

Winkle III, John W. *The Mississippi State Constitution: A Reference Guide*. Westport, Conn.: Greenwood Press, 1993.

Yates, Gayle G. *Mississippi Mind: A Personal Cultural History of an American State*. Knoxville: University of Tennessee Press, 1990.

MISSOURI

Conard, Howard L. *Encyclopedia of the History of Missouri*. 6 vols. New York: Southern History Company, 1901.

Culmer, Frederic A. *A New History of Missouri.* Mexico, Mo.: McIntyre Publishing Company, 1938.

Foley, William E. *The Genesis of Missouri: From Wilderness Outpost to Statehood.* Columbia and London: University of Missouri Press, 1990.

———. *History of Missouri, Volume 1: 1673 to 1820.* (The Missouri Sesquicentennial Edition). Columbia: University of Missouri Press, 1971.

Houck, Lewis. *A History of Missouri, from the Earliest Explorations and Settlements Until the Admission of the State into the Union.* 3 vols. Chicago: R. R. Donnelley, 1908.

McCandless, Perry. *A History of Missouri, Volume 2: 1820 to 1860.* (The Missouri Sesquicentennial Edition.) Columbia: University of Missouri Press, 1972.

March, David D. *The History of Missouri.* 4 vols. New York: Lewis Historical Publishing Company, 1967.

Meyer, Duane G. *The Heritage of Missouri.* 3rd ed. St. Louis: River City Publishers, 1982.

Nagel, Paul C. *Missouri: A History.* Lawrence and London: University Press of Kansas, 1989.

Parrish, William E., ed. *A History of Missouri.* (The Missouri Sesquicentennial Edition). Columbia: University of Missouri Press, 1971–.

Parrish, William E., et al. *Missouri, the Heart of the Nation.* 2d ed. Arlington Heights, Ill.: H. Davidson, 1992.

Shoemaker, Floyd C. *Missouri and Missourians: Land of Contrasts and People of Achievements.* 5 vols. Chicago: Lewis Publishing Company, 1943.

Stevens, Walter B. *Centennial History of Missouri: One Hundred Years in the Union, 1820–1921.* 5 vols. St. Louis: S. J. Clarke, 1921.

Violette, Eugene M., and Forrest Wolverton. *A History of Missouri.* Cape Girardeau: Ramfre Press, 1960; reprint of 1918 edition.

Williams, Walter, and Floyd C. Shoemaker. *Missouri, Mother of the West.* 5 vols. Chicago: American Historical Society, 1930.

MONTANA

Burlingame, Merrill G., and K. Ross Toole. *History of Montana.* 3 vols. New York: Lewis Historical Publishing Company, 1957.

Hamilton, James M. *History of Montana, From Wilderness to Statehood.* 2d ed. Ed. Merrill G. Burlingame. Portland, Oreg.: Binfords & Mort, 1970.

Leeson, Michael A. *History of Montana, 1739–1885.* Chicago: Warner, Beers & Company, 1885.

Malone, Michael P. *Montana: A History of Two Centuries.* Rev. ed. Seattle: University of Washington Press, 1991.

Raymer, Robert G. *Montana, the Land and the People.* 3 vols. Chicago: Lewis Publishing Company, 1930.

Sanders, Helen F. *A History of Montana.* 3 vols. Chicago: Lewis Publishing Company, 1913.

Stout, Tom. *Montana: Its Story and Biography.* 2 vols. Chicago: American Historical Society, 1921.

Toole, K. Ross. *Montana: An Uncommon Land.* Norman: University of Oklahoma Press, 1959.

NEBRASKA

Brown, Elinor L. *Maps Tell Nebraska's History.* Ceresco, Nebr: Midwest Publishing, 1991.

History of the State of Nebraska. Chicago: Western Historical Company (A. T. Andreas, proprietor), 1882.

Miewald, Robert S., and Peter J. Longo. *The Nebraska State Constitution: A Reference Guide.* Westport, Conn.: Greenwood Press, 1993.

Morton, Julius S., et al. *Illustrated History of Nebraska.* 3 vols. Lincoln: J. North, 1905–1913.

Nebraska History. Lincoln: State of Nebraska Historical Society, 1989.

Olson, James C. *History of Nebraska.* 2d ed. Lincoln: University of Nebraska Press, 1966.

Sheldon, Addison E. *Nebraska: The Land and the People.* 3 vols. Chicago: Lewis Publishing Company, 1931.

NEVADA

Angel, Myron, ed. *History of Nevada.* New York: Arno Press, 1973; reprint of 1881 edition.

Bowers, Michael W. *The Nevada State Constitution: A Reference Guide.* Westport, Conn.: Greenwood Press, 1993.

Davis, Samuel P. *The History of Nevada.* 2 vols. Las Vegas: Nevada Publications, 1984; reprint of 1913 edition.

Earl, Phillip I. *This Was Nevada.* Reno: Nevada Historical Society, 1986.

Elliott, Russell R., and William D. Rowley. *History of Nevada.* 2d ed., rev. Lincoln: University of Nebraska Press, 1987.

Hulse, James W. *The Nevada Adventure: A History.* 6th ed. Reno: University of Nevada Press, 1990.

Mack, Effie M. *Nevada: A History of the State from the Earliest Times through the Civil War.* Glendale, Calif.: Arthur H. Clark Company, 1936.

NEW HAMPSHIRE

Belknap, Jeremy. *The History of New Hampshire.* 3 vols. New York: Arno Press, 1972; reprint of 1791–92 edition.

Heffernan, Nancy C., and Ann P. Stecker. *New Hampshire—Crosscurrents in Its Development.* Grantham, N.H.: Thompson & Rutter, 1986.

Jager, Ronald, and Grace Jager. *New Hampshire, an Illustrated History of the Granite State.* Woodland Hills, Calif.: Windsor Publications, 1983.

McClintock, John N. *Colony, Province, State, 1623–1888: History of New Hampshire.* Boston: B. B. Russell, 1889.

Morison, Elizabeth F., and Elting E. Morison. *New Hampshire, a History.* New

York: Norton; Nashville: American Association for State and Local History, 1985.
Pillsbury, Hobart. *New Hampshire; Resources, Attractions, and Its People; a History.* 5 vols. New York: Lewis Historical Publishing Company, 1927.
Sanborn, Edwin D. *History of New Hampshire* . . . Manchester, N.H.: J. B. Clarke, 1875.
Squires, James D. *The Granite State of the United States.* 4 vols. New York: American Historical Company, 1956.
Stackpole, Everett S. *History of New Hampshire.* 4 vols. New York: American Historical Society, 1916.

NEW JERSEY

Fleming, Thomas J. *New Jersey, a History.* New York: Norton; Nashville: American Association for State and Local History, 1984.
Johnson, James P. *New Jersey: History of Ingenuity and Industry.* Northridge, Calif.: Windsor Publications, 1987.
Kross, Peter, *New Jersey History.* Wilmington, Del.: Middle Atlantic Press, 1987.
Kull, Irving S., ed. *New Jersey, a History.* 6 vols. New York: American Historical Society, 1930–32.
Lee, Francis B. *New Jersey As a Colony and a State; One of the Original Thirteen.* 4 vols. New York: Publishing Society of New Jersey, 1902.
McCormick, Richard P. *New Jersey from Colony to State, 1609–1789.* Rev. ed. Newark: New Jersey Historical Society, 1981.
Myers, William S., ed. *The Story of New Jersey.* 5 vols. New York: Lewis Historical Publishing Company, 1945.
Stockton, Frank R. *Stories of New Jersey.* New Brunswick, N.J.: Rutgers University Press, 1987; published originally in 1961.
Williams, Robert F. *The New Jersey State Constitution: A Reference Guide.* Westport, Conn.: Greenwood Press, 1990.

NEW MEXICO

Beck, Warren A. *New Mexico; A History of Four Centuries.* Norman: University of Oklahoma Press, 1962.
Chavez, Thomas E. *An Illustrated History of New Mexico.* Niwot: University Press of Colorado, 1992.
Jaramillo, Nash. *A History of New Mexico.* Rev. ed. Santa Fe: Distributed by La Villa Real, Southwest Books Materials, 1986; text originally published in 1973.
Murphy, Dan. *New Mexico, the Distant Land; An Illustrated History.* Northridge, Calif.: Windsor Publications, 1985.
Nostrand, Richard L. *The Hispano Homeland.* Norman: University of Oklahoma Press, 1992.
Roberts, Calvin A., and Susan A. Roberts. *New Mexico.* Albuquerque: University of New Mexico Press, 1988.

Simmons, Marc. *New Mexico!* Rev., enl. ed. Albuquerque: University of New Mexico Press, 1991.

Twitchell, Ralph E. *The Leading Facts of New Mexican History.* 5 vols. Cedar Rapids, Iowa: Torch Press, 1911–1917.

NEW YORK

Brodhead, John R. *History of the State of New York.* 2 vols. New York: Harper, 1853–1871.

Ellis, David M. *A History of New York State.* Ithaca, N.Y.: Cornell University Press, 1967.

———. *New York State: Gateway to America.* Northridge, Calif.: Windsor Publications, 1988.

Flick, Alexander C., ed. *History of the State of New York.* 10 vols. New York: Columbia University Press, 1933–1937.

Galie, Peter. *The New York State Constitution: A Reference Guide.* Westport, Conn.: Greenwood Press, 1991.

NORTH CAROLINA

Ashe, Samuel A. *History of North Carolina.* 2 vols. Spartanburg, S.C.: Reprint Company, 1971; reprint of 1908–1925 edition.

Bell, John L., and Jeffrey J. Crow. *North Carolina: The History of an American State.* Montgomery, Ala.: Clairmont Press, 1992.

Clements, John. *North Carolina Facts: A Comprehensive Look at North Carolina Today, County by County.* Dallas: Clements Research, Inc., 1988.

Henderson, Archibald. *North Carolina: The Old North State and the New.* 5 vols. Chicago: Lewis Publishing Company, 1941.

Lefler, Hugh T., and Albert R. Newsome. *North Carolina.* Rev. ed. Chapel Hill: University of North Carolina Press, 1963.

Orth, John V. *The North Carolina State Constitution: A Reference Guide.* Westport, Conn.: Greenwood Press, 1993.

Powell, William S. *North Carolina, a History.* New York: Norton; Nashville: American Association for State and Local History, 1985.

———. *North Carolina through Four Centuries.* Chapel Hill: University of North Carolina Press, 1989.

Waggoner, Sara M. *North Carolina, the Tar Heel State.* Bryn Mawr, Pa.: Dorrance, 1988.

Williamson, Hugh. *The History of North Carolina.* 2 vols. Spartanburg, S.C.: Reprint Company, 1973; reprint of 1812 edition.

NORTH DAKOTA

Compendium of History and Biography of North Dakota. Chicago: George A. Ogle and Company, 1900.

Crawford, Lewis F. *History of North Dakota.* 3 vols. Chicago: American Historical Society, 1931.

Dill, Christopher L., and Brian Austin. *Early Peoples of North Dakota.* 2d ed. Bismarck: State Historical Society of North Dakota, North Dakota Heritage Center, 1990.

Gray, David P., and Gerald G. Newborg. *North Dakota: A Pictorial History.* Norfolk, Va.: Donning Company, 1988.

Hennessy, William B. *History of North Dakota . . . Including the Biographies of the Builders of the Commonwealth.* Bismarck: Bismarck Tribune Company, 1910.

Lounsberry, Clement A. *Early History of North Dakota: Essential Outlines of American History.* Washington: Liberty Press, 1919.

Rezatto, Helen. *The Making of the Two Dakotas.* Lincoln, Nebr.: Media Publishing, 1989.

Robinson, Elwyn B. *History of North Dakota.* Lincoln: University of Nebraska Press, 1966.

Rolfsrud, Erling N. *Story of the Peace Garden State.* Farwell, Minn.: Lantern Books, 1990.

Schlasinger, Ethel, ed. *North Dakota: A Guide to the Northern Prairie State.* 2d ed. New York: Oxford University Press, 1950.

OHIO

Knepper, George W. *Ohio and Its People.* Kent, Ohio: Kent State University Press, 1989.

Randall, E. O., and Daniel J. Ryan. *History of Ohio; the Rise and Progress of an American State.* 5 vols. New York: Century History Company, 1912.

Roseboom, Eugene H., et al. *A History of Ohio.* 2d ed. Columbus: Ohio Historical Society, 1986; originally published in 1967.

Wittke, Carl F., ed. *The History of the State of Ohio.* 6 vols. Columbus: printed under the auspices of the Ohio State Archaeological and Historical Society, 1941–1944.

OKLAHOMA

Dale, Edward E., and Morris L. Wardell. *History of Oklahoma.* New York: Prentice-Hall, 1948.

Foreman, Grant. *A History of Oklahoma.* Norman: University of Oklahoma Press, 1942.

Gibson, Arrell M. *Oklahoma, a History of Five Centuries.* 2d ed. Norman: University of Oklahoma Press, 1981.

Gibson, Arrell M., and Victor E. Harlow. *The History of Oklahoma.* New ed. Norman: University of Oklahoma Press, 1984.

Morgan, Howard W., and Anne H. Morgan. *Oklahoma, a History.* New York: Norton; Nashville: American Association for State and Local History, 1984.

Morris, John W., et al. *Historical Atlas of Oklahoma.* 3d ed. Norman: University of Oklahoma Press, 1986.

Thoburn, Joseph B., and Muriel H. Wright. *Oklahoma; A History of the State and Its People.* 4 vols. New York: Lewis Historical Publishing Company, 1929.

OREGON

Bancroft, Hubert H. *History of Oregon.* 2 vols. New York: Arno, 1967; reprint of 1886 edition.
Carey, Charles H. *A General History of Oregon Prior to 1861.* 2 vols. Portland: Metropolitan Press, 1935.
———. *History of Oregon.* Chicago: Pioneer Historical Publishing Company, 1922.
Corning, Howard M. *Dictionary of Oregon History.* 2d ed. Portland: Binford & Mort Publishing, 1989.
Lyman, Horace S. *History of Oregon: The Growth of an American State.* 4 vols. New York: North Pacific Publishing Society, 1903.
O'Donnell, Terence. *That Balance So Rare: The Story of Oregon.* Portland: Oregon Historical Society Press, 1988.
Scott, Harvey W. *History of the Oregon Country.* Comp. Leslie M. Scott. 6 vols. Cambridge: Riverside Press, 1924.

PENNSYLVANIA

Clements, John. *Pennsylvania Facts: A Comprehensive Look at Pennsylvania Today, County by County.* Dallas: Clements Research, 1987.
Donehoo, George P., ed. *Pennsylvania, a History.* 7 vols. New York: Lewis Historical Publishing Company, 1926.
Downey, Dennis B., and Francis J. Bremer, eds. *A Guide to the History of Pennsylvania.* Westport, Conn.: Greenwood Press, 1993.
Dunaway, Wayland F. *A History of Pennsylvania.* 2d ed. New York: Prentice-Hall, 1961.
Jenkins, Howard M. *Pennsylvania, Colonial and Federal; A History, 1608–1903.* 3 vols. Philadelphia: Pennsylvania Historical Publishing Association, 1903.
Stevens, Sylvester K. *Pennsylvania, Birthplace of a Nation.* New York: Random House, 1964.
———. *Pennsylvania: Keystone State.* 2 vols. New York: American Historical Company, 1956.

RHODE ISLAND

Arnold, Samuel G. *History of the State of Rhode Island and Providence Plantations.* 2 vols. New York: Appleton, 1859–60.
Bicknell, Thomas W. *The History of the State of Rhode Island and Providence Plantations.* 5 vols. New York: American Historical Society, 1920.
Carroll, Charles. *Rhode Island: Three Centuries of Democracy.* 4 vols. New York: Lewis Historical Publishing Company, 1932.
Conley, Patrick T. *An Album of Rhode Island History, 1636–1986.* Norfolk: Donning Company, 1986.
Davis, Hadassah, and Natalie Robinson. *History You Can See.* Providence: Rhode Island Publications Society, 1986.

Field, Edward. *State of Rhode Island and Providence Plantations and the End of the Century: A History*. 3 vols. Boston: Mason, 1902.
McLoughlin, William G. *Rhode Island, a History*. New York: Norton; Nashville: American Association for State and Local History, 1985.
Tanner, Earl C. *Rhode Island: A Brief History*. Providence: Rhode Island State Board of Education, 1954.

SOUTH CAROLINA

Lander, Ernest M. *A History of South Carolina, 1865–1960*. 2d ed. Columbia: University of South Carolina Press, 1970.
———. *South Carolina: An Illustrated History of the Palmetto State*. Northridge, Calif.: Windsor Publications, 1988.
McCrady, Edward. *The History of South Carolina*. 4 vols. New York: Paladin Press, 1969; reprint of 1897–1902 editions.
Wallace, David D. *South Carolina, a Short History, 1520–1948*. Columbia: University of South Carolina Press, 1966; reprint of 1951 edition.

SOUTH DAKOTA

Karolevitz, Robert F., and Bernie Hunhoff. *Uniquely South Dakota*. Norfolk, Va.: Donning Company, 1988.
Milton, John R. *South Dakota: A Bicentennial History*. New York: Norton; Nashville: American Association for State and Local History, 1988; published originally in 1977.
Robinson, Doane. *History of South Dakota*. 2 vols. Logansport, Ind.: B. F. Bowen, 1904.
Schell, Herbert S. *History of South Dakota*. 3d ed., rev. Lincoln: University of Nebraska Press, 1975.
Smith, George M. *South Dakota: Its History and Its People*. 5 vols. Chicago: S. J. Clarke, 1914.

TENNESSEE

Corlew, Robert E., and James A. Hoobler. *Tennessee: The Volunteer State*. Northridge, Calif.: Windsor, 1989.
Corlew, Robert E., et al. *Tennessee, a Short History*. 2d ed., updated through 1989. Knoxville: University of Tennessee Press, 1990.
Dykeman, Wilma. *Tennessee, a History*. New York: Norton; Nashville: American Association for State and Local History, 1984.
Folmsbee, Stanley J., et al. *History of Tennessee*. 4 vols. New York: Lewis Publishing Company, 1960.
Hale, William T., and Dixon L. Merritt. *History of Tennessee and Tennesseans*. 8 vols. Chicago: Lewis Publishing Company, 1913.
Hamer, Philip M., ed. *Tennessee: A History, 1673–1932*. 4 vols. New York: American Historical Society, 1933.

Laska, Lewis L. *The Tennessee State Constitution: A Reference Guide.* Westport, Conn.: Greenwood Press, 1990.

Moore, John T., and A. P. Foster. *Tennessee: The Volunteer State, 1769–1923.* 5 vols. Chicago: S. J. Clarke, 1923.

TEXAS

Calvert, Robert A., and Arnoldo De Leon. *The History of Texas.* Arlington Heights, Ill.: H. Davidson, 1990.

Cummins, Light Townsend, and Alvin R. Bailey, eds. *A Guide to the History of Texas.* Westport, Conn.: Greenwood Press, 1988.

Frantz, Joe B. *Texas, A History.* New York: Norton; Nashville: American Association for State and Local History, 1984.

Haley, James L. *Texas: From the Frontier to Spindletop.* New York: St. Martin's Press, 1991.

———. *Texas: From Spindletop through World War II.* New York: St. Martin's Press, 1993.

Johnson, Francis W. *A History of Texas and Texans.* 5 vols. Chicago: American Historical Society, 1916.

McDonald, Archie P., and Richard Dillard. *In Celebration of Texas: An Illustrated History.* Northridge, Calif.: Windsor Publications, 1986.

Procter, Ben H., and Archie P. McDonald, eds. *The Texas Heritage.* 2d ed. Arlington Heights, Ill.: Harlan Davidson, 1992.

Richardson, Rupert N., et al. *Texas: The Lone Star State.* 4th ed. Englewood Cliffs, N.J.: Prentice-Hall, 1981.

Webb, Walter P., et al., eds. *The Handbook of Texas.* 3 vols. Austin: Texas State Historical Association, 1952–1976.

Wooten, Dudley G., ed. *A Comprehensive History of Texas, 1685–1897.* 2 vols. Dallas: W. G. Scarff, 1898.

UTAH

Alter, J. Cecil. *Utah, the Storied Domain.* 3 vols. Chicago: American Historical Society, 1932.

Hunter, Milton R. *Utah: The Story of Her People, 1540–1947; A Centennial History of Utah.* Salt Lake City: Desert News Press, 1946.

May, Dean L. *Utah: A People's History.* Salt Lake City: University of Utah Press, 1987.

Neff, Andrew L. *History of Utah, 1847 to 1869.* Ed. and annot. Leland H. Creer. Salt Lake City: Deseret News Press, 1940.

Peterson, Charles S. *Utah, a History.* New York: Norton; Nashville: American Association for State and Local History, 1984.

Warrum, Noble, ed. *Utah Since Statehood, Historical and Biographical.* 4 vols. Chicago: S. J. Clarke, 1919.

Whitney, Orson F. *History of Utah . . .* 4 vols. Salt Lake City: Cannon, 1892–1904.

VERMONT

Crockett, Walter H. *Vermont, the Green Mountain State*. 4 vols. New York: Century History Company, 1921.

Hall, Hiland. *The History of Vermont, From Its Discovery to Its Admission into the Union in 1791*. Albany, N.Y.: Munsell, 1868.

Hill, William C. *The Vermont State Constitution: A Reference Guide*. Westport, Conn.: Greenwood Press, 1992.

Morissey, Charles T. *Vermont, a History*. New York: Norton; Nashville: American Association for State and Local History, 1984.

Newton, Earle W. *The Vermont Story: A History of the People of the Green Mountain State*. Montpelier: Vermont Historical Society, 1983–.

Sherman, Michael, and Jennie G. Versteeg, eds. *We Vermonters: Perspectives on the Past*. Montpelier: Vermont Historical Society, 1992.

VIRGINIA

Beverley, Robert. *The History and Present State of Virginia*. Ed. Louis B. Wright. Published for the Institute of Early American History and Culture at Williamsburg, Va. Chapel Hill: University of North Carolina Press, 1947.

Billings, Warren M., et al. *Colonial Virginia: A History*. White Plains, N.Y.: KTO Press, 1986.

Rubin, Louis D. *Virginia, a History*. New York: Norton; Nashville: American Association for State and Local History, 1984.

WASHINGTON

Avery, Mary W. *Washington: A History of the Evergreen State*. Seattle: University of Washington Press, 1965.

Barto, Harold E., and Catharine Bullard. *History of the State of Washington*. 2d ed. Boston: Heath, 1953.

Beckett, Paul L. *From Wilderness to Enabling Act: Evolution of the State of Washington*. Pullman: Washington State University Press, 1968.

Clements, John. *Washington Facts: A Comprehensive Look at Washington Today, County by County*. Dallas: Clements Research II, Inc., 1989.

Ficken, Robert E., and Charles P. LeWarne. *Washington: A Centennial History*. Seattle: University of Washington Press, 1988.

LeWarne, Charles P. *Washington State*. Seattle: University of Washington Press, 1986.

Meany, Edmond S. *History of the State of Washington*. New York: Macmillan, 1924.

Pollard, Lancaster. *A History of the State of Washington*. New ed., rev. 1951. Portland, Oreg.: Binfords & Mort, 1954.

Snowden, Clinton A. *History of Washington; the Rise and Progress of an American State*. 4 vols. New York: Century History Company, 1909.

Stratton, David H., ed. *Washington Comes of Age: The State in the National Experience*. Pullman: Washington State University Press, 1992.

White, Sid, and S. E. Solberg, eds. *Peoples of Washington: Perspectives on Cultural Diversity.* Pullman: Washington State University Press, 1989.

WEST VIRGINIA

Ambler, Charles H., and Festus P. Summers. *West Virginia, the Mountain State.* 2d ed. Englewood Cliffs, N.J.: Prentice-Hall, 1958.
Callahan, James M. *History of West Virginia, Old and New.* 3 vols. Chicago: American Historical Society, 1923.
Conley, Philip, and Boyd B. Stutler. *West Virginia, Yesterday and Today.* 4th ed., Rev. and rewritten. Charleston, W.V.: Education Foundation, 1966.
Lewis, Ronald L., and John Hennen, eds. *West Virginia: Documents in the History of a Rural-Industrial State.* Dubuque, Iowa: Kendall/Hunt Publishing Company, 1991.
Miller, Thomas C., and Hu Maxwell. *West Virginia and Its People.* 3 vols. New York: Lewis Historical Publishing Company, 1913.
Myers, Sylvester. *Myers' History of West Virginia.* 2 vols. Wheeling: The Wheeling News Lithograph Company, 1915.
Rice, Otis K. *West Virginia, a History.* Lexington: University of Kentucky, 1985.
Shawkey, Morris P. *West Virginia in History, Life, Literature and Industry.* 5 vols. Chicago: Lewis Publishing Company, 1928.
Williams, John A. *West Virginia, a History.* New York: Norton; Nashville: American Association for State and Local History, 1984.

WISCONSIN

Austin, H. Russell. *The Wisconsin Story: The Building of a Vanguard State.* 3d ed. Milwaukee: Milwaukee Journal, 1964.
Campbell, Henry C., ed. *Wisconsin in Three Centuries, 1634–1905.* 4 vols. New York: Century History Company, 1906.
Gara, Larry. *A Short History of Wisconsin.* Madison: State Historical Society of Wisconsin, 1962.
Nesbit, Robert C., and William Fletcher Thompson. *Wisconsin: A History.* 2d ed., rev. and updated. Madison: University of Wisconsin Press, 1989.
Raney, William F. *Wisconsin, a Story of Progress.* Appleton: Perin Press, 1963.

WYOMING

Bartlett, Ichabod S. *History of Wyoming.* 3 vols. Chicago: S. J. Clarke, 1918.
Beard, Frances B., ed. *Wyoming from Territorial Days to the Present.* 3 vols. Chicago: American Historical Society, 1933.
Coutant, Charles G. *History of Wyoming and the Far West.* Published for University Microfilms. New York: Argonaut Press, 1966; reprint of 1899 edition.
Junge, Mark. *Wyoming, a Pictorial History.* Norfolk: Donning Company, 1989.
Keiter, Robert S., and Tim Newcomb. *The Wyoming State Constitution: A Reference Guide.* Westport, Conn.: Greenwood Press, 1992.
Larson, Taft A. *History of Wyoming.* Lincoln: University of Nebraska Press, 1965.

———. *Wyoming, a History*. New York: Norton; Nashville: American Association for State and Local History, 1984.

DISTRICT OF COLUMBIA

Bowling, Kenneth R. *The Creation of Washington, D.C.: The Idea and Location of the American Capital.* Fairfax, Va., and Lanham, Md.: George Mason University Press; distributed by arrangement with University Publishing Associates, 1991.
Bryan, W. B. *A History of the National Capital from Its Foundation through the Period of the Adoption of the Organic Act.* 2 vols. New York: Macmillan, 1914, 1916.
Fogle, Jeanne. *Two Hundred Years: Stories of the Nation's Capital.* Arlington, Va.: Vandamere Press, 1991.
Green, Constance McLaughlin. *Washington: A History of the Capital, 1800–1950.* Princeton, N.J.: Princeton University Press, 1977; first published in 1962.
Gutheim, Frederick A., and Wilcomb E. Washburn. *The Federal City, Plans and Realities: The History.* 2nd print. Washington, D.C.: published in cooperation with the National Capital Planning Commission by the Smithsonian Institution Press, 1981, 1976.
Howard, George W. *The Monumental City: Its Past History and Present Resources.* 2 vols in one. Baltimore: J. D. Ehlers & Company, 1873, 1880.
Lewis, David L. *District of Columbia: A Bicentennial History.* New York: Norton, 1976.
Melder, Keith, et al., eds. *City of Magnificent Intentions: A History of the District of Columbia.* Washington, D.C.: Published for Associates for Renewal in Education by Intac, Inc., 1983.
Porter, John Addison. *The City of Washington, Its Origin and Administration.* New York: Johnson Reprint Corporation, 1973, 1885.
Tindall, William. *Origin and Government of the District of Columbia.* Washington, D.C.: Government Printing Office, 1903.
Wilson, Rufus R. *Washington, the Capital City, and Its Part in the History of the Nation.* 2d ed. 2 vols. Philadelphia and London: J. B. Lippincott Company, 1902.

AMERICAN SAMOA

The Cyclopedia of Samoa (Illustrated). Western Samoa: Commercial Printers, 1984, 1907.
Gilson, Richard P. *Samoa 1830 to 1900: The Politics of a Multi-cultural Community.* Melbourne and New York: Oxford University Press, 1970.
Gray, J.A.C. *Amerika Samoa: A History of American Samoa and Its United States Naval Administration.* Annapolis, Md.: United States Naval Institute, 1960.
Henry, Fred, and Tofa Pula. *Samoa, an Early History.* Pago Pago: Department of Education, American Samoa, 1980.
Masterman, Sylvia. *An Outline of Samoan History.* Apia, Western Samoa: Commercial Printers, 1980.

Moors, H. J. *Some Recollections of Early Samoa.* Apia, Western Samoa: Western Samoa Historical and Cultural Trust, 1986, 1924–1926.
Rowe, Newton A. *Samoa under the Sailing Gods.* New York: AMS Press, 1978, 1930.
Runeborg, Ruth E. *Western Samoa and American Samoa: History, Culture and Communication.* Honolulu: East-West Communication Institute, East-West Center, 1980.
Watson, Robert M. *History of Samoa.* Wellington, New Zealand: Whitcombe and Tombs, Ltd., 1918.

COMMONWEALTH OF THE NORTHERN MARIANA ISLANDS

Del Valle, Maria Teresa. *The Marianas Islands in the Early Nineteenth Century.* Agana: Micronesian Area Research Center, University of Guam, 1980.
Farrell, Don A., and Phyllis Koontz. *History of the Northern Mariana Islands.* Saipan: Public School System, Commonwealth of the Northern Mariana Islands, 1991.
Fritz, Georg. *The Chamorros: A History and Ethnography of the Marianas.* Mangilao, Guam: Micronesian Area Research Center, University of Guam, 1984.
Hezel, Francis X. *From Conquest to Colonization: Spain in the Mariana Islands, 1690–1740.* Saipan: Division of Historic Preservation, 1989.
Hoyt, Edwin P. *To the Marianas: War in the Central Pacific, 1944.* New York: Avon, 1983, 1980.
Johnson, James B. *Land Ownership in the Northern Mariana Islands: An Outline History.* Saipan: Mariana Islands District, Trust Territory of the Pacific Islands, 1969.
Thompson, Laura. *The Native Culture of the Mariana Islands.* New York: Kraus Reprint Company, 1971, 1945.

GUAM

Beaty, Janice J. *Guam: Today and Yesterday.* Agana, Guam: Department of Education, Government of Guam, 1968.
Carano, Paul, and Pedro C. Sanchez. *A Complete History of Guam.* Rutland, Vt.: C. E. Tuttle, 1965.
Farrell, Don A., and Phyllis Koontz. *The Pictorial History of Guam.* 2d ed. Tamuning, Guam: Micronesian Productions, 1986.
Holmes, Joseph R. *This Is Guam.* Agana, Guam: Pacific Press, 1953.
Maga, Timothy P. *Defending Paradise: The United States and Guam, 1898–1950.* New York: Garland Publishing, 1988.
Nelson, Evelyn G., and Frederick J. Nelson. *The Island of Guam: Description and History from a 1934 Perspective.* Washington, D.C.: Ana Publications, 1992.
Perez, Remedios Leon-Guerrero. *Guam, Past and Present.* 3 vols. Guam: Department of Education, 1946, 1950.
Sanchez, Pedro C. *Guahan Guam: The History of Our Island.* Agana, Guam: Sanchez Publishing House, [1988?].

PUERTO RICO

Dietz, James L. *Economic History of Puerto Rico: Institutional Change and Capitalist Development.* Princeton, N.J.: Princeton University Press, 1987.
Figueroa, Loida. *History of Puerto Rico from the Beginning to 1892.* New York: L. A. Publishers, Neografis, 1978.
Morales Carrion, Arturo, and Maria Teresa Babin. *Puerto Rico, a Political and Cultural History.* New York: Norton; Nashville: American Association for State and Local History, 1983.
Phelps de Cordova, Loretta. *Five Centuries in Puerto Rico: Portraits and Eras.* San German: Interamerican University Press, 1988.
Ribes Tovar, Federico. *A Chronological History of Puerto Rico.* New York: Plus Ultra Educational Publishers, 1973.
Van Middeldyk, Rudolph A., and Martin G. Brumbaugh. *The History of Puerto Rico, from the Spanish Discovery to the American Occupation.* New York: D. Appleton and Company, 1915.

U.S. VIRGIN ISLANDS

Anderson, Lillian S. *Up and Down the Virgin Islands.* Orford, N.H.: Equity Publishing Corporation, 1963.
Boyer, William W. *America's Virgin Islands: A History of Human Rights and Wrongs.* Durham, N.C.: Carolina Academic Press, 1983.
Cochran, Hamilton. *These Are the Virgin Islands.* New York: Prentice-Hall, 1937.
Creque, Darwin D. *The U.S. Virgins and the Eastern Caribbean.* Philadelphia: Whitmore Publishing Company, 1968.
Dookhan, Isaac. *A History of the Virgin Islands of the United States.* Epping, England: Caribbean Universities Press for the College of the Virgin Islands, 1974.
Harrigan, Norwell, and Pearl Varlack. *The Virgin Islands Story.* Kingston, Jamaica: Caribbean Universities Press; Epping, England: Bowker, 1975.
Hill, Valdemar A. *Rise to Recognition: An Account of Virgin Islanders from Slavery to Self-Government.* St. Thomas, V.I.: n.p., 1971.
Jarvis, Jose A. *Brief History of the Virgin Islands.* St. Thomas, V.I.: Art Shop, 1980, 1938.
Larsen, Jens P. M. *Virgin Islands Story. . . .* Philadelphia: Muhlenberg Press, 1950.
Leary, Paul M., ed. *Major Political and Constitutional Documents of the United States Virgin Islands, 1671–1991.* St. Thomas, V.I.: University of the Virgin Islands, 1992.

Index

About the Authors

BENJAMIN F. SHEARER is Vice President for Student Affairs/Dean of Students at Alvernia College in Reading, Pennsylvania. He is co-author of the first edition of *State Names, Seals, Flags, and Symbols: A Historical Guide* (Greenwood Press, 1987). His earlier books include *Communications Technologies and Their Social Impact* (compiled with Marilyn Huxford, Greenwood Press, 1984), *Periodical Literature on United States Cities: A Bibliography and Subject Guide* (compiled with Barbara S. Shearer, Greenwood Press, 1983), and *Finding the Source: A Thesaurus-Index to the Reference Collection* (compiled with Barbara S. Shearer, Greenwood Press, 1981).

BARBARA S. SHEARER is Associate Director for Public Services at Thomas Jefferson University Library. She is co-author of the first edition of *State Names, Seals, Flags, and Symbols: A Historical Guide* (Greenwood Press, 1987).